THE
HOLLOW
YEARS

Also by Eugen Weber

Peasants into Frenchmen

France, Fin de Siècle

Action Française

A Modern History of Europe

THE
HOLLOW
YEARS

*France in the
1930s*

EUGEN
WEBER

W·W· Norton & Company

New York

London

The text of this book is composed in 12/14 Centaur
with the display set in Radiant Bold condensed.
Composition by ComCom Inc.
Manufacturing by The Haddon Craftsmen, Inc.
Book design by Margaret Wagner

Library of Congress Cataloging-in-Publication Data
Weber, Eugen Joseph, 1925–
The hollow years: France in the 1930s / Eugen Weber.
p.   cm.
Includes bibliographical references and index.
1. France—History—1914–1940.   2. Reconstruction
(1914–1939)—France.   3. Depressions—1929—France.
4. Germany—Relations—France.   5. France—Relations—
Germany.   6. World War, 1914–1918—Influence.   I. Title
DC389.W35   1994
944.081—dc20   94–18612

ISBN 0-393-03671-5

W.W. Norton & Company, Inc.
500 Fifth Avenue, New York, N.Y. 10110
W.W. Norton & Company Ltd.
10 Coptic Street, London WC1A 1PU

1 2 3 4 5 6 7 8 9 0

For

JACQUELINE

again

and again

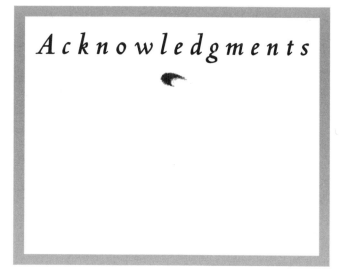

Acknowledgments

I AM MUCH indebted to the following for their help in consulting documents that proved important to my work:

Dr. Charles Blitzer and the Woodrow Wilson Center for a special fellowship that permitted thorough examination of materials in the National Archives, Washington, D.C. Mme. Florence Descamps and the Comité pour l'histoire économique et financière de la France for permission to use their rich store of oral archives. Professor Emmanuel Le Roy Ladurie for permission to use the unpublished memoirs of his father, Jacques Le Roy Ladurie. The Research Library of UCLA for permission to use the papers of Roger Mennevée, as for its consistent helpfulness and its exceptional facilities for the study of the Third Republic. Professor Guy Thuillier, for constant inspiration and unstinting advice.

Contents

T H E
H O L L O W
Y E A R S

66 "*T*

HUCYDIDES OF Athens wrote the history of the war between Peloponnesians and Athenians . . . believing that it would be a great war and more memorable than any previous conflict . . . for the parties to it were in every way at the height of their power. He could see the rest of the Greek world taking sides in the quarrel, and those who did not join in at once prepared to do so. No greater movement, in effect, ever stirred Greece and the world at large. It may be said that the greater part of humanity experienced its effects."[1]

Those are the opening lines of the first political history that the West has known, the chronicle of the Peloponnesian War, written by a younger contemporary of Pericles who died twenty-four centuries ago leaving his work unfinished. Before he died, though, Thucydides had lived the conflict he chronicled: as an Athenian citizen of high station, as a rather unsuccessful general, and as an exile with time to reflect on the experiences of his fellows. In the Greece of his time, armed conflict was practically a way of life, and for every city, war was a continuation of politics by other means. No city-state made this clearer than Athens in the middle of the fifth century B.C.—the century of Aeschylus and Sophocles and Socrates—once Persian power had been shattered and Pericles' city set free to expand its power and its living space at the expense of other Greek communities on the mainland and across the seas. "We are not the first," argue Thucydides'

3

Athenians, "who have aspired to rule; the world has always held that the weaker must be held down by the stronger." Not the first, certainly, but the most clear-sighted.

Many feared Athenian invasiveness, Athenian aggressiveness, and many fell before them. One state felt safe: the great conservative land power of the Peloponnese, Sparta, which all who dreaded Athens sought to stir against it. The Corinthians, close neighbors of Athens and its rivals, tried to wake them up, to remind them "how by slow degrees . . . the Athenians encroach upon their neighbors" and how "when they know that you will-fully overlook their aggressions, they will strike and not spare." The Spartans, the Corinthians argued, thought themselves safe and could not be bothered to take action. "You persist in doing nothing. . . . Instead of at-tacking your enemy, you wait to be attacked, and take the chance of a strug-gle which has been put off until the enemy's power has doubled. . . . You do not see that peace is best secured by those who use their strength justly, but who show that they have no intention of submitting to wrong."

Spartans were old-fashioned where Athenians were modern, irresolute where the Athenians were decisive. Procrastinators, slow to take offense, they were unwilling to fight for themselves, let alone to defend endangered friends. They let their allies down, charged the Corinthians, or "drove them in despair to seek the alliance of others," as long as Sparta could avoid the issue. Things could not go on that way; they didn't. In the end, Thucydides tells us, the growth of Athenian power terrified the Spartans and forced them into war.

The long duel between Athens and its allies, on one hand, and the cities of the Peloponnese led by Sparta, on the other, stretched through three wars that took place between 459 B.C. and 404 B.C. Thucydides fused the last two of these wars together and treated them as a single twenty-seven-year war. That is what some historians of the twentieth century have done, who treat the wars that began in 1914 and ended in Germany's defeat in 1945 as one long thirty-one-year war, in retrospect a European civil war interrupted only by uneasy truces.

Of course, things are not so simple. The temptation to compare Ger-many and Athens—modern, expansionist, efficient, dynamic—France and Lacedaemonian Sparta—agrarian, irresolute, reluctant to act even in its own defense—is very strong. It would, however, lead us astray. Not only because Sparta eventually won the war and its empire, whilst it lasted, was even more oppressive than the Athenian but also because, of the two twentieth-century enemies, France was the democracy. It was ruled, as Athens was, by the will of little people and of middling people, and by the demagogues they elected; it was taught by the Sophists, whom Plato had denounced; it was hobbled less by the unimaginative self-confidence of the Spartans than by moral laziness and fear. In other words, France was both like Athens and like Sparta, and unlike either; historical similes can at best reveal suggestive parallels.

Ineffective politicians also grappled with insoluble problems in the France of the 1930s, just as they do today: refractory economy, intractable immigration, rising unemployment, rabble-rousing xenophobia, swelling taxes, and a contracting tax base. Yet the fear of war that overshadowed the thirties, unbalancing budgets, envenoming social problems, feeding insomnias, is absent in the 1990s, and the material context is vastly different, too. The same applies when we summon up Thucydides to color images of sixty years ago. In the twenty-five hundred years that lay between the Greece of Pericles and the France of Edouard Daladier, the material environment had been transfigured, the capital of sensibility, consciousness, self-consciousness had radically changed. And yet we recognize a sated, stagnant power attempting to avoid war, retreating before a vigorous, ravenous force that presses steadily forward until retreat becomes too shameful and conflict inevitable. Then we round up the usual suspects: foreign entanglements, economic turmoil, moral infirmities, social conflict, and factions that preferred foreign foes to internal antagonists. They look strangely familiar. More so when we remember that it was not the first time that France had faced such problems. Not by far. *Sit ut est, et non erit,* Lucien Prévost-Paradol, a minister of Napoleon III, had warned in 1867: "Let [France] be as she is, and she will not be."[2] That was before the first of France's three Peloponnesian Wars. After the third seemed ended, in June 1940, Paul Valéry noted in his diary: "France expiates the crime of being what she is."[3] But we are all victims of what we are. Athens, then Sparta, and France and Germany in due course, would expiate the crime of being what they had made themselves.

History is a building yard where the building is never done. Structures go up, are torn down, and then rebuilt in different styles. Circumstances differ; interpretations differ; present experience throws an ever-changing light on past events and raises different questions about them. Situations recur that are superficially similar but never quite the same. Bad ages to live through are good ages to learn from. So we are tempted to plumb the past for answers to present quandaries, but in the end, one thing that we learn from history is that people seldom learn from history. Even when they pretend to do so. And that is one conclusion we may draw from the last decade of truce between two world wars on which these pages focus. When the guns of the First War fell silent, peacemakers set to work on a peace to end all peace. No sooner, or so it seemed, than their work had ended, another war began to loom ahead. Those who worked hardest to avoid it did most to make it come, and in the 1930s their work bore bitter fruit.

In rueful retrospect, the 1920s were *l'après-guerre*, lively and optimistic. The 1930s are distinctly *l'avant-guerre*: increasingly morose and ill at ease. Contemporaries varied in their perceptions. A few clear-sighted ones seem to have seen war coming since the negotiations of Versailles. More sensed it in the middle thirties, when German rearmament kicked off in deadly earnest and Hitler began to break even treaties that his country freely signed. By 1936, when the French stood by while German troops reoccupied the Rhineland, France, in some French eyes, began to lose the next war. Internal peace was also badly troubled when the exaltations and anxieties of the Popular Front spurred talk of civil war that might outmatch the bloody war in Spain. Both 1937 and early 1938 made clear to most that the last war would not, alas, be after all the last. By Munich time, all hopes of peace abroad and significant reform at home had collapsed altogether.

That, among other things, above other things, is what this book is about: the inexorable march to war of a society that was, and yet was not, helpless to affect its fate. For men (and women, when they got the chance, which in those days was seldom) are not *objects* of history—playthings of tides, currents, laws that they can't inflect. They are responsible *subjects:* actors who write and rewrite their script while moving from one decision to the next or, failing to decide, resign the script to others. Each choice, each failure to make a choice commit them to a course and set the limits of their further choices. Decisions and events are not the work of fate, and we are not its baubles unless we choose to be. Not individually, but taken as a whole, the French of the 1930s would not, could not decide. They allowed others to forge their destiny and had to pay for this abdication.

In the event, the last decade of the Third Republic may be described by a selection of titles culled from Emile Zola's novels. *Au bonheur des dames* begins the series, followed by *L'Argent* with its money problems, *La Curée* with its scandals, its scramble for spoils, and its hunt for quarries, *Germinal* with the social conflicts that are also the seedtime of changes to come, to bottom out in the collapse of *La Débâcle* (The disaster).

Jean-Baptiste Duroselle entitled his great study of French foreign policy during the 1930s *La Décadence*. In *A Dictionary of Platitudes* that Gustave Flaubert compiled throughout his life one entry reads: "Epoch (ours): thunder against it. Call it a time of transition, of decadence." So the notion of French decadence is hardly new. Only, during these years it came to be in evidence on every front. Before foreign affairs went signally awry in the mid-thirties, internal troubles sufficed to dismay the French. When Depression crept upon them around 1931, later than in other industrial lands, it revealed a brittle economy, fragile edifices of fraud, and lots of investors ruined by their collapse. Everything would work out; it had done so before. But everything worked out badly. France was not an underdeveloped country, but a developed one in an advanced state of decay. The cascade of scandals and the cat's cradle of political and financial corruption they revealed branded parliament as a kleptocracy, squelched whatever respect the public retained for the country's political personnel, stifled the limited confidence they preserved in their state. The crisis of the 1930s was as much economic as diplomatic, as much institutional as economic, as much about public morality, confidence, and self-confidence as it was about economic interests, employment, or the balance of payments.

So there *is* an atmosphere of the 1930s: a mood, a spirit that are distinct from those of the 1920s and justify their treatment as a manifest entity from 1930 to 1940. And yet, quite clearly, the decade is also a continuation of what went before and a preparation of things to come. Looking forward, one is struck by the continuity of demographic concerns that inspired the family legislation of the Third Republic on its last legs and of Vichy, to culminate in *le baby boom* of the Fourth Republic. Continuity also between Third Republic and Vichy policies of protection, tariffs, and import quotas designed to avoid foreign competition. And continuity of interest in plans for a managed economy that prepared the ground for the Fourth Republic's immensely successful Commissariat au Plan, and in collaboration between state and industry, that inspired the technocrats of Vichy and the managers of the postwar economic renaissance.

Persistence, on the other hand, of the "long nineteenth century" which, in terms of modern comfort, household equipment and help, attitudes, legislation, and social structures, ends only with the 1950s. Perpetuation of the 1920s, with their Fascist leagues, their fears about national security, currencies, and savings, and their many politicians blissfully ignorant of economics. Extension, above all, of the fallout—the effects—of the First World War. The war had bled France white. A whole generation of menfolk had been felled or mauled. Sagging demography sagged further. The absence of young and, some contend, of the best and brightest, cut down on the Marne, on the Somme, at Verdun, account for the pacifism, the defensiveness, timidity, indecisiveness, shortage of breath and of initiative that aggravated earlier tendencies to mediocracy and gerontocracy. A book about the thirties must be, directly or indirectly, a book about the wounds and mind-set of a host of survivors—veterans, widows, orphans, parents—grieving for the slaughtered and determined to avoid a repeat performance of the disaster whose ruins were still being repaired in 1939, less than a quarter of a century later. The Maginot Line, symbol of an era, was the creation of a much-decorated, badly wounded war veteran from the borderlands of Lorraine: André Maginot.

But if the shadow of 1914–1918 broods over these years, so does the reader's foreknowledge of 1940–1944. The French of the 1930s entered the future looking back to 1914, forgetting that history depicts circumstances that do not repeat themselves. For this error they paid in 1940, and the years of Vichy were part of the payment. But the suffering and struggles of that purgatory do not figure in these pages. Sufficient unto the day is the evil thereof. It is enough to remember, as mentioned before, that the 1930s provided a mine of ideas and initiatives to be carried out, perfected, developed by the *Etat Français* of Vichy, by the Fourth Republic, and even by the Fifth: social laws, the emancipation of women, cheap housing, existentialism, consumerism, reform of the state, of the Constitution, and of public administration, to name only a few. In a way, the thirties, when Raymond Poincaré and Aristide Briand died and Edouard Herriot was discredited, witnessed the end of generations formed long before the First World War, and the first appearance of men formed in or after the war: Georges Bidault, Pierre Mendès-France, Charles de Gaulle, Jean Monnet, Jean-Paul Sartre.

This string of names gives notice that necessary references to politics, economics, and foreign affairs do not exclude personalities. Events and institutions are made by men and women and lived by them. History that does not feature individuals is a hollow exercise. And history that ignores the everyday aspects of life and culture is even more incomplete than it is bound to be. Thucydides wrote of politics, diplomacy, and their extension—war. We survey more than that. While Athens and Sparta fought, or squabbled, Spartans, Athenians, and their neighbors continued to buy and sell in markets, bring up children, work or look for work, go to the theater, engage in sports, worship, and wrangling. Though sports, sophistry, and Sophocles are still with us, we don't know very much about the rest. Of our own days and the days just before ours we can tell more. This is the time when international conflicts and internal strains play themselves out in the provocations of Surrealists, the design and the delays of the International Exhibition of 1937, as in pacifist and xenophobic books and films. They do so too in Drieu La Rochelle's wild swings from left to right, Paul Nizan's equally desperate pursuit of salvation from right to left, or the popular illusion that André Gide might have the stuff of a political leader. It is a time remarkably like our own: The young produced enthusiasts who immatured with age; the old improved on the mistakes made by their elders. It is a time remarkably different from ours: much transport still unmechanized, government offices only beginning to be equipped with telephones, electric signs hampering the functioning of newfangled radio sets, refrigeration rare, domesticity dense, made-to-measure clothes normal even in modest households, and clogs unexceptional (several murderers of 1937 beat their victims to death with their footwear).

None of this proves anything, except that the people of the decade lived in familiar but radically different times. They lived in interesting times; that's what the Chinese wish their enemies.

In a prize-giving speech delivered in a Paris lycée in 1932, Paul Valéry made the same observation. "You live in interesting times," he told the students and their parents. "Interesting times are always enigmatic times that promise no rest, no prosperity or continuity or security. [In our age] there coexist a number of incompatible forces, none of which can either win or lose. . . . Never has humanity joined so much power and so much disarray, so much anxiety and so many playthings, so much knowledge and so much uncertainty."[4] His comments would be as apposite today as they would have been in the epoch of Thucydides, which was as much a time of transition and of decadence as our own.

The word *history*, meaning "an inquiry," is akin to the Greek verb "to know." Knowledge is power, even if the mediated experience of others is only worth what we can make of it. The historian is not a teacher, and he is not a prophet. He tries to provide an intelligible account of what happened in an area of the past for present readers to use. His history supplies the secondhand experience that can be the beginning of wisdom for those who will face their own experience forearmed by knowing how in other times others have acted in comparable situations. "If those who wish to study the clear record of what happened in the past and what will, in due course, tend to be repeated with some degree of similarity (as is the way of human events) judge this work to be of some help to them, it will content me," declares Thucydides.

To do history is to search for truth. But truth is more than verifiable facts laid end to end. Historians have to choose among a mass of incoherent facts and organize their selection into *their* version of reality: a construct that they hope will be true to events, explain them to a degree, and clarify without oversimplifying. But history also tells a tale; it is a *story.* The best stories are full of action, and so is history which chronicles the actions of men and women moved by interest, greed, and passion, by anger, or by fear, prey to their impulses but also accessible to reason, blundering in darkness but toward the light. History does not predict the perils we may encounter, but it helps remind us that others have undergone similar trials and worse, have lived anxious moments, have erred, have suffered, yet often have survived. Or someone has survived to tell their tale.

I

A Wilderness
Called Peace

Solitudinem faciunt, pacem appellant.

They make a wilderness, and call it peace.

—*TACITUS*

THE 1930s begin in August 1914. For fifty-one months thereafter, 1,000 Frenchmen were killed day after day, nearly 1 of every 5 men mobilized, 10.5 percent of the country's active male population. That was more than any other Western belligerent would suffer: The British counted half as many dead and missing, Germans and Austro-Hungarians, who had incurred heavy losses, never got as far as 10 percent. About 1,400,000 French lost their lives; well over 1,000,000 had been gassed, disfigured, mangled, amputated, left permanent invalids. Wheelchairs, crutches, empty sleeves dangling loosely or tucked into pockets became common sights. More than that had suffered some sort of wound: Half of the 6,500,000 who survived the war had sustained injuries. Most visible, 1,100,000, were those who had been evidently diminished and were described as *mutilés,* a term the dictionary translates as "maimed" or "mangled," and English usage prefers to clothe in an euphemism: "disabled."

Precise figures are unavailable, and anyway, on that sort of scale, they mean either too little or too much. Statistics, above all, offer general impressions that do not take stock of particular cases, like that of Eugène Haensler, a priest, gassed in the war, who died only in 1930 of tuberculosis contracted as a result of his poisoning. Or the amnesiac veteran whom the press discovered in 1936 living in Rodez and featured as "The Living Unknown Soldier." Or the Provençal infantryman Jean Giono, one of eleven members of his company to survive Verdun. Or Jean Giraudoux, wounded several times but wounded more severely still by clumsy surgeons, living for years with enteritis, diarrhea, nervous nightmares, to note: "fatigue, fatigue. . . ." Heroic endurance left behind postheroic letdown and depression.[1]

There was Eugène Dabit, who volunteered for the artillery in 1916, when he was eighteen. Appalled by the physical and moral horrors of the war, he tried to get out of it by simulating madness, then almost threw himself under a train (but didn't), finally came through with only a superficial wound. Returned to civilian life, he remained, as he said, *"malade de la guerre"*—sick with the war, for the rest of his life. "Almost every night since my demobilization, images of the front came back to haunt me, and—a still worse nightmare—I dreamed that hostilities were starting again."[2] Dabit wrote several novels, one of which, *Hôtel du Nord* (1929), brought him real success even before Marcel Carné turned it into a film. But through the thirties his private journals reflect a constant dread: War is coming. Can he escape? In August 1936, thirty-eight years old, Dabit made his escape: to death.

For the unafraid, another kind of deterioration lay in wait. In 1934 Roger Vercel, a frontline officer for four years, won the Prix Goncourt for *Le Capitaine Conan*, the story of a true fighter hero who ends up gross and full of bile, drinking himself to death in a provincial dump. It was people like him who won the war, Conan tells the narrator. "If you should run across them, look closely: they'll be like me." Not all of them were. Far from it. But in the *Gazette des tribunaux*, France's *Police Gazette*, case after case of officers, once decorated for their bravery, now dragged into court for fraud or other crimes, bears out Conan's bitterness.[3]

To those dead, wounded, or in some way maimed, one has to add those who were not conceived. It was estimated that during the years of carnage, 1,400,000 souls had been left unborn. Fewer marriages, fewer babies would mean fewer conscripts during "the hollow years" and a declining population—especially when compared with that of France's neighbors. Falling mortality did not compensate for the falling births whose number, after 1935, was inferior to deaths. Couples married in the 1930s avoided bearing children more deliberately than their forebears had done. Burdens in a difficult world, children were also hostages to fortune: designated victims of adversities increasingly easy to discern. During the decade 23 percent of couples had no child, 32 percent had one.[4]

The French had engaged in family planning earlier than their neighbors, which meant that war losses hit them relatively harder but also that falling birthrates declined from levels that were already low.

Between 1900 and 1939 French population grew 3 percent, and that was only thanks to immigration. Over the same period German population grew 36 percent, Italian 33 percent, British 23 percent. That was depressing enough. More practically, it designated the later thirties as a demographic danger zone when the pool of draftees would be especially shallow. In the last years before 1914, 660,000 young men a year had celebrated their twentieth birthdays and prepared for military service. Between 1935 and 1939 there would be only 400,000 twenty-year-olds each year. During that time more people died in France than there were babies born. Nor were the statistics altogether a question of numbers. France was growing older; it became the European country with the fewest young and most old people. In 1911 under-twenties represented 33.6 percent of the population; in 1931 they represented 30 percent. In 1936, 15 percent of French were over sixty, 10 percent over sixty-five.[5] Not a recipe for enterprise, for enthusiasm or self-assurance.

Though all men born after 1870 sooner or later became liable to conscription for the war, not all died at the same rate. Fewer of those born before 1890 were actually called up; far fewer of them saw active service; far more survived. The bloodbath was reserved for those born in the 1890s, who would have been at the peak of their productive powers in the 1930s had they survived. Heaviest hit of all were the classes drafted between 1909 and 1915, comprising men born between 1891 and 1897. These contributed over one third of those mobilized and lost 26 percent of their number on average: more than one man in four. In 1930 they would have been in their mid-thirties.[6]

Not only men suffered, and some suffered more—certainly longer—for having been left alive. Three quarters of a million orphans became wards of the state, which paid them pensions till they were eighteen. Close to a million aged dependents, unable to help themselves, also drew meager pensions, on which they rubbed along. So did war widows choosing not to remarry or finding no opportunity to do so. But many who drew no pension knew the dry bitterness of having lost loves that could not be replaced. Fifteen at the Armistice, Yves Simon found his mother, who had lost her eldest son, unmoved by victory. "I understood, on November 11, that the mothers of dead soldiers did not want to be consoled."[7]

Women in general had fared badly. On the eve of war France had counted 1,035 women to every 1,000 men; by its end it counted 1,103 per 1,000—a figure that concealed graver disparities: 1,200 women to 1,000 men for those in their early twenties; 1,323 to 1,000 for those in their latter twenties. On the eve of war, men and women between twenty and forty years old roughly balanced each other out: about 6,000,000 of each sex. Twenty years later women in that age-group outnumbered men by more than 1,000,000. France became a country of elderly, and often single, women.[8] Many spinsters threaded their way through the 1920s and thirties; many in a conventional society with conventional aspirations would be frustrated of marriage and motherhood. For a generation France was submerged by the dark weeds of mourning, the veils of the *grand deuil*, the crepe of *demi-deuil*, the somber-colored hats, gloves, shoes, dresses of widows and orphans and parents and kin either inconsolable or unable to afford a more cheerful garb.

The bitterness of women and their suffering made little impact on politics because women were less politically active than men. Even among schoolteachers, in whom one would expect to find some interest in public affairs, only 27 percent of women surveyed claim interest in politics, as compared with 73 percent of the men. But an overwhelming majority speak up for peace and, when they reject politics or express hatred for them, do so because they associate politics with the war that deprived them of fiancé, husband, or son. Mona and Jacques Ozouf, who surveyed over a thousand *institutrices*, even found some women teachers who hoped that the women's vote—for which they had to wait till 1945—would permit the foundation of a "feminist" party dedicated to antimilitarism and pacifism.[9]

But those who lived most visibly—at least most audibly—in shadow of the war were veterans. Half the men in France served in the war. By 1930 just less than six million survived; by 1935 five and a half million. In France of the 1930s one man in two, or almost, was a veteran, and half of these had joined a veteran association: one quarter of the electorate, then still exclusively male. They joined less for old times' sake than for benefits demanded or defended. Veteran associations were about pensions, which went to one survivor out of five, about other payments like the *retraite du combattant* voted in 1930—500 francs a year at fifty, 1,200 francs at fifty-five ($20 and $50)—about protecting these meager tributes. Small sums, but they added up. In 1931–1932 war pensions, indemnities, and the like represented 13.5 percent of the nation's budget. By 1935 some 7 billion francs had been paid out in pensions, more on hospitalization for some or on retraining others to function in the life of every day.[10]

Laws were also voted for affirmative action that privileged disabled veterans: cheap fares, reserved seats on public transport, but also the obligation for employers to reserve a proportion of the going jobs for them. Into the Second World War and sometimes beyond, many positions—some more, most less important—would be staffed by survivors or by widows of those who had not survived. Their incapacities, their bitterness, or simply their ill humor would color public life and make human relations more snippy and contentious.[11]

As one might expect, few veterans cherished warm feelings for the kind of conflict they had by luck escaped or for the military institutions they had enjoyed but little. They had gone off to a fresh and joyous war. They were to be maimed or killed in ignoble butcheries like that which, between July and November 1916, killed 1,200,000 Germans, French, and British soldiers in the cold, rain, and mud of the Somme: more than at Verdun. Most of them, like the future *inspecteur des finances* Jean Appert, who served in the infantry, remembered their service as a massacre and their superiors as stupid. When they marched past, lapels clinking with decorations, they refused to march in step, the better to assert that they were no longer soldiers. Patriotic still, they were not militaristic. They were against military authority, against regular officers, against the murderous nonsense of war. In 1930 a member of the prime minister's cabinet reported to André Tardieu that they were "as intoxicated with pacifism as the [political] parties."[12] As a privileged young woman, the daughter of a conservative senator, noted on the eve of the following conflict, "Father served in the other war. His memory of it is so awful that he speaks of it only reluctantly, that is never. Mother, who was left alone with four children, has kept a sort of grudge ever since. They don't really believe in another war. It seems much too crazy."[13]

The land around them bore witness to the madness. In 1935, when Jean de Lattre, the future general, drove to Metz with his wife, Simone, to take over the 151st Regiment of Infantry, they passed through the Verdun area, where in 1916 a thousand soldiers died per square meter and where de Lattre himself had fought. Nineteen years after the carnage, vast areas, Simone noted, lacked all vegetation; the landscape looked chaotic, nightmarish, marked by a few blackened tree trunks and great lunar craters full of stagnant water. By then the Douaumont ossuary, built with privately raised funds and with American aid, offered a cold reminder of four hundred thousand dead. But for many years after the Armistice the great swath, four hundred miles long, ten or twenty miles wide, where the front had been lay desert, desolate. The ruins ran from the North Sea to Champagne and beyond. A decade barely sufficed for the rebuilding, and some sites that once were villages remained no more than place-names on a post. In the 1930s, when the war zone had been largely rebuilt, 10 percent of the dwellings and 10 percent of the factories in it had not been raised back. In 1933 a businessman from Toledo, Ohio, visiting the north of France was struck by the "devastation." In the Ardennes in 1938 one man had only just finished restoring his war damage. And cases of housing damage suffered over twenty years before were still before the courts in 1939.[14] The First World War was very contemporary history even as the Second loomed ahead.

By the time reconstruction had been officially completed, in 1931, every village and every town in France had raised its monument to the fallen on which interminable lists of names, sometimes two or three per family, marched in dour columns. There are plenty of villages today where the number of World War dead is greater than that of the men remaining there.[15]

Paris, of course, had the tomb of the Unknown Soldier, whose constantly burning flame under the Arc de Triomphe was regularly rekindled in memorial ceremonies. And Armistice Day, November 11, provided annual reminders that the hecatomb it recapitulated should be the last. After 1919 the anniversary of victory in 1918 became not a celebration of triumph but a remembrance of death.[16] Anchored in that gloomy November day, the cult of the dead that loomed so large throughout the twenties and the thirties became an annual reminder that repetition of recent horrors should be avoided at all costs.* The same urgent and solemn message was repeated on other occasions: election speeches, prize-giving ceremonies, dedications (notably of war memorials), commemorations, political debates. The war no sooner won, the French were being confirmed in horror of its cost and dread of its repetition.

The Treaty of Versailles had left France looking like the greatest land

---

*It was. In the parish of Saint-Sernin, at Toulouse, the roll of First War dead runs to 450 names; that of the Second War to 17: 5 in May 1940, 6 in June 1940, another 6 in the fighting of 1944.

power in a Europe that was still, at the time, at the center of the world. The overwhelming determination that the last war should be the last, *la der des dères*, was not evident to all observers, but it runs through these years and offers a key to their understanding. As War Minister André Maginot told the U.S. ambassador, the French had a horror of war: "There is probably no other nation in Europe that [is] less warlike."[17] Events would show that Maginot spoke true, and the reason for that can be found in the preceding pages. As Giraudoux had said, "fatigue, fatigue . . ."

Looking back at her youth in the thirties, Annie Kriegel has attributed the indecisiveness and apparent spinelessness of her compatriots to "a sort of national exhaustion": no time to recover from the trauma of 1914–1918. After exhaustive study of *anciens combattants* Antoine Prost agrees. Among the veterans, he writes, "the war had left a great weariness, an immense lassitude. They have been worn down." Contemporary evidence bears them out. Gaston Cusin, a student doing his military service as an officer in the 1920s, remembers only veterans "who were very tired and wanted only to relax and rest." Edouard Herriot, then prime minister, drew the evident conclusion: "A country like ours can't always be asked to stretch its will to the point where . . . it might break. . . . It needs a rest." Within a few years of this, *Paris-Soir*, the mass-circulation evening newspaper, could use "the state of fatigue left behind by the war" as a natural reference. And if Herriot had not made clear what that meant, Daniel Halévy spelled it out: The public spirit, civic sense were dead. The recent sacrifice of 1,400,000 men, remembered, made all hearts waver.[18]

Perhaps not all. Nor would anyone claim that all had lost their spirit. But enough. There were patriots in France, and they were many, but somehow patriotism was dead. Its demise was not immediately evident, but it had died in the trenches, on the Marne, at Verdun. Patriotism now spoke of pacifism, expressed reluctance to fight—first for others, then for France as well—and it reflected an ever more weary, ever more desperate search for impossible solutions to insoluble problems.

The years before 1914 had been bright with the red, white, and blue of patriotism and its more blustering incarnation: nationalism. The years before 1939 favored other colors: the red of socialism and communism, the white of pacifism. The word *pacifism* and its derivative *pacifist* had been invented in the 1890s by a Frenchman, then officially adopted by the Universal Peace Congress held in Glasgow in 1901.[19] The notion that abolition of war is not just desirable but possible had not filtered far beyond the organized Left until the years following 1914. But slaughter and suffering persuaded many that anything would be better than the bloodletting they had witnessed. Since France suffered more than most other countries, that feeling took firmer and more widespread hold there than elsewhere.

One way in which Right and Left opposed each other was by mutual accusations of warmongering. But of course, in the pacifist contest, the Left was constantly in the van. There were unrelenting pacifist revolutionaries, like the brilliant scholarship boy Georges Soulès, better known as the polytechnician engineer Raymond Abellio. In the Toulouse working-class neighborhood where he grew up, Abellio—born in 1907 and thus too young for the First War—remembers that "the war, its massacres, its scandals, had ruined a certain sentimental idea of the fatherland. No one today can realize the virulence of our hatreds and our rejections; we looked on patriotism as *absolute evil.*"[20]

There were less fundamentalist reasoners, like the young *normalien* Raymond Aron whose pacifism drew him to socialism. And there were perfectly decent apparatchiks whose functions made them go through the pacifist paces that were expected of them. René Belin, secretary first of the Postmen's Union, then of the General Confederation of Labor (CGT), has recalled how in 1933 he had to present to the Trade Union Congress the traditional pacifist resolution that threatened a general strike in case of mobilization. Neither he nor the confederal secretary, Léon Jouhaux, agreed with the resolution, but it was expected of them, so they presented it, and it was ritually passed.[21]

But even agnostic conformism could bear witness to the strength of the pacifist current. That trend was confirmed by the flood of war memoirs and novels that gushed after 1915: 303 works by 252 authors listed in 1928. Some of these sold massively (Henri Barbusse's *Le Feu*, published in 1916, sold over 300,000 copies by the war's end), and many introduced authors—Roland Dorgelès, Georges Duhamel, Maurice Genevoix, Jean Giraudoux, Pierre MacOrlan, Henri de Montherlant—unknown or unpublished until then. Nor did interest flag over time. Published in June 1929, the translation of Erich Maria Remarque's *All Quiet on the Western Front* sold 72,000 copies in ten days and nearly 450,000 by Christmas. *L'Humanité* serialized it, the Dominican *Vie intellectuelle* praised it, a literary critic saw in its sales "a sort of plebiscite in favor of peace. Every volume bought is equivalent to a vote."

In 1928 the Kellogg-Briand Pact outlawing war, which we shall meet again, appeared to answer pacifist expectations. The years that followed blighted the hopes it had aroused. Pacifism became as frustrated, querulous, disgruntled, and defensive as the society it addressed. By the 1930s a Greek statesman, Nicholas Politis, described the country as being in the throes of pacifist depression.[22]

One of the most outrageous representatives of sullen, blustery pacifism was Louis-Ferdinand Céline, whose *Journey to the End of Night* denounced all dehumanizing agencies—capitalism, colonialism, alcoholism—but, above all, the butchery of war that turns men into dead meat. Céline, whom the beginning of war found serving in the cavalry, had been wounded in October 1914, decorated for bravery, and had then trailed from one hospital to another while operation after operation sought to heal his injured arm. The war that he denounces is in the image of the war he knew—pointless, absurd, and murderous on a gigantic scale. His rancorous exaggerations apart, that was the kind of war that pacifists rejected. Peace had to be kept at any price, even at the price of apparent cowardice.

A more attractive and far more sensible figure attests to this. In 1936, after years of silence, Roger Martin du Gard published what seemed to be the end of his great multivolume saga of a bourgeois family: *Les Thibault.* In *The Summer of 1914,* the younger of the two Thibault brothers, Jacques, a Romantic enthusiast, dies trying to scatter pacifist leaflets over French and German troops about to join battle in August 1914. Martin du Gard's message was not that pacifism was a failure but that it must not be allowed to fail again. In September 1936, under the impact of the civil war then raging in Spain, we find the novelist writing to a friend: "Anything rather than war! Anything! . . . even Fascism in Spain . . . even Fascism in France: Nothing, no trial, no servitude can be compared to war: Anything, Hitler rather than war!"* And when, in 1937, *Les Thibault* won the Nobel Prize for Literature, Martin du Gard's speech to the Swedish Academy denounced "the cowardly fatalism which alone permits wars."[23] We shall see that cowardly fatalism can try to avoid wars, too, though not their consequences. But that is another story.

The assault troops of the militant faith were recruited among schoolteachers. Leader of the militant pacifist wing of the Socialist party, Marceau

---

*In spring 1938 Simone Weill, of Jewish origin but a believing Christian, wrote to her friend the Radical deputy Gaston Bergery that she preferred German hegemony to war, even if it should mean "certain laws of exclusion against Communists and Jews." Simone Pètrement, *La Vie de Simone Weill,* (1973), II, 10.

Pivert was a teacher himself, a product of normal schools that taught him first enthusiastic patriotism, then a revolutionary syndicalism just as enthusiastic. Mobilized in 1914 full of patriotic fire, he was gassed in 1917 and invalided out full of disgust for the war and for the High Command, on which he blamed the carnage, an unrelenting pacifist henceforth, whose "revolutionary defeatism" never flinched. But Pivert was only one more eloquent teacher among many others.

Between 1914 and 1918 over thirty-five thousand teachers had been mobilized, more than a quarter of the teaching force. Of these, nearly one in four had died. Léon Emery, a militant pacifist, remembered that of his normal school class of thirty in pre-1914 Lyons, ten had been killed and several more severely injured. No other professional group seems to have known such losses. Be it the butchery, be it an older antimilitarist tradition or equally well-entrenched hostility to the bourgeois state, most French schoolteachers between the wars were pacifist. Before 1914 they had taught love of the fatherland, which could well mean laying down one's life for it. Now they revised their creed, and their schoolbooks, too. Schoolbooks had to be expurgated, and editors had to join in the task, else teachers—free to select their texts—would refuse to use books written on the wrong lines.[24]

Most teachers' unions were dedicated to weaning children from chauvinism and any glorification of war by teaching a new kind of history and civics that would inculcate respect for humankind and love of peace. The first step in this had to be a revision of the old, dark vision of the German neighbors traditionally presented as malevolent and aggressive. This theme had been discredited by the exaggerations of wartime propaganda. What we call brainwashing the French describe as headstuffing—*bourrage de crâne.* The trouble with this sort of thing, whatever you call it, is that excess breeds counterexcess. Intellectuals had learned that descriptions of enemy evil were not to be trusted. They were going to treat news from Nazi Germany with the same skepticism. Minds that were truly enlightened rejected the image of an evil Germany, assimilated criticism of Germans to warmongering, and suspected those who blamed Germans for evils perpetrated in the present as much as those who blamed them for evils past.[25]

Tales of villainy had been trumped up or exaggerated; now their kind was condemned as calumny. Talk of heroism had been overdone; now it was dismissed as a big lie. Calls for patriotism had led to chauvinism and then to butcheries; now they were denounced as dupery. It was time for history to be brought up-to-date, rewritten in a more equitable vein and one more conducive to international understanding. In the mid-1920s a fair-minded historian, Jules Isaac, revised Albert Malet's widely used history texts for secondary schools. The patriotic *revanchard* Malet had been killed in Artois in 1915. Son and grandson of army officers, Isaac, who had been wounded and decorated at Verdun, rewrote the texts of his predecessor to present both France and its enemies in a more balanced light: Napoleon's wars had been aggressions, too; German responsibilities for the Great War were less exclusive than the Treaty of Versailles would have them. In 1933 his equally influential *Le Problème des origines de la guerre* explicitly dotted the *i*'s and crossed the *t*'s of his argument, suggesting—as American revisionists were also doing—that the French too bore some responsibility for the outbreak of war in 1914. More important still, Isaac told his readers, enmity between nations was not historically or geographically determined, conflict was not inevitable, mutual understanding and international cooperation could surmount circumstantial hostility.

Imbibed by generations of teenagers, this revisionist history made unconditional patriotism ("my country right or wrong") less acceptable, certainly no excuse for war. At the same time, children who once were stuffed with ideas of martial glory were now being taken, class by class, to see anti-war films and then invited to put down their impressions. In July 1937 an educational publication surveyed schoolchildren's views. "War is a scourge," answered an eleven-year-old boy; "War is a horror," answered a nine-year-old girl.[26] That they were right is irrelevant. That there's no evidence of a "but" that might be used to qualify their convictions, of a sense that in some circumstances even calamities have to be faced, is significant.

Children brought up in such a moral atmosphere, like Christian de Lavarenne, born in 1911, looked upon war as ultimate evil, upon its harbingers with horror. Son of an officer killed in the war, member of a family whose menfolk became officers from father to son, Lavarenne believed an understanding with Germany essential and watched the rise of Nazism "with terror." Not a recipe for firmness or, really, for straight thinking. His point of view reminds us that pacifism, or something akin to it, was not limited to the Left. Though those who stood in the center or to the right of the political spectrum had been more given to bellicose talk through the 1920s, most of their troops continued pacific. By the 1930s the leaders had learned to follow their followers. In 1933 we find the marquis Régis de Vibraye, great landowner and generous supporter of the royalist Action Française, telling the management of a peace association that a Germany ruled by Nazis did not preclude understanding between the two countries.[27] Vibraye represented a new current of "integral pacifism," more suspicious of German refugees than of Germany's rulers, more opposed to parliamentary institutions than to Nazism.

Between pacifists from the Left, determined to dismiss whatever did not fit their beliefs in international understanding, and pacifists of the Right, who feared the nefarious manipulations of anti-Nazis eager to use the French as cat's-paws, there was ground for accommodation. Both looked askance at the republic and its institutions, the ones because they were not democratic enough, the others because they were too democratic. Both denounced ruling cliques as irresponsible and corrupt. Both hated war and, after war, the carnage of alcoholism and syphilis, the vectors of decadence: *bistrots*, brothels, homosexuals, drugs, degenerate art. Both suspected capitalism and its mealymouthed lackeys of every ilk: moderates, Masons, and Jews.[28] Both felt it a moral duty to face the state with sterile hostility, and both carried out this duty with stubborn fervor. As Raymond Aron (a "passionate pacifist" in his youth) found occasion to comment later, "resisting power when power is moderate: an excellent method to accelerate its ruin."[29] Moderate power makes revolt easy; moderate power encouraged immoderate opposition. In a France that was immoderate only in its moderation, opponents on all sides found many maledictions they could pronounce in common.

Most pacifists of Left and Right did not especially like Italian Fascists or German Nationalists, but they actively disliked France's own established disorder. The real enemies of peace, as one left-wing pacifist put it, were inside France: in parliament, in government, and among those Jews and refugees who sought to embroil the country in war with Germany. René Gérin, who wrote this, was a graduate of the Ecole Normale Supérieure, a lycée professor, a captain of infantry who ended the war with three wounds, four citations, and the Legion of Honor—a genuine war hero who became a martyr to his pacifist beliefs, twice imprisoned as a conscientious objector in the 1930s, imprisoned again after the war for "intelligence with the enemy." Whatever Gérin's feelings about warmongering Jews, his International League of Fighters for Peace was against anti-Semitism, but also opposed those campaigns against anti-Semitism that threatened to set Germany and France at loggerheads. Other pacifists were less evenhanded. Their arguments for Franco-German understanding quickly degenerated into denouncing the occult links among Jewish politicians, Jewish finance, and the arms manufacturers interested in the profits of war. They compared "the bluff of anti-Semitism" to equally mendacious wartime atrocity propaganda and attacked "the Jewish Press" for contributing to the creation of "a war psychosis." Few, however, were as rabid as Céline, who spewed his bile in all directions, not least on those who sold the alcohol "that hands the people over to the Jews" pending its massacre in yet another Jewish war.[30]

A great moment in the pacifist history of the 1930s would come in February 1933, when, only days after Hitler's coming to power in Germany, an impressive majority of the Oxford Union—the prestigious students' debating society—voted that under no circumstances would they take up arms to fight for King and Country. Paris papers echoed their sentiments and wished that other great universities could emulate their moving example. Agree or not with the Oxford debaters, the pacifists' strange talent for matching their pronouncements with events reads like a counterpart of Rupert Brooke's 1914 poem "Peace," where he thanks God, "Who had matched us with His hour." The Oxford vote took place just as Japan, having gobbled up Manchuria, was invading northern China. A year after this a group of *normaliens* adapted the Oxford formula while placing a wreath on the war memorial to mark their opposition to war. The date of their gesture, May 1, 1934, predated by a few weeks Hitler's mass murder of his brown-shirted followers in the Night of the Long Knives and the Nazi murder of Austria's chancellor, Engelbert Dollfuss.[31]

Nearly one third of the *normaliens* who had gone to war had died, and pacifism was well entrenched in the forcing house of France's intellectual elite. That may be why in March 1935, while Germany reintroduced compulsory military service, ninety *normaliens* and over a hundred other students of other normal schools solemnly protested against two-year military service being reintroduced in France. But *normaliens* were not alone. In March 1936 we hear a trade union leader speaking before the Trade Union Congress held in Toulouse that year declare his preference: "Rather servitude than war!" Less than a week later German troops reoccupied the Rhineland, whilst a portion of the French press, like the *Canard enchaîné*, pointed out that in doing so, Germany was simply invading Germany.

In his account of French foreign policy in the 1930s, J.-B. Duroselle refers to a near-unanimous public opinion in 1936 crying, "Above all, no war!" and a feeble government swept off its feet by "a pacifist tornado." He concludes that only seventeen years after the hecatomb's end another conflict was more than the French could face. That being so, Marceau Pivert, leader of the Socialist party's pacifist wing, could draw the obvious conclusion: The army was not there to be used, so why not cut it? In May 1936, two months after the Rhineland crisis and at the height of unemployment, he proposed a reduction in the length of military service.[32]

Pacifists were impregnable. "What's the worst that can happen if Germany invades France?" asked Jean Giono, veteran and veteran pacifist, in 1937. "Become Germans? For my part, I prefer being a living German to being a dead Frenchman." Then, after the Anschluss in March 1938: "Let me continue to struggle against militarism and necessarily begin by fighting against that of my own country." Another pacifist, Henri Jeanson, agreed: The people to battle were not across the border but fellow French at home—class enemies, Fascists, industrialists, politicians, officers of the General Staff. All Hitler was doing was to revise unjust treaties. True, he was revising them unilaterally, but he was doing it without war, which was as true of Munich in the fall of 1938 as it was of the annexation of Austria in the spring. The philosopher Alain was persuaded that Munich marked the beginning of peace. The *Canard*, which had declared its unwillingness to set the world on fire over Sudeten Germans, breathed more easily: "Ouf, we just missed becoming heroes."*[33]

The *Canard* had a lot of company. In late September 1938 postal and teachers' unions had launched a petition, "We Want No War," which gathered 150,000 signatures in a few days. The Radical—that is moderate—*Echo de la Nièvre* had pleaded abjectly, "anything rather than war. . . ."[34] As Proust had written less than twenty years before this, "pacifism sometimes multiplies wars. . . ." If the last war was not the *der des dères*, that may be due to the blind determination to avoid one. But among pacifists few were as ready as Giono to look experience grimly in the face. The possibility of war, said Giono, had set off an indescribable terror. Some had committed suicide to avoid the draft. Others, like his peasant neighbors, sat frozen, waiting to see if they or their menfolk were to be called up: "[F]or three days they waited, not eating or talking or smoking, in dread of war." His logical conclusion: A general disarmament had to follow Munich, of which

---

*Simone Weill was also willing to accept any outcome to avoid war. In 1937 we find her assuring fellow pacifist René Belin, deputy secretary-general of the Confederation of Labor (CGT) and Vichy's future minister of labor, that "a defeat without war is preferable to a victorious war." In 1938 she writes to another pacifist friend, Gaston Bergery: "War in Europe is certain disaster, German hegemony in Europe may not be one." Conclusion: France should disarm even if it has to be done unilaterally. Simone Pètrement, *La Vie de Simone Weill* (1973), II, 133, 188.

France should take the first step. Unilateral disarmament was better than no disarmament at all.[35] And if the government gave little heed to his urgings, Giono and his fellow pacifists could at least proceed with their country's moral disarmament. For those who dreaded conflict, for those who saw little difference between German rearmament and French, for those who found the semblance of democracy at home no better than the brutal populism of the Nazis, servitude *was* better than war. Why not when, as a Socialist pacifist declared at his party's congress in May 1939, "France under [General] Gamelin would be identical to Germany under Hitler"?[36] Danzig, over whose fate war risked breaking out that year, was no more worth fighting for than the Rhineland, Austria, the Sudetenland, or Bohemia had been. The Baltic port was, after all, a German city capriciously cut off from Germany by horse traders at Versailles, a German city longing to rejoin the homeland. In this context the Neo-Socialist Marcel Déat's refusal to die for Danzig sounds very different: not an eccentric challenge but the expression of concerns central to a majority of the French.

We can see now, as some saw then, that the desperate optimism of those who thought peace a simple matter of clearing up mutual misunderstandings was a tragic blunder. Dedicated to Franco-German reconciliation, pacifists continued to argue in its favor after 1933, when illusion turned to disillusion. France should have negotiated, they said, with the Social Democrats and the conservatives of various stripes who ran Germany in the 1920s. That it had failed to do so was no argument for not negotiating with their successor, Hitler. On this score men of good will allied with men of no will, blindly vindicating Nazi policies, rashly minimizing the Nazi menace, and their vehement arguments confirmed the inertia, unease, and fears of their fellows. Most of the French did not want to face the German menace. Pacifists justified this lethargy when they dressed up amoral self-indulgence in moral-sounding arguments. Sometimes they did not even bother to go that far.

The abbé Arthur Mugnier (1853–1944) was a Benedictine priest who, for many years, cared for some of the most fashionable and also some of the most talented souls in Paris. Friend and spiritual adviser to many writers, he has been described as a man of piety, wisdom, and learning. On June 28, 1938, the man of God noted in his *Journal:* "The thought of a war solely about Danzig turns my heart. But we are committed. . . . Well, let's get uncommitted! It's only a stupid question of honor."[37]

Economy,
Economies,
Economists

In the long run we are all dead! Economists
set themselves too useless a task if in
tempestuous seasons they can only tell us
that when the storm is long past the ocean
will be flat again.

—*JOHN MAYNARD KEYNES*

PSYCHIC WOUNDS were aggravated by economic woes. French politicians liked to say that a nation's finances should be managed like those of a family. But households that tended their affairs the way France had since 1914 would end in bankruptcy, and the country skirted that fate in the 1930s.

Between the end of the First World War and the beginning of the Second the franc lost more than nine tenths of its original gold equivalent. The war had been fought on credit and expedients, while inflation crept up and purchasing power plunged. In 1918 wholesale prices were three and a half times what they had been four years before, and six times as many banknotes had been put in circulation. When the artificial props that kept the franc relatively stable were removed in 1919, the exchange value of the national currency reflected its real weakness: From 5.45 to the dollar in January 1919 it fell to 12 in January 1920 and to 15.50 the following January. Thereafter it wobbled, mostly downward, until in summer 1926 it hit its lowest low: A franc worth twenty American cents seven years before was now exchangeable for four.[1]

Exasperation and determination turned the tide. Within a few months with the trusted Raymond Poincaré, ex-president of the republic, at the helm, confidence returned, the franc recovered, but at a cost. By 1928 the franc had been officially stabilized at one-fifth of its postwar value: 25 francs to the dollar, 120 or 125 to the British pound. A triumph, claimed Poincaré's supporters, certainly a relief after the pangs of the last few years, but a disaster for many. For holders of fixed-rate obligations, government bonds, railway stocks, insurance policies; for owners of farmland let on long-term leases or rental property whose rents had been frozen since the war; for all those who had lent money or signed contracts at fixed rates, this was a terrible blow. The country sighed with relief, but many viewed the franc's stabilization as bankruptcy.

Also as betrayal. Where in 1913 some 31 billion francs in government stock had been outstanding, 100 billion more had been bought by 1921. One third of the war's cost had been financed by private savers who bought national defense bonds, and many had given up their foreign obligations to help the government's procurement abroad.* As late as 1920 a state loan had promised a safe 6 percent interest to bondholders who were to see four fifths of their investments' value vanish in a few years. To mentalities formed over generations of monetary stability, investments were even more about security than profit. They were also about patriotic duty. When one's country called, shares, gold, personal jewels flowed into public coffers. In 1921 still, the bishop of Saint-Brieuc, in Brittany, announced a payment of 10,000 gold francs contributed by inhabitants of his diocese, bringing their donations of *or patriotique* to an impressive 1,156,775 francs.[2] None forgot that the gold pieces the civic-minded had exchanged for paper would have kept their value, while paper wasted away.

Coming so soon after the failure of foreign bonds, especially Russian ones, in which so many savings had been invested, the failure of France's government to honor its obligations was the last blow. The leisure class of rentiers (560,000 of them declared in 1910, to be multiplied by family and

*"In no belligerent country have the rich contributed so little during the war as in France, or the poor so much in the way of indirect taxes," observed a well-informed English journalist, Robert Dell, in *My Second Country, France* (London, 1920), 55. But rich and less rich did buy war loans, on which they would take bad losses. The one exception may have been those better-off peasants whose sons at the front discouraged them from subsidizing a war they hated. Ibid., 230.

dependents) was broken beyond repair. Those not entirely ruined in the 1920s were going to be battered through the 1930s as yields were cut by government fiat and as the 6 percent bonds of 1920, their value drastically shrunk, were forcibly reconverted in 1932 to pay only 4.5 percent—a conversion that cost bondholders dear but brought fat commissions to the banks handling it.

When Edmond de Goncourt died in 1896, he had left his fortune to found an academy that would pay a generous annual rente to ten friends (and their successors) who every year would award a prize to a promising young author. The five-thousand-franc prize, first awarded in 1903, was meant to permit the prizewinner to work in comfort for two years on his next book, with no money worries. To guarantee a regular revenue and a safe one, the Goncourt fortune had been invested in government bonds. By 1938 the revenue had shrunk drastically, and the prize would be worth just a bit more than the annual dole of an unemployed Paris workman. By then winners of the Prix Goncourt did not have to worry about its cash value. Others, dependent on investment income for a habitual lifestyle, or simply for retirement, were less fortunate.[3]

With the rentier a certain leisured culture disappeared on which a good deal of literary and artistic life had rested. There would be no more men like Amédée Baumgartner, the brilliant surgeon who limited his practice to make time for classical studies, mountain climbing, the theater (he helped found the Vieux Colombier theater), and music.[4] There would be fewer men like the comte Jean de Pange, landowner-scholar whose revenues were gradually worn away by repeated government welshings. Reading his *Journal* for 1930, 1931, 1932, one senses the mounting sourness of those who lost part of their fortunes not once but several times.

Baumgartner and Pange were wealthy, and while some wealthy families lived like parasites, many had contributed disinterested service to community, to state, to scholarship. Such family traditions were to wane away.* A

---

*On the eve of war one third of the elite state engineering corps, the *Ingénieurs des ponts et chaussées*, left state employment for private practice in the course of their career; by 1928–30 some 55 percent did so. In 1910, 14 percent of the magistrates of the Conseil d'Etat migrated to the private sector; by 1930 more than twice as many. *Inspecteurs des finances*, another elite corps, showed similarly rising defection rates. Traditionally, army officers, magistrates, high civil servants had never relied on their wages. After the war, inflation, the shrinkage of private revenues, the diminution of rentes confirmed the need for an earned income that many had done without and made poor pay a subject of public debate. After 1930 economic crisis would turn the wages of public employees into a political issue and migration from the public to the private sector into a "hemorrhage." Dominique Chagnolland, *Le Premier des ordres* (1991), 242–43, 234.

still more crucial loss was the trust that ordinary French folk had placed in a state they had only recently been taught to think of as their own—a sentiment that did not survive these repeated letdowns. Those who gave up gold, savings, or shares in American companies because the state asked them to help had been told that they could trust the honor of France. Inflation, devaluation, renegation appeared like robberies and deliberate fraud perpetrated by authorities in whom they placed their faith. Disaffection followed, most intense among the solid citizenry that everywhere makes up the firm base of the state. Similar but worse experiences in countries like Germany destabilized society enough to bring revolutionary Nazis into power. In France things never got so bad. Solid citizens continued relatively solid. But most, henceforth, nursed a bitter grudge against the state, nor would they ever trust it.

As if this were not bad enough, there was another debilitating consequence of the franc's failures. The political figures involved in the stabilization of 1928, not least Poincaré, felt as their charges felt that France had let down the French. The trauma had been overwhelming. It should not happen again. Henceforth the franc would remain stable. General agreement on this meant that France would face the world monetary crisis with one financial hand tied behind its back. As first Britain, then the United States abandoned the gold standard and let their currencies float, as Europe began to bristle with exchange controls, quotas, and clearings, in France the first priority continued to be protection of savings. Defending the fatherland meant, first, defending the franc. Devaluation was theft. Maintaining a gold parity that events outdated was the way of wisdom. "Amidst monetary instability," boasted *Le Figaro* in 1933, "France is an island of stability, of confidence, of orthodoxy."[5] Of inertia, too.

Though 1933 was a little late for its high claims, *Le Figaro* exaggerated only little when French economic conditions were compared with those of other countries. After 1927 the French economy rebounded and reached production levels unknown since 1913. As the twenties petered into world depression, France alone seemed to lead a charmed life: the franc stable, the budget in surplus, productivity higher than ever, unemployment slight, and French tennis players leading the world. When, in October 1929, Black Tuesday struck Wall Street, the French had not been impressed. Less than a month after the stock market crash a new French government affirmed "a policy of prosperity." Americans were dismissed as squanderers and speculators; France's economic structure was strong enough to withstand their failure. In 1930 it was France's turn to preen over its brilliant budgetary situation and its gold reserves. "One is always rich when one spends a bit less than one makes," boasted the minister of finance. "Whatever the cause of world depression, France can face it with relative serenity," declared *Le Temps.* Paul Reynaud went one better. "Today capitalism triumphs in the world," he assured the 1930 congress of his party, the Alliance démocratique. "We see its benefits rain down on the working masses."[6] Even as he spoke, the beneficent rain was becoming a destructive storm.

Here it becomes necessary to backtrack, because the economic troubles of the Western world like those of France were directly related to "the peace to end all peace" imposed upon the Germans at Versailles. A crucial part of the Versailles settlement involved the indemnities—reparations— that Germany was supposed to pay for the death, damage, and destruction it had inflicted and for which it was held responsible. Bearing in mind that any discussion of the topic is bound to turn into simplification, one may say that the sum of reparations began by being hugely inflated and ended by becoming irrelevant, because largely unpaid. Still, having fought its war largely on credit, France based its postwar budgets on the hollow (and increasingly unlikely) assumption that its debts would be paid, its budgets balanced, and costs of rebuilding its devastated areas would be covered by German reparations. At the same time, like other Allies but more than most, France had borrowed heavily from others—about fifteen billion francs from the British, over twenty-five billion from the United States— and expected to draw on German reparation payments to pay its American debts.

The Germans, who had signed the Versailles Treaty with ill grace, approached reparations with grace iller still. To demonstrate their incapacity to pay, they set off an inflationary process that made the mark worthless, ruined a lot of Germans by the way, and set afoot the destabilization and the disaffection which, perfected by yet another economic crisis after 1930, made many Germans feel that any change, however radical, was better than the chaos and shame to which they seemed condemned. Americans, meanwhile, who wanted not chaos but trade in Central Europe but who did not want to get involved in European affairs, helped to negotiate two agreements, both designed to rebuild Germany with foreign loans so that it could pay reparations to its victors from which they in turn could pay their U.S. debts.

The flow of foreign credits to Germany and to its Central European neighbors was to be stanched by the monetary crisis that began in 1929 with the crash of the New York Stock Exchange. American banks failed; French and British ones pulled in their horns. In 1931, following a cascade of banks suspending payments in Germany and in neighboring countries, the German chancellor declared his country unable to continue paying reparations. President Hoover suggested a one-year moratorium on all international debts. When the year was over and Hoover's moratorium ran out in 1932, German reparations had been virtually suspended. The French did not see why they should resume paying their American war debt when Germans paid nothing to them. "The French won't pay us a cent unless they collect from Germany," an American diplomat accurately predicted. They had borrowed American money, they argued, to fight a war that was America's, too. The Americans had pressed for an end to German payments while raising their own tariffs to hobble the French exports that might have helped pay French war debts. With patriotic good conscience the French defaulted on their debt as Germans had defaulted on their own, and the French press hailed the default with enthusiasm. "When patriotism and pocketbooks come together," reported the American commercial attaché, "nothing can withstand them."[7]

The French, as we have seen, were feeling virtuous on all fronts. As *Le Temps* observed, "the happy balance of the economy and the virtues of the French people have made France a pillar of world economy." Closer to the grass roots, "the people feel they are better off than we are or than the British or Germans," an American military attaché thought. "They attribute this to their own sterling qualities of economy and simple living. . . ."[8] But living simply proved less simple than it looked. As crash followed crash in Germany, French banking establishments and other firms began to follow suit. Devaluation and inflation in the twenties had encouraged speculation. Small investors seeking safe havens for their savings had entrusted these to banks that lent or invested their money with more greed than prudence, or simply siphoned it off into enterprises of their own. Before the Wall Street crash, the wobbly German financial market depended heavily on French bank loans.[9] Yet German investments were turning out no safer than Russian ones had been. Investment banks like that of the speculative financier Albert Oustric obtained control of smaller provincial banks, used them in complicated stock market jugglery, milked them of funds, and pulled them down when the financial cat's cradle finally collapsed. Oustric's tangled web began to unravel in 1930, and as it did, the Bank of France turned out to have been involved in his shady operations, as were high-placed political figures, senators, cabinet ministers, who had been kept on payroll.

Many complicated financial structures that had in the later twenties risen on kited checks and political tangles cracked under the impact of world depression. In 1931 a respected banking family, the Bouilloux-Lafonts, controlling a major airline, the Aéropostale, was faced with public disgrace. They had dipped into the Aéropostale's government subsidies to prop up other endangered holdings, crashed, and brought the airline down with them. These and similar widely publicized scandals were more than business bankruptcies that threatened ruin for innocent savers, investors, and personnel. The financial failures entailed the moral failure of public figures that had been bought or wheedled into helping the ruined firms. The bankruptcy of Oustric was followed first by the resignations of the minister of justice, the undersecretary of state of public works, and the undersecretary of state for fine arts, all of them on Oustric's payroll, then of the cabinet which they had graced. The Aéropostale scandal brought an end to the political career of an influential deputy, Maurice Bouilloux-Lafont, and almost scuppered the career of a larger figure, the minister of finance, Pierre-Etienne Flandin, who turned out when not in office to function as legal counsel of the airline. Flandin survived disgrace (the Aéropostale didn't) by pointing out how many among those who attacked his ways shared his "indelicate" record. In a quarrymen's convention it was difficult to cast many stones.* The public credit of parliament and of its members was diminished further. So were estimates of business morality. In 1939 the U.S. assistant attaché for air would explain the problems of the aircraft industry in terms of graft and crooked politics.[10] The French had begun to do so a long time before.

Bear in mind that while small firms and small investors suffered, large banks and large investors made hay by coming to the rescue of failing concerns at the expense of previous shareholders and owners. Financial clouds are often lined with silver, at least for a chosen few. But the clouds were darkening fast.

---

*Members of parliament involved in financial scandals were usually cleared by their colleagues for insufficient evidence, and some continued in elective office for years thereafter. Less privileged mortals had to manage differently. The mid-thirties saw so many fraudulent liquidations and other operations breaching the law that the guardian superintending holding cells at the Paris lawcourts set up a special cabinet, appropriately furnished, where for a consideration prisoners of means could meet their—usually female— friends in private. His resourcefulness came to a bad end in 1935, when, with his wife's help, a crooked banker escaped from the low-security cell. *Gazette des tribunaux*, March 5, 1937.

Economic crisis in Britain or Germany had come like a blizzard; in France it felt more like a nagging drizzle. Taking the years 1925–1929 as 100, the General Industrial Production Index for 1930 stood at 97 for Germany, 88 for the United States, 115 for France. In 1931, when Britain registered 85, Germany 79, the United States 74, France still showed 102. In 1932, when every other industrial country touched bottom, France was just beginning to suffer. But delayed crisis meant delayed recovery. The British and the Germans, whose output fell drastically between 1929 and 1932, were back at 1929 levels in 1934 and 1935, well above them in 1937. France did not recover until the eve of war, in 1939.[11]

It is hard for one country to insulate against the winds of surrounding depression. In 1930 already sales were becoming more difficult, competition keener, margins of profit narrower, white-collar unemployment and part-time work schedules more evident. In fall of that year the U.S. commercial attaché noticed that stenographers, impossible to find only some months before, were now looking for work.[12] The year 1931, when the Industrial Production Index began its slow descent, was full of warnings of depression in the offing. It came the following year, when the *Ami du Peuple*, a daily more generally ready to boast about national good fortune, headlined MARDI GRAS DE CRISE. Shrove Tuesday would be glum. Carnival was dead.[13]

So was free or freer trade. The year 1932 resounds with calls for national preference and protection. Consume French goods only, buy only from French firms, urged the press. In February 1932 the fashionable women's monthly *Femina* reminded its readers that elegance should be national and civic-minded: "[D]on't wear old dresses, buy new ones and buy French: buying French proves not just patriotism, but good taste." Soon they would try to make wine fashionable for cocktails—"*l'heure des vins de France.*" In March the U.S. commercial attaché reported "restriction fever." But the quotas, duties, and restrictions on imports that a recent French writer has termed "defensive interventionism" brought few benefits. Freight car loadings plunged as foreign trade faltered; returns on taxes fell; government expenditures rose as hard times counseled intervention; bankruptcies surged. Counting 1913 as 100, the adjusted index of business failures and liquidations, which stood at 116 in 1931, had climbed to 150 in 1932 and continued to rise.[14]

Other grim figures rose as well. Between 1929 and 1936 unemployment seems to have quadrupled; partial unemployment increased even faster as working hours grew shorter. One study estimates a high of 1,000,000 unemployed in 1935, another tells us that that same year, out of 12,500,000 wage earners, 2,000,000 were out of work: about 1 in 6. As the U.S. commercial attaché commented, "official data are practically worthless." Many unemployed, 1,000,000 at least, eked out livings from their savings or with the help of friends and relatives. So official figures provide at best an index of misery, as does the surge of articles about the homeless, about the suicide of individuals and of couples unable to make ends meet, about the unemployment problem waning as the unemployed starved to death.[15] Specific figures about particular places may shed more light. In Troyes, the industrial center in Champagne whose hosiery business had been hard hit, unemployment figures rose by 6 percent between January and April 1933. More revealing, at Clichy, outside Paris, one study shows the number of unemployed receiving aid multiplied a hundredfold between 1930 and 1932, rising another 60 percent by 1935. In 1929 the municipality of Clichy spent 1,839 francs on unemployment relief, in 1931 just over 1,000,000, in 1935, 10,500,000.[16]

The interesting thing about official figures, which most of the time are all we have to use, is that they show the French in 1935, when unemployment was at its highest, suffering less than comparable lands: 2.6 percent out of the country's total population, contrasted with 7.6 percent in Britain, 9.4 in Germany, 12.75 in the United States. That was the positive side of the demographic crisis: Fewer babies born during the war meant fewer unemployed thereafter, simply because there were fewer working-age French folk looking to be employed. But it also meant that there were fewer French overall working, earning, spending.

Between 1930 and 1935 the French, especially those earning less or thrown on charity or on the dole, drew in their belts, cut down on inessential expenditures. Clothes, worn for a longer time, were mended more often; walls went unpainted; upkeep was put off. Fewer children attended holiday camps, fewer families went on holiday, and more admitted that they hadn't gone. There was less entertainment, less smoking (tobacco down 9 percent), less correspondence (letters sent down 5 percent), less heating (gas consumption down 5 percent). Savings and deposits fell steeply. But food consumption remained the same or rose: more meat, milk, coffee, sugar, fruit, significantly less beer, but wine made up for it. Calorie intake, though lower for the unemployed, remained above the dietitians' minimum twenty-seven hundred calories a day—in the provinces encouragingly higher. Suicides climbed, but the mortality rate kept falling, infant mortality by about one third over the first half of the thirties. Unemployment itself turned over, a high proportion of working folk oscillating between no work, some work, underemployment, full employment. We shall see that shortage of jobs bore harder on working women. But few men who were less than fifty experienced the demeaning sense of long-term uselessness that so many felt in the British Isles.[17]

This being said, the effects of depression went beyond the physical sphere. Bankruptcy, which once dishonored families and clans (Flaubert ruined himself to save his niece's husband from dishonor), became a not overly significant commonplace of business life. Widespread bankruptcies sapped confidence in contracts; constant government intervention introduced levels of constraint that encouraged breaches of intrusive legislation; commerce increasingly sought to circumvent laws that it could not respect. Inflation, taxation, tax evasion and other kinds of illegality combined to encourage more deals made in cash, more short-term transactions, fewer long-term enterprises.[18] For a brief spell France had welcomed the twentieth century; it would not fully accept it now until the 1960s.

Recession, depression were attributed to overequipment and overproduction. Too many machines displaced labor; too many goods chased too few consumers. "Mechanization," explained a Radical economist in 1932, "causes unemployment which causes underconsumption which causes slumps." Unemployment, opined *Paris-Soir*, the evening paper, was the result of overproduction; underconsumption reflected prices that were far too high. Charles Spinasse, professor of political economy, Socialist deputy, and future minister of national economy during the Popular Front, concurred. None stopped to consider that lower prices could be achieved only by higher production, and higher production depended on the machinery that noodleheads blamed for overproduction and underemployment. Circumstances confirmed prejudices. Industry was largely self-financing, and possibilities of modernizing equipment shrank as profits did. Banks were fragile (nearly four hundred went under between 1931 and 1935), and they became more so as depositors transferred their cash to mattresses, to foreign accounts, or simply to sustenance.[19]

Nobody really knew what was going on: Industrialists afraid of tax authorities hesitated to provide production data; the first obligatory statistical surveys, introduced in 1938, began offering answers in 1939. In their absence people made do with moral saws. The economic problems of the present would be solved by a return to the moral virtues of the past: thrift, sobriety, renouncing prodigality—except, of course, for the prodigal. Figures of authority like General Maurice Gamelin, chief of the General Staff, blamed the crisis on the appetite for pleasure and possessions unleashed by the development of material civilization, and hoped that the Depression would be a lesson to those who had succumbed. Capitalism *was* in crisis; the crisis of capitalism provided the crucial essay question in the 1934 competitive exam by which *inspecteurs des finances,* the elite of the financial public service, were recruited. "Fine subject! That's all one talked about . . ." remembers one candidate.[20]

As old suspicions of modernity resurfaced, traditional reactions surfaced, too. Hard hit by retrenchment, publishers and booksellers saw revenues plunge with sales. Paul Léautaud, the catty writer, recorded in 1933 that some booksellers did not sell as much as one volume a day. Wages were being cut everywhere. "The man who packs books in the shop," noted Léautaud, "says things are going badly, there's going to be a revolution."[21] We shall see in another chapter that Léautaud's interlocutor was not exceptional. His mood mirrored the widespread surliness apparent in all quarters. In January 1934 Edouard Bourdet's *Les Temps difficiles* (hard times) opened at the Théâtre de la Michodière. Business, its first lines made clear, is a disaster: Two of the hero's factories are closed, one works three days a week, the fourth keeps going only to finish an order for the War Ministry. Theatergoers recognized a familiar situation: "I hear only about catastrophes, families ruined, businesses bankrupt. . . . It's an epidemic." It was more than that: a plague and, as with most plagues, the rich retained the best chances of survival. Bourdet's besieged hero has stopped paying dividends to shareholders, but not his own salary. He has kept his hunt, his paintings, his servants, his château, and Act I ends on the dinner menu awaiting the company: trout in aspic, saddle of lamb, mushrooms, foie gras. . . . As that month's *Femina* confirmed, "What dancing and merrymaking! One dances at Ciro's, one dances at the Ritz, one dances everywhere . . . the tediousness of depressions seems far away . . . one goes out every evening; the jewels, the pearl necklaces, have no time to rest in their caskets."[22]

Some friction between socioeconomic groups is commonplace in all societies. Though often muted, mutual suspicion, resentment, fear more or less concealed between the powerful rich and the powerless poor, between those with the time and means to enjoy life's blessings and the barbarians at their gates, are hardly exceptional. Friction becomes aggravated when conditions make goods more scarce, access to even modest living more difficult than usual. With less to go around, what there is left counts more; the wraps come off the struggle. Hard times sharpen resentments; claims and defensive counterclaims grow more shrill.

Politics, which are always about who gets what and who loses what, focus more sharply on economic issues which, in their nature, cannot be settled swiftly or easily. Democratic politics exaggerate the sound and fury of struggle, exacerbate the instability of inherently unstable situations. Hitherto quiescent folk and social groups begin to stir, and their unwonted mobilization complicates political games normally played mostly by more experienced players. All economic crises since the 1770s had been political crises, and political instability, which always frightens business, only aggravated the economic situation. This is what happened in the 1930s, too, when one financial-political scandal after another disturbed business conditions, exasperated political instability, made a bad economic situation worse. After 1933 the theme recurs in the monthly and annual reports of U.S. commercial attachés who attribute the worsening economic situation to political tensions and instability which themselves feed on economic crisis.[23]

One area where economics and politics intertwined in unexpected fashion was the countryside. Since the end of the nineteenth century the proportion of the country's rural and urban populations had changed radically. In the 1890s France had been two thirds rural; by 1930 66 percent of the population lived in towns. Still, one family in three lived on a farm or in a village and consumed the produce of its fields. Four million farm households were largely self-sufficient, buying only rice, coffee, sugar, and salt. As the saying went, peasants knew how to live heads high and wallets tight. Most baked their own bread; others got it from the baker in exchange for their flour. Soup, still the main meal, was supplemented mainly by home-grown vegetables: potatoes, cabbage, carrots, beans. Butter and eggs were sold in the market. The year's pig steeped in the salt tub. Beyond it, one might rise to a chicken for celebrations, only exceptionally to butcher's meat. There was cider, homemade from local apples, wine cut with water in wine country, and, of course, water from the well, though water—often polluted—had an indifferent reputation. Drinking it made one spiteful, they said in Normandy: *L'eau rend méchant.* So, one might guess, did money, seldom handled, little used. "While urban workers are often paid in cash (notice that *often!*)," explains a report of the 1920s, "rural workers are very often paid in kind." Adding that farmers are not used to accounts or to their keeping. In 1932 a tax inspector found many in the southwest still describing land and real estate taxes as the taille—the poll tax that had been abolished with the ancien régime. In the rich Norman cattle country of the Auge traders in the twenties still counted in ancient pistoles (10 francs) and ecus (3 francs), peasants set prices not in francs but sous—the more accessible 5-centime subdivision of the 100-cent franc: 42 sous the milk pot meant 2.10 francs for two liters of milk.[24]

That was near Falaise, where only the old still spoke patois, the local dialect. Veterans had learned to speak "like everybody else" when war had mingled units in the trenches, and they had continued to use French on coming home. Yet though increasingly they talked like everybody else, they did not think like them, or quite. Producers in a society of consumers, they suffered when prices tumbled, resented dealers and speculators who profited from their ruin, scorned governments that botched their defense. Peasant life has always oscillated from bad years, when drought, torrential rains, hail, murrain hurt what they grew, to allegedly good years, when large harvests brought the prices down. Now government intervention further complicated their circumstances, setting minimum prices by decree, forcing them to sell unstockable stocks on the black market. Peasants were cautious, distrustful, suspicious, timid, wary, and their proverbs reflected long-established convictions:

> Distrust your father!
> Distrust your mother!
> Distrust yourself!
> Believe only in God . . . and even then![25]

The history of agriculture is less about crops than about passions. And prejudices. Rural timorousness was born of long experience, and experience bred rancor. Peasants believed—and they were partly right—that in the war they had suffered more heavily than other social groups. Bourgeois, civil servants, industrial workers had bled less heavily than they and theirs, and even when the disproportion was more imaginary than real, the loss of strong young arms was more blighting on small self-sustaining properties. A village like Couffouleux (Aveyron), population five hundred, that lost more than fifty of its sons killed in four years lost more than 10 percent of the population, the marrow of its youth. It never recovered.[26] Peasants were pacifists, perhaps more intensely than their fellow French; but they were rancorous above all. Contemporary observers use or quote words like *grudge, vengeance, anger, dupery, shirkers.* When depression hit, and it had hit them first, their resentments grew sharper, more articulate, especially against industrial workers whose postwar strikes they blamed for having delayed their demobilization and return to the fields where they were sorely needed. As Henri Dorgères declared, whose Peasant Defense Committees were founded in 1928 and 1929 to fight against the costs of social insurance, "there's no solidarity between peasant and urban worker, there's only exploitation of the former by the latter."[27]

A loudmouthed agitator whose Green Shirt militants provided action in small centers where in the mid-thirties the cinema was still a flickering wonder, Dorgères testifies to hardships readily turned into political hay. His anti-Marxism was an incantation, but he found ready ears when he called upon peasant crowds to raise their pitchforks against "the tyranny of towns," of townsmen, of functionaries (*le fonctionnaire, voilà l'ennemi*), of parasitic foreigners. The ancient virtues embodied in country folk could be recaptured only by a return to the land, an idea that appealed even to moderate minds in disoriented times. Henri Queuille, the Socialist minister of agriculture, wished "that every Frenchman, whatever his job, could own a field however small."[28] Country folk may have felt less sentimental enthusiasm.

Between 1930 and 1935 agricultural prices fell to half; peasant buying power in 1935 was two thirds what it had been in 1929. Farmers could not sell their produce without losing money. They tried stocking crops, but barns and silos ran over. In December 1934 the harvest of 1933 had been hardly broached. They cut back on seed, on fertilizer, on improvements. Between 1932 and 1935 loans issued by the Crédit Agricole of Finistère fell by almost 90 percent. Productivity, no longer related to profit, also fell. Farmhands stood idle; day laborers were stranded without work. In the middle thirties in a Gard village, where three houses out of two hundred enjoyed running water, four heads of household out of six were out of work, and those who worked barely earned their food. "Our neighbors," noted the young Denis de Rougemont, "are privileged to have a garden. Yet the main meal of their day consists of chestnuts, olives, radishes and some garden vegetables that they haven't been able to sell."[29] The farming population had been falling since the mid-nineteenth century. Now it fell further, and if it didn't fall more, that was because so many who had left the land to work in town returned to underemployment on the farm.

God helps those who help themselves. That hard lesson learned in the previous century had helped improve wages and conditions of labor in towns. It was time for peasants to follow suit, but rural organization was not easy. Agricultural associations were in the hands of notables with a mentality and interests that often differed from the grass roots. Peasants were seen, and they saw themselves, as second-class citizens. Ready enough to vote poultices for wooden legs, parliament paid no heed to ordinary rurals. It had, for example, voted to introduce summer time, a measure unpopular with folk whose lives went by the sun, whose labor was gauged by light, not watches. Minimum prices set by government fiat underscored government impotence, made very clear that hope lay not in Paris but with peasants taking their destinies into their own hands. Leagues sparked by the likes of Dorgères helped let off steam but led down dead-end streets. Agricultural syndicates, friendly societies, cooperatives were more promising. Who would found them? Who would lead them?

Bright village children traditionally made their way out of mud and misery by the sort of studies that brought them urban status, turned them into priests, teachers, minor civil servants, residents of towns. The twentieth century, however, had seen the appearance of agricultural colleges that offered bright lads the training that would make them better farmers, more active in the defense of local interests, founding cooperatives, competing with doctors and landowners for seats on municipal councils. The war had contributed to this training. At Jurques, in Calvados, as the thirties opened, the mayor, a carpenter, opposed the syndicate being founded there. But its president, Adrien Geneviève, had learned in the trenches how to care for wounded, to apply splints and perform injections, skills that, when used back home, gave him the prestige of a healer. When Geneviève offered to supply his neighbors with coffins, properly padded yet cheaper than the carpenter mayor could turn out, his battle for the syndicate was won.[30]

Catholics embattled in an anticlerical republic had fought back since the nineteenth century's end by organizing first urban, then rural working people in social and self-help clubs. Their first agricultural college, the Ecole Supérieure d' Agriculture, had opened in Angers in 1898. By 1920 half of the members of the Catholic youth movement, the ACJF (Association Catholique de la Jeunesse Française), were peasants. By the twenties' end a movement catering specially to young peasants had appeared, the JAC (Jeunesse Agricole Catholique), which would provide a cohort of peasant leaders through the 1930s and beyond. Naturally enough, their support, like their inspiration, often came from priests or from local figures interested in progress but not very much in the established order, like Jacques Le Roy Ladurie, promoter of agricultural syndicalism in the Calvados and, by 1937, general secretary of the national union of agricultural syndicates. Unreservedly anti-Marxist, Le Roy Ladurie was also anticentralist, antistatist, antiliberal—denouncing the free wolf in a free sheepfold. But no one else offered to support agricultural cooperatives, suspect to some of hampering free speculation in grain, to others of red collectivism. Since French importers of American and British farm equipment, Deering or Massey-Harris, refused to deal with the Calvados cooperative suspected of socialism, the Normans bought and used German harvesters. That was the idiocy of French business that men like Le Roy Ladurie denounced, as they denounced the foolishness of industrialists at bay ignoring the vast undeveloped market of the countryside.[31]

For nearly a century, in a land where enfranchised men rejected or ignored the Church, the Church had looked to women for worship and support. Peasant organizers, often of the Right, looked to women also. Le Roy Ladurie launched his syndicate in the Calvados by appealing directly to the farm wives. In the peasant economy of the pasturelands, milking, making butter, selling dairy products fell in the women's province, affecting not only profit but personal honor as farmwife and as trader. Milk and butter issues brought women into the union; women brought their husbands. In the process, women's views of the world broadened; they had taken a step to empowerment. They still lacked the vote and would not get it until 1944, but they were more explicitly partners of their husbands, more consciously participants in community enterprise.[32] Self-enfranchisement preceded enfranchisement, as it must if it is to work. And what was true of women was true of men as well. Hard times taught self-help within the market and beyond it, too. Learning to set up and run credit associations, mutual fire insurance, mutual accident insurance provided hands-on courses in politics and participation more effective than casting a vote every so many years. The quest for fertilizer and better produce prices trained more country folk for modern living on their own terms, not those of urban civics.

It made them more active, more conscious citizens. But not necessarily more civic-minded than their city cousins. In 1938 and 1939 most of the peasantry was solidly against the possibility of war, and for the same reason

that ranged their forebears against traipsing off to Russia in 1812: reluctance to enter conflicts that did not concern *their* land. None (or too few)
explained that the fortunes of others might directly affect their own. When,
in July 1940, a few days after their army's collapse and the suspension of
the Third Republic, the Conseil Général of Calvados met in Caen, there
was no mention of Pétain or of the new Etat Français. The main subject of
discussion were the privileges of *bouilleurs de cru:* Should fruit growers retain
the right to distill ten liters of pure alcohol a year free of tax?[33]

Normal people perceive the world in concentric circles that move out-
ward from their household and themselves. They know very well when
things go badly, but the context of problems remains obscure or seems irrelevant. We shall see that only an exceptional few knew more than that.
But hindsight provides broader references. The world trade crisis gnawed at
the national economy. Between 1928 and 1931 French sales abroad fell by
one quarter; by 1936 France exported half what it had sold only eight years
before. French gastronomy continued triumphant, haute couture did well,
but those were lonely stars on a dim horizon. In constant 1914 francs, income from exports was down 61 percent. As confidence plummeted, investments fell: Investment rates in 1938 were barely two thirds what they
had been in 1930; modernization, energy, equipment fell behind. The active population, steadily shifting out of the agricultural sector, seeped out
of industry, too, accounting for 36.6 percent of the total in 1929 and only
32.3 percent in 1938.[34] What statistics call "services" only too often means
taking in each other's washing. But while service workers produced little,
industrial workers produced less, and earned to scale. Industrial wages, on
the whole, had kept up with inflation. After 1930 wages began to fall, but
what bit into income now, for those still employed, were cuts in working
days and hours paid for. In the textile valleys near Rouen, full of factories,
spinners, dyers, weavers, fullers worked three days a week and one week in
two or three. Many women and young people whose wages used to supplement family income were let go. Breadwinners' take-home pay barely supplied a household's needs.[35]

Since the war national revenue per person had grown by a yearly average
of 5 percent. In the thirties it fell twice as fast as it had just risen. A sluggish
economy, stingy banks, timorous capitalists, disenchanted investors, shrinking producers, desperately thrifty consumers, the bears had taken over the
market. The bears growled that horns should be drawn in, belts tightened,
budgets balanced, the franc defended—especially the franc defended,
against budgetary deficit. Those who preferred more active policies were

hamstrung by the country's monetary and financial weakness. A lot has been written, a lot has been said about how little, how badly the political class of those days understood economics. It may be, however, that the leaders of France ignored economics and finance less than it has been alleged, that they were caught in a vise between economic moves some would have liked to make and the political temper of their electorate.

It remains true that the political and economic establishment was underinformed and underarmed to fight a crisis. In the absence of even approximate statistics, no one had a complete picture of French financial life. Budgetary forecasts were based not on hard data but on past experience. Cash flow throughout the nation and over the nation's borders was an unknown quantity. The French distrusted checks or any records that might help a tax collector, and most transactions were made in cash. People queued up to draw or make payments in person: savings, insurance, pensions, taxes. The new social legislation of the thirties raised problems for men and women who did not realize that the slips of colored paper they received represented payments they were supposed to cash. "He had a check," remembers one social assistant; "he didn't know what it was."[36]

Government revenue rested most heavily on indirect taxes—wine and alcohol, tobacco, business activity—and taxes were relatively higher in France than in neighboring countries, because the weight of public debt per head was a good deal greater: more than twice that of Belgium, three times as much as in the United States. As the economy flagged, as shares lost half their value between 1928 and 1932, the tax on business transactions brought in less revenue, investments in stocks and bonds fell further. Taxes on stock exchange activities that used to bring forty-six million francs in 1926 paid something over eight million francs in 1931. The 35 percent paid on the price of automobiles, the 50 percent paid on sugar did not fall, but national revenues fell along with purchases of dispensable goods. Other basic taxes reflected the tax laws of 1791, all of them based on visible references that avoided snooping into private lives: land tax, property tax, *patentes*—licenses to practice trades—and the old tax on doors and windows.* Many a young revenue official began his service by counting doors and windows of structures to be taxed. Income tax, voted in 1914, intro-

---

*Introduced in the 1790s as one of a number of levies on "external indications of wealth," this assumed that the dwellings of ordinary folk would show a minimal number of openings and proved, of course, a self-fulfilling prophecy that discouraged the circulation of light and air. Although the tax was officially abolished at the end of the First World War, oral evidence indicates that tax inspectors continued to take doorways and fenestration into consideration in estimating taxpayers' means.

duced in 1916, applied to annual revenues above twelve thousand francs. In 1932, 350,000 persons submitted such returns. A morning paper pointed out that the country boasted 1,200,000 automobiles and that quite a lot of people with revenues over twelve thousand francs did not even own one. Where had potential income tax payers disappeared?[37]

Municipal income rested on *octrois*, tolls levied on goods entering the commune. Most of the revenue came from food products, alcohols, and fuels. But *octroi* regulations also applied to private individuals, whether residents or travelers, creating minicustoms stations and customs searches at every municipal border. In 1937 travelers arriving at a railway station had to declare the goods they brought. Drivers could be stopped and checked for the gas in their tanks or parcels in the back seats. In the Paris region in the 1920s *octroi* employees entered trams, trains, buses to control and collect their pounds of flesh. By the 1930s this particular practice had been dropped. Shopping and small parcels were "tolerated"; so were home deliveries in the suburbs. But hunters returning home with a hare or a lark or two were supposed to buy a lump-sum ticket *(forfait)* or take out an annual subscription, beside the hunting permit delivered by the state, and lines of trucks and private cars continued to encumber the gates of many towns, where inspections were carried out. Debate about abolishing these feudal levies had been going on at least since the beginning of the century, but their contribution to municipal finances was too precious. Paris in 1929 raised 550 million francs from its *octrois.* Though some left-wing municipalities abolished the *octroi* and replaced it by taxes on automobiles, horses, pianos, mules, billiards, and real estate, a doctoral dissertation of 1937 indicated nearly a thousand towns that still relied on them. As late as 1943 Bar-sur-Aube, in Champagne, published a new tariff of its *octroi* taxes—abolished finally in 1949.[38]

Most towns balanced their budgets by fair means or foul. After 1931 the government never did. The politics of the thirties are about how they tried to, how they failed, and how attempts and failures affected the national mood and the nation's capacity to operate. Repeated attempts to collect taxes due but unpaid produced satirical ditties but little revenue. So did imaginative broadening of indirect taxation: Electrical signs were taxed; so were signboards and advertisements; surtaxes were placed on postage stamps, their proceeds allegedly for the unemployed (forcing us "to feed those who do nothing, encourage them to go on doing nothing," complained one irate citizen).[39]

Among the most lasting schemes for squeezing money out of stones was the development of betting. Since 1887 a proportion of the revenue from racecourse betting (pari mutuel) had gone to local charities and national public assistance. In 1930 the betting system, reformed, became off-the-racecourse betting (pari mutuel urbain), accessible through bars and tobacco shops all over the country. Henceforth millions of bettors could place their wagers through the PMU and contribute to public welfare over their Sunday drinks. Some PMU revenues went, as they had always done, to a variety of good causes, including the installation of water mains, the protection of nature, support for horse breeding and sporting activities. Another portion went to supplement the budget.[40]

An even more effective innovation was the National Lottery: hardly a new invention (Nero used a lottery to rebuild Rome after the fire he set), but a remarkably successful one. Several projects for a lottery had been mooted in the 1920s, designed either to subsidize reconstruction or to abolish the national debt. In 1931 a project destined to help the unemployed proved more persuasive, was voted by the Chamber of Deputies, and the first drawing in 1932 was a great success. In 1933 the sale of tenths of tickets, which made their price more accessible, went so well that the lottery's managers curtailed its publicity budget. The harder the times, the more attractive fantasies of escape.[41]

But lotteries and betting profits did not go far in solving the overall budgetary bind, which grew worse as times got harder and revenues fell farther behind expenses. Scattershot taxation and harsher repression of defensive fraud mobilized taxpayers. The later 1920s, which embittered those whose savings had helped save the franc, evoked taxpayers' movements which in the harder years to come attracted an even more numerous, more agitated following. Subsidized by marginal political aspirants like François Coty, the Corsican perfume millionaire and admirer of Mussolini, or Jacques Lemaigre-Dubreuil, whose fortune rested on a great oil firm—the Huiles Lesieur—the Taxpayers' Federation claimed half a million members by 1934.[42] Compound of exasperation, nostalgia, and common sense, their message appealed to many.

If the government kept its hands off the economy and out of taxpayers' pockets, time would restore prosperity. The unemployed would find jobs when they became willing to work for lower wages; businessmen would sell their products when they decided to slash prices. The weak would fall by the wayside, but competitive adjustment would bring recovery, and good times would return. Shrunken stocks would revive demand; growing demand would encourage investment; rising investment would offer employment once more and refloat the economy on a tide of consumption. Unfortunately it did not work that way. A lot of French investments consisted of bullion and bank notes hidden in piles of linen. The French like savings even more than money. But savings have to be secure. Now capital, frightened or discouraged, went into hiding at home and abroad. Hoarding—*thésaurisation*—offered the preferred escape for little people and larger capitalists who didn't trust the government, its tax collectors, the investment opportunities government restricted, the credit instruments that it failed to honor. For excellent private reasons, tens of billions of francs were withdrawn from the national economy when they were needed most. In December 1932 the issue of silver coins intended to replace small paper notes then in circulation was postponed for fear that it would further encourage hoarding and that despite their very low silver content, the new coins would rapidly disappear into mattresses and cupboards. When new five-franc pieces were eventually struck in 1933, they were made of nickel.[43]

By then John Maynard Keynes had begun to argue that in a depression there was no wage so low as to eliminate unemployment or turn the business cycle around. Only deliberate public deficits could provide the subsidies and investments to get the economy going and tempt hoarders to join in. But Keynes's revolutionary theories were largely unknown in France, and his *General Theory of Employment, Interest, and Money* (1936) was only translated there under the Occupation (1942). The gist of Keynes's ideas, however, presented in earlier works, had become available in translations of the 1920s and early thirties. Left-wing economists, like the Socialist Charles Spinasse or Léon Blum's economic adviser Georges Boris, admired his ideas. Conservative writers, like C.-J. Gignoux, attacked them as early as 1933. Specifically, conventional economic wisdom was aware of the employment possibilities of public works. The minister of finance discussed their utility in creating jobs. The minister of war provided credits to hire the unemployed for work on country roads. A conservative country mayor like Antoine Pinay undertook the urban renewal of his industrial town. A Socialist municipal council like that of Toulouse used public works to moderate joblessness by modernizing local services, hired roadmen, cemetery guardians, garbage collectors, telephone installers, builders, and unskilled workers, yet hardly made a dent in soaring unemployment.*[44] But

---

*Neither did the efforts of the French Red Cross, whose Central Committee, struggling against unemployment in luxury industries, launched a campaign to persuade women to buy an extra dress: *la robe portebonheur*. See *Temps*, December 23, 1932.

public works, welcomed when state coffers had been full, seemed less attractive now that they were empty. Government intervention, many said,
delayed market adjustments by draining off investment capital. It was easier
to keep unwanted labor off the market by easing short-term reenlistments
in the army or raising the school-leaving age from thirteen to fourteen.[45]

Staggering from one issue of Treasury bills to another, from one government loan to the next, the Treasury was running on empty, the market
awash in bills: four billion in early 1932, fourteen billion three years later,
over twenty billion in spring 1936. Rising debt limited the government's
freedom of maneuver. Priming the pump of production, getting the jobless
back to work cost money. What we now describe as deficit financing could
still be plausibly denounced as national bankruptcy. Retrenchment was the
only responsible answer to recession. Expenditure on school construction
was cut by two thirds, on workers' housing by half. Shipyards, arsenals were
closed or cut back. The great ironworks at Trignac, on the lower Loire,
closed their gates, depriving a municipal council already overwhelmed by
unemployment benefits of essential tax revenues. In Saint-Nazaire, next
door, when the last great ocean liners, the *Champlain* and the *Normandie,* were
launched in 1932, thousands were thrown out of work. Hydroelectric development was suspended; the national telephone network remained frozen
in underdevelopment; retirement conditions for public school teachers were
downgraded.[46]

The building industry, locomotive of economic activity, was thoroughly
discouraged. Few private investors could afford the cost of building modern structures; few found much profit in so doing. Investment, speculation
favored office buildings and commercial property on which they were free
to charge higher rents and where capital could be amortized more swiftly.
But such speculative building came to an end with the Depression. Residen-
tial property meanwhile lost money or was sold off piecemeal to those who
lived in it. Many apartment houses turned into condominiums, but many
more landlords failed to persuade their tenants to turn owners. Renting was
too good a deal. Ever since the war successive governments had prevented
rents from keeping pace with inflation or responding to devaluation. Rent-
ers were protected, come what may. When lodgers couldn't pay the rent,
landlords were prohibited from evicting. Property owners were forced to
shoulder the social responsibilities of the nation. Soon rental property cost
more than it brought in. Owners, their real incomes steadily falling, limited
the upkeep of their properties to the bare minimum. Savings could have
gone into building houses or apartments for sale or rent. But rent ceilings

discouraged builders from bringing more rental units on the market, while high interest rates discouraged the building of modest homes. The British recovery of the thirties rose on a housing boom. The French denied themselves that possibility by prohibiting profit. Building industry operation in 1938 was 40 percent below its 1928 level. In Paris building had dropped from 6,470 stories a year in 1914 to 400 stories in 1938–1939. "At this rate," commented the American commercial attaché, "it would take several centuries to renew existing dwellings," let alone add new ones.[47] He exaggerated, but the hunt for lodgings was going to remain a popular pursuit into the 1960s.

The most counterproductive cuts, politically, concerned public employees, whose numbers had grown from 619,000 in 1914 to 745,000 in 1925 to 858,000 in 1932. Government personnel expenditures, not including pensions, accounted for one third of the national budget. Resented by the general public as meddling, finicky, and rude, secure in their tenure and retirement, *fonctionnaires* were favorite targets of taxpayer wrath. Beginning in 1933, recruitment of *fonctionnaires* was slowed, then suspended, and attrition was allowed to diminish their ranks.* Then salaries and benefits became the target of economizing governments, retirement payments, pensions—not just of *fonctionnaires* but of veterans and other pensioners too. Premiers like Gaston Doumergue in 1934, Pierre Laval in 1935 used decree-laws (not subject to parliamentary debate, thus not involving parliamentary responsibility) to cut wages and raise taxes over broad categories. In August 1935 the latest round of cuts reduced by 10 percent all state and local government expenditures, including interest on bonds, and cut rents, mortgage payments, and utility rates by an equal amount. As Julian Jackson comments, a right-wing government dedicated to freeing the economy from controls had produced "the most extensive intervention in economic life ever hitherto undertaken by a French peacetime government" *and* repudiated the state's financial obligation to rentiers to boot.[48]

The decree-laws provoked widespread demonstrations, strikes, and riots the country round. The retrenchments affected not just income but govern-

---

*Writing in 1933, one career civil servant pointed out that since the war, stagnant salaries, inflation, and rising living costs denied public employees the possibility of "honorable subsistence" and discouraged potential candidates from choosing careers in the public service. The best and brightest looked elsewhere. As a result, particularly in the last few years, the level of candidates had fallen, admission standards had followed suit, and the quality of public service was becoming a matter for concern. André Moufflet, *M. Lebureau et son âme* (1933), 9, 12, 139.

ment facilities everywhere: Tax offices were closed; so were registry offices, tobacco manufactories, and warehouses, even courts of law. Where folk had paid tax or filed a suit near home, after 1934 many were forced to make tracks for some larger center. And where traditional unemployed could be politically dismissed as traditionally rebellious, the decree-laws struck at all social levels. Demonstrations against them saw magistrates and army generals march beside schoolteachers and customs agents.[49] Advocates of deflation hoped that if living costs and revenues could both be cut, the budget would be balanced, and the economy free to gather steam again. In fact, what people noticed was their diminishing incomes and waning facilities. That was a perfect recipe to ensure the triumph of the opposition. The French and their *fonctionnaires*, at one for once, refused to accept deflation and punished those responsible for it by voting against them in 1936.[50] Theories divide, declared a Communist in 1936, but claims unite.[51] Enough of the French had claims and grievances that year, apparently state-inflicted, actually self-inflicted, to bring in a government of the Popular Front.

A major cause of economic problems was the franc. Devaluation had been so traumatic that none dared consider it again. That meant that when other countries left the gold standard—Britain in 1931, the United States in 1933—letting their currencies float free, France maintained the value of its money at the cost of its trade. French goods became less competitive with goods of other countries; French services cost more than the same services cost elsewhere. Tourism was especially hurt. In 1930 one dollar bought better than 25 francs; in 1933, less than 20. In 1929 tourists contributed 9.6 billion francs to the economy; in 1933, less than half that: 4.3 billion. Thereafter income from tourism never rose above the 3-billion-franc mark. What such figures meant we can see from the economy of the Côte d'Azur: At Menton eighteen big hotels closed during the 1930s; at Nice twenty-two. Along the Mediterranean coast, like everywhere else, construction flagged. Between 1928 and 1931 the number of building permits fell 45 percent in the department of Alpes-Maritimes. One result: In the fourth electoral district of Nice the Communist candidate had won 3.2 percent of votes cast in 1932; in 1936 he got 50 percent and won.[52]

As exporters slashed prices the world over, the French found themselves in a quandary. In 1929 French prices, all in all, stood 22 percent below the foreign competition; by 1935 they were 21 percent higher than the British, 35 to 66 percent higher than world prices as a whole. Americans, who in

1931 found French cars costing twice what they cost at home, reported that in 1934 they sold at three times the U.S. price.[53] Exports were not alone to suffer; everyday living costs affected the cost of labor and production. Meat, butter, sugar, beans, chicken, cheese were all significantly dearer than in Britain; so was coal; so were men's suits, haircuts, or getting a pair of shoes resoled, not because wages were too high but because the high franc made everything expensive.[54] Suggestions of devaluation were met by scorn, by denunciation, by affirmation of loyalty to the franc stabilized by Poincaré, which, Premier Gaston Doumergue declared in a national radio address in March 1934, "must remain intangible." Parties and public opinion from the Action Française on the Right to the Communists on the Left concurred. Savings were not to be expropriated again. One year later, in March 1935, the Belgians, who had stuck with France and with the gold standard, devalued in their turn. Within twelve months unemployment figures in Belgium fell 24 percent compared with 3 percent in France.[55]

The issue could no longer be avoided, but it was put off as long as possible. In June 1935 parliament voted a law (mentioned above) whose single article permitted the government of Pierre Laval to operate by decree in order to avoid devaluation of the currency. When devaluation finally came in fall 1936, under the aegis of a Popular Front that began by rejecting the idea, it was carried out—a financial official remembers—in fear, in haste, too late to do much good. Too little, too late meant that one devaluation was followed by another and another still. By 1938 the franc was worth less than half what it had been in 1928, drawing the cheerful comment "Falling prices at last! One can find francs at ten cents."[56]

Prices, actually, had been falling for some time. Complaints against *la vie chère* had swelled as the twenties ended. Even the wealthy now wanted to compare prices when they shopped and window-shopped, and expected to see prices clearly posted, a demand to which expensive boutiques responded grudgingly.[57] At less exalted levels, increasingly discriminating buyers incited more sedulous sellers to think afresh. One of the few positive aspects of the Depression years was that in a country little given to competitive marketing, crisis spurred competitive pricing and imaginative sales techniques. Sales and discounts demonstrated the high markups on which wholesalers and retailers had lazily relied. Department stores now advertised price cuts ranging from 15 to 30 percent on all their goods; custom tailors provided made-to-measure suits at almost half the price. Even so, many preferred to get old suits and dresses dyed to look like new at a fraction of what new garb cost.[58]

Few French manufacturers of consumer goods courted the mass market. Carmakers, technically capable of mass production, ignored the potential demand, rejected cheaper models in favor of expensive ones that promised higher profit. French automobile production progressed but slowly, while British sales more than doubled. That was when bicycles equipped with motors gained popularity. Their cost was low; their single-horsepower engine consumed little gas and required no license to operate. Workmen and employees could afford their modest prices, about sixty dollars, and save on public transport fares, which were going up. French makers of radio sets had kept prices high and driven buyers into the arms of German, American, Dutch manufacturers. By 1932 radio stores offered discounts of 30 to 40 percent and still made a living. Electrical appliances had enjoyed little attention from the electrical industry or power companies. By 1933 the American commercial attaché noted intensive advertising campaigns by electrical manufacturers, "particularly in the provinces where . . . electrically operated labor saving devices are not well known."[59]

They were becoming better known thanks to the postwar invention of an innovative man, Jules-Louis Breton, fascinated by new technologies. The first annual exhibition of household appliances, the Exposition des Arts Ménagers, had opened in 1923 and taken up regular quarters in the Grand Palais a few years later. By 1939 the annual show counted over six hundred thousand visitors; by the end of the 1940s, double that many.

Business enterprise did not enjoy much prestige in France: Moneygrubbing was vulgar; profits could be made only at somebody else's expense. Born in 1911, educated by Jesuits, Pierre de Calan remembers that "going into business was not done." But simpler people too regarded trade with a jaundiced eye. "[T]o say of somebody that he's in business," declared Pierre Hamp, a labor writer, "is the beginning of dishonor." Selling on credit was regarded as a form of usury. Commerce and industry were getting used to bank credit; modest folk were transferring habits of consumption credit from the tallies of baker and milkman to the purchase of dishes and furniture. But the middle classes were ashamed not to pay cash. Here, too, things were changing. Slowly. A 1933 study of purchases on the installment plan noted that installment sales, 3 percent of all commercial transactions in 1926, accounted for 23 percent in 1930 and 1931, for 25 percent of car sales in 1932. Yet payments were still preferably made at the store counter. Payment collectors calling at the home could provoke neighbors' comments. Afraid of wagging tongues (*qu'en dira-t-on?*), customers preferred to avoid their visits. And credit establishments made their deliveries in unmarked vans.[60]

Another novelty, discount stores, provided more acceptable avenues for shoppers of modest means. Frank W. Woolworth's five-and-ten-cent stores had flourished all over America since the late nineteenth century, as had Sebastian Kresge's. But discount retail outlets appeared in France only in the later 1920s, probably inspired by German imitations of the Americans. They did not catch the public eye, however, until depression made them so popular that they were identified with it as *magasins de crise*.[61]

Between 1931 and 1933 retail stores promising low single prices blossomed. Prisunic, Priminime, Monoprix, Dimax, Unifix, Fixprix appeared not only in working-class quarters but on posh streets like the avenue de l'Opéra and in the provinces. By 1934 the capital boasted 30 of them, while eighty-five urban centers shared 126 more. Oases in drab settings, they were luminous, heated, crowded, animated, cheerful, their stalls full of inexpensive and attractive goods that one was free to handle but did not have to buy.

Department stores had in the nineteenth century introduced breadth of choice. Discount stores cut prices by narrowing choice, hence their overhead. Their massive orders tempted manufacturers only too glad to employ their machines and their personnel, even if profit margins were lower and labor earned less pay. Often launched by established firms like the Printemps, (Prisunic) or the Galéries Lafayette (Monoprix) eager to attract a new clientele or, as they put it, "to defend the workman's buying power," they featured a selling strategy that brought Zola's descriptions up-to-date. Shoppers were made welcome, were encouraged to browse, to enjoy the bright lights and the canned music, were tempted to buy cheap necessities and small luxuries, too. The unemployed found there a dry place to pass the time, the young a convenient hangout, lovers a rendezvous, the idle enjoyed the action, and all of it was free. "One was OK there from the first. . . . Warm, safe, far from everything. As in a pleasant dream." There weren't many pleasant dreams to choose from for those with empty pockets in those days. Offerings were geared to native taste and habit. In 1932 Woolworth's upper price limit was twenty cents in America, sixpence in Britain—equivalent to about two francs. In France the maximum price, ten francs, sometimes a little more, reflected the higher prices but also "the fear of not satisfying a demanding public and raising suspicions about the quality of goods." The system worked. In 1934 Printemps shares paid less than 4 percent, but Printemps shareholders got 7 percent on their investment in Prisunic.[62]

Bulk buying and loss leaders also paid off for multiple branch chain stores, selling mostly food, another postwar phenomenon to grow in the Depression. The chain stores of the thirties, mostly franchises, competed with other grocers by offering lower prices; but they attracted buyers by rebates, bonus stamps, prizes, and free gifts—*primes*—that, bought in bulk, cost little and retained a faithful clientèle. *Primes* had been imported from the United States in the 1890s and used to attract customers or subscribers ever since. But their extension in the 1930s was exponential. While factory warehouses bulged with unsold goods, gifts in kind could profitably be used for publicity and sales promotions. From groceries, *primes* spread to florists, shoe stores, dyers, hat shops, and other establishments. Furniture emporiums offered free luggage; 250 grams of Brazilian coffee brought a free lottery ticket. The eponymous hero of Gabriel Chevalier's *Les Héritiers Euffe*, a merchandising paladin, had made his fortune by "diabolic cunning in the selection of such gifts . . . carving sets, umbrella stands, baby carriages, furniture. . . ."[63]

Actually the majority of *primes* were modest household objects that housewives on tight budgets would hesitate to buy: tablecloths, napkins, crockery, or towels. They helped the thrifty buyers' budget but also altered homelife, norms of civility, and sociability. The working-class housewife acquired not just plated cutlery or stainless knives but coveted luxuries till then inaccessible to the prudent shopper: lustrous tea services with enamel flowers that opened the possibility of entertaining friends. Families learned to use box cameras to take their own photos at will. Chandeliers replaced bare bulbs hanging from the ceiling. Material life changed aspect, especially in the countryside, where table knives "by the thousand dozens" replaced the pocketknives peasants still used at table. Lampshades had been ignored as too expensive. In one area where the electricity company sold 165, a Maison de Primes distributed 3,000. Where stores had sold 600 electric irons, bonus schemes ordered 8,000 and reduced local appliance prices by 20 percent while electrical consumption rose.[64]

But benefits for consumers and for the retailers who served them could mean trouble for small shopkeepers unable to compete. Small stores were numerous, and their numbers kept growing. Between 1931 and 1939 Paris counted three thousand new bakeries, pastrycooks, and ice-cream parlors alone. There were more groceries too, more barrow boys, more workers self-promoted from industry to shopkeeping. They benefited from industries desperate to dispose of their products on sale or return and from the enhanced dignity of being their own masters.[65] But discount stores, chain stores presented a potent threat. A study of 1934 counted about two million retailers "that the development of single price shops would ruin."[66] Small shopkeepers had campaigned in the 1890s against department stores whose conditions of sale they denounced as unfair competition. They had survived the challenge by living shabbily, working heroic hours, cutting costs and corners, underpaying taxes. Now, with their survival once more threatened, they organized to oppose the plague of cheaper prices. Politicians alleged to support cut-rate stores were hounded; representatives were pressured to abolish the foes of small-scale enterprise.[67]

Both Left and Right lent an attentive ear to shopkeeper appeals. In 1934 the Chamber of Deputies voted the abolition of all discount stores, but the measure that passed almost unanimously (588–2) predictably did not get past the more conservative Senate.[68] In 1936, shortly before the general elections, bills were finally passed prohibiting the opening of new *prix uniques*. Restrictions followed in quick succession on shoe factories, shoe shops, repair facilities that competed with cobblers, the licensing of new taxicabs to compete with the ones in possession of streets. Calls for further restrictions came from hairdressers, butchers, bakers, owners of gas stations.[69] All felt that too much on offer spread the demand too thin; all agreed that overactivity, "overproduction," discouraged sales. Not enterprise but restriction was the answer to economic problems. The spirit of Thomas Malthus ruled over the land.

III

Plus ça change

Plus ça change, plus c'est la même chose.
—ALPHONSE KARR, 1849

"THE CLIMATE is temperate," a succession of Americans reported from Paris, "but the continuous rain and lack of sunshine makes it unhealthy for children and usually difficult for American women."[1] Despite such slurs, New Year's Eve 1929 was favored by springlike sunshine, and January 1 of 1930 would be sunny, too. Good weather on New Year's Day was important for those who continued the tradition of visits, formal and informal, to wish friends, relatives, and superiors a happy new year and to present gifts. New Year rather than Christmas was the season for gifts and tips—*étrennes*. First-of-the-year liberalities continued to present a problem not just within families but around them: servants and friends' servants, concierge, barber, grocer, one's regular taxi driver. . . . The list was long, expectations were vast; budgets were narrowing. No wonder, noted *Paris-Soir*, that such rituals were giving ground, visits thinned out, there was less room for manners in the agitated existence one led in 1930.[2] Cakes and pastries had gone up in price; so had carriages for the social tour, smaller lodgings hampered entertainment, shortage of staff forced hostesses to open the door themselves. . . .

Abundant by today's standards, servants were becoming harder to find and to afford.[3] The war had offered escape from dependency and subjection; better opportunities in the twenties carried men and women into preferable employment in factories, stores, offices, for which better schooling prepared new generations. Whatever the perceptions, though, numbers shrank but slowly: 20 or 25 percent smaller in the thirties than they had been before the war, fifty-seven domestics per thousand families. A middle class lifestyle could hardly dispense with personnel to fetch and especially to carry water, coal, firewood in homes where electricity, gas, and often running water took their time appearing. Being served at table by a maid marked out the petty bourgeois from the working class; being attended by a maître d'hôtel, black-suited and white-gloved, set aristocrats and upper bourgeoisie apart from mere bourgeois. "It was unacceptable until 1939," remembers a woman born in 1920, "to be served by a woman."[4] She means at table, and she means "in my social circle"—for women provided the mass of home employees as they had always done: nearly seven hundred thousand against one hundred thousand men.

Those who could afford it continued as they had done before. American military attachés in Paris seem to have employed two to four servants: cook, housemaid, butler, and chauffeur. As late as 1939 the household of Edmée Renaudin, wife of a high official, mother of five children, counted a cook, a Swiss governess, a lady's maid, a scullery maid ("You need a girl, said mother, to carry dishes and clean shoes"), a washerwoman, a *frotteur*, who came once a week to polish the silver, and Mme. Robert, who took the older children out for walks and supervised their homework. But such stability was less usual than the shrinkage and downgrading of domestic help: fewer live-in servants, more charwomen, and help by the day. By 1936 more than a third of servants were *femmes de ménage*, who came in as needed, and the language of employers was shifting from "service" to "help."[5]

Another postwar custom evolved slowly. Hairdressers, manicurists, seamstresses, parfumers even used to come to the home. After the war the habit persisted in provincial towns and for the better-off in Paris, where barbers too came to the home to shave or to trim the men's hair. Increasingly, though, specialized shops catered to middle-class and working women alike, beauticians sold glamour and youth by the package, manicure shops spread from the place Vendôme all the way to Belleville, hairdressers sprang up in country towns where coiffeuses had done most of their work in homes. There had been 61,700 registered hairdressers in France in 1926; there would be 99,400 in 1931 and perhaps 170,000 a decade later. More care about appearance, greater fastidiousness, higher expectations even for women (and for children) of quite modest means created new possibilities of employment and novel facilities that soon became part of the urban landscape. Just as domestics turned into help, so purveyors of services turned into shopkeepers.[6] As with tailor, haberdasher, or shoemaker, so with hairdressers, manicurists, artisans providing personal services to familiar clients shifted to less exclusive, more impersonal activities.

Structures of sociability also evolved. Fewer people offer dinners or throw parties, noted one observer in the later twenties. Thrift and shortage of help play their part in this, but so does fear of cigarette burns on furniture or carpet, of glasses leaving rings on varnished wood, of chair arms broken by guests who perch on them rather than on the seat. "There was no longer enough wealth to receive well, there was no longer enough tact to behave well when invited."[7] It is tempting to view such comments in the perennial light of "Things ain't what they used to be." Certainly the drinking and smoking alleged to discourage receptions had increased since the war, especially among women, who bought more and more cigarettes while men preferred to roll their own. Proper young women who had concealed their tobacco habit now kept their cigarettes on the edges of the plates they ate from or even wore rings that doubled as cigarette holders. But life continued leisurely for many. Since most people took two hours or more for lunch, aperitifs thrived, and so did midday papers like *Paris-Midi*. Even the wives of Communists were shocked when husbands did not come home for lunch. And for those who were far from the Communists, social activities prospered as before.

Until 1939 hostesses listed in the *Bottin Mondain*, France's Social Register, went on listing their regular reception days (*jours*): first and third Saturday of every month, first Tuesday and last Friday, or simply every Friday. Masked balls that only the wealthy could afford also continued to the eve of the Second War, some very splendid. And though the busy night life of the twenties declined somewhat, there was still time for a lot of it, and opportunity for Mme. de Noailles to appreciate the sight of Georges Auric, the avant-garde composer, at the bar of the trendy Bœuf sur le Toit, raising his pretty little closed fist in honor of the Popular Front.[8]

Society as usual continued to operate on several levels at once. Phoenix-like at levels where money becomes fortune, fashion for the fashionable continued to self-destruct the better to revive, changing with the times the better to mirror them. Bare arms, beach pajamas, then shorts for holidays, *robes sport* for the morning, *robes de ville* for shopping in town, cocktail dresses for the late afternoon, evening dresses and splendid jewels thereafter. "It's natural for people of modest means to dress as they can," opined *Paris-Soir*, "but inconceivable that the better-off should take this as an excuse" to avoid the expected *tenue de soirée*.[9] That was in 1931. By 1933 a chill in the air provided not excuses but inspiration: fewer formal dinners, more snack and buffet dinners informally enjoyed in *le living room,* along with newly popular Scotties—terriers whose rectangular build fitted the sober, "clean," architectural designs of the day.

In the new architectural esthetics buildings, apartments were "machines for living": not furnished with furniture but equipped with equipment—standardized and structured not in old-fashioned wood and fabric but in the sort of metal used for office furniture. Nothing decorative about them; nothing very comfortable either: Art was incompatible with decoration, let alone with relaxation, but aspired to be "truly social, pure, accessible to all," as a manifesto of 1930 put it. Accessible at least to those rich enough to accept the discomfort of naked walls and hard, straight lines, the impracticality of flat roofs that leak more easily than inclined ones, the indiscretion of glass walls that afford little privacy, the cold and heating costs of reinforced concrete slabs and more exposed surfaces than could be found in old-fashioned dwellings, for the sake of spare modernism—stark, cubic, "functional," and up-to-date. Completed in 1931, the Villa Savoye, which the Franco-Swiss Le Corbusier (born Edouard Jeanneret in 1887) built near Paris, chock-full of innovations, creative, utilitarian, good to look at and hard to live in, explains why in the straitened thirties the architectural avant-garde was condemned to write rather than build. The rich were less rich than in the twenties; the politicians who controlled the funds for public projects were old-fashioned; the plastic progressives appealed to intellectuals and to esthetes, not to the masses that dreamed of lodgings less social than comfortable.

The design, imagination, experimentation that stayed on architects' drawing boards expressed themselves more successfully in the decoration that progressives spurned and in fashion. Elsa Schiaparelli, friend of Surrealists, designed the first siren suit, a *robe sirène:* straight up and down, its length a compromise between afternoon and evening gear, allowing the elegant wearer to pass from afternoon to nightfall without a change of dress. Imaginative accessories, plastic zippers, eye-catching buttons in the shape of peanuts, insects, musical notes, berets shaped like lamb chops or like inverted pumps, economical turbans, consoled for fewer changes. By 1936 *Femina* was touting *caches-misères*—details (for those who could afford them) designed to modify or liven a dress that had been seen too often. Soon

Princesse Amédée de Broglie would be quoted deploring the unfortunate tendency to standardize fashion.[10]

Fashions, in fact, became less standardized, less formal. Women's lingerie grew more skimpy, also more wearable. Prewar abundance of body linen was mitigated by the *combinaison*—the nineteenth-century British combination garment that came into its own in France between the wars, replacing the chemise in its upper part and petticoats in its lower. Rayon underwear followed the "natural" figure. Constricting corsets gave way to suppler elastic girdles that promised softer contours, then to roll-ons and panty girdles for younger, lither shapes. Hats, required wear for respectable parties of both sexes, were sometimes replaced by light *voilettes* or abandoned altogether in the case of men. Men's morning coats gave way to suit jackets— not without a struggle; waistcoats retreated as three-piece suits became subject to pullover incursions. In November 1932 Count Jean de Pange ran into the minister of education at the Bibliothèque Nationale and thought the occasion worthy of record: Anatole de Monzie, "negligently dressed," wore a pullover in guise of a waistcoat. Stiff collars and cuffs slowly gave way to soft ones. Collars and ties were worn even on excursions until sport shirts appeared in 1936 that could also be worn on nonsporting occasions, while plus fours trickled from golf courses to become current wear. Eventually abandoned to children and adolescents, *culottes de golf* marked chic informality. When, in 1935, a high-ranking security operative is sent from Paris to solve a crime on the Ligne Maginot, he wears knicker-boker *(sic)*, sports shoes, and woolen socks.[11]

Matching the simpler garb and less formal living, bodies grew less lush, slimmed down to fit the two-piece swimming suits that shocked and fascinated older generations. *"Grossir c'est mourir un peu."*[12] Diets were in: Grapefruit replaced steak, spinach replaced stew, tea came without sugar, salad without oil, ham without fat, café au lait without milk, toast without butter. The new oracle, Colette complained, was the bathroom scale,[13] but she herself paid little heed to it. Men's tummies flattened out; women's bosoms swelled above abridged remains. "Flat chests are out of fashion," *Marie-Claire* advised its readers, "develop your pectorals." Schiaparelli launched padded bras; busts were in ("You're the age of your breasts"); plumpness was out. So was aging. Face-lifts and other esthetic enterprises became fashionable enough to appear in a play with Gabrielle Dorziat. But those who couldn't afford tummy tucks drank vinegar as their grandmothers had done to pull a corset on or, more up-to-date, replaced alcohol with *quarts Vittel.*[14]

The fashions of the rich were not entirely useless. Appealing or absurd, they were also decorative, and entertaining to more than to each other. They provided employment, of course; more important, they fed aspirations. Conspicuous consumption generates envy, which generates attempts to imitate. Relayed by the daily press, by illustrated weeklies, and by the cinema, they offered suggestions, models, patterns that others would follow when they could. Most French, meanwhile, had other more pressing concerns, like the necessities of life, their maintenance, or their slight improvement.

CONTEMPORARIES FEEL change more sharply than historians who take a bird's-eye view. From that elevated perspective, change came to France only hesitantly and in patches. One is struck, for example, by the slow pace of electrification and by the reluctant manner in which electricity, when available, was used. It was natural enough that some should reject newfangled utilities that they found less useful than bothersome, avoid the glare of electric light and retain gas or oil lamps until they died. Others simply could not afford costly energy. Normal rooms lit by a forty-watt bulb, a Paris evening paper pointed out, would look much better under a seventy-five-watt light. The trouble was that the current used by the latter cost nearly twice as much. Electrical costs were prohibitive.* The price of power for the light used to sell an article was higher than the cost of the work that had gone into the item. By 1939 some hostesses had installed "elegant" toasters in their salons to prepare *rôties* for tea, but no one else could afford such ruinous luxuries.[15]

Beyond Paris the situation was generally worse. The provision of electrical power was in the hands of hundreds of private companies, some better capitalized, some more efficient than others. State subsidies encouraged rural electrification, much of which was undertaken in the thirties, but many isolated localities would not be reached by power lines until after the

---

*The same was true of gas, whose consumption stubbornly stagnated between the wars: 40 cubic meters per head of population in 1925, 45 m³ in 1931, 42 m³ in 1938, by which time Switzerland used 59 m³ per inhabitant, Germany 174, the United Kingdom 222, and the United States 600. This despite the gas industry's publicity designed to popularize the "comfort, cleanliness and economy" of central heating and of water heaters and its offer of a cookbook by Edouard de Pomiane to every buyer of a gas oven. Alain Beltran and Jean-Pierre Williot, *Le Noir et le bleu* (1992), 14.

Second War.[16] Traditionalists opposed electrification because it would keep country folk carousing till all hours; some peasants resented power lines that trespassed on their land carrying God-knew-what evil forces.[17] The real foes of rural electrification, however, were the power companies, whose installations failed at the slightest provocation. As the *Petit Troyen* complained, just where the rates were highest, power failures were most frequent. "Only too often electrical current enjoys a Sunday rest."[18]

Even with such drawbacks, experience of electrification was exciting. In January 1936 the *Semaine religieuse* of Nantes welcomed the bells' being rung by electric power; in February, altars lit by electric light. But what seemed delightful luxuries in an urban setting served more serious needs in a rural one. In many villages its coming called for popular celebrations. In homes the effect was electrifying. At Plozévet in Brittany, where the process begun in 1928 was completed in 1959, the Hélias family home had electricity installed in 1932. The whole neighborhood came to admire the new electric lamp with its own glass lampshade, but the family was most moved of all. The first evening "we can hardly eat our soup for the light in the house that seems far bigger, far too big for us who are used to do what we have to do within the circle of the petrol lamp. We have to learn other gestures, to measure our steps more broadly. . . ."[19] Though in the country propane or butane appeared only in the fifties, a good few kitchen stoves shifted from wood to coal and then, in the thirties, to gas or electricity. Where it became available, passage to gas (or electricity) in cooking and heating did not mean just greater comfort and more heated rooms but also less drudgery: no more fetching coal and firewood, no more cleaning and clearing out ashes, less coal dust, less dirt, less heat in summer from permanently lit hearths or stoves. Servants and their mistresses both benefited.

It wasn't so much thrift or avarice on the consumer's part that limited prewar use of electrical appliances. It was the power companies' inefficiency and lack of enterprise that made their access difficult, their use awkward. The first "mechanical" washing machines, moved by a handle, were put on sale after the Great War, but automatic washers run on electric motors appeared only after 1950. Until then the laundry was done in the traditional washtub, or by washerwomen collecting the laundry at intervals, rubbing and rinsing it in the local river (as at Nevers till the 1950s), the municipal washhouse (kept up until the sixties), or from a *bateau-lavoir* such as the *commissaire* Maigret could gaze at from his office on the quai des Orfèvres.[20]

The weekly wash for a family of four called for eight hours of manual labor—about forty-nine eight-hour days a year for housewives or for drudges. And refrigerators were as rare as washing machines. But a washer-dryer or a refrigerator cost the equivalent of twelve hundred hours of a cleaning woman's wages. In the United States the equivalent machine cost three to four hundred hours. Replacing labor by machines continued uneconomical until after the war. The market was smaller, of course, than in the States, but the main problem lay, most likely, in the number of producers: Fifty-four firms made gas stoves, forty-five electric stoves, fifty-three washing machines; more than fifty made refrigerators, thus guaranteeing higher prices for all.[21] No wonder that keeping food fresh continued a problem into the 1960s; drinking cold drinks in hot weather remained a luxury. Those aspiring to such facilities used or dreamed of iceboxes, but as *Marie-Claire* wrote in 1937, "not everybody can enjoy the convenience of an icebox." "It's nice to drink cool drinks in summer," confided the lower-middle-class *Confidences* in 1938, but it was not always possible for lack of ice. By then the better-off aspired to refrigerators, and the posh monthly *Femina* carried small ads for Kelvinators: "cold in the service of comfort." *Match* reassured the less sanguine: Iceboxes were just as good.[22] What changed by then was less availability than aspirations. Films, magazines, *primes*, publicity familiarized the public, women especially, with what they could have had but didn't. Women's magazines began to ask why they didn't, then to demand they should. The washing machines, the bread loaves ready sliced and wrapped, the other conveniences Americans and Scandinavians took for granted should be available in France.[23] They were not, of course, but once the French learned to want them, they stood a better chance of getting them.

Less rare than refrigerators, telephones also functioned as symbols of conspicuous consumption. Available since the 1880s, they were beginning to be automated half a century later. By 1939 Paris subscribers (but few in the Paris suburbs) enjoyed dial telephones. The provinces followed suit more slowly: industrial centers like Saint-Etienne (1931), Lille (1933), Clermont-Ferrand and Strasbourg (1937), holiday centers like Deauville (1931), Biarritz (1934), the Côte d'Azur beginning in 1936. Vichy got its new telephone equipment in 1937, and Catherine Bertho points out that its quality would be one argument for picking the watering spot as capital of the *Etat Français* in 1940. But interurban communication continued primitive to the end of peace, and Vichy would find it harder to call prefectures in its southern zone than to call German-occupied Paris. As for the countryside, most of it relied on the ingenuity of telephone operators—or of the operators' children when the mothers cooked or shopped.[24]

The country's telephone network remained underdeveloped, restricted budgets limiting installation and equipment, high subscription rates discouraging subscribers. Telephones too were subject to frequent breakdowns and equipment failures. In 1931 one subscriber sued the PTT, responsible for the service, for shock and light burns suffered when her receiver exploded on being picked up. But injuries inflicted by the instrument were less evident than its absence. In 1929 and 1930 the Paris Courts of Justice were equipped with phones; in 1930 Jean Cocteau presented *La Voix humaine*, the first play whose chief character is a telephone; in 1933 the Horloge Parlante offered the first automatic time information; in 1937 Elsa Schiaparelli, inspired by Dali, designed a handbag shaped like a telephone. But in the provinces administrative offices, like those of tax collectors, ignored the instrument.[25] The *Bottin Mondain* had been launched in 1903 to list subscribers to the telephone at a time when the privilege was restricted to members of high society. A survey of its 1928 edition, based on the first 500 names listed under B, produced 286 subscribers. The same repeated on the 1939 edition of the *Bottin* shows 323 subscribers out of 500, with many more listing a phone in their provincial or country residences. The telephone was obviously catching on, but not as an indispensable piece of everyday equipment.

Machines in general were not in much demand. *Inspecteurs des finances* on tour through the provinces remember few or none in banks, post offices, tax bureaus; no typewriters and no typewritten reports, no calculators. The Ministry of Foreign Affairs, until 1940, employed an official calligrapher to produce accreditation papers. Insurance companies had mechanized their offices in the 1920s, with typewriters, calculators, and dictation machines. But the hero of a popular novel of 1938 is employed in a bank where he copies letters by hand. One machine, however, proved popular from the start. Paul Léautaud indicts in one breath the vulgarity of the telephone and the trashiness of wireless radio. But he is in a minority. When the abbé Mugnier, dining with Paul Valéry, was treated to a concert relayed by "wireless telegraphy," he found it extraordinary "to hear these distant voices that one would think in the next room . . . a pure fairy tale . . . marvelous, a creation of genius."[26]

The first daily news broadcasts had begun in 1925. By the 1930s radio had progressed from early stammers and static to professional programs. Nearby electrical installations, tram lines, or luminous signs still created interference, but this did not discourage those who could afford one from buying a set, or the state from taxing them. In 1933, after Hitler and Ramsay MacDonald, French politicians had begun to exploit the political possibilities of the medium; by 1934 the Paris police had introduced radio cars; in 1937 radio had its own pavilion at the International Exhibition of that year. Officially inaugurated on June 23, it had to wait till July 15 for the electrical connections that permitted its exhibits to function.[27]

France counted one million sets in 1932, over five million in 1939, mostly owned by city folk. The price of sets kept falling, so that by 1936 a passable one could be acquired for the equivalent of twenty to thirty days' worth of a worker's wages. If France lagged in the radio density stakes, way behind Germany, Britain, Belgium, and the United States, that may have been because large parts of the country were ill served by broadcasting stations or were not served at all. Technical equipment was poor, power weak, fading frequent, sound indifferent, blurring, scrambling, interference, failure of broadcasting stations frequent; programs were unsophisticated and uncoordinated.[28] But the marvel that fascinated the abbé Mugnier delighted his fellow French as well. It enabled millions to hear voices only thousands heard until then: Tino Rossi or Charles Trenet trilled popular songs to fame, from *"Parlez-moi d'amour"* to *"Tout va très bien, Madame la marquise,"* nationalized publicity and publicity jingles about apéritifs or soaps. It also supplemented flagging conversations, filled the families' long deserts of silence, established relations between isolated homes and the wider world, smoothed family relations, replaced bickering. Léautaud's trash offered something for almost everyone.

"Street musicians are disappearing," complained *Paris-Soir* in January 1930, "people have no time to listen, the traffic makes it awkward to hear. . . ." Gramophones first, then radios cut into the public of musicians in the street, but the noise and bustle of traffic were also a factor in their waning. For every automobile on the road in 1900 there were two hundred in 1920, seven hundred in 1930; there would be thirteen hundred in 1940. Observers commented that unlike carters, wagoners, teamsters, car drivers were courteous. "They hardly ever exchange insults—their speed is too great." But they caused other problems. Traffic jams, real enough in the days of horse cabs, became a plague. January 1930 brought parking regulations that kept streets free for traffic, paying parking lots, better circulation. In 1931 pedestrian crossings appeared; in 1932 luminous traffic lights (activated by a policeman's hand), which seem to have fascinated the public but to have tamed drivers little.[29] In 1933 the last trams disappeared from the streets of Paris, removing an obstacle to motor traffic but also the fairylike mystery of men polishing tram rails at night, their blowtorches striking festive showers of sparks from the metal.

Beyond Paris, driving conditions were worse. Roads were poor; roadside equipment was nonexistent. Toll roads had been rejected as too costly to use, hence undemocratic. Also as Fascist.[30] In 1929, when Georges Clemenceau died, the car that brought his body to the Vendée from Paris ran out of gas about two hundred miles from the capital, at Langeais, then got stuck in the mud and had to be pulled out by oxen not once but several times. In 1931 driving from Lyons to Bordeaux in nine hours was still an exploit that some would bet against. Cars and their components, not least tires, were subject to frequent breakdowns, one reason why those who could afford it employed chauffeurs. And driving claimed its victims: In 1930, 2,042 men and women died, nearly 5,000 in 1934. There were four times as many bikes as cars in France, but mortality from automobiles was seven times more numerous than that from bicycles and three times more than related to railroads. Driving tests were not hard to pass. When Jacques Le Roy Ladurie took his test, he banged into a wall, ran over a chicken, narrowly missed a pedestrian, was congratulated by the examiner, and obtained his permit. But driving schools multiplied and insurance companies grew; by 1935 most drivers carried insurance.* Newspapers published advice to pedestrians hoping to avoid being hit by cars (pin or tie white cloth or paper to your clothes or hat); lawyers battled over the responsibility of owners of cars stolen and then used to kill someone; theater critics blamed cars and the bad new habit of weekend driving for the theater's doing badly.[31] Familiar territory.

Car owners remained a minority, and not everyone who owned a car could drive one. Maigret, model of middling Frenchmen, never drove. He had tried but gave up. A bank inspector traveling regularly through the country between 1934 and 1939 took the train: "[I]n those days we had no cars." A 1936 survey of writers, conducted by a literary magazine, reveals

---

*Even impecunious priests had their own Automobile-Club Saint-Christophe, which helped them acquire cars and insurance within their means. Beginning with eight hundred members in 1932, the club boasted a membership over five thousand by 1936. J. Brugerette, *Le Prêtre français et la société contemporaine* (1938), III, 608–09.

that many couldn't drive, and far from all owned cars.[32] Those who did, like Georges Duhamel, were middle-aged and successful. Also dubious about the benefits of modernity—at least for others. In 1932 Duhamel contributed a preface to Denys Amiel's curmudgeonly *L'Age de fer* (The iron age). The world was going to the dogs: Stables were lit by electricity now; peasants were going to the market by bus. . . . One wonders what fly had bit Amiel to make him condemn such slivers of comfort. Denis de Rougemont came closer to reality when, about the same time, he celebrated the *autocars* that changed provincial life, meandering conveniently through the countryside, introducing competition and price-cutting where rail's monopoly had reigned.[33]

Peasants and modest people were actually beginning to buy cars and vans. In a Provençal village without running water, Léonce Chaleil and his father bought a nine-horsepower Citroën truck for more money than they would pay to buy a house, but it served for thirty years. In 1936 a schoolteacher bought his first automobile—a Peugeot 301—because his wife yearned to see the sea she'd never seen. They could afford such exceptional luxuries because they had money saved, because they regarded the vehicle as an investment, but also because the auto industry was more up-to-date than others. Publicity, market studies, credit sales had been imported from the United States; more sales were being made on credit: more than a quarter of transactions in 1939. Cheap cars as such did not as yet exist: The moderately priced six-horsepower Peugeot 201 compact, launched in 1929, sold for around twenty-one thousand francs, equivalent to about seventy weeks' of a workman's wages; the marvelous 2HP Citroën, planned for 1939, would be put off for years.* But two thirds of cars sold every year were secondhand, hence cheaper. In 1920 there had been more telephones than automobiles; by 1940 these proportions had been reversed.[34]

Automobiles were both exceptional and familiar. When people dreamed, they dreamed of flying, still an uncommon experience few had tasted, hence open to fantasy, or else they paid a few francs to go to the cinema. Hireling of our dreams, Céline called it in 1932, there to be bought like a prostitute for an hour or two of make-believe.

The cinema was as old as the century—indeed a few years older—but long remained split between a popular attraction akin to music hall enter-

---

*Bertrand de Jouvenel, *Un voyageur dans le siècle* (1979), 107, claims quite plausibly that it was Citroën's idea that inspired Hitler's project of a people's car: the Volkswagen.

tainment and an intellectual plaything for a few. The 1920s had seen the appearance of *ciné-clubs* catering to the latter, as of cheap brochures, "books of the film" sold as *ciné-romans*. But cinema in 1930 accounted only for about a third of national entertainment. Then came the talkies. Sound films, launched in the United States in late 1927, wrought a revolution. The cinema had appealed largely to intellectuals and to the lower classes. Sound films turned movies into mass entertainment the country over. Not at once. Thousands of small theater owners who found it impossible to pay for sound equipment survived by continuing to show silent films. In 1935 nearly a sixth of picture theaters still did so. Bigger cinemas rewired and installed sound insulation, attracted a large curious public, but faced costs so high that they barely broke even. Time brought adjustment: By May 1934, 1,738 houses had been wired for sound, 2,077 by December. New cinemas opened: fifteen thousand new seats in Paris, bringing the capital's total to twenty-two thousand that year, and thirteen thousand in the provinces. By 1935 the U.S. commercial attaché estimated a total of four thousand motion picture theaters in France, thirty-three hundred of them wired for sound. Two hundred million, then three hundred million men, women, children went to the movies yearly, and school principals began to complain of the effect this had on children's attitudes, fantasies, propensity to violence. . . .[35]

To this tide of popularity the Depression made one significant contribution: double features. Eager to attract a poorer public, theater managers offered greater value for the money: two feature films, a newsreel, a cartoon, and perhaps a short. It worked. Cinema's share of Paris entertainments rose from 40 percent in 1929 to 72 percent in 1939, when more than 220,000,000 went to see a show. In May 1940, as the Germans advanced through northern France, Paris cinemas counted over 3,000,000 admissions; in June, with a lot of cinemas chillingly closed, 835,000 still found time to sit in their flickering darkness.[36]

The cinema's meat was the theaters' poison. Less than a quarter of cinema receipts in 1936, the intake of legitimate theaters fell below one-fifth in 1939, but desperate voices had been raised to deplore theatrical decadence since motion pictures found their tongue. The material reasons were clear: The cinema offered greater comfort, better seats, more legroom, easier access, cheaper prices. There was no need to dress up; there were no intermissions during which one had to spend more than one had already spent on coatroom, program, and tipping the attendant who showed you to your

seat.[37] Was it coincidence, or the natural drift of talent to greater opportunities and better money? Just as cinema came into its own, theater seemed
to cast its last lights but dimly. The experiments of Max Reinhardt, Erwin
Piscator, Konstantin Stanislavsky, Gordon Craig were being carried out on
other than French stages. André Antoine and Jacques Copeau, once heroes
of the avant-garde, survived from earlier eras. Few French authors of importance now flourished on the stage. Paul Claudel was declamatory and static.
Only Jean Giraudoux seemed both original and attractive. Only Louis
Jouvet—director, producer, actor-manager, inspiring entrepreneur, who introduced Giraudoux to the public—gave the impression that the live stage
breathed.

BORN IN 1910, Julien Gracq evokes the Nantes of his youth: traffic light,
servants and peasant women in their Breton bonnets, *octroi* stations, wash
barges for laundrywomen, lamplighters with their long sticks at dusk. . . .
Also the social distance that divided manual workers from the petty bourgeoisie precariously poised above them.[38] Manual workers between the
wars seem to have been better off than they had been during the so-called
Belle Epoque before 1914. They had more money and were less afraid to
spend it. More modestly priced shops catered to their needs. They ate
more, and they ate more meat—even though it might be horsemeat[39]—
they dressed better and, on the whole, more cleanly. There was less mending, patching, cutting down, less knitting socks and stitching clothes at
home; there were fewer seamstresses who came in by the day, more readi-
ness to turn to professional tailors and to ready-mades. But living quarters
had not followed suit. Lots of neatly turned-out women and men lived in
pitiful lodgings, narrow and comfortless. Few thought to comment, let
alone complain, about physical conditions long taken for granted and that
even unions seem not to have mentioned.[40]

The norm was the norm. When Henri Sellier, mayor of Suresnes, outside Paris, built cheap housing equipped with central heat, bathrooms,
proper kitchens boasting proper sinks, and incinerators for the garbage,
critics accused him of "trying to house workers as if they were bourgeois."
The new schools of Sureness were denounced as *des écoles-palace* that would
inculcate tastes for luxury that children of the people would never be able
to satisfy. In 1935, when the architect of the new Open Air School visited
his showpiece, teachers refused to open its windows, even on the sunny

side: "The children would catch cold." Fresh air was bad for health. Drafts were worse. The windows were only cracked in 1936, but Sellier went on abuilding; nurseries, leisure centers, old-age clubs, a swimming pool made Suresnes a guiding light of modern urbanism, but a lonely one. Sellier remained an exception, and so did his eccentric notions.[41]

In 1936, Françoise Cribier has told us, more than half the poorer young Parisians lived in one room or in a kitchen-bedroom. Most of these had no toilet, no light, no heat, no "comfort" (usually meaning water); but what people said they missed most was space, and by that they meant a little privacy and modest esthetic satisfaction. About one tenth of these people were forced by the rental shortage to live in quarters that had been condemned as insalubrious: humid, vermin- and rat-infested, impossible to heat in winter. The two rooms where the future teacher Jean Vial grew up with his parents—no water, no gas, lit by one oil lamp—were still there in the 1940s. Cribier, researching conditions in the thirties, cites one informant—Mme. S, born in 1911—who lived in a waterless garret until 1940 when she found another garret with a water tap. The case of Mme. S, remarks Cribier, was exceptional. But only round 1940 did nearly all Parisian buildings enjoy running water and direct-to-sewer drainage.[42]

In rural areas electrification came later, as we saw, water service later still—unsurprisingly, since stringing wires takes less time than laying pipes. Into the 1940s only about one child in five had access to running water. In remote areas, like the Lozère on its high plateau, small towns and villages began to get running water in the thirties, but mostly for hotels. Plenty of villages and small towns got water only after the Second War. Until then almost half the rural population and its cattle depended on ponds, wells, pumps, village fountains, or a rain barrel in the yard. Even towns with water services faced variations in pressure and in service—as at Rennes, where, in 1939, many buildings in the center of town enjoyed no water in their upper stories.[43] As for small-town hotels, with their privileged water, they were almost uniformly lousy: unheated, uncomfortable, lacking elementary facilities.[44] In 1935 a country newspaper rejoiced that approachable water closets began to appear, but continuing propaganda for *politesse et propreté* suggests that both were in short supply.[45]

Jean-Pierre Goubert, who has traced *The Conquest of Water*, found slop buckets and chamber pots in regular use into the 1950s in towns like Toulon, Marseilles, Saumur, Beauvais, and others where many dwellings counted only one toilet for all, and where many a housewife eased her labors by chucking the family slops and night soil out of a window into the street. Goubert's evidence is borne out by Marie Rouanet's recollections of growing up in Béziers after the Second War: no conveniences, the gutter for a sewer, ice sold from an ice cart and used sparingly. . . .[46]

Public health reflected material conditions. A medical man discussing mortality in the mid-thirties commented on the impressive rarity of deaths from old age: "a striking fact that dominates mortality statistics." Statistics are unreliable, of course, the medical statistics were primitive, and certain crimes (rape, incest) or causes of death (madness, suicide) were considered dark secrets seldom to be divulged. But if we go by what came to light, some formal causes of mortality were declining. As misery receded, so did one of the oldest forms of family limitation: infanticide. As more babies got their own cradles, fewer were overlain and stifled by the parents they were sleeping with. Fewer babies were abandoned by their parents; fewer killed by elders altogether. At least as recorded by the courts, private and public brutality also waned. Sexual violence against women and children fell away. The assizes judged fewer cases of assault with serious bodily harm and fewer assaults leading to involuntary manslaughter. French homicide rates were low, and while they rose during the troubled thirties, they remained three times less than Italian murder rates, one tenth those of the United States.[47]

There were five doctors in 1936 for every four practicing in 1921, eight dentists where there had been three, and 20 percent more pharmacists as well. Average mortality fell from 17.2 per thousand in 1920 to 15.8 per thousand in 1932. But if the French died less, French males died more and earlier than their neighbors. British males lived more than three years longer, the Dutch as much as seven more. And the general health of the French was worse. In 1918 French and Germans had comparable proportions of men not fit for military service or invalided out: 26 percent for the French, 27 percent for the Germans. Twenty years later, in 1938, the difference was depressing: 33 percent unfit in France, 17 percent in Germany.[48]

Some of the morbidity was caused by ill-mastered plagues like typhoid and diphtheria. More was attributed to venereal disease, which preoccupied the authorities and the media. Seemingly official statements referred to eight million syphilitics and to astronomical death rates comparable to those of Charleroi and Verdun. There were no precise statistics, but a work of 1932 attributed eighty thousand adult deaths every year and some sixty thousand stillbirths and miscarriages to the "public calamity." Attempts to close brothels in garrison towns merely shifted the trade to cafés, brasseries, and "pensions," whose clandestine activities proved more dangerous than those subject to official oversight and regular health inspections. The venereal tide appears to have ebbed slowly through the thirties, but economic pressures did not help. Rising unemployment went with rising prostitution, as at Nancy, where, just in the first nine months of 1932, unauthorized prostitution soared from sixty to over two hundred women, and sexual enterprise went with sexual disease.[49] Still, most experts agreed in tracing most of the country's health problems to alcoholism.

With over five hundred thousand cafés, bars, wine cellars, taprooms, and dramshops in 1937, France boasted one drinking facility for every 81 men, women, and children, compared to one for 225 in Italy or one for 425 in Britain. The decades between 1920 and 1940 would see the highest consumption of wine in recorded history—approaching 250 liters per adult per year. Of the 13,500,000 Frenchmen over twenty, 800,000 drank 3, 4, or more liters of wine a day, 1,300,000 drank between 2 and 3; 4,300,000 consumed only 1 to 2 liters a day.[50] Vintners gladly catered to demand or helped create it by turning out more rotgut by the year. At Soulland in the Vendée, where allegedly thirty-eight cafés served 2,200 inhabitants, the vineyard surface quadrupled between 1920 and 1940. A local doctor writing in 1933 draws a charming sketch of little men traipsing off to school, the neck of a wine bottle protruding from each satchel.[51] But gurgling liters of wine tell only part of the story. One must also count beer, cider, distilled alcohols, all of which contributed to the rise of mental disorders, of brawls and blows exchanged, of stomach and liver ailments. Between 1930 and 1936 the mortality of Frenchmen over twenty rose by about 4 percent; deaths from alcoholism and cirrhosis went up 30 percent.[52]

More deadly still, tuberculosis, which accounted for about one third of male deaths between the ages of thirty-five and fifty, was closely related to drinking. *"La tuberculose se prend sur le zinc,"* one expert declared: TB is caught in bars.[53] No one thought to contradict him, but the relation between alcoholism and consumption was minimized or ignored. A National Committee of Defense against TB had been founded in 1919 with the help of the Rockefeller Mission; schoolchildren and scouts were enlisted in national campaigns to sell anti-TB stamps, and the National Office of Social Hygiene (founded in 1924) launched nationwide campaigns against TB as well as typhoid, diphtheria, and venereal disease. But the antialcoholic campaigns that flourished before 1914 were forgotten, the Office of Social Hygiene was abolished in 1935 as part of that year's budget cuts, and the media, friendly to jolly social drinking and hostile to barbarous Prohibition, largely ignored the alcoholic menace.[54]

Vine plantings increased, wine prices fell, government subsidies encouraged distillation of alcohol from grapes, beets, and fruit, and publicity in favor of "hygienic" drinks like wine and cider and less hygienic ones like aperitifs, whose manufacturers showed record profits. In many parts of France home distillers accounted for half or two thirds of the adult male population, and hence of the electorate. No politician could challenge them and survive. Attempts to restrict or control distilling were abandoned; fraud flourished. Desperate to increase wine consumption, successive governments promoted its drinking in schools, in the army, in hospitals and even considered offering it to the Salvation Army. A Ministry of Education directive ordered that health classes should stress the benefits of wine, frustration of which would drive abstainers to "alcohol" and, worse, to "infamous drugs." As this suggests, most French people, not least medical men like the perennial minister of agriculture, Henri Queuille, believed in the blamelessness of boozing and considered wine the best antidote to alcoholism.[55]

They did their best to live up to these principles. A law of 1931 created a National Committee of Propaganda for wine, and Queuille himself opened the wine industry's House of Wine in Paris in 1933. Laws of 1931 and 1933 eased conditions for home distillers, whose numbers almost doubled. The best that society seemed to do, besides expanding lunatic asylums, was to promote consumption of fruit and juices, distribute them at fairs, open grape bars throughout the country (including one *station uvale* in 1933 at the Gare Saint-Lazare in Paris), where temperance advocates and wine bibers could toast each other in unfermented grape juice. There were also remedies like the Poudre Montavon, guaranteed to cure drunkenness without the drinker's even knowing. Altogether, despite the appearance of medico-social centers, of social assistants, of district nurses in rural areas, medical conditions improved but slowly; information about medical facilities and availabilities continued as inadequate as the facilities themselves.[56]

For those who lived and died in such conditions, and too many did, the example and the opportunities that schools offered were just as crucial as they had been in the nineteenth century. It was often from schools that vaccination campaigns against smallpox and diphtheria took off, in schoolrooms that the vaccines were administered, and schools led campaigns for cleanliness still crucial in days when ablutions continued rare. "The Saturday shower has become a reward for the girls," observed one teacher in the Vosges, while many colleagues noted that children smelled more sweetly on Mondays than they had at the week's end. Considering that a recent survey of Paris medical practitioners 1930–1970 shows most of them washing their hair weekly, but only a minority their feet, one gets an idea of the state in which doctors found their patients. By 1976 patients who smell offensively or who wear dirty linen are "exceptional," but the change is described as recent. In the 1930s some patients had to be sent away to take a bath before being examined, and the doctors' chief recommendation seems to have been to wash.[57] The refrain was general. Columns of advice to readers insist on what remained a chore. "Nothing can estrange husband from wife or wife from husband like a strong smell," writes L'Œuvre in 1933. "To be beautiful you have first to wash," insists a fashion column in the Canard enchaîné—preferably with water. The first thing that the very middle-class Marie-Claire sought to teach its readers was to wash themselves and take off their makeup before they went to bed.[58]

That was easier said than done with water scarce, warm water scarcer, quarters unheated (one ad for gas radiators pleads that buyers would henceforth dress and undress without shivering). Which may be why Henriette Nizan, when away from home, relied on a good rub with eau de cologne. Others did so at home, along with a lick and a promise. "You keep talking about baths and showers," a reader of Confidences writes in. "But you don't think of those who don't have the means." Miss Lonelyhearts, Bellyne in Confidences, responds that a primitive rig-up in the kitchen and a jug of hot water is what most people use. As late as 1954 only one dwelling in ten enjoyed a tub or shower, and those who had them did not necessarily employ them. In 1931, at Bourg-en-Bresse, the Nizans' neighbors in a newly built HBM (habitations à bon marché—cheap housing) used their tub to store firewood. And Jean Giono did not bother to install a bathroom until 1952.[59] Into the 1950s the sour-sweetish smell of fresh sweat reinforcing the old in clothes that were seldom cleaned permeated bistros, theaters, schools, and public transport. Popular wisdom echoed habit. "You'll spoil your eyes," it warned those who read; and those who washed: "You'll wear out your skin."

In Brittany the real revolution in living conditions came only in the 1950s. That's when ordinary folk began to eat white bread, eggs, butchers' meat, and processed cheeses like Camembert or Vache qui rit. That's when the first trousers for young women appeared, pending cigarettes for women in the 1960s.[60] That is also when small portable gas rings (*réchauds*) spread, though proper cooking stoves (*cuisinières*) continued rare, as did hot-water heaters. Still, life had steadily become less austere. The thirties brought permanent waves and short-sleeved dresses. Children had almost no more patches on their clothes, and their clothes now tended to be their own: bought off a rack, no longer hand-me-downs. After 1936 there were lots of strangers about, holidaymakers unknown till then in a land whose Breton language knew no word for holiday—*vacances*. Little ones could no longer roll their marbles in the roadway because there were too many cars going far too fast. On the other hand, they played with store-bought toys and presents brought by Father Christmas, who gradually took over from Child Jesus—born so long ago, as one tot explained, that he had grown a beard. A lot of houses had installed doors with glazed glass panels, closed not just at night, as the old doors were, but in the day as well, on which one had to knock and which did not always open even when one knocked. The woman who sold lollipops now had a shop with windows, the baker sold fewer ten-pound loaves and more baguettes, tomatoes—suspect as poisonous in the 1920s—came in cans that could be opened without waiting for special occasions, and oldsters noted that people were eating less; they didn't even bother to finish the leftovers.[61]

Times change and we change with them. But change comes only slowly. So it would be with bakers, baker's apprentices and journeymen, deliveryboys, and pastrycooks. The hero of Marcel Pagnol's film *La Femme du boulanger* (1938) explains to his village neighbors that he prepares everything in the evening, around seven; then he goes to bed. At one in the morning he comes down to knead the dough and mold the next day's loaves by hand. Then he puts them in the oven, by which time it is four or five. He takes forty winks, and his wife wakes him at six or just after, when it is time to take out the first batch and prepare two more that would be ready by ten. So it goes. In his country village Aimable Castanier, the baker played by Raimu, works alone. In 1938 he still fires the oven with kindling and firewood that he must gather and chop up, he still bakes several batches made up not of baguettes but of two- and four-pound loaves, and of the occasional oven cake (*fougasse*) that men pick up to eat when going hunting or into the fields.

In less isolated venues, demand by the 1930s had evolved, and so had the bakery business; but the lot of bakers who worked in France's fifty or sixty thousand bakeries continued grueling. Aimable must have served his apprenticeship at the turn of the century, when nearly half the boys in France and one third of the girls went to work at thirteen or before. We can only assume that the conditions of labor then were no better than in the 1920s, when the twelve-year-old R, born in 1909, began a three-year apprenticeship, during which he worked fifteen hours a day, seven days a week. Things had improved by 1935, when the fourteen-year-old D started to work eighty-four hours a week (7×12), twenty-one hours fewer than R but still without a break, days of rest being few before 1936 and fewer still for bakers. When he became a journeyman, at twenty, D began to work only eleven hours a day for six days a week. He still did so in 1979.[62]

B, who appears in the same survey made in 1979, was thirteen in 1934. Apprenticed in a village of the Sarthe, he would wake up in the dark, at 2:00 A.M., and end his labors fourteen hours later at 4:00 or 5:00 in the afternoon, not before having sawed his firewood and piled it in the oven to dry, whence he would take it out again to chop it in the small hours of the morning. Around 11:00 A.M. he harnessed the horse to trot out into the neighboring countryside to deliver orders, sometimes by himself, sometimes with his master. His pay was bed and board. A law of 1928 prohibited night work for the young, but it was generally ignored. Another lad, entering his apprenticeship at fourteen, in 1971, would get his day of rest but was still expected to work seventeen hours a day during the other six. Worn out after a year, he found a place in a relative's bakery where he need work only eighty-five hours a week. When he became a journeyman, he could expect to work as few as sixty-six.[63]

Bakery imposes its demands on those who serve it. Hours are hard to change. What about conditions of labor? Kneading took time and energy; so did the need to fire the oven and to supply it with firewood or coal; so did the use of leavening, which forced the baker to keep an eye on molds and broke up his rest. Mechanical kneading machines appeared before the First War but began to spread only in the 1920s. Numbers of bakehouses were improved, and modernized: ovens fired by gas, then by electricity made them cleaner and lighter; yeast replacing leavening eased the journeyman's watch. He no longer leavened every evening, even on his "free day." Batches that had called for six to nine hours' labor took only three with modern equipment. On the other hand, the cost of buying out a bakery kept new owners from altering or replacing the old ovens with new, more modern equipment. By 1939, though gas was spreading, as was cheap oil fuel, coal and wood were still being widely used.[64] So Aimable, who fired his oven and kneaded by hand in a wooden kneading trough, remained far from exceptional into the 1950s.

More to the point, modern material saved effort on one front only to increase it on others. New ovens that never stopped heating encouraged continuous baking, while the facilities of yeast encouraged fancy products—*bâtards*, baguettes, *ficelles*, rolls—to replace the large standard loaves. As shop sales grew in importance, home deliveries waned, an afternoon batch replaced the delivery round, but each batch represented more work: Where the baker once put 80 two-pound loaves into his oven, he now put in 150 baguettes.[65]

Urban and urbanized taste did not just desert plain for fancy. It became increasingly finicky. Diets recommended eating no bread, or less bread, or at least healthier bread: whole wheat, rye. Those who could afford it had long eaten white bread. By the late thirties, as one observer put it, "delicate eaters felt safe only if they spread their butter on the black bread that peasants considered a sign of misery." Bakers made bigger profits from black bread snobbery. "They make customers pay more for bran than for wheat flour, and give people food for pigs in order to please their fancies."[66]

The critic was treating exceptions as the rule. A professional observer, writing in 1939, still found it necessary to reassure his readers that fresh bread was not bad for the stomach: "[N]ewly baked bread is as good as stale bread, whatever they say. If the digestion takes longer, that's only because one eats more of bread that one likes better." That had been the point of feeding large households on stale bread: keeping consumption down. Now it turned out that consumption was going down even with bread that folk liked better. In the 1920s the French had consumed 628 grams of it per person per day. By the 1930s that figure had fallen, and it kept going down. By 1960 the French ate less than half that much, and a decade later half of that again.[67] A baker's life is not an easy one.

ONE DOMAIN where change moved with positively glacial speed was the condition of women. The 1920s publicized the emancipated woman who wore her hair as short as her skirts and demanded as much freedom as the men she bedded. In 1922 Victor Margueritte's tomboy *La Garçonne* had scandalized a public eager for scandal, deprived its author of his *Légion d'honneur,* and brought him six hundred thousand readers. But the new woman was no longer new. On January 1, 1930, the novel that *Paris-Soir* offered its readers as a serial presented a young woman picking up her boyfriend in her car and asking him to give her boxing lessons. The following day's "Courrier," answering readers' letters, recommended light *voilettes* to a reader who wanted to be seductive: "[*V*]*oilettes* soften the gaze deliciously." Between seduction and pugnacity, a woman's choice was narrower than it seemed.

In parts of the countryside, menstruating women still did not visit cellars, where their impure presence could have spoiled preserves, did not bake cakes, whip cream, beat egg whites or a mayonnaise: "It won't come out." Well beyond that level, the hoary debate about feminine intellectual capacities continued. In 1930 the dean of the Sorbonne's Faculty of Letters bravely asserted his belief that women were capable of rising to men's ranking. But a woman writer, arguing the scholarly capacities of her sex against Stone Age critics who dismissed women scholars as abnormal, hedged her bets: "One has to admit it, few women are capable of intellectual labor." *Marie-Claire* plied its public of women emancipated enough to read it with advice on how to attract men and avoid "Solitude." Male avant-garde activists agreed. Before the war macho Futurists had made a business about despising women and soft feminine qualities. After the war Surrealists fascinated by the marquis de Sade reified or angelized them.[68]

The postwar years *had* seen more feminine claims to mastery over their own bodies, and this embittered the struggle against the rule of men who were busy legislating against birth control. Fear of waning numbers sapping national security had brought punitive legislation against the dissemination of contraceptive information, let alone contraceptive products, and against abortion, which continued as the principal method of birth control. Removed from the province of juries and handed to more ruthless petty sessions judges, sentences for abortion grew heavier and more frequent.* Between 1880 and 1910, 72 percent of abortion cases had ended in acquittal. Between 1925 and 1934 fewer than one in five did so. Stubborn propagandists like Bertie Albrecht—a Protestant from Marseilles married to an Anglo-Dutch broker—persisted in arguing for sex education, mothers' rights, children's rights, birth control, sterilization, abortion. But they were crying in the wilderness and increasingly liable to criminal prosecution. Feminist, Socialist Madeleine Pelletier, who was a medical doctor specializ-

---

*After 1920, attempted or successful abortion was penalized by six to twenty-four months' imprisonment. Sentences for those carrying out an abortion ranged from one to five years. The law was finally abolished by Simone Veil, minister of health in a cabinet headed by Jacques Chirac, in 1974 when "the voluntary interruption of pregnancy" became legal.

ing in mental ailments, published several works suggesting that a bit more "depopulation" would improve the quality of life and advocating the right to contraception and abortion. In 1939 she was arrested as an abortionist and interned in a mental clinic, where she died.[69]

France counted scores of feminist organizations, almost all led by society ladies who called for political but not sexual liberation. Sex was immoral, advocating freedom on that front was as unpatriotic as it was licentious, and the trajectory of *La Garçonne* and of its author reflects this unfortunate conjuncture. Monique, the free woman, works, attends a gym, listens to *jazz-bands*, drives, dances in *dancings*, drinks "irish and soda." She is also sexually promiscuous, tries drugs, smokes opium, has lesbian encounters, and, what is worse, finds them emotionally satisfying; but she is also an internationalist and a pacifist. Victor Margueritte (1867–1942), her creator, had himself evolved from patriotic militarism to unexpected but profitable progressivism. Longtime partisan of more flexible divorce legislation (eventually introduced in 1975), of fair alimony and legitimation of illegitimate children, and of the feminists who argued in their favor, Margueritte had found fame (some called it notoriety) in a series of novels about adultery, rape, prostitution, and alluring orgies that shocked, titillated, and sold well. But pornography concealed or spurred a social conscience. Feminist progressivism went with other nonconformist positions: pacifism, nudism, birth control, abortion, eugenics, all on the agenda of a radical and sometimes anarchist Left that argued in the same breath for emancipation of women and that of the masses. In 1927 Margueritte's *Your Body's Your Own* (*Ton corps est à toi*), preaching "Malthusianism," sexual selectivity, an end to "bestial copulation" and to the propagation of congenital ills, TB, and venereal disease, provoked the ire of all right-thinking folk, not least the League of Fathers of Large Families. Slogans like "Grow but do not multiply" and "Multiplication means war" were clearly subversive.

So, repressive laws were abrogated only in 1967, and even then antinatalist propaganda was banned. Until that time or, at least, until after the Second War, contraception was practically nonexistent. Women, Henriette Nizan remembers, tried to be careful, some men practiced coitus interruptus, herborists sold little sponges on a thread that could be dipped into some liquid like vinegar, or pomades containing quinine, supposed to prevent conception. "There were also condoms. I've never met a man who used them."[70]

In the old days pilgrimages had offered pious pretexts to flee the conju-

gal nest. The Church's prohibition of relations between man and wife unless to procreate encouraged abstinence. So did overbearing and its discomforts. Marcelle Auclair pioneered the women's page of *Paris-Soir* before
founding *Marie-Claire*, a cheerful women's weekly that the Church denounced as a menace to chastity and marital fidelity. Auclair's marriage to
Jean Prévost was happy and productive, but with her parents things had
been more difficult: After the birth of the second child the mother-in-law
decreed separate bedrooms; one son, one daughter were enough. That had
been the old lady's method; her second boy brought into life, she barred her
bedroom with bolts.[71] Was that why Pierre Andreu remembered a petty
bourgeois world where, honeymoons past, "sexuality counted for very little"? Social commentators rued waning virility.[72] It looks more like a desperate attempt to spare women the horrors of repeated childbirth and families its burdens. The differences in living conditions between working-class
families with many children and families with none or few was clear for all
to see. Many experienced it. A baker born in 1913 at Le Creusot remembered how his mother "had let herself die" at sixty-nine after nine children.
He and his wife had two after having vowed to have only one and slipped
up. "I didn't want any . . . so sickened we were to see the life my parents
led."[73] Abortion continued.

Writing in 1935, one supporter of birth control felt that eight hundred
thousand might understate the number of illegal annual abortions and cited
one young woman who had four a year. Working in a hospital himself,
Pierre Bassac estimated abortions and legal births to come out roughly
even.[74] Catholics too interrupted pregnancies abruptly, which may be why
the Church could no longer evade the problem. Catholics in good standing
searched for ways of family planning that could get around the condemnation of sex with no conception in view. The findings of Dr. H. Knaus, an
Austrian, and of Ogino, a Japanese, were going to provide a method of
"periodic continence" that promised safe intercourse beyond its monthly
limits. After 1931 a spate of books, articles in Catholic publications, and
brochures printed in Dominican convents attempted to vulgarize the ex-
panded limits of permissible sex.[75] Demographers and politicians meanwhile moved to supplement sticks with carrots. Family allowance plans had
been introduced by private enterprises as early as 1919. The state would
make them part of the panoply of inducements offered by a decree-law of
1939. The Code de la famille subsidized marriages, offered loans, family
allowances, bounties for children, encouragement for mothers who did not

go out to work, aid for rentals paid from a single salary, and lighter inheritance taxes for larger families. Above all, the code made some of these allocations payable directly to the mother, an important step in the emancipation of wives from the dominion of their husbands. Across great wastes of inertia, modest victories were being recorded.

A softer, kinder version of marriage began to be put about. For Antoine Prost, the thirties see the emergence of novel affective solidarities: *couples,* tenderness, mutual affection, a new appreciation that happiness in marriage and in the family is important—the happiness of children, the happiness of parents and children living together.[76] Marriage was more, *Marie-Claire* argued, than physical or sentimental attraction that is bound to wane; friendship, collaboration, camaraderie must last even after love has died. The naïve historian remains baffled before such views of marital affection. Perhaps they worked. Yet man remained the designated provider, responsible for his wife's turnout, her elegance, and her allowance, too. No wonder *Marie-Claire* supplemented its lenifying lessons with advice more stern. Make yourself familiar with the law, it told its readers, and, more immediately, don't be helpless, learn to defend yourself against aggression or insolence.[77]

In this respect boxing, as in the *Paris-Soir* serial cited earlier, could come in useful. Earning your keep was more effective still. World War I, said an eminent barrister, had been the women's 1789. In the absence of so many men they did not just increase their numbers in run-of-the-mill jobs—12,000 in the PTT (Postes, Télégraphes, Téléphones), 130,000 working for the services—but in more desirable ones as lab researchers, factory engineers, hospital administrators, officials in some ministry. For daughters of the bourgeoisie, remarks Guy Thuillier, diplomas replaced dowries.[78] In 1924 high school curricula for boys and girls became identical. The number of adolescents passing the baccalaureate did not rise vertiginously, but what increase took place may be attributed to the competitiveness of middle-class maidens, who by the thirties' end accounted for one third of graduates. In the Paris Faculty of Law, where there had been 46 French women students in 1913, there were ten times as many in 1920, 921 by 1927. By 1935, 10 percent of lawyers before the Paris bar were women. Young women became members of ministerial cabinets; they came in first in prestigious competitive examinations like the *Concours Général* and the *Agrégation.*[79] Significantly, one book of 1932 about women by a woman, Yvonne Ostroga, would be entitled *Les Indépendantes.*

We shall see that women were not as independent as all that. Still, circumstances drove them to gainful employment, and the drive was an uncertain one. In 1929 the Estates General of Feminism organized by the Conseil National des Femmes Françaises had raised the question "Why are women forced to work instead of devoting themselves solely to their home?" and answered that necessity forced them to it. The way the question was formulated suggests that the National Council of French Women was drawn from the leisured class. For a lot of women work in the home was no less wearying than work for wages. Until the Second War, fetching water from the pump that stood in street or square, washing, pressing with a coal-fired iron, mending clothes, housekeeping were full-time activities that left men indifferent but kept housewives busy and, often, uncomfortable. The simplest tasks like cooking were complicated by equipment designed with no thought of the user's convenience.* If a feminist reformer like Pauline Bernège, an enthusiastic admirer of American "domestic science," praised the appearance of stoves and cookers "at the level of the housewife's hands," it must have been because so many stoves were difficult to work at. But the ladies of the national council thought of work in other terms.[80]

An American reporting on France testified that paid work for women of the upper classes was a very recent phenomenon. An *inspecteur des finances,* René Frédet, concurs: It was ill considered to have a wife who worked—at least, who worked for money. Among the upper classes, volunteer work was perfectly all right; income-producing labor was for the men alone. Devaluation, then depression had encouraged girls of good family first to obtain degrees, then to attend courses in useful skills that could be applied at home, like sewing to cut down dresses or to reuse the sumptuous prewar gowns of mothers or of aunts. So the idle rich were no longer quite as idle, but seldom in a profitable way. *Femina* reassured its readers that the pretty young women who danced the night away passed days in study, social work, or practicing "arts of amenity" like making lampshades or binding books.

---

*Even in middle-class apartments charcoal stoves ruled the roost; gas ones made only timid breakthroughs. On the other hand, the media were beginning to pay attention to the simplification of cooking and of menus. In one of his broadcast talks on Radio-Paris, Dr. Edouard de Pomiane referred to the *"crise de la technique culinaire"* created by the progress of feminism: "One loves simple cooking as one loves a simple study by Matisse or Fujita." Pomiane dedicated his cookbooks to the wonders of gas (*La Cuisine en six leçons,* 1927), to speed and efficiency (*La Cuisine en dix minutes, ou l'adaptation au rythme moderne,* 1930), to modernity (*Radio-cuisine,* 1933, where the views quoted above can be found pp. 21, 22).

One result was that the general public assumed that the social assistants beginning to appear in hospitals, factories, and the poorer quarters were simply new-model *dames de charité*, ladies bountiful facing no material problems and needing no salary.[81]

The assumptions were self-fulfilling: Social workers were paid a pittance on which they could not live. Many lived with their parents. Many a woman who worked or studied dreamed of having a room of her own long before she got one. Even so, few, isolated, and misprized as they were, women social workers and social assistants suggested the possibility of alternatives for women. In 1936 the social assistants visiting Ardentes, in the Indre, found peasants despised by city folk and despising themselves, with peasant women at the bottom of the scale. "We're stupid in the countryside," a young girl explained, and, of course, inferior to the men. The assistants taught the girls how to tend the sick, how to learn so they could better their lot, how to take correspondence courses, how to escape an apparently inescapable destiny. The response was enthusiastic: "[T]hey suffered to feel themselves inferior."[82]

The daughters of the rich were limited by codes that restricted profitable endeavor; those of the poor or poorer had broader possibilities. A few industries employed them in growing numbers—chemicals, leatherwork, food processing—and statistics suggest a stronger feminine presence as subordinate salary earners in hospitals, clinics, insurance companies and banks, or as shop assistants. But those who did not want to derogate found possibilities limited: Milliner, teacher (especially in a private school), governess, or lady's companion pretty much exhausted the list. Catholic unions pioneered courses in cutting, sewing, pressing (menial tasks), shorthand, and accounting. Municipalities founded technical schools that taught French and commercial English, accounting, shorthand, women's hairdressing. These were women's jobs, and women knew their place. At a time when all working hours continued extensible and unregulated, those of women workers were most subject to stretching, just like a housewife's schedule.[83]

Wise secretaries kept needle and thread in the drawer to sew their employers' buttons or to mend a tear. In more skilled employment—laboratories, for example—work was hard to find, and men resented the competition. In any case, in times when access to jobs was often obtained by personal intervention, women of merit, just like men, more often entered a career by way of family influence or on a husband's coattails. At Nevers, for example, when the curator of the town's museum was called up for the war, his wife took over, approved by the Municipal Council. Working first in her husband's name, then as secretary, finally as temporary curator after her husband died, Marguerite Duran managed the museum until 1943, by all accounts far better than her successors were to do but always at a lower salary than a male could earn.[84] Among many others, a 1933 book on careers open to women testified to the enduring superiority of males and to the need for women to resign themselves to it. And resignation would be just as well, since the Depression set off "a tide of antifeminism."[85]

"Never has life been the object of more arduous combat," declared a 1935 book by a professional woman, *Women at Work;* "never has daily bread been so rare or so hard to earn." With the labor market overcrowded, the struggle in it was hard but especially hard for women. Welcomed during and after the war, tolerated as times got harder, by 1934 and 1935 women found themselves brutally sidelined or expelled with a minimum of formalities or excuses. Official measures closed administrative careers, admitted to competition only candidates who had performed their military service (hence excluded women); liberal professions "boycotted" them. The struggle, wrote Suzanne Cordelier, would have been less brutal if women "by taste for independence rather than real need" had not challenged men in careers that their mothers would never have envisaged because they regarded them as the preserve of men. But "what ten years ago seemed a charming whim takes on the aspect of criminal trespass. . . . The traditional conflict of the sexes is doubled by an almost malignant rivalry. . . ."[86]

Contemporary evidence suggests that male students rebelled against women invading their courses. Teachers more or less automatically eliminated them from exams and competitions. Women lawyers found the atmosphere of lawcourts increasingly unbearable as men no longer bothered to hide their irritation in the presence of a female colleague conducting a case. The Conseil d'Etat, France's highest appellate court, denied women access to the magistrature. Enlightened literary weeklies declared women less useful than men in high positions, "which is why they seldom reach higher levels and why examiners favor male candidates." Even Socialists, Thuillier reminds us, when they launched their project of a National School of Administration in 1936, excluded women from it.[87]

Cordelier suggested that women should look to careers where they would not face such problems. But careers of that sort were getting fewer and more difficult. The postal service, for example, had long harbored and valued women workers, *Damdad (dames d'administration),* who, like their male colleagues, made their way by competitive examination. In July 1935 an article in the postal union bulletin restated priorities in pious terms: "Emancipation doesn't bring happiness, it merely destroys family feeling." The thing to do was to "return women to their natural destiny, guarantee them a haven, let them give our children life in peace; let them fill their role of wife and mother without asking them also to perform exhausting work.*[88]

It is not clear that whatever work was left was less exhausting, only worse paid. In spring 1938 Henri de Montherlant noted the mass of women crowding round newspaper offices where they could get the paper hot off the press and hurry to be first at any going job. "One understands why these poor girls are loath to prostitute themselves rather than work."[89] Unfortunately many who worked only made ends meet by prostituting themselves on the side. A plethora of articles through the middle thirties denounced the low salaries—especially in department stores—that forced salesgirls onto the pavement after they had left their counters. But there was always domestic service. As a Grenoble lady is made to say in 1939, "One good thing about this war—now one can find charwomen and maids of all work who are less demanding. . . ." And there was still marriage, if you could get it. In 1937 France Weiss, twenty years old, the younger sister of a well-known hostess and feminist, graduates first from the financial section of the Institute of Political Studies and declares that what she wants is a husband and children.[90]

So nothing is univocal, nothing is clear, except that women are not as good as men: second-class workers, second-class citizens. Recourse against that sentence was difficult since women had no vote, hence no access to political power, at least in its formal and most obvious form. Projects and variants of projects for the emancipation of women were endless, ranging from notions of a family vote to that of giving them a voice in municipal elections. Approved by the Chamber of Deputies in 1919, 1925, 1932, laws granting voting rights to women had been repeatedly blocked by the

---

*It was in this spirit that in state and local administrations where almost one third of employees were female, women became subject to quotas and dismissals. After 1934 the rule would be: Last hired, first fired. In the postal service, of 1623 agents dismissed, 1,400 were women. The militant Socialist deputy mayor of Elbeuf, René Lebret, demanded that women workers should be replaced by jobless men. In 1935 the National Congress of Mayors, Socialists and Communists included, voted unanimously in favor of working women's return to the home, where they could do most good. Laurence Klejman and Florence Rochefort, L'Egalité en marche (1989), 250–54.

Senate. As *L'Echo de Clamecy*, which claimed to favor votes for women, sagely commented in the midst of one more such debate in 1935, woman was not created for struggle. Emancipation, if it ever came, could only bring disappointment. We know that women were spared the disappointments of emancipation until after the Second War. Louise Weiss, Lucienne Boyer, Françoise Rosay, and many others continued to campaign for it.[91]

Louise Weiss's memoirs are one long dirge about the cause of women's rights. In 1929, 1931, 1937 the Estates General of Feminism, which preached to the converted, evoked much publicity and little action. Suffragist demonstrations before parliament, at the Opéra, at the Bastille tied up traffic but stirred scant support. Partisans of Weiss's *Femme nouvelle* sent red balloons drifting on the wind toward the presidential box at the soccer cup final at Colombes Stadium in 1936, taunted and lampooned hostile senators, delayed the start of the Grand Prix at the Longchamps races, obstructed the rue Royale by chaining themselves across it ("I can't arrest this lady," moaned one policeman; "she dresses at Molyneux."). But the established feminine—and sometimes feminist—organizations were reluctant to work together and tepid about political action. In the public sphere, charity, not politics, was the domain of women.[92] Political men agreed. Léon Blum, an old acquaintance of Victor Margueritte and advocate of women's rights, appointed three women undersecretaries of state to his first Popular Front cabinet but did little to advance the cause of woman suffrage. His party's enthusiasm for the cause was moderate at best; Radicals and Radical-Socialists feared the danger of women casting votes for obscurantist candidates. As Clemenceau had said, "We already have universal [male] suffrage. No need to aggravate a futility."[93] The Pope had announced that he was in favor of the women's vote, so Radicals were against it, but it is hard to tell how many Catholics actually favored enfranchisement.* Officially, Communists, like Catholics, stood for emancipation, but even they had their reservations. Women should be seen but not heard. Certainly not in the political arena.

---

*They certainly did not favor women working—pleading family values, effect on children, the pressure on working women to work in the home as well—and, like the Catholic feminist Andrée Butillard, campaigned instead for decent lodgings, family allowances, better pay for men, part-time work for mothers. More direct and certainly more brutal, Joseph Danel, professor of law in the Catholic University of Lille, argued that "one should progressively eliminate women . . . from all jobs where their presence has no reason except to lower male salaries by its competition. The economic crisis is an opportunity not to be missed." Andrée Butillard et al., *Le Travail de la mère hors de son foyer* (1933), 14, 49–50, 53.

So, emancipation was slow, patchy, and largely indirect. Where in 1900 a woman could not serve as a witness or go to court on her own behalf, where in 1930 a married woman had no control over her earnings and needed her husband's authorization to apply for a passport, by 1937 *Marie-Claire* exulted that all this had changed. Prenuptial agreements about separation of property were coming into fashion, and under this *séparation des biens* women could act more freely. A law of February 1938 ended the legal "incapacity" of women to engage legal actions without their husbands' consent, replaced "the duty of obedience" by a declaration that the husband was the family head, took a few steps to free women from their husbands' oversight of property, savings, wages, personal income, gave them the right to work without their husbands' express permission, though that was still required to open a bank account or safe-deposit box.[94] Limited though it was, the law of 1938 was, in its way, a landmark measure. It coincided with greater physical mobility for women, with more participation in public activities (like strikes and demonstrations), with less of visible modesty, with a disturbing rise in the use of makeup and in disputes about its use between parents and teenagers. Society, clearly, was beginning to go to pot. But women continued to die from botched abortions. And a survey of 1947 still showed women who worked spending six or seven additional hours a day on housekeeping, while women without paying jobs spent ten hours a day. Some things never change.[95] Much.

IV

Foreigners

L'amour de l'humanité est facile. . . . Les
hommes ne se détestent que de près.
Love of humanity is easy. . . . People only
detest each other from nearby.

—*JACQUES CHARDONNE*

N EVERY country in the world, Arthur de Gobineau once wrote with sublime modesty, "when one is not French, one is a foreigner."[1] The more the twentieth century advanced, the more France was to attract foreigners, benefit from them, resent them, reject them.

When the century opened, the large, underpopulated country—only thirty-eight million—counted over a million aliens. Then came the war, the dark swaths it cut, the opportunities it created. Immigration boomed. In 1921 foreigners made up less than 4 percent of the country's population. Ten years later they counted almost double that number. France had become the world's leading host of immigrants, ahead of the United States. In Paris, where in 1921 foreign residents represented 5.3 percent of the capital's population, ten years later they stood at 9.2 percent and accounted for a quarter of all persons arrested by police.[2]

Inevitably, critical voices arose to denounce the dregs of the world flowing into the hexagon, too numerous to assimilate, too barbarous to keep the peace, weighing on the country's jails, on its medical resources, poisoning the race, or using [foreign] gold to buy and parcel out the unspoiled countryside.[3] When in 1928 the perfume millionaire François Coty set out to challenge the established press by bringing out a daily that sold for ten cents instead of twenty-five, his populist *Ami du Peuple* specialized in chauvinism, and the editorial articles that Coty signed were mostly written by a professional anti-Semite, Urbain Gohier.[4] By 1930 *L'Ami du Peuple* printed a million copies and claimed three million readers. So xenophobia always found a public.

One regular contributor to Coty's papers *L'Ami* and *Le Figaro* was a wild art critic, Camille Mauclair—symbolist, anarchist, and early Dreyfusard reconverted to the anti-Semitism of his Alsatian parents by hatred of art merchants and of speculators. Mauclair had his work cut out hounding the false esthetics of so-called modern painting, the pictorial Soviet of the Ecole de Paris, the metics busy spoiling French taste,* the importers of hideous Expressionist works, the Jews (Kisling, Chagall, Pascin, Soutine, Lipchitz), half Jews (Picasso!), Masons, Communists (Signac), and other Bolshevik agents. "One really does not have to be xenophobic," he explained in *Les Métèques contre l'art français* (1930), "to feel concern at the growing number of metics who, brandishing a naturalization certificate whose ink is scarcely dry, install themselves in France to judge our artists without an intimate sense of our race. . . ."[5]

But the Gohiers and the Mauclairs remained marginal, their xenophobia more derided than influential. What Ralph Schor describes as national egocentrism could express itself in benign and hospitable ways as long as national comfort was not challenged. France had welcomed immigration; indeed, encouraged it. Russian, Greek, and Armenian refugees were outnumbered by Italian, Spanish, Belgian, Polish immigrants attracted by job opportunities. In 1921, one and a half million foreigners lived within French borders; by 1931, nearly three million, almost 7 percent of the country's population. One third of these carried Italian passports; more than another million had been naturalized recently or born to Franco-Italian couples. The next most numerous group were the half million Poles, concentrated mostly in the north and the northeast: miners, workers in heavy industry and on the land.[6]

Welcome, or not made too unwelcome while times were good and unemployment low, outsiders were swiftly resented once jobs became

---

*Metic (Gk *metoikos*; Fr *métèque*) was the word ancient Greeks used to designate aliens with no citizenship or other rights in a Greek city. Revived by the nationalist Charles Maurras in 1894, it became the generic pejorative term for aliens in France, equivalent to *gringo*, or worse.

scarce. In moments of crisis minds adrift grasp at stereotypes: corruption, betrayal, mischief. If unemployment rose, that could be blamed on now-unwanted strangers, intrusive, parisitic, speaking in strange accents and cooking with strange smells. By the end of 1931 "a wave of xenophobia" was sweeping over France. Unions, legislators, political and administrative authorities, had to react to grass roots hostility that media and press campaigns helped stir but did not originate.[7]

Most Italians working in France continued to identify themselves as Italians. Reception was cool, integration slow, and the Fascist authorities did their best to maintain ties between emigrants and their home country. Consulates distributed Christmas trees, offered cheap fares, holiday camps in the peninsula, free travel and hospital care for mothers who returned to bear their children at home in Italy. They also dispensed geography textbooks that presented Corsica as an Italian island. *Fasci* were implanted in better than twenty towns, and some of the blackshirt meetings echoed disturbing claims. In 1927 the *Progrès de Lyon* reported one meeting that resounded with ritual cries: "To whom does Savoy belong? To us! To whom does Nice belong? To us! To whom does Tunisia belong? To us!" Ten years after this, Italian youth organizations in France boasted twenty-four thousand members and Mussolini's secret police, the OVRA, over a hundred operatives, not counting unofficial agents and provocateurs.[8]

Anti-Fascist Italian activities were equally perturbing. Where in 1930 few *Fasci* numbered as many as the fifteen hundred members to be found in Paris, some twelve thousand Italians had joined the Communist CGTU (Unified Confederation of Labor). By 1936 the French Communist party counted five thousand Italian members, the Italian Communists in exile more than that. The immense majority of the immigrant community was apolitical, but it was its politicized members who attracted attention. Acrimonious clashes between Fascists and anti-Fascists were easily perceived as intrusive. Fights between Italians of the Left and Right were common; murders—in a society where violence still shocked—too common. History recalls the murder in June 1937 of the anti-Fascist activist Carlo Rosselli and his brother, but most victims of the political violence tended to be supporters of Mussolini. A French scholar has counted twenty-eight murders of Fascists in France between 1923 and 1933.[9] The diffuse resentment against sober and hardworking foreigners competing for work in France was aggravated by resentment of political conflicts that affected national security at home and abroad. The rising number of Italian workers returning home after the economy started to flag in 1931, the falling numbers of the Italian colony overall were greeted with relief.

Poles presented fewer political problems, but what Janine Ponty calls conjunctural xenophobia affected them as well. As partial unemployment crept ahead in 1931, 1932, 1933, conditions for workers in mining and industry became increasingly difficult—especially so for foreigners without access to unemployment benefits or retirement pay, such as they were. More foreigners became involved in labor conflicts, more of them were expelled from France for political causes (meaning left-wing activity). In the Pas-de-Calais in 1931, 70 foreigners, 53 of them Poles, were expelled from France; in 1932, 93 foreigners, of whom 68 were Poles; in 1934, 178 Poles and only a few others.[10]

As mining companies began to fire Polish employees outright, arrivals from the homeland fell, returns increased. In 1930, fifty-five thousand Poles entered France and ten thousand left the country; in 1931, twenty thousand entered, twenty-five thousand left; in 1932, six thousand entered, thirty-seven thousand left. Although they show a less precipitate rise in exits, Italian figures for those years reveal the same decline in entries. By 1932 the minister of labor, Pierre Laval, referring to foreign labor as a whole, could boast that new entries had been practically suspended.[11] The general reaction seems to have been: Good riddance!

Foreigners could do no right, and prejudice seized on them coming or going. Some refused to assimilate, kept themselves to themselves, intermarried, jabbered incomprehensible gibberish, held fast to their religion, their rabbis, their priests, and their clannish ways, draining the country of its substance and yet demanding assistance when unemployed. Others assimilated too readily, "ruined French artisans by their competition, undersold small shopkeepers, developed intellectual pretensions, wormed their way into all the liberal professions, married local girls and spread their physical or moral blemishes throughout the land, overran hospitals, clinics, lunatic asylums, prisons, making for national decadence and decay."*[12]

---

*To understand the popularity of such views, one might refer to the now-classic dissertation of Georges Mauco, *Les Etrangers en France*, published in 1932. Even this sympathetic (or at worst detachedly objective) geographer expresses concern that "this crowd of immigrants, many of them uprooted and ill-adapted, work to increase criminality by one third and unarguably contribute to demoralization and disorder. No less pernicious is the moral delinquency of certain Levantines, Armenians, Greeks, Jews and other 'metic'

No matter that a lot of foreigners took jobs the French were not there to perform or would not envisage. Isolated voices raised to argue the usefulness of immigrant contributions were lost in the general concert of imprecations. The Right, of course, was vocal, but the Left was not far behind. The *Action Française* denounced "The French under a foreign yoke"; the Hatmakers' Union thundered against the leprous immigrant rabble, the Hotel Workers' Federation campaigned against "the invasion of foreign labor."[13] Language offered a treasury of pejorative locution: metic, "undesirable," *macaronis, Polaks, sidis,* or *bicots*. . . . Calls to keep France for the French rose on all sides, not least among industrial workers. "How do you expect unemployed workers not to look with hatred, or at least with envy, on foreigners with a job?" asked a Socialist, without waiting for an answer.[14]

By the end of 1931 French musicians were beginning to picket and to interrupt foreign orchestras, explaining to sympathetic bystanders the desperate conditions that justified their actions. Other labor actions were less pacific: Up in the Nord repeated clashes between striking textile workers and Belgian strikebreakers left numerous wounded and one Belgian dead. Violence thrived the country over: Italians were killed in Savoy, Moroccans in Lyons, Poles in Flanders. . . . Working-class needs made hay of working-class solidarity. In the working-class suburb of Saint-Denis, cinemagoers cheered the news of taxes imposed on immigrant wage earners. The General Confederation of Labor's newspaper, *Le Peuple,* denounced foreign workers and their sweated labor to call for a diminution in the number of foreigners. Before too long the Communists learned to clamor, *"La France aux Français!"* (Maurice Thorez explained it meant not xenophobia but a call to rid the country of spies and provocateurs), and on the eve of war syndicalist marchers still cried out the slogan.[15]

Reducing the foreign workforce was a mainstream proposal. One of Blum's trusted aides, Georges Monnet, Socialist deputy of the Aisne and future minister of agriculture under the Popular Front, joined Edouard Herriot and many others in calling for quotas, which parliament voted by 1932. Right- and left-wing governments had encouraged immigration. Now they encouraged outmigration. Some 43,000 foreigners left France in

---

tradesmen and traffickers." Mauco concludes by warning against "the peril of a pacific invasion less brutal but more subtle than that of barbarian hordes." Op. cit., 558, 560.

1930; they would be 93,000 in 1931, 108,000 in 1932. In the five years after 1931 half a million foreigners left the country; the number of foreign residents in Paris shrank by over a third.[16]

Some of the shrinkage was due to the rising level of naturalizations, which provoked as much revulsion as did the alleged burden of aliens themselves. In 1927 a newly passed law had simplified the Byzantine process of naturalization. Many took advantage of the new facilities: ten times as many in the eight years beginning 1927 as in the eight years before that. By 1936, 70 percent of naturalized French citizens had got their papers in the decade since 1927. How really French were they? How French were they perceived to be? When in 1935 the newly elected Miss France turned out to be a recently naturalized young German, Mlle. Pitz, "hostile reactions" persuaded the winner to resign. Her title went to the runner-up, Mlle. Giselle Préville. *"Miss France sera française!"*[17]

All along the line the professional classes rebelled against foreign competition. Students flowed into France, many from Eastern Europe, graduated from law or medical faculties, then stayed on in the country to undercut good French lawyers, or more especially doctors, and steal their practices. In 1934 access to the French bar was regulated; naturalized foreigners were prevented from practicing law for ten years after becoming French. In 1939 the Paris Faculty of Letters counted 28 percent foreign students, the Faculty of Medicine 34 percent. One medical student in three came from abroad; too many planned to stay. With one doctor for every 1,650 inhabitants France was seventeenth in the world of medical rankings, way behind the United States with one doctor per 753 inhabitants or the U.K. with one per 822 inhabitants. But the profession clamored for protection against foreign invasion of a field it described as overcrowded, and the Right, always strong in medicine, pressed the case. In winter 1935 the Action Française called for a strike in medical faculties, to exclude foreigners from competition for internships or externships, prohibit them from temporarily replacing interns, prohibit doctors naturalized for less than ten years from practicing at all. *Je Suis Partout* (February 9, 1935) denounced *"Les métèques médecins"*; the Latin Quarter erupted in its high-spirited fashion *("A bas les métèques! La France aux Français!")*. In summer 1935 the exercise of medicine—already hedged in 1933—was further limited, medical and dental practice restricted to naturalized foreigners who had performed their military service in the French Army.[18]

Ralph Schor points out that these restrictive laws were among the few measures that the general public was able to extract from its elected representatives and that "it was only in suspicion and hostility" that a relative national unanimity was realized.[19]

The entertainment industry had led the field in denouncing foreign invasions. *L'Illustration*, the influential weekly, published cartoons showing French composers driven to produce their creations in the street because theaters were monopolized by foreign shows, or featuring French actresses unemployable in France because they lacked the requisite foreign accent, or describing truly Parisian operettas: "of American origin, with an Austrian tenor, a Spanish baritone, an Italian diva and a Russian ballet." *L'Intransigeant* launched a campaign against foreign films, good for raising sales even though the *Canard enchaîné* pointed out that the cinema owned by the newspaper screened mostly German and American films. The daily press competed to denounce movies made by foreigners with unpronounceable names or the use of special effects the French could not afford (*King Kong* was one example), all working to corrupt the public's fragile taste.[20] In 1938 (late in the day) Marcel Pagnol's *Le Schpountz*, depicting the film industry, featured a relatively sympathetic Jewish producer and Glazounov who, with a Russian name, a Turkish passport, a strong Italian accent, represents "a great French director." But not everyone was as good-natured as Pagnol. French movie personalities too competed with one another in denouncing the hold of Americans and Jews over the profession—not too tight, it seems, to let them prosper, but irritating when a competitor got himself decorated before his turn. Marcel L'Herbier complained bitterly when Paramount's Georg Zuckor preceded him into the Legion of Honor: "*On honore les métèques et l'on ignore les créateurs de chez nous.*"* Jacques Feyder explained that he filmed abroad more often than he wanted because "Jewish invaders had taken over the French cinema." The popular comic Fernandel called for a purge of the industry to clear out foreigners. Better than words, a host of films reflected these resentments. Especially after 1935, foreigners were pretentious, insidious, corrupting, encroaching, arrogant. That was the image, that was the message that films conveyed.[21]

---

*Lambasting "the barbarian invasion of French cinema," L'Herbier's memoirs, *La Tête qui tourne* (1979), 207–08, 244–45, refer to a France overwhelmed by "a cloud of Balkan producers" and "more submerged than ever by an invasion from the West" that fed the public's craze for films "which adulterated by their exhibition of Yankee ways the healthy traditions of our own way of life." In 1933 L'Herbier's friend Jacques Catelain had published a series of articles in *Le Journal*: "Hollywood-Vampire." Some things never change.

One other dread threat that the French had to face during these years was the American menace. Taking a deep breath, *L'Ami du Peuple* denounced *le cocktail* and *l'art nègre*, along with the sadistic contortions of American hoofers, nudism, Freudianism, all the aberrations of a delirious society that betokened the end of a civilization. Everything, as *Paris-Soir* complained in February 1931, everything was becoming Americanized—from machinery to love. And Professor Harold Laski of the British Labor party, after talking to a group of French Socialists, noted his amazement "at the intensity of their dislike for America." He added that "of course, their attitude is based upon sheer ignorance." It was based on interest too.[22]

After 1920 Prohibition, which hit French vintners hard and roused the hackles of the press as well, was regarded as an infantile form of protectionism camouflaged by native American puritanism. The French, who bore their own protectionism lightly, were shaken by the malevolent protectionism of the Americans. When in March 1921 a Republican Congress pushed through an emergency tariff bill, President Woodrow Wilson had vetoed it: "If we wish to have Europe settle her debts . . . we must be prepared to buy from her." That wasn't obvious to all and never had been. The Republican twenties bristled with high tariffs that culminated in the Hawley-Smoot bill that President Hoover signed in June 1930. None of them improved the state of the American economy or the American image abroad.

The French also bore their own racism lightly. They were, however, shocked, as well they might be, by American racism. They noted that Josephine Baker, a star in Europe, could find no hotel in New York City to give her a room. They judged that America's original—racist—sin was an inescapable social destabilizer and that the country was condemned to live with the incurable wound it had inflicted on itself. But racism was not an exportable commodity, hence nothing to worry about, only to criticize. Jazz, chewing gum, soda fountains appeared more intrusive, more characteristic, too. Americans were young, rich, generous, physically seductive, mentally deficient, culturally detrimental. They represented a modernizing, rationalizing influence that upset the traditional order and landscape of social life.[23]

Americans, noted André Siegfried, a distinguished political scientist who was not unfavorably disposed, had created a consumer society, a productive economy that provided workers with homes, bathrooms, and cars but drained out personality and turned them into robots. In America automated productivity produced automatons. That was what Georges

Duhamel—already a doctor and a novelist—found when he visited the United States as the twenties ended: a farrago of inspections, forms, controls, queues, calorie counting, canned music, material comforts, hypocritical prohibitions, industrial luxuries, produced by soulless machines for crowds drained of their spirit.[24]

In America Duhamel found a model of the society of the future which he presented to his fellow French in all its horror. The future was soiled by jazz (barbaric silliness), movies (a pastime for illiterates), and advertising (directed at sedentary mollusks). Inhabited by stupefied drudges steeped in materialism, conformism, and uniformity, it was ruled by boredom and collective illusions. The model of America was best found in movies—"a diversion for helots"—too often shown in palaces that displayed "the luxury of bourgeois brothels." Here was a nation utterly given over to the excesses of industrial civilization: regulation of images, of health, of self-indulgence even; mass production of sausages, people, ideas. "[T]he antheap prevents me from seeing the ants." America was not a society but a system; Americans who thought themselves free were the slaves of their own benevolent despotism. Was this what awaited Europe?[25]

Europeans apparently, at least the French, shuddered with delightful apprehension. By August 1930, *Scènes de la vie future* published that spring (and soon translated as *America the Menace*) had gone through 150 printings and evoked several imitations. Before long it got its author elected to the Académie Française. *Scènes de la vie future* clearly appealed to fears that an older, better France was dying. Poincaré praised it warmly. Duhamel noted in his *Journal* how the older man referred to the Americanization of France—the new rhythm of life, motorization, advertising—"with real despair."[26] Despair was nobler than vulgar optimism. Both Duhamel and Paul Morand, who had committed his own American book, the novel *Champions du monde*, painted the United States in dark colors—a sort of police state, prohibitionist and moralistic, an anthill inhabited by soulless insects. For Morand, Americans worked too much, only to avoid having to think. "Why don't they dare to think? Because they are weak in the head, infantile, lacking natural curbs or morality." Pierre Dominique, reviewing the two works in the *Nouvelles littéraires,* found them superior to and more convincing than the more positive picture painted in a rival work, Paul Achard's *A New Slant on America.*[27]

A reporter for the generally anti-American *Ami du Peuple,* Achard had visited the United States about the same time as Duhamel but found there a truly new world, as different from Duhamel's horrors as from that which both had left behind in France. The scale of people, like that of streets and buildings, impressed him, as did the national character ("No one complains, no one is envious"). He liked the cleanliness and comfort, admired the individual liberty and respect for law, understood the relation between standardization and prosperity, low taxes and hard work, enjoyed the movie theaters that provided both entertainment and vicarious luxury for very little money, appreciated a technology that worked: "When I got home I found the elevator out of order. I tried to phone my family to tell them of my return, but I gave up."[28]

No wonder that Dominique dismissed such rank prejudice as superficial. Threats were more titillating: "[T]he overwhelming spiritual mediocrity" that lapped across the ocean, Latinity itself about to be gobbled up by Yankees, as Francis de Miomandre direly warned and, worst of all, the attraction that this vapid but seductive world exercised upon so many young.[29]

The most eloquent of the young, however, knew how to look after themselves. Finished in August 1931, published in October, Robert Aron and Arnaud Dandieu's *Le Cancer américain* denounced America's colonization of Europe by credit *(vampirisme)*, competition (unfair), methods of production that elbowed aside native ways *(délire tayloriste)*, to establish "a secret protectorate over the old world." It argued that the sickness of the times should be attributed not to the war but to a cancer associated with America: the supremacy of industry and banking over the rest of life, of "rational mechanisms over concrete and sentimental realities" representing truths more profound than the bustling sterility that American modernity offered, and that led only to economic crisis, unemployment, and war. The American economy, with its "myth of production and credit," produced unemployment, and unemployment produced war, because only war could eliminate the unemployed. Meanwhile, "this country where all say yes" infected the saner, older world it touched with the conformism, the lack of critical spirit, the anti-individualism that flourished in its bustling universities. And universities (their teachers and students powerless hostages of the money power represented by trustees) were no worse than American philanthropy (manipulative), free public libraries (stupefying), or the thought police serving a regime that pretended to liberate but actually prostituted and enserfed.[30]

Eloquent, sensationalist, and hitting home often enough for a good read, Aron and Dandieu fumbled toward the future while keeping their eyes steadfastly fixed on past mirages. As in *La Décadence de la nation française,* the companion volume published the same year, *Le Cancer américain* reflected growing anxiety about French confusion, purposelessness, decline—both absolute and relative. But the authors' verve was resolutely reductionist. Both books equated "militaristic Fascism" and Anglo-Saxon "economic imperialism" to reject both as equally bad for France. "American" industrialism was America's version of fascism—as totalitarian, as oppressive, as poisonous for the national organism, but more insidious. In fact, the American "myths" Aron and Dandieu denounced—credit, production, consumption, "pseudo-needs"—deserved better than outright rejection. And the unequivocal condemnation of alien forces masked the impotent rage of children challenged to step out of a cozy nursery into a world not preferable but simply more competitive.[31] By 1933, when the duo's third and last book together, *La Revolution nécessaire,* was published a few months after Dandieu's untimely death, this refusal to face facts had reached the heights of petulance: "Fascism, Bolshevism, Hitlerism, Americanism—dictatorial regimes all—are born of our absence: because France threw in its hand."[32] There was a lot to say about French responsibility for the deteriorating international situation, but to attribute the rise of Bolshevik dictatorship in Russia or Fascist dictatorship in Italy to French errors was to overestimate the influence of the nation. Exorbitant estimates of French stature produced exorbitant estimates of French decline. Even when bewailing national decadence, the French could not help exaggerating national capacity.

But there was more to it. In 1899 already, Octave Noël of the elite School of High Commercial Studies had warned against *The American Peril,* deplored "the fierce selfishness" of a people all of whose energies were dedicated to the indefinite increase of riches, comforts, and material goods, denounced their "overheated and artificial civilization," their hypocritical policies, and, not least, "their system of excessive production." Times change, the scolding changes little, and its persistence suggests enduring tensions and dilemmas. Behind debate about virtues and vices of cultures far away lay live (and lively) issues much closer to home: the war between traditionalists and modernizers or, if one prefers, between the comforts of inertia and the disturbing challenges of productivism, rationalization, standardization, more efficient management, whether in industry or in public administration.

Keeping up with the modern world, forging ahead in it, involved more than technological innovation: The scientific management of labor, the concentration of capital, the organization and cooperation of productive enterprise were as difficult to face as to carry out, because they went against the national grain.* Custom and inclination privileged artisanal values, personal relations, moderation in scale, deliberation in rhythm and performance, all of which turned out more admirable than profitable. Standardization—the key of modern industry—went counter to an economy used to operating in fruitful disorder, threatened existing interests, habits, and assumptions. Yet standardization, identified with the United States, gave American business a great advantage over less adaptable economies. Published in 1931, Charles Pomaret's *L'Amérique à la conquête de l'Europe* is one long argument about the advantages of "simplification" and the "subjection" to which France condemned itself by refusing to adapt.[33]

But Pomaret was an oil engineer, and Pierre Brossolette, who wrote the book that Pomaret signed, was a young man in his twenties. We know about the generation gap, though not as much as we need to know; we know almost nothing about the role of engineers in twentieth-century France, or about the clash between engineers and humanists between the wars, the differences between graduates of the Ecole Polytechnique and those of the Ecole Normale Supérieure, the latter visible and dominant, the former laying the groundwork for France's glorious renovation after the Second War. Understandable in terms of interwar frictions and discomforts, anti-Americanism deserves to be understood, too, as a coded version of more profound national dissensions.

An overview of twentieth-century anti-Americanism in France never becomes very tragic because there's no imagining the unhappy ending without which tragedy is incomplete. Criticisms of America or of "Americanism," however harsh, read more like aspersions on aspects of French character and society: part of an intra-French debate. Even when unwarranted, the

---

*The fate of Henri Fayol, himself a successful mining engineer and manager, reflects the scanty hearing doctrines of rational management could expect. Son of a mechanic, Fayol (1841–1925) developed an "administrative science" that would become known after the War as *Fayolisme*. Having denounced the state's incapacity to run a business (*L'Inapacité industrielle de l'etat: Les PTT,* 1921), Fayol recommended the "industrialization of the state" that presently lacked continuity or competence in management, ignored long-term planning, refused responsibility or accounting, provided no incitement or reward to its personnel linked to their performance. Rational management based on basic rules—foresight, organization, leadership, coordination, and control—would include long-term planning, market studies, the scientific organization of labor, and constant contact between management and labor. This *Doctrine administrative* (1929) excited a few disciples, but the absence of wider interest is more symptomatic than Fayol's commonsense recommendations.

American image at the most popular level remained one of plenty or else a medley of colorful stereotypes. When traveling through the States, in 1932, Hergé's *Tintin and Milou* found just what moviegoers would expect: fallible gangsters, clumsy cops, inept Indians, kidnappers, dognappers, bootleggers, credulous capitalists, and journalists outlying each other. But ignorance is a great stoker of twisted images: President Hoover would have been surprised to read about his Farm Board as a terrible example of planned economy, and even André Tardieu, America's admirer and friend, blamed economic crisis on the United States[34] when it had come largely from Central Europe and from the imprudent speculations of French bankers themselves.*

A more awkward cause of friction between the two countries could not be put down to mere ignorance. France's American debts were going to bedevil relations between erstwhile allies, ruffle a historical friendship, and cast Uncle Sam into a new role as Uncle Shylock.

The European allies in the war against Germany had negotiated large loans from American bankers to pay for weapons, munitions, supplies, without which they could not continue to fight. When they bid up German reparations at Versailles, they hoped that a part of these could be used to pay their American debts. It did not work out that way. The Germans wriggled out of paying (most) reparations and did so in part with American help. Americans wanted a prosperous and stable Germany to trade with and to hold the fort against Bolshevism. The Dawes Plan in 1924, the Young Plan in 1929 were named after the American experts who presided over the scaling down of Germany's international debts. "America declares a plan," commented a French journalist, "the way Germany declared war."[35] That was in the twenties. Soon the Hoover moratorium of 1931 brought reparations effectively to an end, but not American claims for the repayment of debts that they were owed by other than the Germans.

An accord of 1926 between U.S. Secretary of the Treasury Andrew Mellon and Senator Henry Bérenger had renegotiated France's war loans, largely reduced the sums involved, set interests at a low 1.6 percent, and fixed 1988 for the final annuity payment of the consolidated debt. The French continued to try to connect the debts they had contracted in the war with German reparations; Washington never accepted this, and the Mellon-

---

*More sensibly, in the *Dépêche de Toulouse* in summer 1931, Heinrich Mann denounced the Franco-German conflict by arguing that the United States had been the true winner of the last war and that the political situation would find no solution until France and Germany came to an understanding, permitting them to dispense with transatlantic interference. See Albrecht Betz, *Exil et engagement* (1991), 113.

Bérenger accord made no mention of any such relation. That may be why parliament took three years before it ratified the repayment schedules agreed in 1926. Those in the know, however, believed France got a good deal, and it was ratified in 1929 with Poincaré's strong support.[36] We know that payments would not go on for long. Suspended for a year in summer 1931 by Hoover's plan for an international moratorium, they should have resumed in 1932, but didn't.

Reluctant to divorce debts and reparations when the burden of repayment would have been slight, the French were even more reluctant to do so now that their funds ran low. The United States, which had imposed an end of German reparations, had added insult to injury by doing it practically in tandem with the Hawley-Smoot tariff, which practically closed its market to foreign imports. How could the French pay their American debts if the American creditors made exports prohibitive? "Interdependence of reparations from Germany and debts due the US is ludicrous," wrote the commercial attaché from Paris, "but President Hoover is blamed. . . . America has taken away the reparations from which Europeans would pay their American debts, and must suffer the consequences."[37]

As a matter of fact, by 1932 Americans demanded less the actual repayment of debt than its recognition. But nuances of this order were no longer much use. To the Americans, the French were welching on commercial debt freely assumed. To the French, the Americans were unfeeling usurers. They had never ceased taking the German side, and they were doing so again. When, in December 1932, the prime minister, Edouard Herriot, pleaded France's honor and the word it pledged, parliament gave him a very dusty hearing, which was no more than he had expected. Herriot's government fell, and with it the American debt dropped down the trap of history, to be exhumed only as nagging memories. For J.-B. Duroselle, the Socialists and the Right, who joined their votes against repayment, stood for "the national spirit, chauvinistic, avaricious, and alien to the shifts of Anglo-Saxon moralism."[38] In fact, both nations come out of the imbroglio badly: Americans, as ever, invoked legalistic evasions to give themselves a good conscience; the French, just as typically, fell back on rodomontade. They forgot their own denunciations of Lenin for repudiating debts underwritten by the czars; they applauded their own repudiation of debts they had themselves underwritten.[39] But politics and international relations are not about ethics; they are about perceptions of current interest, and they run on rationalizations that make us feel in the right.

International relations, furthermore, are also about personal relations, and French diplomacy during those years did not bother to maintain truly effective links between Paris and Washington. Jules Jusserand, the French ambassador in Washington from 1902 to 1924, was a Shakespeare scholar married to an American and spoke English as fluently as French, though with a terrible accent. Good friend of Theodore Roosevelt, the two men once crossed the Potomac swimming together naked, with Jusserand keeping his gloves on "in case we meet a lady." No man since Tocqueville understood the United States so well, thought Jacques Lacour-Gayet, then a young financial attaché; but Jusserand was replaced first by an old fuddy-duddy so ignorant of things American that he had no ideas of Democrats, Republicans, or what they represented, then by the eminent Senator Bérenger. Neither man knew English. Paul Claudel, who replaced Bérenger in 1927, was a career diplomat but did not care for the new post, where he would spend six years. For those in the know, Lacour-Gayet remembered, there were for Claudel two kinds of Americans: those he did not know and those he did not recognize. But, then, Washington was hardly a major post to compare with London, Rome, Berlin, or even Brussels. Contacts between the Quai d'Orsay and Washington or New York were *"très espacés,"* and few French diplomats bothered to learn English. Georges Bonnet, ambassador in the mid-1930s, knew no English either, any more than Georges Duhamel had done.[40]

What sense of the country could such men develop before they went home again or to a better post? What kinds of interpreters would they make of their country's views or those of the land in which they served? No wonder that the debt queston was allowed to grow, to fester, and to rankle. Talking to General de Gaulle in the 1940s and 1950s, Georges Duhamel found him still resenting the Americans' insistence on collection of their debts.[41] To what extent did memories of the early thirties affect the hostile suspicions that queered relations between Washington and the Free French in the early forties?

If the American position was so resented, the issue was not only money but frustrated affection, too. The French understood selfishness, even that of others. What they found harder to stomach was the feeling that Americans cared more for German welfare than for French, for the prosperity of foes than for that of friends. No wonder that was so, an old nationalist explained, when the American press and American opinion were dominated by German Jews, and Jews notoriously were sympathetic to Germany.

Younger nationalists found the theme appealing: *L'Ami du Peuple* revealed the shenanigans of "Judeo-German-American finance," opening the way to endless speculation, threatening the stability of the franc. Even as Hitler's irresistible ascension placed it in serious doubt, the identity of German and American interests, umbilically joined by Jews, became more of an evidence to true believers. By 1938, when Louis-Ferdinand Céline published his *Ecole des cadavres,* talk of "American Judeo-Gangsterism" led naturally to more specific references to "Judeo-Americans (that is, in short, all Americans . . .)."[42] And this, in turn, leads us into a realm far less benign than anti-Americanism, and far more tragic.

THE JEWISH population of France, less than ninety thousand at the turn of the century, had more than doubled by 1930 and stood around three hundred thousand in 1939.[43] Yet even at its highest the proportion of Jews in a French population forty-one million strong remained unimpressive: about 0.7 percent. Most of the French never saw a Jew or wouldn't know one if they saw him, but few, if challenged in 1930, would lack a view of Jews. Churchgoing Catholics knew them as the people who killed the Son of God—a faux pas of which Easter Week provided annual reminders. The urban populace, especially in Paris, connected them with capitalism and capitalist exploitation or else with low-paid competition that cut even closer to the bone. But there was too—above all—the diffuse prejudice that a well-informed Jesuit described as "anti-Semitism of principle—latent and quite general."[44] One did not have to hate Jews to think ill of them, to prefer to avoid them, and, of course, not to want one's offspring to marry one. Emmanuel Berl remembered the father of a girl he courted who would not want her to marry him because he was Jewish, "but he would not have wanted him if his father had been a dentist or a bailiff . . . anti-Semitism had a certain innocence."[45]

Many well-known intellectuals quite innocently reflected their negative image of Jews on one level or another: André Gide, François Mauriac, Romain Rolland, Georges Duhamel . . . Some probably had honed their prejudice abroad, like Paul Morand, who married a Romanian, Princess Soutzo; some, like Paul Léautaud and Marcel Jouhandeau, spilled bile on Jews among many others; some fitted native stereotypes into their writings, like Georges Simenon, many of whose minor unpleasant characters are Jewish; some, like Jacques Feyder or Robert Brasillach, resented Jewish success greater than their own; some—Brasillach again—let homosexuality drive them into the arms of Rexists and of Nazis; some, like Marcel Arland, found anti-Semitic criticism good in parts, just like the curate's egg; some, like Edmond Jaloux, didn't much blame the Germans, explaining "that the Jews had taken all the money in Germany and kept the Germans from living."[46]

Reasons or rationalizations there were many. Yet it all came down to one thing. For Jean Giraudoux, as for so many others, the Jews were not as other French; they were not French whatever passport they might carry; they were simply "other." They also—whatever the exceptions—did not belong at certain levels of society or of administration, which may be why in 1930, when Jean Filippi passed the competitive examination to the Financial Inspectorate, of nineteen "admissible" candidates, one who had been well placed in preparation was simply excluded for his Jewishness.[47] That was our Jesuit Father Joseph Bonsirven's *"antisémitisme de principe,"* latent and mostly dormant when not challenged. But it took little to stir the embers.

The Right, of course, had been actively associated with anti-Semitism since the 1880s. In 1930 the main anti-Semitic rag of those far-off days, *La Libre Parole,* was revived: a straw in the wind. In 1931 Georges Bernanos, Catholic dropout of the Action Française, reburnished the memory of Edouard Drumont, France's anti-Semitic pope. But where the Right led, the Left was not slow to follow. Anti-Semitism offered licit opportunities for xenophobia and patriotic ire that did only modest violence to internationalism. Jews had long been the resident aliens par excellence. In France they were associated with the German enemy. War had exacerbated chauvinism, and Jews were its first and most obvious focus. In 1920, for example, the afflux of Jews fleeing East European upheavals coincided with a plague epidemic that made fifteen victims in the poorer parts of Paris. Socialist and royalist legislators agreed in blaming Jewish refugees for turning the capital into a nest of microbes; the Communist *Humanité,* the radical *Œuvre,* joined the carping chorus.[48]

When, in 1923, Emile Delavenay left his native Savoy for the lycée Louis-le-Grand in Paris to prepare for the competitive entrance examination of the Ecole Normale Supérieure, he was struck by the aggressive anti-Semitism that some of his fellow students showed. Attending the lycée Montaigne a few years later, the future Cardinal Lustiger, son of poor Polish immigrants who always spoke French badly, had to face fights and insults because he was "a dirty Jew." Yet at a girls' lycée a student from Martinique "with skin the color of coffee with very little milk" was tormented and ostracized worse than any Jewess. Being Jewish simply made tricky situations worse.[49]

Jews were not especially prominent among the foreigners that flowed to Paris in the 1920s. Good Frenchmen could focus their prejudices as easily on Ruritanians or on Yankees. Bécassine, at Clocher-les-Bécasses, was shocked by the parakeet accent of a South American, *Rastaquéros;* a slightly more sophisticated observer, Paul Morand, objected to the flood tide of Cubans and Brazilians. . . . And when the more or less financial, more or less conservative *Petit Bleu* denounced the strange foreign faces filling the terraces of Montparnasse cafés, its description, explicit enough, nevertheless avoided specifying to whom "the circumflex noses, overdark hair, coppery skin," belonged.[50]

Then, early in 1933, Germany went over to Nazism, and by the end of the year over twenty thousand Germans had sought refuge in France. Between 1933 and 1939 some fifty-five thousand Germans passed through the country—not many compared with the more numerous representatives of other nationalities, but a bone of contention in those contentious times. Many of the exiles had an international reputation: Heinrich Mann, Lion Feuchtwanger, Alfred Döblin, Bertolt Brecht. Others, like Walter Benjamin, Arthur Koestler, Hannah Arendt, and Giselle Freund, whose camera was her only fortune, were going to acquire one. Numbers remained small: twenty-five thousand or so year in year out, about one third of them in Paris; and Jews represented less than one third of that until 1938.[51]

Their output was prodigious. Concerts, ballets, public lectures sprinkle the contemporary press but cannot hold a candle to the printed word. Between 1933 and 1939 about three hundred books by exiled German authors were to be translated into French, besides a mass of articles in French newspapers and periodicals. Albrecht Betz, who studied their activities has counted a remarkable yearly average of forty books and two hundred articles in France during these years. More relevantly, most of these were oriented to the Left, whether Socialist or Communist, which meant that the politics of German emigration melded with the internal politics of France. Even Lion Feuchtwanger, better known for his historical novels, published *Moscou 1937,* the story of his trip to Russia that detailed the comforts and joys he and his wife had discovered in the land of the future. For the intellectuals whom German nationalism had rejected, the modern world and modern civilization began with the French Revolution, with the rights of man the Revolution had proclaimed, with the democracy to which its heirs aspired. For Jewish refugees, intellectual and nonintellectual, emancipation and progress identified with it. No wonder that conservatives of all stripes, however disgusted by Hitler's treatment of dissenters and Jews, did not want to see the ill treated taking refuge in their country. No wonder that the governments of a Third Republic already riven by dissension did not want it aggravated by more sources of mischief. By fall of 1933 the first sympathy had waned; the refugees' welcome had cooled to more restrictive policies. Official statistics show that 616 political refugees were expelled or refused admission in 1933 alone.[52]

As the years passed, *Jewish* and *refugee* became synonymous: "[F]irst one, then ten, then a hundred, then fifty thousand . . . Paris absorbs them all." Paris was turning into a New Zion, insinuated Paul Morand, into Canaan-on-the-Seine, suggested *Candide*, while *Candide*'s more vociferous sidekick, *Je Suis Partout*, spread alarm about "Foreigners in France," "The Exodus of Israel," and "France Invaded." France, Paul Morand made one of his Jewish characters rejoice, had become "God's own concentration camp" for Jews who, no sooner sheltered, knew only to cause trouble for their hosts.[53]

"Invasion" was a favorite image,* and though most German Jews only used France as a staging area before moving on, their German associations served them ill. For Emile Buré, Clemenceau's old associate of *L'Aurore*, now master of his own republican and nationalist publication, *L'Ordre*, the immigrants were "the Uhlans of German revenge." And why not? As François Coty pointed out in his *Figaro*, if French Jews claimed to be French, German Jews could hardly claim they were not German. Curiously this seemed to be borne out by the way some Jews behaved. In her contribution to the multiauthored *La France et l'Allemagne 1932–1936*, Rita Thälman mentions one German Jew—Alfred Rosenthal—distributing Nazi films like *Horst Wessel*, another—Samuel, better known as Lucien Leuman—who used his position as publicity director of a film company to aid Nazi propaganda in France, and a third, the American Walter Ruthmann, whom she describes as an agent of Goebbels.†[54]

---

*The Jewish "invasion" was also featured in a series of articles by Raymond Millet, published by the authoritative *Le Temps* in spring 1938 and reprinted by the author under the title *Trois millions d'étrangers en France* (1938).

†Not all these Jews were from abroad. In 1934 Marc Hély, president of the Professional Union of Authors and Composers, visited Germany, where he was well received. In *Le Franciste* of July 29 and December 9,

Of course, reactions to the refugees varied widely. When, in 1933, Albert Einstein decided not to return to Berlin, the French government at the behest of the minister of education, Anatole de Monzie, created for him a chair of mathematical physics at the Collège de France. We know that Einstein went to Princeton instead, but the offer of a chair at France's premier institution of higher learning had evoked almost unanimous approval. The only false note came from the likes of Coty, who denounced him as an agent of the international Jewish-Bolshevik conspiracy, like his patron Monzie, "the most active agent of the Soviets in France." Coty was thinking of Einstein's reluctant involvement in 1932 with Henri Barbusse's world antiwar congress, which the physicist criticized as a waste of time and from which he dissociated himself when he learned it was Communist-dominated. But Einstein was indeed for peace, as he was against fascism. His pacifism, his antifascism, his Jewishness would have got him into hot water had he not sensibly opted to leave Europe for the United States.[55]

Not all Jewish refugees were Einsteins; not all French observers were Cotys. Some traditionalists objected to wealth or vulgarity far more than they did to Jewishness. Some sympathized with Jewish victims of German barbarism because their oppressors were German. Some good Catholics, like the comte Jean de Pange, hoped Hitler was less awful than he seemed, while they also tried to defend his prey. But most attempts to evoke sympathy for Jews abutted on stubborn prejudice: Anti-anti-Semitism simply did not sell.[56] Paul Morand's *France la doulce*, first published in the leftish weekly *Marianne* in 1933, then as a book by Gallimard in 1934, turns about a French film industry colonized by interlopers. The film producers are all foreign—Jews, Greeks, Romanians, Armenians—and ignorant of French or Western culture. But they know their business. The German Jew, to take one example, rejects the idea of a film friendly to Jews, because it would not sell in Germany, and would prefer an anti-Semitic script with more public appeal.

If anti-Semitism sold better, and increasingly well with time, that was less because Jewish numbers grew in some frightening fashion (we have seen they did not) than because Jews became associated in the public mind first

---

1934, he denounced "the calumnies and lies" of the anti-Nazi press and praised Germany (and Italy), where "no foreigner can take the place of a native worker! But in our sweet and democratic fatherland artists starve to leave room for the rabble of the world!" Quoted by Richard William, *La Question juive entre les deux guerres* (1992), 159. This despite a decree of April 1933 designed to protect French labor in places of entertainment, cinemas, theaters and music halls.

with disturbances of the peace, then with directly threatening the cause of peace itself.

Stephen Schuker has pointed out how "recent Jewish immigrants . . . belonged to Communist-affiliated groups that appeared to be sapping the State from within." Many of them had come not from Germany—whose Jews dressed and behaved in "respectable" fashion—but from farther east, where both Jewishness and anti-Semitism were more obtrusive and crass. Many of the poorer, less Orthodox immigrants from Poland picked up their political training in rough left-wing schools. They suspected the "Jewish fascism" of middle-class French Jews and preferred to emphasize the worldwide war against working-class oppression rather than "the insignificant struggle between Germans and Jews." Eastern Jews spoke Yiddish and joined Communist cells. The Yiddish Workers' Theater put on "revolutionary" plays; Yiddish schools and choirs sang songs like "We are workers' children . . . our father is on strike: the police fires on workers in the streets . . . when I grow up I'll be a hero, a soldier, a Communist." The *Croix Angévine* did not have to tell the truth in order to sound plausible when it claimed that metics predominated among the Communists demonstrating in February 1934. But Jews represented a further menace still. Militant Jews, more aggressive than their native fellows because more desperate, "actively campaigned for a boycott against goods from Nazi Germany and proselytized in favor of various forms of intervention to aid their persecuted brethren abroad."[57] Scarcely a way to endear themselves to French pacifists, and a perfect excuse for xenophobes to argue that foreigners whose own legal position in France was in doubt were trying to embroil the country in their private quarrels.*

Symbol of this dangerous drift was Léon Blum, head of the Socialist party and, after the elections of 1936, of the French government, too. Some Blumophobes, of whom there were many and of many kinds, attacked the Socialist leader as a warmonger. In fact, he had spent most of his early career arguing for moral disarmament and leading his party in voting against defense budgets. That did not prevent his enemies from denouncing his antifascism as aggressive and his politics as likely to lead to war. It stood to reason: Blum was Jewish; Jews wanted war. *Candide* called on the French to

---

*Thus *L'Ami du Peuple*, November 20, 1933: "The metics of the Judeo-Masonic Revolutionary International who live at our expense and abuse our hospitality . . . may lead us straight to the most awful war where France would fight on behalf of Israel."

oppose the war Blum wished to wish on them; *Je Suis Partout* illustrated the grave of Private Durand, killed in the coming war: "Died for F~~ran~~ce Is-rael."[58] Such views were not limited to the Right. Raymond Abellio, then active on the Left, makes clear that the anti-Nazism and the "bellicism" of Blum and of his—often Jewish—friends were attributed by more stead-fastly pacifist comrades to Semitic prejudice. Semitism and bellicism ap-peared to coincide; so, increasingly, would antibellicism and anti-Semitism. Like the pacifist wing of the Socialist party ranged behind Paul Faure, a growing portion of the Left came to associate its search for peace with op-position to Jewish warmongering.[59]

By 1936 Alain himself, the peaceful rationalist, assumed that all German refugees "preached Holy War. If it breaks out under Blum, anti-Semitism will rule in France. . . . Beyond this double fanaticism, I see no possibility of war. . . ." For Alain, the Jewish fanatic and the anti-Jewish fanatic were as one. For many others, anti-Jewish fanatics presented no particular problem; Jewish ones were a present threat. As *L'Echo de la Nièvre* complained, it was just the foreigners who fled their own country like cowards who were most obstinate in pressing their foolish hosts to battle. "They, of course, would stay behind, providing company for French women. . . ." "Don't defend Benda, don't defend Blum," wrote André Suarès to Jean Paulhan. "When war breaks out, civil or foreign, you will see an explosion of anti-Semitism and they will be largely responsible for it."[60]

By 1938, when Suarès traced his lines, anti-Semitism was exploding—precisely because old prejudices were stirred up by new fears. The more disturbing the apprehensions of war, the livelier the gossip about Jews working to stir fear and hatred of the Germans.* During the Munich crisis rumors of Jews secretly working for war were particularly rife. There were demonstrations against the Jews in Paris and in provincial centers like Lyons, Dijon, and Epinal; Jewish shop windows were smashed; foreign-looking individuals were attacked in the streets. Near the Gare de l'Est two Jews speaking Yiddish were surrounded by a hostile crowd accusing them of defending Hitler; in working-class Belleville two immigrants alleged to have cried, "Long live Hitler! Long live Germany!" got away by the skin of

---

*Thus in May 1938 Emile Roche, the influential director of the Radical *République*, wrote his friend and patron Joseph Caillaux that the "Franco-Russian" supporters of Czechoslovakia were simply out to sink Hitler, who was "guilty only of having put German Jews in concentration camps, for the motor of all this campaign, if it is Russian, is also Jewish." See his letter in Emile Roche, *Avec Joseph Caillaux* (1980), 187.

their teeth; other Jews were charged with inciting young people to avoid mobilization. The hostile crowds—and apparently police, too—were using Jews as mirror images of their own discontent.[61]

Emmanuel Berl remembered Céline's explaining his father's business failure, which led the old man to blame Jesuits and Jews: *"Crois-tu qu'il était con!"* Then, in 1937, came *Bagatelles pour un massacre*, and in 1938 *L'Ecole des cadavres*—paroxysms of fear and loathing for those who, in Céline's eyes, were leading France back into carnage. The democracies wanted war, they would have it, and the Jews had drugged and dragged them into it. "War for the bourgeoisie was shitty enough; but now war for the Jews!"[62] Desperate, exasperated, outrageous, torrential, frenzied, raging, Céline was as ferocious as he was frantic—snarling, ranting, roaring, sneering, spitting his fury, his spite, his bile, too malignant to be funny, too excessive to be taken seriously, untranslatable, untranslated, and yet reviewed with the sort of respect a professional deserved when unbalanced, with the sort of detachment that suggests that, by then, almost nothing shocked. In the *Nouvelle Revue française*, Marcel Arland regretted the excessive tone of *Bagatelles:* A little more equity and nuance and the book's indictment (of a society hopelessly tainted by black and Jewish blood) would have been more effective.[63]

Colonel de La Rocque, who opposed the anti-Jewish tendencies of some Croix de Feu, was savaged for it by the Action Française and by some of his more militant adherents. Pope Pius XI, who, in September 1938, declared anti-Semitism "inadmissible," was ignored by many faithful, including the Assumptionist Fathers of *La Croix.* Who could blame them when the grim prayer Pro perfidis Judaeis continued to impress the faithful on Good Fridays?[64] It would be only in April 1939 that a decree-law prohibited incitements to hatred for reasons of religion or race.[65] Six months before that, almost coincident with Hitler's *Kristallnacht*, the activities of resident aliens had been restricted, the hunt for the arrest and expulsion of illegal aliens had become more urgent. One has the impression that by late 1938 and early 1939 anti-Semitism had become endemic. And yet even in 1940 the sons of anti-Semites still fell in love with Jewish girls, and Jewish families like the Lazards refused to believe that the German-occupied zone held any threat for them. In September 1940 a demobilized professor, Claude Lévi-Strauss, asked his superiors at Vichy to send him back to his post at the lycée Henri IV in Paris. The following month, October, most Paris shops were sporting signs excluding Jews.[66] But Paris and other urban centers were sophisticated. In the depths of France, as in the Lot of Anatole de Monzie, the rural populations looked with as much suspicion on all *étrangers*—outsiders whatever their provenance, even French—as it had done half a century before.[67]

V

The Decadence

See how it is written in the destinies of this
country to find its men always inferior to
circumstances! There is the implacable sign,
the chronic revelation of our decadence.

—*JULES FERRY, 1871*

FOR *SHAKESPEARE'S* Duke of Gloucester, the future Richard III, winter of discontent was turned into glorious summer by the sun of York. But that was a delusion. Doom and gloom reigned over the last years of the house of York, as they did over the last years of the Third Republic. While Jean-Baptiste Duroselle's *Decadence* fits both the mood of those years and our impression of them, one cannot help wondering why political shenanigans not very different from those of the early Republic should so bedevil its later years. Scandals and parliamentary instability had scarred other periods without bringing about collapse. The seven years from 1913 to 1920 counted twelve cabinets trying to hold the country together, nearly two a year, yet France had won the war. In retrospect, what followed looked much the same only a bit more so: fifteen cabinets under the presidency of Gaston Doumergue, 1924–1931; three in the eleven months of Paul Doumer's presidency before his murder in 1932; seventeen under Albert Lebrun, between 1932 and 1940—though only eleven prime ministers and ten ministers of foreign affairs led the musical chairs. Chronic instability, yes. Yet why should more of the mixture as before feel like decadence? Or so much more like decadence?

One obvious reason for this must be that the early Republic rode out its crises, overcame its scandals, and finally won the Great War, too, while the late Republic collapsed in defeat that confirmed its disgrace. Another explanation, not exclusive of the other, is that in the thirties internal disarray combined with foreign crisis to an unbearable degree, without any respite to draw breath. Business as had been usual before 1914 became less acceptable. The war had sapped authority at all levels: military leaders discredited by demonstrated incapacity, intellectual leaders discredited by their propagandistic eyewash, members of parliament discredited as incapable of coping with crisis, and moral values discredited by hard experience. Bravery, reason, foresight made less sense in the trenches, where the weak, the birdbrained, and the cowardly fared as well or badly as the strong or wise. Hard work and thrift could not prevail against inflation or the collapse of investments made with the greatest prudence. The old moralities did not disappear, but they were placed in doubt. The tug-of-war between acceptance and rebellion became rougher, and louder the demands for reassurance. The more dubious the value system came to appear, the shriller its affirmation, the sharper the denunciations of its failures.

The mixture as before no longer seemed tolerable because times were different, and so were the folk that lived them. Aspirations were higher, expectations greater, tempers shorter, nerves more frazzled, challenges cut closer to the bone as crises shifted from ideology to interest, from politics to economics, as margins for error shrank along with stability, security, and confidence. While depression drained their pockets and crisis grabbed their throats, men (women, too, sometimes) looked for decisive action but found only muddled parliaments running around in circles. Strip the verbiage from parliamentary politics, and the economic materialities are left. Balancing the budget and keeping the franc safe were the main stated goals of every government. Since the latter goal made the former unattainable, neither was achieved. Contradiction between public works and budget savings, budget savings and armaments, more trade and more protection, lack of confidence in a currency on the brink of devaluation, lack of confidence in governments pledged not to devalue it made governing akin to Penelope's shroud, woven by day, unraveled by night. The public, yearning to have its cake and eat it, blamed its representatives. The representatives in public blamed each other, in private disparaged the electorate they wooed.

A brilliant little book of 1932 by one of the country's foremost literary critics, Albert Thibaudet's *French Political Ideas*, begins with the affirmation *"La politique, ce sont des idées"*—literally, "Politics is ideas." That should suffi-

ciently illustrate the muddle of a country whose literary class could field
such silly notions without raising a howl. But one could add, at least, that in
a society professing to believe that politics are about ideas, political confusion was bound to grow along with the gaggle of ideas struggling to be
heard.

Duroselle indicts "the extraordinary incapacity of the French to let
themselves be governed. . . ."[1] What seems more striking is how extraordinarily difficult the governors made government, and how tenuous. Their
time and energy drained in endless jockeying and parliamentary maneuvers,
political figures found less opportunity to address issues that clamored for
attention but got less of it than did "the intrigues and machinations between parties and groups which unfortunately play such a large part in
French political life."[2] The Republic, parliament, politicians were already
connected in the public mind with scandal, corruption, shifty demagogy.
Harold Laski had been struck by "the degree of discredit into which parliamentary institutions have fallen. . . . To take a politician as dishonorable *a
priori* is a commonplace wherever one goes."[3] That had been in 1927. But
what most had stomached while bent on normal living stood out more
sharply when times turned hard. Troubled citizens sought someone to
blame and settled on those whom they had elected to manage the nation's
business and who, on a closer look, managed mostly their own. To jaundiced eyes politics looked increasingly like a conspiracy that professionals
engaged in, ever less like a way to tackle and to solve the problems of the
nation.

The problems of the nation might have looked clearer if the nation had
been more clearly one. Unfortunately, as Daniel Halévy wrote in 1931,
simplifying the situation rather, two nations faced each other the country
over, "each with its great men, slogans, books, newspapers, soon with its
own language and its syntax too." Halévy and his readers were aware that
this was nothing new, that the country numbered many families that would
not recognize each other, let alone intermarry; many estates where decent
folk would not set foot because they had been acquired as national property
in the 1790s, many clans, clubs, schools, cafés, and shops that ideology,
religion, and immemorial tradition made mutually exclusive so that in
country towns like Caen, Right and Left even frequented different brothels.[4] That was the geology of politics, above which a more provisional geography can be mapped.

Beginning at the left of the map, Communists regarded all to the right of them as class enemies, with special animosity toward their immediate neighbors of the Socialist party, whom they denounced as Social Fascists or Social Cops. By the late 1920s the Communists' specially selected audience, those proletarians with nothing but their chains to lose, were mostly foreign immigrants without a vote to cast. There was no mass of revolutionary-minded workers, and major unions until the later thirties were of a moderate bent. But Communists had managed to bring together a mixed bag of all the discontented: evicted tenants, embittered veterans, bankrupt householders, dissatisfied journeymen and small landowners, students ashamed of bourgeois origins, artists at war with the established arts, as well as a hard core of Moscow-approved revolutionaries. This disparate and unstable conglomerate whose only common trait lay in being *against* could only be held together by rigorous discipline and draconian dogma, capable of swift tacks, yet unyielding on the straight.

If Communists were dogmatic, Socialists were bureaucratic. The Marxist ideology that they continued to spout had little link with French circumstances or with their social base of teachers, civil servants, and skilled workmen. Before the Communists appeared to claim it, Socialists had been about revolution. They continued to talk about it, but the presence of Communists diminished them into a sort of center left of Marxism—rejecting contact with the bourgeoisie from which they drew their leaders, ritually refusing to vote budgets and military credits, even when tacitly supporting governments deemed as being of the Left. Revolution—like Reformation—begins in utopia and ends in orthodoxy. The less revolutionary the Socialists felt, the more terrible their revolutionary verbiage became. But the revolution that they favored in principle was not meant for tomorrow. This opened them to flank attacks from Communists and made their spokesmen even greater sticklers about doctrine. But electors who cast ballots for parties of the revolution discounted their verbiage, which was more likely to impress timid moderates and to confirm the worst suspicions of conservatives.

Socialists, at least so they said, were for economic and social change. Radicals were for traditional political programs. The party officially favored nationalization of private monopolies like railroads and insurance, supported profit sharing and a planned economy, opposed capitalism, trusts, and large-scale enterprise, and firmly avoided any steps that could advance such "grandiose social fantasies." That did not mean they did not talk about them—talk was what Radicals did best—but since traditional programs had mostly been enacted or abandoned, and since the small towns and rural districts electing Radicals thought more about preserving than creating, few political formations looked as conservative. Peter Larmour, a reliable student of this period, finds "no indication that any Radical during the thirties ever envisaged putting a single reform into effect."[5]

That may have been because they had been discouraged in the twenties, when Radical successes at the polls had foundered before the hostility of the Church and of high finance, whose interests they threatened, and when the franc's crisis had finally driven their leader, Herriot, out of office. Deputy and mayor of Lyons, France's second city, Edouard Herriot was a traditional Radical politician: immensely cultivated, an enthusiastic gastronome, as vain as he was portly, more interested in show than substance, caring less about long-term politics than about day-to-day maneuvers and more for his studies in literary history than for his party, he was an individualist, indifferent to economics, too lazy to prepare his files or else too bored by them, and his program consisted largely of getting reelected. Traditional political programs for his fellow Radicals were chiefly about letting sleeping dogs lie, unless their growls sounded clerical in their sleep. Even their anticlericalism, to many, looked like an excuse for avoiding more serious issues. But anticlericalism apart, did Radicals have principles? Some surely did. Were their principles clear? Some surely were muddled. Should politicians have principles that do not bend or go into suspended animation? Surely not. But Radicals instinctively felt a need to set boundaries to the administrative state that was creeping forward. Exploiting administrative agencies while trying to restrain them is a natural instinct of conservatives. Most Radicals most of the time followed their instinct.

The most positive message of the best-recognized Radical philosopher Alain* was negative: Democratic citizenship meant relentless opposition to the powers that be. What really counted in life was private. Public activity turned on maintaining the private sphere against assaults of the state ma-

---

*Emile-Auguste Chartier (1868–1951) was a lycée teacher of philosophy all his life and a regular newspaper columnist who specialized in short, thoughtful essays. These *Propos* and his teaching made him famous for clearsighted independent reflections that encouraged students and readers to think for themselves, free from the stereotypes and commonplaces that clutter and distort judgment. Chartier's pen name was inspired by a fifteenth-century fellow Norman, the poet Alain Chartier, whom a queen once kissed on the lips while he slept, explaining that it was for the beautiful words and thoughts they uttered. One of Alain Chartier's best-known works, destined "to correct and improve Gallic ways" during a period of foreign occupation and internal strife, exhorted the French to courage, unity, and cooperation. Alain, the philosopher, tried to do as much, with no more success than his predecessor.

chine—regulations, taxes—and, of course, against clerical obscurantism, no less reactionary than bureaucratic oppression.[6]

The Radicals were unlucky. Core party of the Left, they grasped at power in the elections of 1924 and lost it to financial crisis two years later, grasped it again in 1932 to lose it in economic and political scandals. Their chief talents were political when the country's chief problems were financial. After 1932 economic crisis aggravated ongoing fiscal problems, and fiscal problems aggravated political difficulties. With production declining, it was no longer enough to cut spending and raise taxes. Miracles might have helped, but Radicals did not believe in miracles. Budgets could not be balanced by reducing official salaries or freezing recruitment into civil service. Taxing property holders to pay bondholders when the two were practically identical made no more sense than imposing higher taxes on business turnover when the economy was slowing down. The deficit continued to grow. Socialists wanted a levy on capital. Radicals, who sought Socialist support, shunned Socialist ideas. Electoral coalitions between Radicals and Socialists kept breaking down under the pressure of parliamentary realities. That mattered little at election time, when few voted *for* much and most voted against, but it counted a lot when political victory was (as an old Socialist, Pierre Renaudel, once put it) about "all the jobs and all at once."

Political action is about practical things—office, power, laws that help your friends and irk your enemies—and ideology is of small consequence that doesn't address such matters. Renaudel, at whose side Jean Jaurès had been shot in 1914, had been a Socialist leader during the wartime years of national union. After the war Communist pressure persuaded the Socialists to shun coalitions that might confirm Communist charges that they were social traitors, betrayers of their class and of the workers' cause. Renaudel and his friends steadfastly maintained that the cause would be better served by working with Radicals in coalition governments that might get things done. As the thirties opened, new voices began to be heard endorsing this point of view.

Young Turks, both Radical and Socialist, argued that class politics were as anachronistic as traditional, deflationist economics. The answer to France's problems lay not in parsimony but in production, not in prudence but in planning, deficit financing, and government intervention to increase consumption. The problems of the Left were to be solved not by honing sharper ideologies but by maintaining working coalitions. In 1930 a Socialist deputy and old *normalien*, Marcel Déat, published *Socialist Perspectives*, in

Robert Capa

The rather joyless couple here portrayed
are holding or wearing small bunches of
muguet—lily of the valley—traditionally
bought on May 1 to mark the coming
of spring. Rich, poor, or simply modest,
French families came in all shapes and
sizes: thin and fat, large and small. The
ideal seems to have been to have two
children, but that was a rule of the thumb,
and sometimes even small families had
trouble making ends meet.

Public schools had worked hard since the
1880s to improve the hygiene, diet, and health
of children. In the 1920s and 1939s, they
acted as a conduit for new initiatives: medical
examinations, destined especially to combat
TB, cheap school meals, holiday camps . . .

Roger Viollet

In the midst of depression, luxury continued to thrive. The rich are seldom richer than when the poor are poor—at least visibly. They gathered at garden parties, whose informality looks very relative; for late-evening drinks or dinners providing opportunities to show off bodies, gowns, and evening wear as sleek as money could buy; and at functions like the annual competitions of automobile elegance, where beauties and their pets teamed up with machines to demonstrate stylish wealth. The blonde equipped with a borzoi dog and a 54 hp Hispano-Suiza is a popular actress, Alice Cocea, photographed in 1934. The bar scene here portrayed illustrates the fashions of 1936. Both demonstrate that fashion marches unruffled past economic and political crises.

February 6, 1934. The place de la Concorde at dusk, with horse guards trying to clear the square while rocks are being thrown at their retreating backs. Another angle of the same square a few months later shows a more peaceful demonstration of republican veterans protesting the government decrees that threatened to cut their pensions.

Fallouts of economic and political crisis: Adversarial politics grew more virulent. In October 1934, speaking to the national congress of the Radical party, Edouard Daladier had declared: "Two hundred families are masters of the French economy and, in fact, of French politics. These are forces that a democratic state should not tolerate. . . ." The image of a new—financial—feudalism was eagerly taken up by the rest of the left.

**Avant toute chose
DU PAIN
pour les vrais Français**

A la porte
les Juifs
les salauds
qui
exploitent
les
Travailleurs

Tous debout pour la Révolution Nationale !
Contre la Pourriture Parlementaire

POUR LA FRANCE AUX FRANÇAIS ADHÉREZ
au
Parti Socialiste National
seule organisation intégralement anti-juive
27, rue des Petits-Champs, Paris 1er

JUIF

Lisez ce
Leaders et
Staline, russe, marié à
Lénine, dem JUIF.
Karl Marx, Trotsk
Rosenfeld, etc.

Dirigeants
Victor Basch, Kah

Hauts Dign
FF∴ Antonio Coe
dit Fabius de Cham
Hauser, Dalir

Gros Banq
Rothschild, Finaly

Grands Pr
Marthe Hanau, F
affaire Stavisky, C
Fonctionnaires: Is
deuberg et M
Natan, Keim et

Exploits é
Dreyfus, Ullmo, L
Switz, Marjo
dovici, Moïse
Cohen Sande

Comp
nous s

On the other side of the political spectrum the exploitative enemies of the people were defined, just as traditionally, as Jews, a focus convenient for the Socialist Nationalists of the once-Socialist Gustave Hervé and the *Francistes* of the veteran Marcel Bucard, both subsidized by richer patrons.

Women *Francistes* were also active or, at least, vocal, as shown by the photograph of the meeting of a *Franciste* women's branch. Meanwhile, a quieter revolution sought to advance the equality of women on less destructive fronts, though with not much greater success.

The strikes of spring and summer 1936 began like
a holiday: Women danced with women at a biscuit
factory; men dressed up as women to prance at an
automobile factory; labor on the march or affirming proletarian solidarity acted good-tempered, as
if on a family party, picnicking on bread loaves
and sardines. But the workers who bunked down
beside their machines never thought to make them
turn, and the masters who wanted machines to
turn too often thought of workers as machines or
foes. Industrial relations remained adversarial, not
fertile, and the prolonged vacations away from
home soon palled.

David Seymour/Magnum Photos

David Seymour/Magnum Photos

With the thirties, electric trams were put out to grass, leaving city streets to wheeled traffic—especially cars that crowded thoroughfares unprepared for their demands. Witness this traffic jam in the busy square fronting the St. Lazare railway station.

which he argued that Socialists should no longer focus on a working class fast moving beyond their ideological ken but look to all exploited classes, not least the middling middle class, which works as hard and suffers as much from capitalist concentration.[7] Déat's ideas appealed to ambitious Socialists attracted by the more effective policies he proposed and also by better opportunities for office in coalition cabinets: Paul Ramadier, reformist mayor and deputy of Decazeville; Barthélémy Montagnon, a deputy of Paris, and, especially, Adrien Marquet, deputy and mayor of Bordeaux.

The same search for effectiveness inspired Young Radicals like Pierre Cot (born 1895), Gaston Bergery (born 1892), Bertrand de Jouvenel (born 1903), Jean Zay (born 1904), Pierre Mendès-France (born 1907) to abandon their party's favorite stamping grounds (anticlericalism, secular schooling) for positions closer to those of Socialists. They called for abolition of wage slavery, for a society all of whose members controlled their own instruments of production, for more effective trade unions, more state planning, a stronger state. But none of these initiatives carried very far against the opposition of the party machines. Addressing the Socialist Party Congress of 1933, Adrien Marquet insisted that his party's first priority should be the salvation of the middle classes and the reinforcement of the state. That's where the urgency lay, and the votes too, but it was dangerously reminiscent of Fascist interests. Marquet's formula, "Order, Authority, Nation," appalled Léon Blum and the party stalwarts; within a few months the "New Socialists" or *Néos* were expelled from party ranks. While the Young Radicals operating within less rigid structures fared better personally, many of them attaining cabinet office, their quest for a more radical Radical policy did not. Perhaps Alain, the Radical guru, was right in thinking that only moderates could carry out the policies of the Left.[8] Unfortunately, moderates were hard to find.

Standing out from an uninspiring field, the nearest to a reforming conservative, André Tardieu was the best leader that French conservatives never had. Eleven times a minister, three times prime minister, extraordinarily able and extraordinarily aware of it, Tardieu refused to suffer fools gladly—a fatal flaw in any politician. In a republic where all successful parliamentary leaders were provincial, he looked down on the provinces. Nor did he believe in the institutions he did not serve but used: "[B]ourgeoisie, parliamentarism, democracy are as hollow as nobility, royalty, Estates General were 150 years ago."[9] In 1930 Tardieu proposed an American-style industrial policy—technology, productivity, profit—but also institutional reforms that would strengthen the executive and weaken the hold of parliament. Had prosperous times continued, Tardieu's plans for prosperity and public works might have fared better, but, then, conservatives would not have needed the reforms he proposed. As it was, the political Right found his ideas too timid, probably too intelligent also, certainly short of its customary antiparliamentarism and anticapitalism.

Just as the Left ran the gamut from revolutionaries to antirevolutionaries, the Right stretched from old-fashioned liberals and moderate conservatives to wild-eyed radicals and reactionaries. The safest description of the Right is that it accommodated people who voted against the Left. But many of these held certain antipathies in common: distaste for liberal democracy, hostility to inert conservatism and to commercialism rampant, disgust with mass society, protest against bureaucratic uniformities. Not everybody on the Right subscribed to all these points of view (some held by members of the Left as well), but all could sympathize with those who held them. And almost all looked benignly on the most aggressive representatives of their camp: the leagues of the radical Right.

Oldest among these and most blatantly subversive of what it denounced as Established *Disorder* was the royalist Action Française. Looking back from exile in 1941, a Liberal Catholic felt that the role played by the Action Française in French political life could never be exaggerated.[10] But after 1926, when the Pope excommunicated its un-Christian doctrines, its influence over the strongly Catholic Right had much diminished. What counted still was its undiminished verbal and sometimes physical aggressiveness, and its role as nursery and training ground of right-wing intellectuals.* Nevertheless, despite its vigorous activism or perhaps because of it, the other leagues looked to a more prestigious model: the fascism of Mussolini. The Jeunesses Patriotes, founded in 1924 by Paris deputy and Champagne magnate Pierre Taittinger to compete with royalist Camelots du Roi; the Solidarité Française, founded in 1933 by another millionaire, François Coty; the Francistes of Marcel Bucard, also subsidized by Coty, all sported berets and often colored shirts, brandished canes or pickaxe handles, showed off in riding boots of the Italian model when they or their parents

---

*The future actor François Périer remembered joining the Action Française while a student at the lycée Janson de Sailly in order to get away from the "apartheid" of snobbish, wealthier fellow students and "to inflame the disgust with which they filled me." In the Action Française "we hated the bourgeoisie;" but when he looked back, their activism reflected "more provocation than conviction." Not an unusual stance for adolescents, this would prove counterproductive in adult activities. *Profession, menteur* (1989), 66.

could afford them.* But the most impressive league was the Croix de Feu, founded in the 1920s by a veteran, for veterans, developed after 1930 by a handsome, reputedly honest colonel, Count François de La Rocque de Sévérac. A poor public speaker, an incoherent writer—shortcomings designed to promote trust in a society where verbal facility was common—La Rocque proved himself a great recruiter, an effective organizer, good at planning exciting maneuvers and at keeping his troops on their toes long enough to become the Fascist nightmare of his political foes.

Leagues that denounce politics, politicians, and political parties are the mushroom growth of crises when familiar institutions can no longer cope, when exasperation or desperation call for action or, at least, activism. The crisis of the franc in the mid-twenties spawned several violent protest movements, all vowing to impose a new authority capable of reuniting the nation, mending the breaches opened by liberalism and its democratic brood, restoring the fellowship of the trenches, in a national community mobilized by faith, force, and struggle. All of these deflated once the good liberal republican Raymond Poincaré had restored the franc, only to reappear under different colors and mostly different leaders when depression struck.

Raoul Girardet has described fin de siècle nationalism as a contemplation of decadence.[11] If nationalism is the excessive distortion of patriotism, fascism is a similar distortion of nationalism: militaristic, aggressive, totalitarian in its exclusion of alternatives. In moments of distress, it can appeal to sections of the Right with which it shares some ideological affinities, to disillusioned members of the Left who appreciate enthusiasm and activism over substance, and to nonconformists in general who reject bourgeois materialism, egoism, rationalism, and hedonism for more heroic, more theatrical, and less pedestrian utopias. In this respect, the potential of "fascism" as protest and illusion is always with us, but its attractions are at their most acute when things go badly, when normally conservative and timid classes feel that they have nothing to lose, that anything would be better than what is. Such circumstances—which paved the way in 1922 to Mussolini's coming to power in Italy—did not develop in France. Political instability was never insuperable; economic distress never drove a majority to despair. Fas-

---

*One unexpected aspect of league activity was the prominent role of women. In a 1933 news photograph of Marcel Bucard inspecting a Franciste guard of honor, three out of nine members are women. In 1938 they would figure as visibly in parades of Doriot's Parti Populaire Français.

cist or Fascist-style leagues persisted through the thirties, and we shall come across them as we go. But they never conquered the great veteran associations, they never offered serious competition to established political formations, and they performed shabbily at the polls.[12]

France was a sated nation; it had no territories to reclaim, no oppressed minorities to redeem, no lost honor to reconquer. The militaristic accents of the Fascists held no appeal to those with little sympathy for sergeant majors. Veterans who would not march in step for national parades were just as reluctant to do it in a league. Last but not least, while Fascist projects were built around a leader, in France leaders were in short supply. Authoritarian personalities found other opportunities of self-expression, would-be *chefs* like François Coty were easily turned to ridicule, and La Rocque—the only man who could have hoped to imitate Mussolini—was too much of a gentleman, hopelessly legalistic and republican. "The leagues did a lot of marching; they did not endanger the Republic."[13]

The bark of fascism was lost in a babble of voices proposing recipes for salvation, voices raised most shrilly when discomfort knocked hardest at the door. In 1927 Julien Benda denounced *The Betrayal of the Intellectuals* who had deserted the ivory towers of pure speculative thought for the arena of political passions. Instead of exploring abstract principles as their great predecessors had done, complained Benda, intellectuals whetted the asperities of fighting creeds, exalted the particular at the expense of the universal and the practical at the expense of the spiritual. Benda's argument was nonsense. Intellectuals had always participated in the world and in its conflicts, taken sides, forged arguments that bred or sharpened bickering. Nevertheless, Benda's essay and its lasting impact reflected more intense, more active participation of scholars and intellectuals in worldly affairs. Benda denounced what he described as the intellectual organization of political hatreds, and it is true that greater political involvement, a larger and more literate public led to greater demand for intellectual wares, greater consumption, greater production, greater activity in a marketplace broader than it had been before. But if political hatreds could be intellectually organized, so could political, social, economic institutions. At least one could try.

Young people, as usual, but more than usual, blamed their elders for not doing better. They were right. As usual they believed that they could do better, and as usual they were wrong. But that was not evident at once. They too, like their elders, would reflect upon decadence, they too would cry out against it, and they were voluble. In 1927, during the crisis of the franc, two brash young men, Emmanuel Berl (who would become editor of the major Left weekly *Marianne*) and Pierre Drieu La Rochelle (whose Surrealist tendencies appropriately carried him to fascism), published a short-lived periodical ominously entitled *The Last Days.* Drieu's opening article declared: "Everything's gone to pot.—What? A whole world."[14] In 1929 Berl set about announcing the demise of his social class: *Death of Bourgeois Thought* (1929), *Death of Morality* (1930), *Brother Bourgeois, Are You Dying?* (1934). Meanwhile, in 1928, one of their friends, Bertrand de Jouvenel, scion of a distinguished clan who would himself run the gamut between extreme Left and Right, published *The Planned Economy: Program of the New Generation.* The French are great traditionalists, and by this time, as Robert Wohl observes in his *Generation of 1914*, generational writing had achieved the status of a genre in which one group disowned its predecessors and set forth to assert nonconformities and achieve disillusions of their own. Hansel and Gretel too, abandoned by their elders, had tried to find their way out of the darkening forest only to end in thrall to a wicked witch. Hansel and Gretel, characters in a fairy story, surmounted adversity. Jouvenel's generation, lost in contemporary history, faced a harder task. They drew many maps without escaping their slough of despond.

Like the leagues of the middle twenties, the spate of publications evoked by the franc's troubles dried up with that crisis only to start again in a few years. Until 1931, sometimes 1932, the tone of comment continued sanguine: France was the acropolis of humanity's temple of order; the French were the foremost people in the world; the future looked beautiful. France, Raymond Abellio sums up his recollections of those days, believed itself to be a great country capable of deciding the destiny of the world.[15] Then awareness of decline took over; the search for culprits and for cures began again.

Brought down to essentials, the argument opposed two schools of thought: individualistic and moral against pragmatic and technocratic. The great representatives of the former school were Robert Aron and Armand Dandieu, whose *Décadence de la nation française* had lambasted Benda's flight from concrete reality but taken issue above all with "American anti-individualism" and French defeatism before it. Fascism was a menace to be faced all right, but it was no more than a caricature of the American spirit: the oppression of inhuman categories, the cult of rational constructs, the sterile reign of credit, the mystique of productivity, the regimentation of intelligence. France was deep in decadence, proclaimed the authors; it would soon

be in agony. It suffered from mediocre well-being, fear of risk, bourgeoisifi-
cation, lack of higher aims or long-term goals, a day-to-day existence, an
ostrich policy. The world respected France as a monument—a museum
country. For Aron and Dandieu, though, France was the sick man of
Europe, as Turkey used to be. Symptoms were similar, and one could recognize the same process of economic and financial colonization at work in
both, the only difference being that France's colonizers were the United
States. It was only by struggling against them, against Henry Ford and his
French imitators and the oppressive rationalizations and depersonalizations
such firms stood for, that France could rediscover the reason of its being,
the means of its salvation.[16]

The point of view diametrically opposed to this might be described as
Saint-Simonian: substituting the administration of things to the government of people, reaffirming the superiority of productive bees over parasitic
drones, presenting social service, social utility, competence, the scientific
organization of labor as superior values, and technocrats as the new ruling
class. "Soon technicians would rule the earth," remembers Simone de Beauvoir; "the word technocracy had been invented." Like Ford's manufacturing
methods, "technocracy" too had come from America. In this perspective,
however, Americans were no more villains but redeemers; the managed
economy associated first with American business, later with the New Deal
seemed an attractive model. The Socialist *Néos* notoriously admired it; Barthélémy Montagnon, one of their number, had specifically praised the "capitalist socialism" of the economy of the United States.*[17]

But advocates of mixed, managed, planned economies could point to
much closer examples. The Belgian Socialist Henri de Man had long cast
Marxist purity overboard, insisting that "not beautiful dreams but beautiful
actions make life beautiful" and that a new sewer in a working-class quarter
was worth far more than a new theory of class war.[18] True revolution,
thought de Man, would be achieved not by conflict but by planning; and
planisme was going to engender magazines like *Plans*, to which contributed
Hubert Lagardelle, the friend of Mussolini and of Georges Sorel, Arthur

---

*Admirers of the United States did not know more about it than did its critics. Maurice Bardèche remem-
bers the early 1930s, when young *normaliens* like Robert Brasillach and himself were fascinated by the
construction of new societies in Russia and Italy, by Hitler and Roosevelt: "We saw a renewal, a sort of
American fascism; a transformation of America that seemed to us of precisely the same order as what
excited us about Soviet Russia, or about Italy or Germany." Alice Yaeger Kaplan, *Reproductions of Banality*
(Minneapolis, 1986), 184.

Honegger, Fernand Léger and Raoul Dufy, René Clair, and Le Corbusier; or *Révolution constructive*, where contributors, like Robert Marjolin, a future vice-president of Europe's Common Market, Maurice Deixonne, who would preside over the Socialists in parliament after the Second War, and Claude Lévi-Strauss, sought to devise "a transitional economy" in which, following selective nationalizations, private and public sectors would henceforth coexist. Then, in 1933, the Belgian Labor party adopted de Man's *Plan* intended to introduce a mixed economy involving not nationalization of property but its control, the nationalization of credit that would permit this, and a broader social base than the working class alone could furnish. In France a number of Socialist unions and the Socialist Confederation of Labor (CGT) found these ideas intriguing.

Néos in those days could be found on all sides: around the Young Turks of radicalism, among Communists like Paul Marion, among rightists like Pierre Andreu. "Right? Left?" commented a graduate of the Action Française, "so many words henceforth without meaning for a large section of the young elite."[19] Undivided by political allegiance, united by rejection of things as they were, everyone who was anyone or expected to become someone was talking to everybody else. At the Brasserie Acacia, near the great boulevards, the dissident Socialist Eugène Frot met the dissident Communist Paul Marion and the dissident royalist Claude Jeantet. At the Brasserie Lipp, over on the Left Bank, a group of graduates of the Ecole Polytechnique founded X Crise, which brought together followers of Léon Blum like Jules Moch and Charles Spinasse, opponents of Blum like Montagnon, liberal civil servants like Jacques Rueff, progressive conservatives like Ernest Mercier, and rightists like Pierre Pucheu. All were interested in encouraging enterprise and raising productivity. None got very far. The year 1933 overflowed with plans and talk of plans designed to organize the national economy and save it. By fall of that year an editorial in the weekly *Je Suis Partout* chuckled: "I have a plan, you have a plan, he has a plan, etc."[20] There would be more next year: a Radical plan in May 1934, then a separate one by the Young Radicals, one edited by the writer Jules Romains in July, one by the CGT in October. . . .

Then a new Belgian cabinet included five Socialist ministers, among them Henri de Man in charge of public works and unemployment. Within a year Belgian unemployment had been cut in half, and de Man had shifted to the Ministry of Finance, where he devalued the currency, cut taxes, and, his French admirers alleged, balanced the budget. Not even such success, however, did much to change French economic vision. What changed was the mind-set of those involved in public discussions or exposed to their fallout. Richard Kuisel concludes that planning "failed to become a substantial political movement despite, or perhaps because of, its fadlike quality."[21] He is right, but the idea of a mixed economy made its way. Industrialists and syndicalists, used to viewing each other across barricades of prejudice, made contact. The CGT learned that nationalization was less important than control. Public employees learned from their trade union publications about the ideas of Henri de Man and Marcel Déat, about the initiatives of Americans, Fascists, Russians. Those who believed that politics were all, discovered the possibilities of finance. The public officials who served Blum, Auriol, Paul Reynaud, or their Vichy successors read de Man as they read John Maynard Keynes and came to believe in state intervention and planning. As one of them said to Paul Reynaud, "Let's be neither Liberal nor Socialist, let's be intelligent."[22] The intelligent classes were becoming less provincial—culturally, and geographically, too. One cannot help feeling that enthusiasm for plans so marked after the Second War had been learned a decade or two earlier, in the tormented years before Vichy. Robert Marjolin, Jean Monnet's assistant commissioner for the Modernization Plan that revitalized France in the fifties, was an alumnus of *Révolution Constructive.* Other members of Monnet's team of 1946 had learned its lessons in their youth. "We took over their ideas after the Liberation," remembers François Bloch-Lainé, who would become the master of French credit in the 1950s, "without adding anything very much."[23]

IN A collection of essays published in 1932, Jean Mistler, a young Radical, approvingly quoted Alain: "Since the end of the war, the only two ideas to really affect public opinion have been restoration of credit and organization of peace."[24] One, we have seen, was in dire straits. The other would fare no better. In 1925 presidential elections in Germany had brought Marshal Paul von Hindenburg to the head of the German Republic: the incarnation, many French believed, of German militarism and revanchism. Yet it was in that year that a nonaggression treaty between Germany and France was signed at Locarno which seemingly put an end to strife between the two nations. France and Germany mutually guaranteed the existing border between them and the demilitarization of the Rhineland, which was intended to provide France with a margin of security against a sudden attack. Henceforth, as the Versailles Treaty had provided, the river's German left bank and a right-bank strip thirty miles deep were to be permanently free of German troops. Britain and Italy guaranteed the treaty, whose preamble referred to "the desire for security and protection which animated the peoples on whom the scourge of the 1914–1918 war had fallen." But the security was short-lived, the protection an illusion pulled out of a hat by that old magician Aristide Briand.

It was said of Briand that while Poincaré knew everything and understood nothing, he knew nothing and understood everything. He certainly understood how to put a deal over. "Incredibly subtle," Harold Laski found Briand. "Like a benevolent snake." Duroselle, speaking of him, uses terms like *foxyness* and *petty trickery*.[25] And certainly Briand had worked his way over the years from the extreme Left, where he had started out as a law student at the turn of the century, to far more moderate positions. That was hardly an exceptional course. His success was more striking: Since 1906 his ability as negotiator, reconciliator, creator of compromise solutions had made him twenty-six times a minister, eleven times a premier. Did subtlety and artfulness account for his success, or did success feed tales of craft and cunning? At any rate, the structure that the artful dodger patched together in 1925 was more fragile than it seemed. France had so far relied on East European allies to divert and counterbalance German might. Locarno, entirely focused on the West, left Germany's eastern borders up for grabs. France signed a treaty of mutual assistance with Czechoslovakia that it could only honor by disregarding the safeguards of Locarno. It would come back to haunt it. But Poland, Romania, Yugoslavia understood that they were now left to their own devices. France itself was left dependent on German goodwill and on the dubious support of the pact's guarantors: Italy and, above all, Britain, whose interests did not always mesh with those affirmed in Paris. Security was still far over the horizon. That was where it stayed while French military occupation of the Rhineland shrank year after year until, in 1930, it ended altogether.

Then, in August 1928, the French foreign minister, who was still Briand, the U.S. secretary of state, Frank Kellogg, the German foreign secretary, Gustav Stresemann, and the representatives of fifty-seven other nations affixed their signatures to a pact that was to usher in universal harmony. The leading signatories of the Peace Pact for which Secretary Kellogg would shortly be rewarded with the Nobel Prize for Peace, were themselves in a bad way. Stresemann required the constant attendance of a doctor and a nurse; Briand, though only sixty-six, tended to drift off to sleep at the drop of a soup spoon; Kellogg, whose hands were partly paralyzed, had to guide his right hand with his left to sign; and Poincaré, who attended the signing ceremony as premier, was a few months away from the prostate operation that would begin his end. Their pact was no better. It prohibited war as an instrument of national policy but provided no sanctions against anyone who might break the peace. Even so, it evoked great popular enthusiasm and almost unanimous approval in the press. Few discordant voices were raised to point out, as did *L'Ami du Peuple*, that sheep may sing of peace but wolves decide just what its definition is: "The reasoning of the strongest always proves the best."[26]

That was not a message the public wanted to hear. Three months before the Kellogg Pact Jean Giraudoux's *Siegfried*, with its tidings of Franco-German reconciliation, had triumphed on the stage. Significantly, Siegfried was amnesiac. For those who applauded, his loss of memory applied to national grievances they felt it was high time to leave behind. In retrospect, the amnesia, like the play's success, reflects stubborn determination to ignore the warnings of history and of events. Jacques Bainville, the professional pessimist of the Action Française, had long predicted that a peace as ill contrived as that which Versailles imposed could only lead to another war.[27] But as the twenties turned into the thirties, gloomy predictions seemed far off the mark. While Germany counted its unemployed in the millions, west of the Rhine the economy flourished. France appeared prosperous and powerful. It could afford to be generous; indeed, given prevailing spirits, it could not afford not to be. On June 30, 1930, the last French battalion left the Rhineland, which had been occupied since 1918. On July 1 the *Deutsche Allgemeine Zeitung* (admittedly a publication of the Right) commented: "Germans respond only with scornful silence to those who regard the evacuation as a generous gesture."[28] In the German elections of September Hitler's National Socialists, with seven times more votes than in the last, passed from 12 deputies to 107. That seemed poor reward for French benevolence, but Briand was untroubled: Hitler will not go far, he assured the press while doing his best to keep news of German militarism reviving from the French public. Parades and demonstrations of the German Right were "completely suppressed in newsreels shown in French movie houses," reported the American military attaché.[29]

The postwar years were limping to an end, and some speculated that the prewar years were now beginning. Specialists of German affairs on the

French General Staff considered the Nazis' coming to power "a certainty," and German rearmament with it.[30] Briand was losing his grip. In 1931 he failed to win election to the presidency of the republic, which, given his tendency to lunch heavily, then fall asleep and snore in the middle of conversations, was probably just as well.[31] In 1932 he died.* In April 1932, one month after Briand's death, Hitler drew thirteen million votes in the German presidential elections against nineteen million cast for Hindenburg. The French were left to congratulate themselves that an old nationalist had triumphed over a radical supernationalist.[32] What did it matter that German nationalism was more vital and more forceful than the French, explained Jacques de Lacretelle, who was noted for the psychological acumen of his novels; their errors of judgment would simply be greater. The tortoise would always triumph over the hare. One more month, May 1932, and Paul Doumer, the conservative who had been elected against Briand, fell to the bullets of a deranged Russian refugee after eleven months in the Elysée and was replaced by an equally moderate but more insignificant figure, Albert Lebrun. Lebrun, who would be reelected in 1939, just in time to facilitate the obsequies of the republic he presided over, was a man of goodwill: gauche, timid, and myopic. "Never in the history of French republics," comments Duverger, "has void been more absolute."[33]

The tangled web of treaties and agreements supposed to maintain peace was unraveling fast. In new German elections the Nazis became the largest party in the Reichstag, but the French press was not impressed. President Hindenburg had brought in General von Schleicher to hold the fort against the house painter-demagogue. Newspapers from Left to Right celebrated "the piteous end of Hitlerism" (L'Œuvre, January 1, 1933) and "the decadence of Hitler's movement" (Paris-Soir, January 1, 1933). The German Boulanger had missed the boat, exulted L'Echo de Paris (Nov. 7, 1932), forgetting how law-abiding the populist nineteenth-century general had been. The Socialist Populaire and the royalist Action française agreed: Hitler was henceforth excluded from power. But Schleicher resigned as January 1933 ended, and the demagogue found himself in power after all. A pacifist dedicated his latest book, Peace on Earth, to Adolf Hitler. Suzanne Buisson, of the Socialist Federation of the Seine, warned against overreacting: "The more

---

*"With Christian Fouchet," a country gentleman remembered, "I went to pay my respects to the mortal remains of Briand. He lay, a small corpse dressed in his Sunday best, in a modest room on the avenue Kléber. We found no one there." Charles d'Aragon, La Résistance sans héroisme (1977), 95.

you complain about the Fascist peril, the better its chance of coming about."[34] The chances of the French fully realizing the Nazi peril diminished further when a translation of *Mein Kampf*, in which Germany's new leader designated France as the hereditary enemy to be crushed before his plans could be fulfilled, was ordered destroyed by a Paris commercial court. Only expurgated versions would be available to the few who bothered to press past Nazi propaganda blowing hot and cold.[35]

Foreign affairs and international news had never attracted much sustained attention either before or since the war. From now on this changed. A gaggle of weeklies directed at the general public offered regular comment on the international situation. Unfortunately the weight of circulation lay with periodicals sympathetic to Mussolini (who, as we know, made trains run on time), admirative even of the suspect Hitler, whose authoritarian policies they envied. Printings of the apolitical *Lu* and of the mildly progressive *Marianne*, edited by Emmanuel Berl, whom rightists praised for his objectivity, ran far behind the sales of ever more virulent publications like *Gringoire* (over 600,000), *Candide* (350,000), and *Je Suis Partout* (60,000–80,000). And while right-wing reviews reflected Right opinion reinforcing it, those of the Left, when not pacifistic, voiced only their words.[36] In the international competition the battle of beliefs was being lost at home before it could be engaged across the country's borders.

Attention meanwhile was shifting back to the first concern Mistler had cited: what he called the question of credit and what we loosely call the economy. While nationalists gave way to supranationalists in Germany, the French Assembly discussed a new budget involving modest tax raises, cuts in the civil service budget, in pensions and veteran allocations, and the prevention of tax frauds practiced on a spectacular scale by all who could. Such proposals evoked indignant opposition, soon organized and channeled by taxpayer protest groups. Most notable among these were the Committee for the Defense of Taxpayers, subsidized and manipulated mainly by the director of an oil and petrol firm, the Huiles Lesieur, Jacques Lemaigre-Dubreuil; and the Economic Salvation Committee, subsidized by the Employers' Federation. As usual the legitimate interests of shopkeepers, clerks, and other small folk who suffered in recession served as screen and catspaw for the selfish interests of big money. On January 30, 1933, as Hitler was appointed German chancellor, a meeting of the Economic Salvation Committee turned into a noisy demonstration against treacherous politicians: "No more taxes, not a cent! no more parliament! no more deputies! dictatorship! dissolution!" Cries like these were not exceptional in Paris, but hard times and a discredited political class make a flammable combination. In the thirteen months between December 1932 and January 1933 five cabinets succeeded each other, while protest movements sprouted on all sides: Farmers, veterans, civil servants, shopkeepers, war widows, taxi drivers filled streets and meeting halls.

What the country needed, argued *Paris-Soir*, was a spectacular crime to take people's minds off present problems. It got not one but two. In February two sisters working as housemaids in Le Mans massacred their employer and her daughter: "She tried to beat me, I tore her eyes out." Quite literally. Fourteen years after the trial of the Papin sisters Jean Genet's *The Maids* (1947) was going to turn sordid horror into theater of the absurd. More absurd still was the story of Violette Nozière, determined to poison her parents to get her hands on a small inheritance. The eighteen-year-old bungled her first attempt when rat poison in the soup had simply made her genitors vomit. She botched the second try a few months later, bumping off the father but letting mother survive to accuse her. It turned out that the boyfriend Violette tried to retain by her exertions was a militant royalist Camelot du Roi, but not even such succulent news fare could keep the public eye off parliamentary politics, which offered still sharper sensations.[37]

"*POLITICAL REGIMES* in France," the Englishman Robert Dell had written, "have a habit of foundering in an ocean of scandals." Dell wrote in 1919, in the wake of "a huge crop of scandals during the last two years," to predict the end of the then regime by reference to the scandals that preceded 1789 and 1830.[38] But if republicans did not govern very well, they knew how to survive the results of their failures. It would be hard to find a decade of the republic's history unmarked by scandal, and we have seen that the 1920s had been fertile in them. The novelty about new model scandals was the great role the press now played in concocting, publicizing, and exploiting them. The Third Republic was no more corrupt than its predecessors, but corruption got more publicity in the press. The new model scandal grew to a great extent from a coincidence of interests between a section of the press that had something to say and other, larger sections that had something to sell: wares they could peddle faster in the excitement of lurid revelations.

If the revelations worked to the disadvantage of the regime in place, so much the better. The vast majority of the Paris press was on the Right, and the Right, when not dedicated to opposing the Republic, worked to discredit republican governments in office. A detailed American review of Paris newspapers[39] lists twelve publications of the Right and extreme Right that sold a million and a half, six of the Left or extreme Left selling about seven hundred thousand, with the many-million-strong mass-circulation dailies centrally situated, but most of the time unfriendly to the Left. The major characteristic of the Paris press was that few of its members were self-supporting. Advertising revenues were thin and in the thirties falling, sale prices too low for them to make ends meet, few owners like Jean Prouvost of *Paris-Soir* and *Paris-Midi* were enterprising enough to make their holdings profitable. The rest, like François Coty, depended on their private fortunes and on subsidies from banks, industry, the French and foreign governments. Since news were more convincing than advertisements, most papers sold their news columns to anyone that paid. "No paper," declared Pierre Cot, "is independent of financial powers" or, one might add, of a political faction. "Corrupt, its news tendentious, even false," Dell had described the press after the war, evoking no contradiction. "Notoriously venal," thought the American Embassy twenty years later:

> In reporting a sporting event, a French newspaper will mention the name of an auto, airplane or bicycle only if the company puts up the cash. Speeches of distinguished men are "overlooked" unless the required sum is forthcoming. Exhibitors in the various salons are at the mercy of the slush peddlers, foreign propaganda (influenced by foreign slush funds) is usually coupled with political publicity. This Embassy, of course, has no fund available for propaganda. This fact is well known and deprecated in Paris journalistic circles. Despite this the Embassy has frequently been approached by representatives of *Le Matin*, *L'Intransigeant*, *Le Radical*, *La République*, *L'Illustration* and a horde of . . . less important sheets. In every instance it was intimated that if a sum was subscribed the anti-American campaign . . . would be attenuated. . . .[40]

Given such circumstances, readers had no way of knowing whether facts had been distorted, suppressed, even invented; nor did they seem to care. When, in 1932, Paul Gorguloff murdered President Paul Doumer, *Le Matin*'s Prague correspondent, the young Hubert Beuve-Méry, sent back evidence of Gorguloff's madness and his earlier plans to murder Hindenburg,

Lenin, and Czech President Thomas Masaryk. The paper suppressed his findings because it preferred to feature imaginary tales of Gorguloff as a Soviet agent. And if the press was for the buying, so were journalists trying to make ends meet. The gentleman who directed at the same time a patriotic sheet that called for protection of French industry and the publicity magazine of Ford in France was only one of many.[41] Readers had no way to tell the true and false apart, but they went on reading. Since more people read than ever read before, the printed message, even when taken with a pinch of salt, had wide-ranging effects. Like plagues carried by rats, news carried by newspapers affected lives far beyond their places of publication.[42] Disorder, anxiety used to be limited and local; they became broadly shared perceptions—national, even international maladies.

Amid the shrill protests of taxpayers, *fonctionnaires,* and others, against the dull thuds of crashing cabinets, the avid press now found a scandal to its measure: a tale of lowlife in high places that would destabilize the fragile coalitions of Left and Center-Left which tried to hold the fort since 1932. The first hint of fruity scandal came in December 1933, when proceedings began against one Serge Alexandre Stavisky, diversely represented as being of Russian, Romanian, or Hungarian origin, in connection with fraudulent activity based in the municipal pawnshop of Bayonne. With the blessing of that small town's mayor, who was also its Radical deputy, the Mont de Piété had issued many millions' worth of bonds, which another Radical deputy, Albert Dalimier, minister of colonies in the Camille Chautemps cabinet of the day, had warmly recommended. Losses involved in the scam affected mainly insurance companies that had followed Dalimier's advice, not the small investors who had been so badly hurt in previous failures. But the bankruptcy scandals of the late 1920s were recent, and Stavisky himself provided a splendid example of pernicious metics—foreigners of prey— that the Right loved to hate. Police spy, gambler, and confidence trickster on a grand scale, Stavisky was corrupt and corrupting. His police record went back to the twenties; he had been pursued but not indicted for the past six years, while the relevant files and documents of his case had been lost, juggled, or tucked away. His case had been pending since 1928 (some said 1926[43]), to be postponed nineteen times. The Paris Parquet—the chief prosecutor's department—which was supposed to prosecute him and had not, was headed by Premier Chautemps's brother-in-law Georges Pressard, and both men were eminent Masons. Stavisky had contributed, heftily it was said, to Radical election funds; Radical politicians and journalists had intervened with the authorities to keep Stavisky from harm; a number of Radical bigwigs were expelled from the party under a cloud. Radicals, the parliamentary system, and the judiciary were all tainted with the brush of corruption.

Condemning the system or the Radicals within it was excessive. It was not entirely unjustified. Politicking cost money: Donations, banquets, help for the local party sheet, even if it only came to life on election eve, weighed heavily on the funds of provincial lawyers, doctors, veterinarians. Elections also cost: posters and handbills to be printed, opponents who withdrew before the second ballot to be paid off, partisans to be cheered by free drinks. Traditionally the Right relied on wealthy supporters and the private incomes of its candidates; Socialists and Communists taxed party members and representatives heavily. The inchoate Left Center, notably Radicals, short of both private wealth and party funds, scrambled around for money. The party, it was said, got help from insurance companies eager to avoid nationalization.[44] Individual members got it where they could, which made them more independent and more indifferent to voting discipline that never held much water anyway right of the Socialists.

In the absence of a two-party system, party discipline was slack, continuity nonexistent, effective government difficult to achieve. It has been said that there are too many laws in France for there to be any law. Certainly the only law the French truly respected was private law—*privilege*—as it suited them. The administration of justice, far from independent, came under the control of the minister of justice—the keeper of the seals. His department allocated cases, transferred them at will from one court or judge to another, fixed dates of trials or postponed them, decided the advancement and the posting of all magistrates. "A magistrate making use of the freedom that the law affords him would be regarded by our rulers as a formidable freak," *Le Figaro* declared. A highly centralized administration gave great power to ministers and to those who could influence them or their services. In late January 1934 the American Embassy in Paris reminded Washington of "the contempt in which the better class of Frenchmen hold their elected representatives." The many who did not despise them regarded them as necessary facilitators and conduits.[45]

The enormous amount of patronage at the government's disposal—from subsidies and derogations to tobacco shops—meant that government was regarded primarily as a dispenser of favors. As the main channels through which such favors flowed, senators and deputies spent most of their time answering letters and receiving visits from constituents and influence peddlers, the rest of their time jockeying for power. Every cabinet crisis offered new opportunities for office. Cabinets played musical chairs; ministers came and went; the representatives of the sovereign people enjoyed neither authority nor continuity. Radicals were hardly responsible for this state of affairs, but they had stood at the crossroads of political action since the beginning of the century. Their philosophy rejected state power because of its potential for oppression; their practice parceled that power out to petty potentates to peddle or demean. *The Republic of Cronies,* as Robert de Jouvenel—Bertrand's uncle—had called it in a book that denounced politicians as accomplices in a vast conspiracy to pull the wool over the public's eyes, "meant that rigorously honest men were on good terms with shady men who were on good terms with despicable men."[46]

So the furor of winter 1933–1934 sprang from belief in politics as a business conducted on the principle "If you can't beat 'em, bribe 'em." Postwar reconstruction had involved billions of "politico-financial graft"; the liquidation of the vast stocks that Americans left in France after the war produced more embezzlement and fraud; then there had been affairs like those of Oustric and the Aéropostale. Stavisky's swindles were unexceptional, but they were quickly blown up. Stavisky, wrote the press, was one of the greatest adventurers of the day, his fiddles were formidable affairs, his personality came straight out of the pages of Balzac, 132 politicians had figured on his payroll, he had even planned to endow a literary prize that would encourage moral publications. Stavisky was on the run, Stavisky was in hiding, Stavisky had committed suicide, no: He had been suicided. Crooks, Jews, Masons were covering up the cover-up.[47]

Public confidence in the police that had tracked down Stavisky and reported his suicide was just as shaky as confidence in the administration of justice. Intensely unpopular even with honest people, Robert Dell had called them, and nothing had occurred to change that situation. From Right to Left the press scoffed at the idea that the political crook had not been shot by police eager to stifle embarrassing revelations. The trade union daily, *Le Peuple,* found the very notion of suicide a lark; the Action française pronounced it a bad joke; the American Embassy agreed: "[S]uch events are not at all unusual in France."[48] The royalist Camelots first, the other leagues following in their wake, came down into the streets to riot, tearing up cobbles and the cast-iron grates protecting trees, stopping the traffic, setting kiosks on fire. Riots were limited to the Left Bank, near the Chamber of Deputies, but they drew sympathizers and curious onlookers, many of whom joined in for fun. Soon they were affecting other parts of Paris. Trams could not make their way; tempers flared; political arguments led to duels; a crowd rioted at the Gare du Nord when a commuter train underwent delay; middle-of-the-road publications like *Paris-Soir,* having tried to treat the affair in perspective, began to call for "The Necessary Purge"; the illustrated magazine *Vu* titled a number "Fin de régime?"[49] Nor would the rioting had mattered so much had it not worsened bad business conditions, discouraged flagging tourism further, and undercut a newly launched government loan.[50]

All this time the most prestigious theater in France, the Comédie-Française, had been staging Shakespeare's *Coriolanus* with its would-be dictator hero and its derogatory remarks about democracy. Coriolanus, wrote André Suarès in the *Nouvelle littéraires,* "tramples on politics, despises parties, rejects popular stupidity and the imposture of political leaders as he rejects the perfidious equality that seeks to level out differences." For those too fond of comfort to rampage through the streets and for some who did, *Coriolanus* became the focus of opposition to parliament, to democracy, to the corruption that had taken on—so demonstrators alleged—a national dimension.[51]

In January 1934 the first issue of the popular magazine *Détective* featured a cover showing the terrified face of a blonde: "1934 opens anxious, panicked eyes on a future heavy with hatred, tragedies and catastrophes." Jitters spread fast. In the last days of January the cabinet of Camille Chautemps finally fell, and Edouard Daladier took over the task of forming a cabinet of Republican unity, meant to include Socialists (who refused), dissident Socialists like Déat and Marquet (who also refused), moderate Nationalists (who accepted), around a kernel of young and not so young Radicals. A professor like Herriot, Daladier was like him a son of the people and a scholarship boy; also a veteran and known to be honest. But where the older man glad-handed easily, Daladier was sullen; where Herriot orated, he made abrupt declarations. His thickset build produced a nickname, the Bull of the Vaucluse; his brooding gaucherie created an impression of vigor and determination. In fact, he was indecisive like Herriot, and weak when push came to shove: a bull with the horns of a snail, one trade union leader called him.[52]

The cabinet's first task would be to reassure the nation by purging out corruption, and Daladier's first visible step in that direction was a series of

administrative moves: Pressard, head of the remiss Parquet, was kicked up-
stairs to higher judicial office; the director of the Comédie-Française, guilty
of programming the unfortunate *Coriolanus*, was dismissed to be replaced by
the head of the investigative Sûreté d'Etat—a man with more theatrical
than detective interests. Finally Jean Chiappe, the Paris prefect of police
who, as a favor to a Radical friend, had squirreled away one of Stavisky's
files and thus afforded crucial protection to the crook, was offered one of
the Republic's plums, the governorship of Morocco, refused it, and resigned.

While highly suspect to the Left, Chiappe had many friends among the
Right, who saw in him an effective foe of left-wing agitators. During seven
years as head of the capital's police and administration he had much improved traffic control, made pimps and prostitutes less visible, given police
a strong esprit de corps. Of course, the police in France are less about public order than about public power, which may occasionally benefit from
some disorder. Instrument of the ruling power, or else of those who seek to
overthrow it, police may serve either interest by tolerating some outbreaks
while suppressing others. Chiappe who showed no mercy to left-wing
demonstrators had his men go easy on *camelots* and *ligueurs* throughout January, arguing that tactful handling limited their turbulence.[53] He may have
been right.

At any rate, Chiappe's going, which triggered the resignation of his right-
wing friends from Daladier's coalition, destabilized the new cabinet. What
may have been more serious, it weakened police riot control just when it
was most needed. A taxi strike and the threat of more rioting caused the
postponement of the year's major social charity event, the Bal des Petits
Lits Blancs, which had been scheduled for February 6. Then, in the late
afternoon of that Tuesday, while Daladier sought and received majority
approval for his cabinet, all the forces of discontent marched on the Chamber of Deputies. Leagues, veterans heavy with decorations beneath a sea of
banners, down-at-heel taxpayers converged on the place de la Concorde
from which a bridge that had just been broadened crossed the Seine to the
Palais Bourbon. On that bridge, at least during the first crucial hours, stood
a thin screen of guards, fewer than two hundred, with no weapon heavier
than the regulation pistol, to bar the way to thousands of demonstrators
determined to break into the Assembly. Many recalled how, less than eight
years before, in July 1926, Edouard Herriot's two-day old government had
fallen before equally stormy masses and how the mayor of a city that

boasted two great rivers of its own (Rhône and Saône) barely escaped an ignominious ducking in the Seine.[54]

For the past few days the right-wing press had been intoxicating opinion with false news of machine guns, tanks, and savage black soldiers mobilized to protect parliamentary corruption against the ire of honest desperation.[55] Violence falsely predicted on the part of the defenders guaranteed violence on the aggressors' part. That Tuesday evening and long into the night, as one rioting wave after another broke on the Concorde bridge, as kiosks and overturned buses flared on the square and near it, as the "Internationale" of participating Communists mingled with the "Marseillaise," fifteen people died and fifteen hundred were wounded. The following day Daladier's government, though constitutionally endorsed by a vote of parliament, resigned. Paul Léautaud, the reactionary curmudgeon, declared himself in seventh heaven. A revolution really was on its way; the regime was on the skids. "I rejoice with all my heart."[56]

His rejoicing was premature. The rioting in central Paris took time to reverberate. Pending the appearance of morning papers and with no radio to make them known, news circulated by word of mouth. Lilian Mowrer, wife of the *Chicago Daily News* correspondent and a bit of a newshound herself, spent the sixth attending dress shows in the salons of Paris couturiers. The public at Fouquet's posh restaurant and café, half a mile up the Champs Elysées from the Concorde, had no idea that anything out of the ordinary was going on. The comte Jean de Pange, for his part, attended an inaugural lesson before a full hall in the Collège de France, crossed the Seine to the Bibliothèque Nationale, went home for tea, then found no taxi (there was a strike) to take him to dinner with friends—Paul Valéry, Jacques Bainville, François de Wendel, the painter Bonnard—and only learned of the fighting from his hostess: "It's abominable, they're shooting at vets." To which Wendel, the great industrialist, reacted with indifference: "We're looking on. It's a dispute of the Left."[57]

Beyond Paris excitement at first was even more moderate. The thousands that turned up Tuesday night in the center of Rennes had come to learn the results of the *Lotérie nationale* drawing. Le Havre, reported the U.S. vice consul, was calm: "Politics are not taken seriously in this part of France." As the *Journal de Montélimar* reminded its readers, perspective was better than passion: The Action Française, Croix de Feu, Jeunesses Patriotes had not been mobilized in the wake of earlier political scandals. The indignation they expressed presumably screened a political operation.[58]

Although provincial centers had followed the affair and many put on demonstrations and counterdemonstrations of their own that busy Tuesday, interest in Paris doings seems to have been proportional to scale: The larger the center, the greater the attention that national politics attracted, though always as seen through local spectacles. The riots of February 6 were followed by counterdemonstrations and strikes of the Left on February 9 and 12. These, when business was already slow, struck provincials more than the rioting: No mail, shops closed, trade lost cut closer to the bone.[59] A change of premier was going to reassure them.

In 1926, having forced Herriot's Radicals out of office, the nation in distress appealed to Poincaré, who had been president from 1913 to 1920. In 1934, Daladier's Radicals having been thrown out of office, Lebrun appealed to another father figure: Gaston Doumergue, once known as *La Joconde* for his perpetual smile, who had been president from 1924 to 1931. Called back like Cincinnatus from his Gard estate, Doumergue formed a coalition cabinet "of respite, appeasement and justice" that lined up representatives of all parties to the right of the Socialists, to the left of the extreme Right, in a geriatrist's dream. It was too much to say, as some were doing, that France was ruled by men of seventy because the men of eighty were all dead. But governmental luminaries were well into their sixties; Doumergue himself seventy-one, the foreign minister, Louis Barthou, seventy-two, Marshal Philippe Pétain, minister of war, seventy-eight. Like Poincaré, Doumergue was a moderate republican (though not moderately republican); like him, he tried to govern by decree under emergency powers voted by large majorities eager to avoid political hot potatoes. But respite was short, and appeasement dubious.

Party politicians were troubled when the old man began to exploit the possibilities of radio by broadcasting a series of reports to the nation billed as fireside chats. When Doumergue submitted projects aimed at strengthening the executive, turning the premier into a real prime minister, limiting the Chamber's capacity to overthrow cabinets at will and giving the president powers of dissolution, those who had welcomed him as a savior prepared to send him back into retirement. In October one of France's major allies, King Alexander of Yugoslavia, fell to Croat terrorists at Marseilles. Alexander was just beginning a state visit to France, but arrangements for his protection had been bungled badly. The Ministry of the Interior and the Quai d'Orsay could not agree on how to share expenses, and so a planned cavalry escort did not arrive. In the panic following the murder of the king, Louis Barthou who, as foreign minister, had received Alexander and who had been wounded slightly, was left unattended to make his way to hospital on foot and lost so much blood on the way that he died on arrival.[60] Barthou had a personality as attractive as a prison gate, but also as powerful. With him ended the hope of a firm French foreign policy or of the survival of the February coalition. "Barthou killed yesterday at Marseilles," Léautaud noted in his diary. "Duhamel loses a vote for his election to the Academy."[61]

Doumergue's moderate ministers had found their Radical colleagues uncomfortably immoderate when Edouard Herriot, trying to get back into favor with the Radical left, launched the potent image of "Two Hundred Families" alleged to hold France in the thrall of their wealth. Radical ministers, led by Herriot, were sick of being denounced as murderers by the Right, as traitors by the Left. Radical and Radical Socialists were still being booed when they appeared on newsreels and howled down as assassins, the U.S. Embassy reported in November.[62] And Doumergue was pressing them to help ban strikes by government employees, limit the number of ministers in the cabinet, agree that future budgets would contain no expenditures without corresponding revenues. Impossible demands. In November 1934 the Radical ministers resigned; Doumergue's cabinet dissolved.

ACADEMIC AND party politics apart, the really interesting action had shifted to another level. American observers thought that they saw "an economic and social revolution brewing in France."[63] Most of the press focused such anxieties on the Red menace. The Left focused its anxieties on the "Fascist" Right. Frightening to many, the sixth of February had been traumatic for those who felt it as a defeat of the Republic and as a premonition of even greater menace. Bertrand de Jouvenel, who lived through the times, has written of *The Great Fear* that seized republican personnel after the sixth.[64] Gaston Cusin, a customs official and a unionist, remembers the secretary of the Civil Service Union declaring on that day "we've got to do something to stop the rise of Fascism." Socialist party bulletins denouncing "the Fascist and reactionary offensive" and calling all good men to aid the Republic were circulated the country over. Even non-Socialist republicans regarded the sixth as a Fascist insurrection, and many expected a coup d'etat to follow. Syndicalist leaders, political militants went about armed and kept arms in their homes to defend themselves. Within ten days of Daladier's resignation, a number of intellectuals, most of them from the universities, had organized an Intellectuals' Vigilance Committee against Fascism to hold the line.[65]

Unrest continued, and unease. Before the end of February the body of Albert Prince, a counselor in the Public Prosecutor's Office who had been a bit too kind to Stavisky, was found mangled by a train in a spot charmingly called The Fairy Dell (*La Combe aux fées*). The Right clamored that Masons, of whom Prince was one, had murdered him to prevent further revelations. "Free Masonry is on its last legs," crowed *La Croix Angévine*, mixing its metaphors. "It has been caught red-handed." *Paris-Soir* hired first Maigret's popular creator, Simenon, then a brace of British detectives—Sir Basil Thomson of the British Intelligence Service and "Mr. Wesley, the iron man of Scotland Yard"—to clear up the mystery. They got nowhere.* "Horror . . . subversion . . . immense anxiety," complained Jacques Copeau, the actor-director. "All the talk is either about the next war or the next revolution," noted Léautaud.[66]

Faced with the cascade of events, we have to make an effort to remember how many put the need to make ends meet before the political crisis, focused on passing exams, shopping, saving, homework, courting, before considering the sins of politicians or the cat's cradle of international affairs. The Bal des Petits Lits Blancs, postponed from the sixth, was held at the end of March in the Opéra, with five hundred guests, five hundred performers, two hundred waiters, and nine orchestras. The taxi drivers' strike having ended on March 4, the *bal* was declared a triumph. The same month *Femina* featured *"Les manifestations de Février,"* which referred not to riots but to sport and elegance. Sports pages, the best read as always, took their politics lightly, too: "The day of the Leagues" turned out to be about football leagues; "The Two Crooks," not about politicians but about football clubs where, as in the Stavisky affair, the scandals of rugby called for a purge.[67] Emotions that strained everyday life were being drained off into sports pages that bristled with fighting words: combat, coalition, struggle, battle, raid, arms, attack, alarm, wounds, triumph, revenge.

The spirit of battle animated both camps. The Paris of the Right elected Jean Chiappe first to the Municipal Council, then to its presidency, and it cheered La Rocque and his Croix de Feu, who promised to sweep out an-

---

The New Yorker's Paris letter (March 17, 1934) suggested that French politics were being run by Edgar Wallace. Though the world-famous mystery story writer had died in 1932, that cannot be excluded.

tipatriotic subversives. Communist mobilization on February 9 had ended in clashes that killed nine and left hundreds of wounded. Then, on February 12, a general strike called by unions and by the Socialists brought out over a million workers in Paris alone and additional masses in hundreds of other towns. But even as its public reached toward unity of action, the Left remained divided by Communist dogma and Socialist suspicion, not to mention Radical distaste for violence of any kind. In June 1934 at last, the Communists, hearkening to their masters' voice, decided to work for unity regardless of class divisions. In July Socialists and Communists agreed on common action "to defeat Fascism."

The Dreyfus Affair had put an end to (overt) anti-Semitism on the Left. February 6 would put an end to the antiparliamentarism until then widely current in left-wing circles. The Republic was in too much danger, it appeared, for its friends to go on squabbling. The Common Front that a few farsighted men like the young Radical Gaston Bergery and the Communist Jacques Doriot had long called for was taking shape, to face the National Front coalition of extreme Right leagues. Arms outstretched in Fascist salutes on one side, fists upraised on the other. "Common front against National Front," wrote the *Ami du Peuple* (May 24, 1934): "a summons to battles in the street." After the bloodshed of early February there would be fewer battles (thirty-seven dead on Feb. 6, 9 and 12; only nine in the two years that followed) but much activity. Between mid-February 1934 and early May 1936 a French scholar counted "1,063 riotous assemblies, processions or demonstrations"—more than one a day and most of them organized by the Left.[68] This competitive defiance and display culminated on July 14, 1935, when—while coincidentally Alfred Dreyfus was being buried in Montmartre Cemetery—Paris divided between rival demonstrations: some thirty thousand Croix de Feu marching from Concorde to the Arc de Triomphe while ten times as many Radicals, Socialists, and Communists (some claimed half a million) paraded along the classic route between the squares of Nation and Bastille.

That was the doing of February 6. The overthrow of a duly empowered government against the background of legalized Nazi terror across the Rhine had underscored the Fascist menace. In fact, a Fascist menace in France was slight. Good at making trouble, the leagues were impotent in exploiting it.[69] The only mass organization among them, the Croix de Feu, was led by a soldier respectful of republican institutions and the law. No leader caught the fancy of a public that looked for authority figures but distrusted any that appeared. Fascism is militaristic and aggressive; the French were pacific and defensive. They were patriots, of course, and many retained the chauvinistic nationalism of the prewar years. But in France that never turned to fascism. Nationalism is a kind of inferiority complex: reaction to loss, perception of weakness. Fascism, which is exacerbated nationalism, the weak turning on the weaker, can sprout only from the sort of political and economic rubble that was not to be found in France. There was economic suffering; there was no economic collapse; there would be no fascism.

February 1934, which stirred the Left with fear of right-wing forces, actually revealed the weakness of the Right, except as spoilers. It revealed also the social pacifism of the broad middle-class public revolted by the bloodshed of the sixth, ninth, twelfth. But it set off a mass reaction activated by fear of fascism that was to spawn the Popular Front. It also aggravated and confirmed political polarization: the politics of either/or. For the next few years there would be no more constructive debate between people of different political stripe. Only clashes.[70] It has been said in France that scandals produce clamor but not votes. This was not true of the great political scandals of the Third Republic; it certainly was not of the Stavisky Affair and its violent fallout. For Jacques Bardoux, journalist, political scientist, and veteran politician, "a new period begins after February Sixth" and "blind are those who do not see it." As for the scandal that began it all, the trials of those accused of making 238 millions' worth of bonds vanish ended in January 1936 with nine of the accused found guilty, including two deputies, both Radicals and both reprieved; and eleven of the accused released, including Stavisky's widow.[71] Few by then were paying much attention to ancient history. Since Stavisky's death, five cabinets had walked the plank, and a sixth was preparing to follow. France was heading into fresh elections; the world was heading for trouble.

In Germany, Hitler was affirming his grip, murdering his rivals, cowing the opposition, marshaling the economy, putting his subjects back to work, and filling their hearts with pride at his defiance of foreigners. In 1933 Hitler had walked out of the Disarmament Conference and out of the League of Nations; in 1934 he had closed the German economy the better to control it within its borders and suspended all cash transfers on debts abroad. That summer, following President Hindenburg's death, he had become his people's undisputed "chancellor and leader." In January 1935 Saarlanders, temporarily detached from the German Reich by the Treaty of Versailles, had freely voted to rejoin their homeland. A month after this the French government, faced with a long-expected deficit of young draftees, proposed to reestablish two-year military service. This gave Hitler the pretext he needed to repudiate the military clauses of the Treaty of Versailles, reestablish compulsory military service, and send German rearmament full speed ahead. The French, U.S. Ambassador William Bullitt reported to his president, "now regard [war] as inevitable."[72] In fact, only some French were beginning to do so. Within one year they would be more fully persuaded.

The reassertion of German aggressiveness had convinced Louis Barthou, an old-fashioned politician, that Russia—however Soviet—had to be brought back into world affairs to redress the European balance of power. He had obtained the Soviet Union's admission to the League some months after Germany's departure and was working on an alliance with it when he was murdered. Barthou had also been drawing closer to Mussolini, who had reacted very firmly when, in July 1934, Nazi plotters had murdered the Austrian chancellor and sought to effect an Anschluss—the annexation of Austria to the German Reich. Barthou's successor, Pierre Laval, as foxy as Briand but clumsier, was less firm-minded. As an ex-Socialist and as a pacifist Laval distrusted armed conflict and wanted to avoid it at all price. He eased Hitler's success in the Saar, which French troops occupied at the time of the plebiscite. He signed the alliance with Russia that Barthou had prepared but made sure it would be ineffective by avoiding all military entanglements.

On the other hand, the mutual assistance pact Laval and Stalin signed in Moscow in May 1935 marked a reorientation of Soviet policy, hence a crucial change in the attitude of the French Communist party, too. The common statement issued in Moscow declared that those who were sincerely committed to peace could allow no weakening of their defenses. Stalin, the communiqué insisted, understood and fully appreciated the French policy of national defense.[73] That was a blow to pacifists of the Left—not least to the Communists, who had to wait four years before they could once again revile wars of imperial conquest. It was a blow to the Right as well: When part of the Left reluctantly abandoned pacifism, many nationalists began to see its virtues. The newfound patriotism of the Communists persuaded anti-Communists that resistance to fascism went against national interests. The true enemies of peace were not Nazis in Germany or Fascists in Italy, but those who wanted to oppose them, if need be by force of arms.[74]

Events in Africa were soon to make this clear. Foreign Minister since Barthou's death and stubborn partisan of peace, Pierre Laval tried hard to make friends with Mussolini—a lapsed Socialist like himself. But Mussolini's idea of friendship was that France would stand by when, in October 1935, Italian troops invaded Abyssinia. Laval, more concerned to retain an ally than to assert the rights of an African monarchy, would have complied. But the Conservative cabinet in London, its overseas interests challenged by Italian ambitions, its electoral position threatened by opponents of Italian aggression, would not allow it. Collective security had to be enforced by sanctions against Italian aggression. Yet collective security meant no security. In France the integral pacifists denounced the colonialist conspiracy of Britain, Italy, and France and rejected any effective sanctions against Italy because these might lead to war. Armed force must not be used to oppose the use of armed force, certainly not to imperialist ends. And Italian counterprotests could be used to discredit Ethiopian allegations that the Italians were using poison gas. Clearly both Ethiopians and Italians ignored the highest standards of warfare, and clearly force as an instrument of policy was bad; but happily there would be no need for noncombatants to exercise force. At the behest of Britain and France, the League of Nations decreed sanctions against Italy that would discomfort the Italians without affecting their capacity to make war. In May 1936 Emperor Haile Selassie left his realm, and Mussolini proclaimed the birth of a new Roman Empire. In June Neville Chamberlain condemned sanctions as midsummer madness; by midsummer they had come to an end. Franco-Italian friendship, what there had been of it, foundered on the rocks of ineffective sanctions. France was left to lean on unreliable British friends, while Italy and Germany began to draw closer together.

Coming hard on the heels of the Franco-Russian pact, the Abyssinian war reinforced the newfound pacifism of the Right without doing much to diminish that of the non-Communist Left. It wasn't just the Right which feared the possibility that sanctions could lead to war. All over Western Europe, dread of hostilities' breaking out was widespread.[75] But even the pacifists of the Left were anti-Fascist, while friends of fascism on the Right were aggressively for their friends' aggressions. There was more enthusiasm for the feats of the Italian Air Force than sympathy for the victims that it made. The Catholic Church distanced itself from mayhem far away on the ground that Abyssinians were mostly godless or else worshiped the wrong kind of god.[76] Students of the Action Française and other nationalist groups disrupted the courses of a law professor, Gaston Jèze, who had served as consultant to Haile Selassie. Their winter-long campaign would end in the resignation of the Law School's dean.

The Left meanwhile, avoiding all idea of intervention, called only for ineffective sanctions to be enforced. No one cared much about the Abyssinians. The division was between those who sought Italian friendship and those, like Pierre Cot, who preferred British support, "without which we could not resist German aggression." In the event, Italian friendship was an illusion, British support did not do France much good. Looking back on that nervous winter, André Suarès would write to Jean Paulhan: "We should have gone to war at the end of 1935, and we would have had fifty years of peace."[77] Henceforth everyone would have his favorite date when France should have gone to war but failed to do so.

Laval's internal policy of deflation fared no better. Doumergue had cut the budget by decree; Laval cut more. August 1935 witnessed violent reactions against *décrêts-lois* that cut the salaries of all government workers from high administrators to stevedores and fitters in government shipyards and arsenals. In Paris and in the great port cities, strikes, demonstrations led to clashes, shots fired, dead and wounded, to stoke the fires of left-wing resentment. Clearly, at least in retrospect, no mere budget cuts could either balance the budget or get the economy back in gear. Devaluation, avoided as the devil, became ever less avoidable. But no one coveted the power, or at least the office, where such decisions would have to be faced, and Laval remained in office until the "petty huckstering and trafficking" with Italy of which Léon Blum accused him persuaded his Radical ministers (the Radicals again!) to walk out on him. The Radical rank and file had joined the drift toward left-wing unity; their leaders had to follow. Besides, it was time for the Left to get its hands on the large slush funds every government controlled, which could be used to influence the outcome of elections. In January 1936 Albert Sarraut, part owner of the greatest Radical provincial daily *La Dépêche de Toulouse*, came to head the first left-leaning cabinet since February 1934.

And so it was that when, on March 7, 1936, Hitler sent German troops to reoccupy the Rhineland, demilitarized by a treaty the Germans freely signed, he found before him a caretaker government headed by a sixty-four-year-old Radical Socialist expert in political dodges. Personally brave—he had fought several duels and won the Military Medal at Verdun when he was forty-four—Sarraut was a discriminating art collector, a veteran of coalition cabinets, better at doing nothing than at doing something. Inaction is a talent that students of politics underrate, but a talent that has to be used at the right time. The spring of 1936 was not that time.

Jean Zay, a junior minister, recalled the Cabinet Council held on Sunday, March 8, the day after the Germans violated their engagements: The foreign minister had nothing to suggest; the service ministers reflected a public opinion that was indifferent or opposed to action. The government had been forewarned by military intelligence and by its ambassador in Berlin, yet it was ready for nothing.[78] French military leaders, prepared (that is, ill prepared) for different kinds of conflict, refused to move. The chief of the General Staff, General Maurice Gamelin, had proved himself a champion at passing competitive examinations. Competent, disciplined, brilliantly intelligent, he was incapable of real initiative. While German generals trembled at the prospect of French reprisals, Gamelin, stoutly ignoring the advice of his own intelligence, believed the German forces superior to the French and refused to move against them unless the government ordered mobilization. But a mobilization—even a partial mobilization—was unthinkable on the eve of elections.[79] Unilateral action would not be envisaged. It could lead to war, and war could not be faced without Allied support. The French appealed to reason, to treaties, to the British, all broken reeds; naturally they got nowhere. German troops held the left bank of the Rhine and began to fortify it. Demilitarization of the Rhineland never made France vastly safer, but it exposed German territory to French attack on behalf of France's allies. Reoccupation and subsequent fortification left protégés and allies in Eastern Europe in the lurch.[80] Gamelin went back to what he did so well. In April, when the crisis had died down, he inaugurated a splendid monument at Lille in honor of carrier pigeons.

As Pope Pius XI told the French ambassador, had the French moved, they would have rendered an immense service to all—not least to themselves. But the French were no longer a great power, and this perception accelerated their decline. Many would testify that the events of March 1936 were for them the prelude to war. Like Hervé Alphand, after the war ambassador to Washington, they realized that "whatever the policies . . .

war had become inescapable. Had we resisted then . . ." But France did not resist. "France wants peace," the American Embassy explained to the State Department, "fears war, does not conceal that fear, and will be forced to take the consequences."[81]

VI

A Famous Victory

"But what good came of it at last?"
Quoth little Peterkin.
"Why, that I cannot tell," said he,
"But 'twas a famous victory."

—ROBERT SOUTHEY,
"THE BATTLE OF BLENHEIM"

"ALL GREAT movements are popular movements," Hitler wrote in *Mein Kampf*, adding that such movements were stirred into activity "by the ruthless Goddess of Distress or by the torch of the spoken word cast into the midst of the people."[1] Distress there was in France aplenty, and 1934 and 1935 would see it rising to a peak, helped in good part by stubbornly conservative deflationary policies. As for the torch of the spoken word, it had flamed brightly since the violence of February 6, when a government that parliament endorsed had been replaced by one that seemingly threatened democratic institutions—worse still, democratic order. With parliament discredited, politics had moved into the streets. The nationalist leagues, which their opponents denounced as Fascist, provoked riots in Paris and in other towns. Philippe Henriot, the rightist Catholic deputy from Bordeaux, toured France, passionately attacking Radicals and Masons and democracy, leaving a trail of fighting and of bloodshed behind: Lyons, Grenoble, Toulouse, Lorient, and Roubaix, where sixty persons were injured in the turmoil.[2]

League membership was small, their public impact hardly overwhelming. But they attracted violent fools and violent idealists (which came to the same thing), both dedicated to disturbing the public and the private peace. More menacing because more disciplined, hence more attractive to the respectable middle class, were the Croix de Feu, their numbers and their tactics based on the premise that La Rocque had learned from his mentor, Marshal Hubert Lyautey: "Show your strength and you will not need to use it."[3]

That principle would have served France well; it served La Rocque less so. Displays of Croix de Feu dynamism, displays of muscle by the other leagues only helped mobilize those whom they filled with loathing and with fear. The general strike of February 12, 1934, had been a first demonstration against "the Fascist menace." Swift on its heels had come a rapprochement between Socialists and Communists; then, in July, a pact between the two for united action "to beat Fascism" and to defend democratic liberties. Communist militants were not afraid of action. In April 1934 a Communist miner died after a fight with members of the leagues. That same month Gaston Bergery, the brilliant Radical deputy of Mantes near Paris, who had resigned his seat after the sixth of February and lost it to a rightist, set up the Common Front to fight what he called the prefascism of the leagues. Late on a night in June 1934 at Lyons, which was a stronghold of the Common Front, pre-Fascists broke into the Common Front premises, and in the fusillade that followed, one of the attackers died, four were wounded.[4]

Pre- or proto-Fascist violence was turning against those who wielded it. The Left was frightened, but it was dispersed, and mutually suspicious. Socialists and Communists had clashed and denounced each other over fifteen years as traitors to the people. For Socialists, the Communists were dupes and puppets of a foreign dictatorship; for Communists, the Socialists were Social Fascists. Louis Aragon's poem of 1931, "The Red Front" reflected their sentiments: "Fire on Léon Blum, / Fire on the performing bears of social democracy!" Socialists, on the other hand, who disagreed violently among themselves on many issues, were overwhelmingly anticlerical and irreligious. In Paris in the years up to 1936 some four in five party members opted for civil burial. When Maurice Thorez, the Communist party leader, offered his hand for Catholics to grasp (the Catholics did not), Socialists insistently continued to sing the offensive song "La Jeune Garde," which warned "bourgeois swashbucklers, gorged [capitalists], and priests" that they had better look out; the Communists replaced "priests" by "Jeunesses Patriotes."

Radicals and Socialists also rubbed each other the wrong way, the former participating in governments that the latter denounced as bourgeois. Many left-wing Radicals were farther to the left in views and voting than right-wing Socialists. But Léon Blum denounced Radicals as Fascist or proto-Fascist. Edouard Herriot responded by pointing out the folly of well-heeled Socialists who called in the same breath for the defense of democratic institutions and the dictatorship of the proletariat. There was no foreordained coalition of left-wing clans. Without orders from Moscow in spring 1934 the Communists would have made no advances to Catholics or Radicals; without league violence the Radicals would not have dreamed of an electoral pact including Communists. Radical ministers took part in the coalition governments that followed the sixth of February: those of Doumergue, Flandin, Laval. But the leagues zeroed in on them as the party of swindlers first, then of murderers and, in due course, verbal violence turned physical. Radical deputies, their wives and families were attacked in political meetings, in trams, or on the street—a process culminating in spring 1935, when a deputy of the Vosges, Paul Elbel, had an eye knocked out, while Pierre Cot, a member of the cabinet that fell on February 6, had acid thrown in his face.[5]

Resentment of the leagues dominated the Radical Party Congress of that year. Some Radicals may have been corrupt; all abhorred violence and feared it. Moreover, Radicals were republican: Their wallets were firmly on the Right, but their hearts were on the Left. Willy-nilly, they shuffled toward a Popular Front that they had long resisted because they couldn't overcome a fundamental belief that no republican should have enemies on the left. As soon as Communists gave up being spoilsports and learned to talk like Jacobins, the Radicals recognized them as fellow republicans. Not for long, but long enough for an electoral alliance. In republican regions, like the Lot and the Corrèze, reported *Paris-Soir* in April 1936, electors of the center were now expected to vote pink and red. "The Popular Front is nothing but the old republican discipline that has operated for forty years," explained Camille Chautemps. But the impulse had come from the leagues. As Raoul Aubaud, general secretary of the Radical party, declared, "There would have been no Popular Front without the Fascist menace."[6]

True enough. But would the Popular Front have been carried by the same ground swell of votes without a hand from "the ruthless Goddess of Distress?" The shrinking take-home pay, the swell of disaffection among those whom first Doumergue's, then Laval's decrees hurt in their pockets and their way of life fed the protest vote. Landlords hurt by cuts in rents, shopkeepers hurt by cuts in prices and grumbling at the competition of army and railroad cooperatives, state and municipal employees hurt by cuts in wages, all vowed to vote for the Popular Front. Trouble broke out even before they did. Between mid-July and mid-August 1935 nearly a million protesters came out into the streets. At Brest three days of rioting left three dead and two hundred wounded; at Toulon, a night of barricades and looting accounted for fifty wounded and two dead. The winter of 1936 also saw a spate of strikes and demonstrations in the streets against the loss of 10 percent in pay. The north, especially, was hit by a tram workers' stoppage that shut down transport and disrupted life in Roubaix, Tourcoing, and Lille for well over a month. In Paris taxi drivers struck in April because lower rates threatened their wages, too.[7] And in the thick of the campaign an old proletarian Marxist true believer, Adéodat Compère-Morel, showed enterprise of truly capitalist proportions by launching "*Le Popu*, the true red aperitif."

On Sunday, May 3, while the Racing Club of Paris won the national football cup, red aperitif drinkers came out on top of the second ballot. This was no left-wing tide: It was 37.3 percent of registered voters against 35.9 percent for the Right. Yet the Right's National Front had elected 222 deputies (*Paris-Soir* said 238), the Popular Front 380, of whom 147 were Socialists (they had been 97), 72 Communists (they had been 21), and 106 Radicals (they had been 158). The Right lost nearly 40 seats, but the major transfer, as the figures show, had taken place within the Left itself, where Communists gnawed at Socialists and Socialists at Radicals. Pierre Laval, talking to the American ambassador, described the vote as a protest vote, and the ambassador seems to have agreed when he ascribed results to three factors in the following order: depression and unemployment, opposition to Laval's decrees (Radical support of the deflationary policy helping to explain their losses), and fear of fascism.[8] So much for victory. Now, the fragile alliance, compound of economic resentments and political fears, was going to crumble under the impact of the very factors that had brought it together.

The first of these was the discomfort of disorder. Within three weeks of the electoral victory and before a new cabinet had time to take over the reins of government, a wave of strikes and sit-ins hit the country. Most of these were spontaneous and reasonably good natured, accompanied more by songs like "Auprès de ma blonde" than by the "Internationale." But no sooner was one strike settled than three others broke out. On Sunday, June 7, one day after the Chamber approved the new Socialist-led cabinet, representatives of the government, of unions and of employers, meeting in the splendid palace of Matignon, which had just been taken over by the prime minister's offices, agreed on the introduction of collective bargaining, freedom to unionize, and general wage raises ranging from 7 to 15 percent. It was, as the Socialist *Populaire* boasted on the morrow, "Victory! Victory!" In the next few days laws on the forty-hour week and holidays with pay topped the winning streak, along with the dissolution of the leagues.

But strikes did not go away. Instead the minister of labor counted 12,142 strikes in June—two thirds of them sit-in strikes—involving nearly two million strikers. Restaurants and cafés closed (legislators queued up with their families to eat in the Chamber restaurant), hotel staffs struck, forcing unhappy guests to make their own beds, hairdressers laid scissors and curlers aside, and work contracts in department stores and dime stores were only settled at the end of the month after an eighteen-day sit-in. At the modish Trois Quartiers department store, near the fashionable Church of the Madeleine, a great banner listed miserable salaries with the comment "Our Future is a Sanatorium or Prostitution." Many sympathized with the movement of those early days: There were concerts for the strikers, there were contributions in cash and kind, and there was no violence. As Ambassador Bullitt wrote to his president, "People forget how politely Frenchmen can riot." Sometimes. Paul Léautaud's journal of that time is full of rumors and excitement, gangs of strikers forcing nonstrikers to fall in line, gas pumps shut down and cars short of gas, red flags fluttering briefly over assorted ministries, tingling exhilaration.[1]

But the tingling of a holiday from authority and legality was moderated by growing exasperation and a suspicion that industrial action now was dominated by ulterior motives. When strikers had settled their own claims, they downed tools again to show their solidarity with comrades that had not, or with foreign regimes in distress, or with the rights of man. Justified claims were giving way, it seemed, to political manipulation; professional aims, as Catholics sympathetic to the workers' cause began to point out, were being replaced by political ones, and collections to help strikers and their families began to feel, "in the absence of police which had disappeared," like being held up to ransom by extortioners. For some, as for the right-wing *Echo de Paris,* the strikes were a German plot. For others, more numerous, they were a Communist one. Neither connection was designed to endear them to a public that grew less sympathetic and more jaundiced as discomfort and insecurity grew more acute.[11]

Society became ever more politicized, more polarized; ordinary people learned to display their political sympathies like badges. In the little beach town of Cayeux (Somme) where Annie Kriegel's family spent their summers, holidaymakers were identified by the newspapers they bought, children from local holiday camps by the songs they sang and the berets they wore: red for the municipal colony of Vitry in the Marne, black for the Catholic colony of Saint-Rose, neutral green for the departmental colony of the Somme itself.[12]

The leagues dissolved, their menace apparently banished, fears of disorder shifted. In July 1936 General Francisco Franco started his insurrection against the Popular Front government in Spain. The French Communist party, hitherto all for class conciliation, began to use industrial action to press Blum's government to intervene. French politics were contaminated by Spanish interests. By September 1936 Maurice Maréchal, founder of the *Canard enchaîné* and normally nobody's fool, had been persuaded by his friends that Franco was about to take Madrid, La Rocque Paris, and Léon Blum was packing his bags to take refuge in England. The Jesuit *Etudes* feared civil war. Comte Jean de Blois, lunching with Jean de Pange, believed the country on the eve of a revolution. The U.S. ambassador reported "the many rumors flying around about the imminence of revolution." The Vieux Colombier Theater offered its version of *The Marriage of Figaro,* in which Figaro, a red scarf around his neck, threatened the *classes possédantes.* Jokes circulated about queues of old women eagerly inquiring, "Where does one rape?" An *Œuvre* cartoon showed a plump maiden: "In my quarter, they're not raping yet. . . ." Old maid (disgusted): "In mine neither."[13]

Joking apart, no one felt safe. Workers feared employers; employers feared workers; small employers feared ruin.* Readers of the middle-class

---

*Labor relations, largely hit or miss, tended to be contentious and cross-grained. In 1936 the authorities of the Ecole Libre des Sciences Politiques, realizing that no courses existed concerning social problems in general and labor relations in particular, asked twenty-eight-year-old Pierre Laroque, *planiste* and self-taught labor expert, to offer one the following year. To everyone's surprise, 450 students turned up in January 1937, and the course maintained its popularity until the war put an end to it. Laroque, *Au service de l'homme et du droit* (1993), 106.

intellectual *Nouvelles littéraires* declared themselves "pursued, trapped, victimized," candidates for the scaffold. In November the minister of the interior, Roger Salengro, Socialist mayor of industrial Lille, pursued, trapped, victimized by a relentless campaign of scurrilous slander, committed suicide. The Right was not so helpless after all; the Left found itself in trouble on two fronts.[14]

More important of the two was the failure of the government's economic policies. On election eve the American Embassy had sketched a grim picture of the situation: unbalanced budget, incomprehensible financial methods, towering deficits in railways and in shipping, rearmament already enormously expensive. "Above all, there appears to be almost as much tax evasion, through graft and carelessness, as in Mexico." After losing the elections, Laval had confided to Ambassador Jesse Isidor Straus (about to leave the post to William Bullitt) that he could not understand how Blum could promise to restore pension and pay cuts, spend large sums on the unemployed, balance the budget, and maintain the franc—"even in politics 2 plus 2 are not 6."[15] Laval was right: Blum followed a demand economy designed to increase employment by cutting hours of work and to increase consumption by spreading the wealth. He did restore pension and pay cuts, limited working hours, but failed to balance the budget in the end or to maintain the franc. Socialists who had so long argued for a reduction of military expenses, had to increase them radically instead. Plans for public works became a casualty of budgetary problems. Pared down to allow for extraordinary military expenses, the imagined mountain turned into a mouse. Government drainage on investment capital continued and grew greater. Stubborn defense of the franc broke down after a few months and led not to one devaluation but to three.

At first things seemed to go according to plan. The slump appeared to bottom out before the elections, and at the end of summer 1936 attempts to anticipate price rises expected when the forty-hour law went into effect encouraged business activity. Price rises followed as expected, not only because of wage increases agreed at Matignon but also reflecting social charges, which increased about 50 percent. Payrolls already inflated by shorter working hours reeled. As costs rose and publicity shrank with business, periodicals and daily newspapers had to raise their prices: in August a weekly like the *Nouvelles littéraires* passed from 75 cents to 1 franc. The tax on books rose from 2 to 6 percent, and booksellers added this to other costs they passed on to their customers. The government offered credit for modernization of equipment, but the government also tried to borrow a great deal. Many businessmen reasoned that they might make more money by buying into government loans than by investing in new equipment. The more government borrowed, the scarcer and more costly money became. The national debt soared. It was calculated that annual debt charges cost the average French family 1,500 francs in 1936, 1,870 francs in 1938. In May 1936 total labor costs in the Paris plant of Louis Renault had been 35,000,000; francs; by December they had risen to 57,000,000. The average cost per hour of labor, 6 francs in May, had become 7.80 in December, while plant productivity per worker fell by an average of 12 percent.[16]

Nor, while employers grieved, did workers feel that much better off. Since 1931 falling prices had improved the real value of their take-home pay. After 1936 rising pay clashed with inflation that gnawed at the value of wages, and wages came off worst. Early in 1938 the U.S. commercial attaché reported that "the situation is no better than at the end of 1935." By then even the forty-hour week was being abandoned, the full or half holiday—*Blumsday*—abolished in a newly stringent economy. Yet, even the less than sympathetic Daniel Halévy admitted, unlike other cartels and blocs, the Popular Front left its mark on people and their ways.[17] The Popular Front abolished gratuities as humiliating, replacing them by a percentage added to the bill. Tips, of course, continued to be given and expected, but the spirit changed. In 1937 rail transport was nationalized into one company that curiously retained three classes of voyagers (they would be cut to two after the Second War), but that was destined to greater efficiency than private companies had shown. Price control committees were introduced—not very effective, but destined to become more so over the decades. A Subsecretariat for Scientific Research was invented and did not last very long, but the National Center for Scientific Research (CNRS) persisted. The Bank of France was nationalized; so were the war industries, and grain prices were regulated by a Wheat Board that eliminated speculators and middlemen. Grain prices, which had fallen steeply, were fixed at almost twice the rate of 1935 and rose higher still in 1937.[18] A government of Reds brought prosperity back to the land—and also to wine growers (Blum represented the wine country around Narbonne), whose products were bought in large quantities by the services to be soaked up by troops.

Then there was the forty-hour week. In 1936, seventeen years after the vote of the eight-hour day in 1919, many workers still ignored the forty-eight-hour week. In hospitals and hotels, cafés and restaurants, bakeries and other small enterprises, in factories working overtime even in an age of unemployment, personnel could be on the job sixty hours a week and more. Others, on the other hand, worked a good deal less and didn't like it. By 1935 most metalworks in the Paris area closed several weeks in summer; others like Citroën closed three days a week, all without pay, of course. By June 1937 most industrial workers worked forty hours a week, five days a week, and were paid at the old rate for forty-eight—or better. Labor preferred the five-day week because it allowed a long weekend; certain employers liked it because it spared them from hiring more hands. On the other hand, the rule that forced all but the largest shops (or tiny family ones) to close two days a week caused serious friction, especially when it was carried out in whimsical and haphazard fashion. Lilian Mowrer, who ran a Paris household at the time, remembers what historians seldom bother to point out: "[I]magine the effect of this on a nation of housekeepers who did their shopping day by day. Although all butchers closed from one till five o'-clock, some shops closed Saturday and Sunday, others Sunday and Monday, others in the middle of the week, yet others a few hours every day, and those not always the same ones. The temper of the most complacent cook was sorely tried when she discovered her favorite vegetable store closed, while her dairy next to it was open, or vice versa. In the kitchen I heard nothing but abuse of Blum."[19]

Nor did larger businesses bother to coordinate. Publishers closed Saturday and Sunday; bookshops that placed orders with the publishers closed Sunday and Monday. Result: not two but three days a week without business exchanges. It was, the *Nouvelles littéraires* complained, a scandalous mess, but there was little to be done about it. Hospitals, bakeries, ships of the merchant navy, none of which could close down at weekends, faced problems of adjustment, conflicts, and costs. So, as we saw, did the retail trade. That being said, the offensive against the forty-hour law was in the first place more political than economic. *Le Temps* and other right-wing publications denounced not losses in productivity—by 1936 a great many workers in industry were forced to work less than forty hours a week—but the immoral sloth and idleness associated with a two-Sunday week.[20]

American observers looking back from early 1938 provide still another perspective. The shorter workweek meant to create employment had squeezed few jobs out of an arid economy. Industries—and they were many—whose labor force had been on short time continued at the same rate, which now counted as full time, or speeded up operations slightly, or—in a few cases—introduced laborsaving machinery to save hiring more workers. In any case, observed the Americans, the pool of unemployed was not easy to reabsorb. About one third of those on relief were unemployable because of handicaps; another third were unskilled laborers and construction workers thrown out of work by the decline in building, who could not hope to find their kind of job in other industries. The minister of labor, Paul Ramadier, presented a similar picture: When you discounted the aged and the infirm, "hardly 200,000 may be recuperated," and those needed retraining for which no credits could be found.[21]

In fact, raising production costs and confirming France's long-standing problem with high prices, the forty-hour law was less significant than the mutual distrust of workers and employers. Statistically the argument seems irresoluble. Did the forty hours' rule nibble down the number of unemployed, or was that the result of attrition, of workers growing old, dropping out, dying off over the years? It seems as if only war production and mobilization solved the jobless problem in France, as elsewhere. Until that time unemployment persisted even among qualified workers, in part because supply did not always match demand. An electrician might be out of work in Normandy while jobs were going begging in Lorraine. So, as mines, metalworks, naval construction, aviation, electrical industries started to turn again, qualified workers proved hard to find.*

In mining, for example, productivity had risen through the thirties by dint of closing less productive seams, firing less productive hands, and making sure that miners' pay did not reflect higher output. The forty-hour law meant that less productive men were hired or rehired, but also that miners were slow to turn out more because they did not trust employers to reward them. In the first five months of 1937 France had to import more than thirty million tons of coal. The iron and steel industry, meanwhile, which had done well from postwar reconstruction, had been less interested in competition than in assured sales in a protected market at home. The family firms that made up much of the industry sought to avoid risk and maximize protection. Investment, modernization, enterprise were as discouraged

*Yet the reluctance of working folk to move in pursuit of work must have been less than has been alleged. In 1937 many dioceses adopted a new national catechism inspired not by changes in the spirit or the content of instruction but by the desire not to confuse children whose parents changed dioceses in the course of their careers. Guy Devailly, *Le Diocèse de Bourges* (1973), 228. There was mobility in France, and the Church adjusted to it. Industry found it harder to adjust because the qualified workers were often simply lacking.

by this cast of mind as they were by recession. As a result, in 1938 the year's output of cast iron was 58 percent that of 1929, the production of steel 64 percent that of 1929. French ironworks could have produced twice as much, and the demand was there. But plants were obsolete, gear old, tools out of date, and while employers continued reluctant to invest, labor continued hostile to automation or to attempts to improve performance. Both could be understood, but neither helped.[22]

HOLIDAYS WITH pay, on the other hand, however much they cut into routine or profits, evoked less hostility. Taking a holiday at all was an upper-class privilege, hardly available to many working members of the middle classes, but projects for such annual breaks for working people had come before parliament since the 1920s. The Chamber had voted in favor of holidays with pay in 1928 and again in 1932, probably relying on the Senate to kill them—as it did. When the measure finally passed in summer 1936, it evoked enthusiasm and good feeling. "Leisure! Leisure!" one newspaper rejoiced. Not everybody took to the road at once on bicycles and tandems, but workers were delighted nevertheless. "We didn't dare think of it," recalled a glassworker of the Loir-et-Cher, but when holidays materialized, he and his mates used the free time to earn a bit of cash helping to bring in the harvest. "Between the garden and the fields, I had no time for boredom."[23]

Closely related to the new gift of leisure time was an unheard-of official interest in its enjoyment through cultural and physical activities. Playing unprofitable games had long been recognized as upper-class self-indulgence. Henri de Montherlant's love of soccer has become part of literature. It is less well known that Jean Giraudoux was a champion runner and amateur of sports or that Fernand Bouisson, president of the Chamber from 1927 to 1936, was an enthusiastic fencer and a first-class rugby player, as was Camille Chautemps. Advertisements for Marsala wines showed lissome female golfers taking curvaceous swings. But golf was a foreign import, tolerable for the eccentric André Tardieu, less so when Briand allowed Lloyd George to coach him in it. Tennis, of course, stood for conspicuous consumption. In 1936 an advertisement for Perrier showed a lively woman in appropriate costume sipping "the elegant and sporting" beverage beside a tennis court.[24] By 1936, however, the only reminder that not long before France led the world in tennis were Lacoste shirts, which are still with us.

Three times champion of France, twice winner of the U.S. championship at Forest Hills, and married to a textile manufacturer's daughter, René Lacoste had invented a light shirt that would enable him to bear the humid heat of American tennis courts. A Boston newsman dubbed him the Alligator because of his penchant for suitcases in alligator hide. In France the alligator turned into a "crocodile"—attributed to his tenacity on the court, and crocodiles ended up on the shirts that were eventually marketed.[25]

But few society sports reached far beyond society. The state cared not a fig, it seems, for sports in general; municipalities were little interested in spending scarce cash on sports facilities; moralists and social critics condemned the exciting and sometimes profitable activities that exhausted young workers and apprentices. It was true that the taste for physical exercise counteracted the pull of drink and cards. But too many lads earned more from Sunday boxing matches or cycle racing than they did from their job, so they focused on the former when their minds should have been on their work. "The abuse of physical exercise makes negligent and mediocre workers."[26] This does not tell us much about the effects of popular sports, as alleged, but it does indicate one reason for their attraction: Cycling, boxing offered a chance for poor young men to escape their straitened circumstances. Of thirteen French world champion boxers, ten won their titles between the wars. Of the six gold medals the French won in the Olympics of 1936, two were in boxing, three in cycling, the last in weight lifting.

And popular sports could benefit from popular chauvinism. In 1930 Henri Desgranges, inventor and manager of the Tour de France bicycle race, decided that national teams would from then on replace factory teams in the Tour. To finance the new system, he introduced the publicity caravan that added color and profit to the annual race. The procession of publicity cars and trucks, preceding the battalion of riders or following in their wake, further brightened their festive passage. The vans advertising Chocolat Meunier distributed hundreds of thousands of paper hats, tons of chocolate bars, lashings of hot chocolate. Colossal bottles of aperitifs, gigantic pots of mustard and cans of shoe polish, piles of free newspapers, song sheets, and brochures, the florid pageantry of desire cruised through a France alerted by regular broadcast bulletins, excited by patriotic appeals—jingles and songs which to the competition between riders added the spice of competition between nations. Happily French cyclists won the Tour in 1930, 1931, 1932, and 1933. That was when Desgranges's sporting daily

L'Auto, promoter of the Tour, reached its highest sales: 364,000 a day, 730,000 a day during July, when the race was run.[27]

Cycling apart, the great popular game was soccer. Thousands of amateurs kicked balls and each other on evenings and on Sundays. The personnel of banks, mines, ironworks, insurance companies, railway depots played in company clubs. Women also played, although their matches did not attract many spectators: twelve thousand for a Franco-British encounter in 1920, only twenty-five by 1925, when activity seems to have petered out. But Socialists and Communists had their own football federations, and so did Catholics. Mass soccer meant more than an inert public cheering from the stands. In years when amusements were few and Sundays lay long and empty, soccer meant keen participants and dozens of local teams: over twenty in Montpellier in 1934, fifteen in Nîmes in 1935, village teams in profusion—a fillip to local patriotism. Between 1925 and 1939 the number of active soccer players doubled to nearly two hundred thousand, and so did the number of clubs: five thousand clubs in 1928, eight thousand in 1932, ten thousand in 1935.[28] Gaston Doumergue, who made a point of attending Cup Final matches became *le président des footballeurs*. Even more suggestive, the popular Socialist deputy mayor of working-class Puteaux, who was active on both the financial and the sports commissions of the Chamber of Deputies, advocated football pools as a means of easing the country's budgetary straits.[29] Georges Barthélémy's repeated suggestions came to nothing—then—probably because of fear that the competition of pools would hurt the revenues of the National Lottery and the *pari mutuel urbain*. But the future lay before them.

Private enterprise too, responding to new demand, provided facilities that had not been there before. Lilian and Edgar Mowrer, returning to France in 1934 to cover the local scene for their Chicago papers, canoed along the Seine and marveled at the artificial beaches and "bathing establishments erected all along the banks, where hundreds of young people camped, swam and sunned themselves." Gay awnings, diving boards, clean white sand had been for the rich alone, yet here they were being enjoyed by modest young men and women from nearby industrial centers "and obviously within the reach of everyone."[30]

So the French were becoming more interested in sports and in fresh air. But little or none of this seems to have been reflected in official actions. No sporting installations had been built in Paris since Olympic Games had been held there in 1924, and very few beyond the capital. By 1938, when

Popular Front policies had had time to affirm themselves, the country boasted about a thousand football grounds, a hundred velodromes, and one hundred all-weather swimming pools. Not much to show.

Léo Lagrange set out to change all that. Lagrange was a Girondin— boxer, footballer, army volunteer at seventeen, then lawyer. In 1932, just thirty-two years old, he had been elected deputy of the Nord. In 1936 he had campaigned with the slogan "Bread for the unemployed, ropes to hang the thieves." A few weeks after he won reelection, Blum appointed him to a newly created subsecretariat of state: Leisure and Sports. He would hold the fort there over two years and through three cabinets. Broad-shouldered, broken-nosed, young, loud, cheerful, determined, Lagrange was just the man to carry through a piece of the revolution that the Popular Front had been elected to achieve. His ideal, and that of his friend Jean Zay, his nominal superior as minister of education, was "the improvement of the race" (Zay in his memoirs called it its "salvation"),[31] and to do this, he used methods that had been pioneered by far more rabid racists in the Nazis' Strength through Joy leisure and sports organization.

Zay and Lagrange's job was far from easy, though Lagrange made it look so. When he became undersecretary of state, Lagrange's offices on the rue de Tilsitt near the Champs-Elysées had no tables, no chairs, no paper, no typewriters, no budget. Until 1937 the Subsecretariat for Sports and Leisure, regularly denounced as a Ministry of Idleness, operated on handouts and credits from the Ministry of Health next door, the presidency of the Council, and other state departments with "secret" funds to spare. "Leisure" extended as far as it could be stretched, and that meant that the subsecretariat became the country's first ministry of less than elite culture: popular playhouses, itinerant theaters, strolling players, festivals, a *cinémathèque*, above all youth hostels. There had been 45 hostels in 1933, and they had offered six thousand nights' lodging to visitors; there would be 229 hostels in 1936, hosting twenty-seven thousand nights' visitors, and they went on expanding. "For the first time in centuries," observed a foreigner in 1937, "French youth is beginning to improve its physique, take to the open road. Girls are not afraid of getting sunburnt, carrying rucksacks . . . on the weekend hikes that are all the rage everywhere in France."[32]

Those who did not hike cycled, and those who cycled often hiked as well. Bicycles had been the luxury of the working class, affording transport, independence, opportunities for socializing and for courtship in Sunday sorties. Young men dreamed of a pretty girl perched on the crossbar of their *vélo*, *biclo*, *bécane*, and sometimes jollied one to that uncomfortable perch.* The sporting comradeship that men could build around them evoked a rich literary imagery that movies like Julien Duvivier's *La Belle Equipe* (1936) perpetuated. Between 1936 and 1938 the number of bicycles in the country grew by almost one third, from seven to nine million. That was when Charles Trenet wrote "La Route enchantée" (the enchanted highway), which sings of cycling, hiking, hitchhiking, nature, and adventure:

Pars! Viens avec nous—tu verras	Leave! Come with us—you will see
Les joyeux matins et les grand chemins	Joyful dawns and spacious roads
Où l'on marche à l'aventure	Where you wander as you please
Hiver comme été, toujours la nature, la route enchantée.	In winter as in summer, it's always nature, always the spell of the road.

The pastimes of the rich—ski, tennis, flying—also became more accessible. Pierre Cot, air minister, had founded popular flying clubs; Lagrange gave them what support he could. By 1937 the flying clubs counted ten thousand members, by 1938, four thousand amateur pilots had been trained in them. And a good many young men who could not afford to fly could dream of it while building model airplanes on a dining room table. Skiing too had been rare even among the rich. At Christmas 1936 Paris railway stations counted fifty thousand passengers leaving for mountain holidays. By late autumn 1938 the popular *Confidences* urged its readers to try skiing, "now accessible to all." They could take advantage of cheap fares, cheap boardinghouses, and, *Confidences* advised, pullovers could be knit at home. "A few days, even a weekend" were good for their health. The race was beginning to improve, and Lagrange's success could be gauged by the alarm of morality's guardians. In February 1939 the *Semaine religieuse* of Besançon reprinted a warning of the archbishop of Paris about the serious dangers of winter sports and skiing holidays where facilities for sin lay dangerously near to hand.[33]

One of Lagrange's great achievements was to introduce cheap fares that

---

By 1934 a bike that a quarter century earlier had cost 300 hours' worth of a workman's wages took only 62.5 hours of labor to buy. The Monoprix sold Hutchinson bicycle tires for only 10 francs ("une honte!"*), and Fernandel enchanted the *populo* when he sang about his little Antoinette: *"Elle fait de la bi-bi, de la bicyclette . . . et ça fait mon bonheur."* By 1936–37 such happiness could be purchased for only 55 hours' work. Jean Fourastié, *Le Grand Espoir du XXe siècle* (1963), 299; Claude Jamet, *Notre Front populaire* (1977), 24–25.

made not only sportive sin but greater mobility available to very ordinary folk. Hardly installed in his unwelcoming offices, the new undersecretary had called railway managers together to ask special prices for the holiday-makers expected that very year. Their first reaction had been to refuse: *"Monsieur le Ministre, c'est antiferroviaire"*—cheap fares went against railway interests. The minister insisted, the managers gave in; holiday tickets, family fares, special trains, all at serious discounts would be available beginning on August 3. That month six hundred thousand tickets were sold at prices reduced between 40 and 60 percent, and the railway companies made a profit for the first time since 1928. There were weekend tickets, too, day trips, and package holidays of a few days for agricultural workers and their families to see Paris: one hundred francs for the three-day trip, including food, lodging, guided tours, a visit to the theater. Men, women, children who had never been farther than the county town, discovered the capital, the mountains, the seaside that they had never seen; and many the International Exhibition of 1937.[34]

Most of the French in the 1930s traveled little. Four out of five did not know what tourism meant. Depression had encouraged a trickle of unfashionable holidaymakers to try the beaches of the Côte d'Azur, not in winter, when the posh folk went, but in the heat of summer. Beginning in 1936 and especially 1937, popular tourism and paid holidays produced an influx of small and middling voyagers eager to use L'Oréal's new suntan lotion, Ambre Solaire, or to drink the new soft drink, Orangina, both of which made their bow in 1936.[35] Seaside resorts closer to the capital benefited even more than Mediterranean ones. "Thanks to holidays with pay," wrote a municipal councillor of Le Touquet-Paris-Plage in 1937, "business at Le Touquet, which had suffered like other resorts, has improved. In 1937, Le Touquet makes more than it had made in prosperous 1929." The following year a twenty-six-year-old typist who had never traveled wrote to *Confidences* for advice: She wanted to visit the Auvergne, with its spectacular extinct volcanoes. Could they help her to find a boardinghouse suitable for a single woman? *Confidences* recommended a serious, moderately priced Catholic home for ladies with shallow pockets, and the young typist was able to enjoy the rugged sites of central France.[36] The fact is that normal folk faced more than money problems: Traveling itself was unfamiliar, daunting, and managing in strange circumstances was something of a mystery. Local and regional tourist offices were rare, especially off the beaten track, and travel agencies rarer still. Without the Popular Front's enthusiastic push, French provincialism would have persisted far longer than it did.

HAD THE affairs of the Popular Front been managed as efficiently as those of the Ministry of Idleness, with as much vision and attention to detail as were provided by Lagrange or by his friend Jean Zay,[37] its record might be different. Unfortunately they were not. Ambassador Bullitt reported back to Roosevelt that no French leader combined intelligence and character: Blum, Mandel, Tardieu had the former; La Rocque the latter. Bonnet was clever but shifty, Chautemps a jellyfish with lots of common sense, and Daladier was distrusted by everyone except by Daladier.[38] Of the men on Bullitt's list, Tardieu was out of politics, La Rocque soon would be, and Mandel, Clemenceau's tough-minded heir, was too tough-minded even for his friends. Daladier, whom we have met before, on February 6 and 7, when he behaved less than well, we shall meet again. Honest, indecisive, he had been a brave soldier; he became a poor leader; redoutable in a rough house, tough except in tight spots, he gives the impression of an impulsive, erratic man.* Chautemps, like Daladier, served in Blum's cabinet; Bonnet had been sent out of harm's way to be ambassador in Washington, whence he returned to wreak his havoc later. The problem lay not with them but with Léon Blum.

Coming to power in less critical times, Blum would have made a fine leader. But would he have come to power in less critical times? Born in 1872, a Jew and an early supporter of Dreyfus, he had held the Socialist party together since 1920 by using immoderate rhetoric in the cause of moderation. He never, it would seem, saw what he did not want to see. He had dismissed Nazism as irrational, its anti-Semitism as a manipulative ploy, and refused to take either seriously. He had rejoiced in the end of Hitler just a few months before the Nazis reached power; he had denounced moderates as Fascists and praised Communists as defenders of liberty. Soft-voiced, seductive, scrupulous, tortured, fragile, passionately committed, quietly confident, personally brave or, at least, proud enough to act bravely, he had a sharp analytic mind, a sophisticated intelligence more sub-

---

*As Tacitus said of Galba, *Omnium consensu capax imperii nisi imperasset:* "Had he never become emperor, everyone would have agreed that he had the capacity to rule."

tle than profound, more charming to those he charmed than truly convincing.

Blum has cast his spell over many students of the times. Contemporaries seem to have found him less enticing. André Delmas, leader of the powerful teachers' union, was struck by his sense of guilt at being a bourgeois and an intellectual, his lack of taste for power, his lack of will to hold on to it. Emmanuel Berl regretted the absence of a left-wing physique (Laval, swarthy, short, and stocky, had that in abundance): "He did not have the looks of his ideology." Bullitt noted "the sort of quicksilver intelligence and the little fluttery gestures of the hyper-intellectual queer ones." Was he "queer"? Abellio hinted as much.[39] I doubt it. A close, long-lasting marriage speaks against it. But it matters little. What mattered is that Blum (as Zbigniew Brzezinski would say of another negotiator) shied away "from the unavoidable ingredient of force," cherishing "an excessive faith that all issues can be resolved by compromise." That often left an impression of indecision. But poor decisions are sometimes preferable to no decisions, especially when one is paid to make decisions. And conflicts can be solved by compromise only when the parties involved are willing to reach a bargain. If they are not, conflicts must be solved by fighting or by the abdication of one side.

Blum's inclination to avoid decisions worked fatally when he skirted the decision to devalue the franc. Bright young men like Jacques Rueff and Paul Leroy-Beaulieu had argued for the move, partly to make French prices more competitive, partly to avoid cutting salaries by cutting instead the currency in which the salaries were paid. The old guard opposed such economic heresy and the moral betrayal it involved. The Popular Front platform had promised to defend the franc, and Communists, keen to placate little people, defended it keenly. A devaluation in June 1936 would have made up for the price rises that the government's special measures brought about. By September, when it was reluctantly accepted as unavoidable, devaluation had already been discounted, investors sold francs short, funds sought safe haven beyond the country's borders. The government's social policies, desirable as they were, touched off price rises of such magnitude that competitive power, which devaluation improved, soon ebbed again. The chief effect of the measure, approached irresolutely and too late, was to inflate the cost of imports, further increasing the trade deficit, further depressing the economy. In January 1936 the dollar brought 15 francs; in January 1937 it brought 21.50 francs. By July 1937, after a second devaluation in June, the dollar stood at 26 francs; one year later it oscillated between 37 and 38 francs, where it remained until the war.[40] In three years and three devaluations the franc lost more than half its value. There must have been a neater, perhaps a less costly way to proceed.

The devaluations, especially the third and last in 1938, were not entirely useless. After October 1938 the economy began to improve; average working hours grew slightly; unemployment shrank; industrial production grew; the industrial production index—100 in 1928, 83 in 1938—climbed back to its 1928 level by summer 1939. Yet in June 1939 average weekly hours worked swung only between 41 and 42.[41] Abolition of *Blumsday* had liberated no economic forces that social legislation had repressed. The timid recovery was connected rather with rearmament, which, on the eve of war, accounted for one quarter of industrial production, with a revival of luxury industries in building and automobile production, and with the cheaper franc, now actually undervalued, which helped the export balance to improve.

In Britain, economic recovery had come in the middle thirties by way of lower taxes, cheap money, renewed consumption. Greater social security meant that people saved less when they could have saved, and they spent more. Greater consumption by individuals meant more work. Less government borrowing meant cheaper money; cheaper money suggested investment—whether in cars or houses that produced more pleasure and sometimes more profit than governments ever did. Houses were built for rent also, because renting in Britain, unlike in France, was a profitable investment, and no one thought his money or investments safer abroad than they were at home. By 1934 Neville Chamberlain, having reduced the rate of income tax and restored earlier cuts in pensions, government salaries, and unemployment benefits, could claim that 80 percent of British prosperity had been recovered. A. J. P. Taylor believes that he was too modest.[42] Production was higher than it had been in 1929, and while wages were lower, the costs of living were a good deal lower, too. Even on the dole, British life became a little better, and rearmament had not even begun.

The Popular Front approach was quite the opposite: interventionism, but of a timid sort. Its economics were about buying power, about re-creating demand and a demand-driven recovery. But when the Popular Front raised the revenues of farmers and employees without blocking prices or imposing currency control, it entered an inflationary spiral that more thoroughly interventionist Nazis had known how to avoid in Germany. There

Hjalmar Schacht had frozen wages and prices, controlled capital and currency, negotiated imports against exports, balanced wages against productivity. In France public works never went anywhere, unemployment did not seriously diminish, currency was devalued but never controlled, prices rose but wages did not follow. Blum was to fall on economic issues, and it was the refusal to devalue in time that programmed his economic policy for failure.

But it was not the economy alone that condemned an experiment deserving of a better fate. Statesmen, regimes may be capable, wise, hard-driving; without a dose of luck they get nowhere. Blum was not lucky, and the proof of this came within weeks of his first success with the military revolt in Spain. France's Spanish neighbor had a tradition of pronunciamentos, driving out one government, replacing it by another. This time the easy turnover did not occur; the walls of Jericho held before Franco's trumpets. Too many Spaniards resolved to stand and fight. So it wasn't Franco's rebellion that doomed Blum's Popular Front; it was the rebellion's failure to settle things swiftly and the civil war that ensued south of the Pyrenees to loom over French politics (and those of other countries) for three years. Would the Left coalition ruling (though hardly in power) in Paris lend aid to the Left coalition threatened by Franco's rebels? Of course. And then, no. German and British pressures played their part in the policy of nonintervention, which meant that while Germans and Italians intervened openly on Franco's side and Russians on the side of Spanish "governmentals," the French closed their eyes to volunteers and matériel crossing the Pyrenees.

With Spain in the headlines, fashion featured boleros and swathed sashes, the *grands couturiers* offered Castilian styles for evening wear, yellow and red, the Spanish national colors, dominated the color schemes of 1936. But if Lanvin and Patou made hay, the mood outside their showrooms was more grim. Even as couturiers displayed their collections, fear stalked the capital and the provinces, already torn and dismayed by strikes. Was France, asked *L'Echo de Clamecy*, safe from the vandalism and the atrocities rife across its border?[43] The Abyssinian War in 1935 had emphasized fears of being sucked into a foreign conflict, divided rightists, leftists, centrists over questions of morality and national interest, driven influential Catholics to argue that Christians need not concern themselves about a people in the majority pagan or Muslim. Only months later and much closer to home, these and other questions reft France even more deeply.

The Radicals divided: Jean Zay, Pierre Cot in favor of aid to Spain; most others dubious or hostile. Socialists also differed, some valuing peace more highly, others comradeship. Blum rejected "the fatality of war," arguably bringing a war nearer. Only the right unanimously rejected what the Action Française called the *Frente Crapular* (blackguard front) and the Communists defended it just as unanimously. The result was national fears exacerbated, division dug yet deeper. Inspired by what went on in Spain, talk of civil war grew rife. In autumn 1936 the bishops of Versailles and of Montpellier ordered their priests to prepare passports and civil garb to use as a disguise: If fighting broke out in France, they could escape abroad.[44] Those who disliked Communists and anticlericals more than they feared mayhem were in their element. As they had argued that Christianity in Abyssinia was either nonexistent or irrelevant, now they argued that atrocities in Spain were perpetrated only by the other side. When, on April 26, 1937, German bombers destroyed Guernica, the historical sacred center of the Basques, the right-wing press—*Le Jour, L'Echo de Paris, Action française*—insisted that the devastation had been perpetrated by the Basques themselves. The *Canard enchaîné* went one better: Joan of Arc, it suggested, died in a fire she herself had lit.[45]

Picasso, as we know, painted his *Guernica*, destined for the Spanish pavilion of the International Exposition of 1937. He was inspired by photographs that he saw in *Ce Soir* a few days after the bombing; the blacks, whites, and grainy grays of his searing canvas picked up from newsreels and from newspapers. But while Picasso painted, a fervent Catholic and anti-Communist novelist, Claude Farrère, author of *La Bataille* (1911) and other classics, whom the Académie Française had just elected in preference to Paul Claudel, visited Spain. Ignoring the testimony of the local Basque clergy that witnessed the air attack, Farrère testified that Guernica was never ravaged from the air. "At Bilbao," which he visited under the aegis of Nationalist rebels, "the Marxists, retreating, have blown up all six bridges, as they blew up Guernica which those who hadn't seen it imagine with touching naïveté to have been destroyed by the bombing of victorious nationalists."[46]

Not all believed Farrère. Did he believe himself? Certain French nationalists, torn between loathing of anticlerical violence and of revolution and their revulsion against Mussolini and Hitler, broke with the Action Française and other rabid friends of Franco. The interventionists within Blum's government meanwhile decided to perpetrate some nonintervention of their own to balance that of Germans and Italians. Daladier was "prudent." But

Vincent Auriol, the minister of finance, who had been born at Revel (Haute Garonne), not far from French Catalan Roussillon, was a strong Catalanophile. Admiral François Darlan, the navy secretary, was strongly for resistance to Italian hankerings after the Balearic Islands. Blum, eager to deliver orders of military matériel that the Spanish government had placed before the insurrection, picked a customs official, Gaston Cusin, to direct a large-scale smuggling operation that continued until the collapse of the Spanish Republic.[47] Cusin knew nothing about Spain but a great deal about customs regulations and about how one could get around them. He had been an active syndicalist most of his life and could call on friends throughout the customs service as well as on the aid of other services—above all, the navy. Under Cusin's direction, a Service des renseignements des douanes was set up, hostile or uncommitted personnel weeded out and replaced, international controls avoided using information from the ministries of Foreign Affairs and War. Ships were renamed; funnels were added to change their silhouettes; false documents listed cargoes of machine guns as potatoes, munitions as sewing machines or uniforms. "For national and strategic reasons" French warships escorted Atlantic shipping to Spanish Republic ports, while, to avoid indiscretions, the crews of Spanish ships putting into French harbors were conveyed for shore leave to Clermont-Ferrand, where no German, Italian, or British spies hung out.

The smuggling operation quickly took on an international dimension, the French sending matériel to Romania in return for the Romanians' sending wheat to Spain, establishing contact with Russian agents, and negotiating with Catalonian anarchists (before these were destroyed) who wanted their pound of armaments "less to fight than to suit their fancy." One interesting aspect of the operation was the opportunity to test French armaments in combat. Hence keeping French weapons from falling into enemy hands when Republican troops retreated was an essential part of Cusin's job. His customs men pressed deep into Spain, to Segovia and elsewhere, to gather up French matériel, and Soviet planes as well. Recuperated armor was shipped to the Mareth Line abuilding on Tunisia's Libyan border against possible Italian attack. Rifles and lighter arms were sent to China for use against the Japanese invaders. Jean Monnet, who reorganized the French economy after the Second War, was, says Cusin, in charge of aid to China and participated in other "crafty" enterprises. Captain—later General—Raoul Salan, connected with the ministries of Colonies and War, was co-opted into sending dissident Ethiopian tribes guns and fake Italian bank notes. So the French were not inert, but they had to hide their light under a bushel.

Official nonintervention, however, never convinced the Right. Primed by Franco's government and by assorted Fascists, its press and its parliamentary representatives repeatedly denounced the smuggling operations.[48] The Communists, on the other hand, choosing to take nonintervention at face value, revolted against it. Their slogan, "Guns and planes for Spain," moved many people of goodwill. But the real pressure came from industrial action. Communist union leaders and party militants stamped strikes out of the ground where no industrial friction had existed, or aggravated labor conflicts where they did, bearing out conservative accusations that alleged labor conflicts masked political motives. The culmination of this exercise in cutting noses to spite faces came in the spring and summer of 1937, around the International Exposition of that year.

THE EXHIBITION of 1937, first to be held in Paris since the beginning of the century, had been planned and announced for years. For reasons of prestige—also of national profit—Blum's government was keen that it should be inaugurated on the official opening date: May 1, Labor Day. The enterprise provided employment to some twenty-five thousand workers, and to ten thousand more in businesses supplying builders on the site. Speaking to workers in the building yards, Blum had called on them to win a victory of the proletariat over international fascism by completing their work on time. The Communists were in two minds about that. They first opposed the sumptuary expenditures as futile; then, after the government in February decided that all labor should be hired through unions, they cheered the enterprise.[49] Then the labor force learned that the government's expected program of public works was to be scuttled and concluded that when their present employment ended, the likelihood of finding other work was slight. They reacted by slowdowns and by strikes, and Communists egged them on. This bedevilment became more combative at the end of winter, when, on the evening of March 16, the authorities committed the serious error of allowing a meeting of La Rocque's PSF (the Parti Social Français, reincarnation of the dissolved Croix de Feu) in a cinema in Clichy which was a Communist hotbed. When hostile crowds menaced La Rocque's public, police trying to avoid a riot created a disaster: They fired into the crowd, killing six persons and wounding a lot more, including

Blum's cousin and assistant, who was trying to restore order. Blum, who had been at the Opéra, rushed to the scene in his dress suit and top hat, which only made matters worse. His critics accused him of fumbling a clear provocation, falling into a PSF trap. The Communists now bayed for the blood of Blum as loudly as the Right.[50]

After the clash at Clichy a general protest strike was called for March 18: public transport hogtied, delivery wagons turned back, taxis stopped and made to unload passengers. The U.S. military attaché described the atmosphere as "somewhat tense in spite of the fact that the French public will stand an awful lot." About a third of the workmen at the exposition—six or seven thousand—also suspended work "to protest against government violence." They found a lot of reasons to protest thereafter. When Blum agreed to make a closed union shop of the exposition, he asked building workers to return the favor by working overtime and weekends to get the job done on time. After March work rules were less easily stretched, and closed-shop hiring caused frictions of its own. Some firms wanting to use their own personnel were prevented from so doing, as were those who wanted to employ members of Catholic unions. Working-class solidarity carried a long way: One cement worker who refused a weekly five-franc contribution to help the Spanish government was forced out under threat of a strike. Other incidents arose when workers found work rhythms too fast or when use of machines to replace men provoked Luddite reactions: The expo building yard saw nothing but sit-ins, slowdowns, work-to-rule, meetings, delegations, stoppages, strikes, and sympathy strikes.[51]

Spring 1937 turned out cold and rainy. The exhibition site was all mud and puddles. The press, Parisian and provincial, reflected growing skepticism whether the exposition would, could open on time or ever. This was replaced in time by stiff-upper-lipped cheer about the bits and pieces that did open. The official opening was put off from May 1 to May 25, when the inaugural party did most of its tour on the Seine. Scaffolds around the new Palace of Chaillot—from whose terrace three years later Hitler surveyed Paris—were removed for the inauguration, then replaced. Only five among scores of pavilions were completed (Germany, Russia, Italy, Denmark, Holland), the rest concealed behind miles of tricolor bunting. Paths and passageways, lampposts and lighting fixtures were still under construction; likewise public conveniences, only available for public convenience in July. "Ask for the guide of pavilions still abuilding," cried right-wing hecklers. "National shame," lamented *L'Echo de Clamecy.*

It was not the work force only; the exposition's organizers had problems with a hotel industry that refused special terms to group tours and, indeed, refused all assurances that it would not *raise* prices at the slightest provocation. As the official report could not forbear remarking, "France was the country of unexpected supplements, of surprise taxes, of tips solicited a bit too visibly. . . ." In July 1937, just as visitors were flowing in, an additional tax was imposed on foreign *autocars* entering the country, and railway fares were raised with no forewarning despite promises that increases would wait till after the exhibition. Various pavilions continued to be inaugurated through July, some in August, whilst visitors from out of town were plagued by sporadic strikes: hotels, restaurants, cafés, and, of course, taxis. In the end an enterprise expected to cost three hundred million francs ended by costing nearly a billion and a half. The 31,500,000 visitors registered in 185 days were fewer than in the exhibitions of 1889, 1900, or the Colonial Exhibition of 1931. Still, over 27,000,000 had paid six francs each to get in (the rest got in free), and the influx of foreigners and provincials had refloated theaters and museums, filled shops, given a fillip to railroad, shipping, and postal traffic. Even the late opening, argued the general commissioner in his report, was par for the course; previous exhibitions, too, had opened late: "All in all, the delay for which we are blamed was, if one may say so, practically normal."[52]

Yet tempers were on edge. In 1937 courts were still judging claims for damages over injuries suffered on February 6, 1934, as well as suits for loss and damage that plants claimed they had suffered during the factory occupation of the previous year. Working-class quarters the country over witnessed sporadic fights between militants of the Right and Left, few of which the newspapers reported.[53] Meanwhile, "respectable" people and their press were kept on edge by articles and rumors warning against Communist preparations for a coup. Stories to this effect started to circulate in the late summer of 1936, beginning at which time American dispatches, most based on faithful reading of the right-wing press, conveyed disturbing tales of Soviet plots and propaganda, plans to seize public installations, spying activities in postal and telephone services, the likelihood of Communist or army coups or countercoups. We now recognize these as part of an "intoxication" campaign designed to destabilize further a disturbed situation. That was not clear then.

Nor was it clear when, late on a Saturday evening in September 1937, at the height of the exhibition, terrorist bombs blew up two buildings in the center of Paris: the headquarters of the Employers' Federation, on the rue de Presbourg near the Etoile, and the headquarters of the metal industries of the Paris region, not very far from there. Two policemen died in the explosions, which the press variously attributed to Red agitators, foreign revolutionary elements, or Fascist provocateurs. The police investigation led to an underground conspiratorial network of men dissatisfied with the inaction of Right and extreme Right organizations to which they once belonged. They called themselves CSAR—Secret Committee of Revolutionary Action. The press dubbed them *Cagoulards* (hooded ones) and their organization, the Cagoule. The CSAR had grown out of a "union of Defense Committees" organized in late 1936 by one of La Rocque's lieutenants in the Croix de Feu, the duke Pozzo di Borgo. Designed to resist the expected Communist take-over, the so-called Defense Committees had turned into a gang of murderers and terrorists for hire, pursuing Gaston Cusin when his smuggling activities fluttered too many dovecotes, murdering Italian anti-Fascist refugees—the Roselli brothers—who had entrusted their security to France. So the conspiracies attributed to Communists had actually been hatched by rightist hoods who had stockpiled arms and ammunition destined to oppose Red risings or to support their own. The public took the sensational news calmly, but they did the Right little good. The *Croix de Feu* (or PSF) were torn by internal feuding; so was the Action Française.* La Rocque was disconsidered; so were the *Cagoulards.* "Curious malady of French nationalism," commented Robert Brasillach to his brother-in-law.[54] The minister of the interior Marx Dormoy, whose police uncovered the Cagoule, would be murdered for his pains in 1941.

But if the Right was sick, the Left was sicker. The Popular Front dreamed, and dreaming is no sin even in politics, of solving the country's problems. Even had it come close, and it never did, the problems that other countries raised were going to prevent this. Decent pacifists, most of them on the Left, had never doubted that pacifism and antifascism could be reconciled. Jean Zay remembered a meeting in Orléans where a leftist at-

*La Rocque was caught between his own loyalty to the republic and the *simili*-fascism of more adventurous followers, between his rank and file's antipathy to big business and the loathing that more militant supporters entertained for left-wing foes of big business. "La Rocque does not want to appear to defend employer groups or the Right," noted Wendel, quoting the colonel's explanation that "his troops are more to the left than ours [the Democratic Republican Union, a conservative group]. . . . His program, too!" Jean-Noël Jeanneney, *François de Wendel en République* (1976), 568. Royalists, too, hesitated between fighting the republic "by all means, even legal ones," as Maurras had put it, and overstepping the bounds of legality in Fascist-style activism.

tacked him: "How can you be an anti-Fascist and vote money for national defense?"[55] Blum himself had been of that mind until the responsibilities and accidents of power persuaded him that the French should "arm to prevent war." The pacifist rationalization cloaked a new realization, a new determination, a new resolution, too. Blum realized that the billions required for rearmament imposed hard choices: Social policies had to make way for sterner priorities. That was when public works were placed on the back burner. There would be "a pause" while France joined in the arms race. Calculated in constant 1930 francs, military expenses rose from 18.5 billion in 1936 to 21 billion in 1937 to 25.5 billion in 1938.[56] By then they had doubled in four years, and so had Blum's problems with those of his own camp.

But throwing money at problems is only a beginning. Over years of belt tightening, the military had become timid and unenterprising even when it came to requesting funds. In 1936, when the government initiated a first four-year army plan, the General Staff had asked for nine billion francs, Daladier had raised the bid to fourteen billion. It is not clear what good they did. Procurement was medieval. Armaments and aviation industries were artisanal and underequipped. The Air Staff was semicompetent. Aircraft programs were incoherent, inefficient, based largely on spreading orders among as many manufacturers as possible. Prototypes swarmed. In 1928 the navy used 400 planes of eight different makes: twenty-seven models, forty-four types, powered by eleven kinds of engine. In January 1930 the Air Ministry placed orders for 115 planes of thirty-seven different models. Mass production only came in with Pierre Cot, and by then it was late. The Germans started to rearm their air force in 1934, the British in 1935; the French only really got going in 1938, by which time the Germans had three times as many hands at work in aircraft industry as France. After the defeat of 1940 Antoine de Saint-Exupéry, looking back, attributed French shortcomings to the contrast between a nation of peasants and one of industrialists.[57] But the nation of peasants was blessed with numerous skilled workers, technicians, engineers, brilliant intellectuals, able technocrats. The clash was not between rurals and urbans, but between men of the nineteenth century and men of the twentieth century, which the French and their leaders, however sophisticated, only entered in the late 1950s and the sixties.

In 1924 and 1932 elections had returned left-wing majorities whose coalition governments lost power within two years or less. The same proved true after 1936, except that then the more or less leftish coalition began to unravel even before a government was formed. Radical enthusiasm for the Popular Front, hardly overwhelming, soon waned further. Radical support for a government one third of whose ministers were Radicals splintered through the summer; by autumn the Radical Party Congress reflected widespread disaffection, even hostility. Radicals had worried about the violence of the leagues; now they worried more about the militancy of strikers who challenged public authority and order more depressingly than leagues had ever done. In October 1936, at the Biarritz congress, an influential party leader, Emile Roche of the Nord, demanded that Radicals affirm their will against "Red and White Fascism and all enemies of the Republic" whether these came from Right or Left. What Roche really meant was that the principal enemy was to be found no longer on the right but—something unthinkable a few years before—on the left flank, among those whom a left-wing Radical would shortly describe as the "Communazis."[58]

It followed that when Léon Blum was finally voted down after 382 uneasy days in office, the cabinets that succeeded him, though they included Socialists, were headed by Radicals: Chautemps and Daladier. The power to legislate by decree that parliament had refused to Blum was granted to Chautemps, who went ahead and raised taxes, while prices rose and kept on rising. Social reforms and wage concessions were brought to an end; productivity trod water; social protest fermented; armaments soaked up what taxes could bring in; the franc oscillated—always downward. Trade unions became unmanageable, and so did small businesses irate at the unions' impossible demands. "The vital factor," Premier Chautemps confided to William Bullitt, "was that the French government could not reduce its expenses or increase its revenues." That had been the problem since the slump washed over the country; rearmament made it worse. Nor did rearmament help where it was supposed to help. "The Quai d'Orsay sees no possibility of preserving the peace and nothing to do but wait," quoth Bullitt; "helpless in the face of events, all they can do is bury the dead."[59]

Peter Larmour calls Chautemps's government a long wake for the Popular Front.[60] One wake gave way to another as Chautemps resigned on March 10, 1938, and then, on March 11, the Germans occupied Austria. No one knows for sure, but most believed that Chautemps's resignation preceded the imminent crisis in order to avoid having to face it. The Left fled from responsibility; responsibility was going to pursue it. After the Anschluss, the Popular Front that had been dissolving on the hoof became irrelevant. Foreign affairs became the crux of politics, and their focus shifted from Spain, which represented an internal French debate, to Germany, which represented a clear and present danger.

In practice little changed. When in March 1938, in the midst of political uncertainty and financial hemorrhage, Blum formed his second cabinet, the Americans found "no more than a handful of deputies interested in anything else than jockeying for political advantage." By March 22 "people have forgotten about Austria." Blum lasted twenty-six days. An unnamed ambassador commented wryly: "They will go on playing politics until the Germans attack the Maginot Line." They went on doing it even after that. Billboard signs were going up calling for Pétain to head one more government of national union, and the U.S. commercial attaché reported that a jittery industrialist was taking steps to send his fourteen-year-old niece who had been studying in Paris back to the United States. It was still only March, but clearly, where Austria had fallen others would follow. Bohemia would be next, and the French military dreaded becoming embroiled on behalf of the Czechs. The High Command envisaged massive losses. For General Edouard Requin, commanding the French forces opposite the Siegfried Line, attack against the Germans meant "the death of a race." His superior, General Gamelin, was of like mind. The last war's bleeding had not been forgotten, Americans reminded their superiors back in Washington: "[A]nother comparable jolt . . . would be pretty close to the end." *Je Suis Partout* agreed: "Should the French get themselves killed for Beneš, the Free Mason?" The question was: Would they risk being killed for France?[61]

An American lunching with Marcel Cachin found the Communist leader expecting war any day. Charles Lindbergh doubted "that a war will start this year. I am afraid, however, that one is very likely to begin in 1939."[62] Lindbergh, of course, was right. French leaders let the British persuade them that their treaty obligations to the Czechs could be disregarded.* Be-

---

*Or was that what the French foreign secretary Georges Bonnet wanted? Emile Delavenay, who worked in London for the semiofficial news agency Havas, recalls that on September 26, 1938, Lord Halifax made public a strong note declaring that if Germany attacked Czechoslovakia, France would be forced to come to its ally's aid and Britain and Russia would certainly support France. The Havas agency immediately transmitted the text to Paris, where it was denounced as false and largely suppressed at the instigation of Bonnet and the Quai d'Orsay. The London head of Agence Havas offered his resignation and was quelled with the award of the Legion of Honor; Delavenay resigned and moved to the BBC. For him, the tale of French dependence on the British offered a convenient excuse for *Munichois* defeatism. Emile Delavenay, *Témoignage* (Aix-en-Provence, 1992), 160–61; P. L. Bret, *Au feu des événements* (1959), 68; and Andrew Roberts, *The Holy Fox* (London, 1991), 119.

tween mid-September and September 30, when, the Munich capitulation signed, Daladier returned in shamefaced triumph, France lived two weeks of crisis. Partial mobilization, when it began to look as if Hitler would force a showdown, set off panic just as the holiday season was drawing to an end. All over the country, overloaded telephone circuits gave up the ghost. In a dress rehearsal for events to come, Parisians who owned cars piled what they could in them, tied mattresses on top, and fled the capital for less menaced havens. Holidaymakers making their way back to Paris encountered a tide of automobiles, and trucks, and vans, rolling the other way. "It was not departure, it was flight; and people ran away in a disarray that reflected a general liquefaction: cars loaded with anything, even with wardrobes, bewildered drivers ending in the ditch, abandoned objects strewn over the roads."[63]

Henry Miller, who had lived in Paris through most of the crises of the thirties without heeding them much, had taken off for the southwest. From Bordeaux he wrote to his friend Anaïs Nin, advising her to get out of the capital (she went to Le Havre): "If it starts on October 1, as predicted . . . I prefer getting out of France: I'm cured of Europe." Then, the crisis past, "anybody who was not 'neurotic' during this period must be abnormal," Miller insisted. "For me it's just as though the war did take place."[64] Cowardice knows no fatherland.

"I don't wish that any generation should experience circumstances like those we lived that September," the future Gaullist prime minister Michel Debré remembered: "a crushing diplomatic defeat and the delirious popular enthusiasm that greeted it." Georges Duhamel summarily dismissed the dreamers who believed Chamberlain's fantasy of a peace with honor: "It isn't peace; it is an armistice." For Bernanos, France had been raped by hooligans while she slept. Munich was the miscarriage that followed. Most revealing, *L'Echo de Clamecy* accurately described what it dubbed a capitulation: "We have betrayed the dead of the Great War, we have betrayed our commitments, we have brought back a factitious peace and left behind our honor."[65] But critics of Munich, then, were in a minority. An opinion survey found only 37 percent opposed to the settlement, and that sounds like an overestimation. The rest shared Léon Blum's "cowardly relief," joined in the general "explosion of joy," or argued like the general secretary of the Socialist Party, Paul Faure, that "Fascism would die of its own success to be replaced by Socialism." In abolishing one anachronistic border after another, Hitlerism was turning out to be "a true internationalism." A seriously disabled and heavily decorated veteran, Edmond Millet, Radical deputy of Belfort on the German border, remembered Munich as the great moment "when Frenchmen finally had been united." No wonder that Winston Churchill found "poor" post-Munich France "corrupt, divided, floundering, without compass" and Lindbergh dismissed it as a "corrupt and demoralized nation."[66]

The official reaction to humiliation at Munich was to negotiate a nonaggression treaty with Germany.* Meanwhile, a Jewish refugee from Germany, distraught at his family's fate, murdered the third secretary of the German Embassy in Paris. The crime was followed shortly, on November 9, by savage organized pogroms throughout Germany. The *Kristallnacht*, as it was called after the shattered glass of Jewish stores, synagogues, and homes, and the horrors that followed it were going to turn the stomachs of most civilized Westerners. They did not discourage French Munich fans one bit. The nonaggression treaty was concluded on November 22, and the German foreign minister, the vapid, pretentious Joachim von Ribbentrop, was invited to Paris for the signature. He would enjoy a sumptuous reception. Tactfully, though Jewish ministers like Mandel and Zay had been invited to the reception offered by the German Embassy, they were forgotten in invitations to the gala the French government offered for Ribbentrop at the Quai d'Orsay.[67]

Those who opposed this lickspittle policy thought less of fighting Germans than of calling Hitler's bluff. Rightly persuaded that the dictator could have been faced down in 1936, they thought that a challenge in 1938 would have the same effect. They did not stop to consider that France in 1938 was relatively much weaker not only in armaments but in manpower during the years when draft contingents were at their hollow worst. Higher civil servants in the know judged France so inferior and so unprepared (*"Nous sommes foutus!"*) that it had better give up anything to avoid fighting. The military, even the best of them like Jean de Lattre, agreed, and Daladier was not a good enough historian to recall Clemenceau's remark that war was too serious a matter to leave to the generals.[68]

French fliers were convinced that Germans enjoyed "a crushing superior-

---

*It is important to recall, as does Anthony Adamthwaite, *France and the Coming of the Second World War, 1936–1939* (London, 1977), 353, that "the principal aim of French foreign policy was the search for an agreement with Germany. French prime ministers from Blum to Daladier worked consistently for an understanding with Hitler." The same, of course, could be said of the British cabinet that signed a nonaggression treaty with the Germans two months before the French.

ity" over them "in numbers and in thought." The Germans had deliberately allowed French air force officers to admire their military installations— some of them Potemkin airfields—and had succeeded in depressing their guests. Military authorities all the way to the air minister were persuaded that the Germans had ten aircraft to their every one and that they could and would bomb Paris as they had Guernica. There were no planes for the defense of the capital, Air Minister Guy La Chambre told Bullitt two days before the Munich Conference, no antiaircraft artillery to speak of, no protection, and the destruction of Paris would be beyond anything one could imagine. La Chambre had sent his wife and child to Brittany and thought that everyone else should do as much (but didn't say so in public). Bullitt, impressed, issued instructions that embassy staff should be quietly advised to follow suit.[69]

The failure of military intelligence, of judgment, and of nerve all came together that mild and sunny fall. "It is difficult to exaggerate," Bullitt's report on the events concludes, "the degree to which the leaders of French political life did not (repeat not) rise to the demands of a tragic occasion." The men who should have governed France, he said, had died on the Marne and at Verdun. It certainly looked that way. It would be fairer, though, to leave the last word to a soldier. Calling up some six hundred thousand reservists in partial mobilization cost the country at least ten million francs reported the military attaché. "The critical financial plight of the government makes it imperative that demobilization proceed rapidly." Money, as ever, called the tune.[70]

That was something that Daladier understood. Already before the crisis, deep in the summer doldrums, he had called for fundamental modifications to the forty-hour law. On November 1, 1938, Paul Reynaud, ambitious, vain, and immensely able, had taken over the Finance Ministry. Less than two weeks later he told the cabinet that France was at the very bottom of world financial rankings and could only escape from that situation by taking drastic action: abolish the two-Sunday week the better to compete with an opponent that knew no Sundays; lower costs for overtime to shrink production costs; dismantle the social legislation of the last few years; introduce family allowances meant to increase the number of future taxpayers. A series of decrees applied Reynaud's program and once more raised taxes. When the unions called a general strike for November 30, their protest was a failure. Big capital and small supported Daladier. In 1938 government loans raised on the financial market covered 3 percent of government expenses; in 1939 they covered 27 percent. In 1935–1936 savings banks had shown a deficit of 1,315,000; in 1936–1937 deposits grew 36,000,000; in 1937–1938 they grew by 640,000,000, in 1938–1939 by 4,282,000,000. Other results were no less striking. Between October 1938 and June 1939 industrial production rose 20 percent overall, 36 percent in the building trades, 40 percent in metallurgical industries, while the number of jobless fell 10 percent where, until then, it had been rising.[71]

Center and Right of course exulted. *"La révolution de juin 1936 est finie, bien finie . . ."* crowed the right Radical *Ere nouvelle.* But they were not alone. Throughout the French provinces, where want was as moderate as unemployment and most people looked to Paris for trouble, not inspiration, peasants, shopkeepers, small manufacturers, and employers were all heartily sick of alarums and excursions. Strikes delayed mail or lost it, closed banks or public offices when you needed to use them, held up deliveries, thwarted travel plans. When the government faced down a Left increasingly perceived as threatening and obnoxious, its success seemed like the end of a two-year nightmare. The mayor of the city of Orange, in Daladier's own department of Vaucluse, wrote to tell him of the immense popularity that he had acquired: "After Munich it was enthusiasm, after November 30 it's better than that: It's the real people who approve you, men and women, the latter often the most enthusiastic and most vocal. . . ."[72]

November 30 brought Daladier yet another gift. That day, with the French ambassador in the visitors' gallery, the Italian parliament had burst into wild calls for the return of Corsica, Savoy, Nice, and Tunisia, while Fascist demonstrators carried the slogan into the streets of Rome. Here was a foe at last that France need not worry about too much, one that civilians and military agreed was fatuous and absurd. Verbal aggression by Mussolini's minions helped to unite a country that was disunited on many other scores. The Left rejected Fascist claims on national territory; the Right reluctantly abandoned hopes of Franco-Italian friendship. Through December 1938 and January 1939, Daladier's travels and his speeches reminded his fellow French that however ready to sell foreigners down the river, France would never give up its own.[73] Daladier's speeches and the controversy with Italian neighbors also reminded a lot of French of a colonial empire that had got little notice until then.

Apart from colorful stories that newspapers printed when they were short of copy, the French electorate had long treated overseas adventure with indifference or hostility. Colonies cost money and brought in little except cocoa, bananas, and troublesome immigrants. Colonial policy was justified as a civilizing mission, part of the white man's burden, but it provided little employment and less satisfaction. In 1931 the Colonial Exhibition celebrated France's generous expansion and the pride of having carried schools, medicine, liberty, equality, and fraternity to the four corners of the world, whose costumes and cooking one could enjoy within the exhibition grounds, where mosques, souks, temples, dancers, camels, and canoes testified to the Greater France, whose empire, on which the sun never set, compensated for the temporarily flagging metropolis. But the fact that the colonies remained underdeveloped, underindustrialized, and underpaid meant that despite protection, native purchasing power for French goods was pitifully small. In 1932 Simenon, returning from a long African trip, wrote a series of articles on his experiences for the weekly *Vu*. Citroën had just organized an African rally publicized by a film called *L'Afrique vous parle* (Africa talks to you). Simenon subtitled his series *L'Afrique vous parle: Elle vous dit merde* (Africa talks to you: It says go to hell). Colonialism was a fraud, colonialists were corrupt, Western civilization for Africa was a mistake, Africans should be left in peace. Peace was the last thing that Africans or anyone else would be allowed to enjoy.[74]

Depression, which dried up so much of foreign trade, increased the economic importance of the colonies. Before it, less than one fifth of French exports went to them; by the late thirties one third of French exports did, and colonial investments had pretty much quadrupled. Yet for the average Frenchman the colonial image, if any, was that of a grinning black man advertising a sweet chocolate drink: Banania. It would be after Munich that more public figures learned to pay compensatory attention to an empire that promised to turn the 42,000,000 weakling into a giant 109,000,000 strong. It was after the Fascist threats to Corsica and Tunisia that imperial horizons beckoned. "Imperial policy will save France," a provincial journalist promised. But no one and nothing could save France except the French themselves.[75]

After the Germans entered Prague in March 1939, breaking engagements they had taken only months before, a new series of decrees raised working hours in plants that worked for the national defense. The minister of Labor, Charles Pomaret, a centrist operating under vague Socialist labels, hesitated to add his signature. He had already protested vigorously the previous November at the decree that eased the application of the forty-hour law, arguing that no enterprise actually worked as much as that. When told that 81 percent of employees in plants with more than a hundred workers labored a full forty-hour week, Pomaret asked where such absurd figures had been obtained and was stupefied to hear they came from the statistics of his own ministry. Now there was more debate between Pomaret and Reynaud, the two men visiting each other in their respective offices. Michel Debré, at the time a member of Reynaud's cabinet, remembered that on his wall Reynaud had a map of Hitler's territorial gains and of his future plans for expansion. As for Pomaret, "on his salon wall are hung twelve or fifteen portraits of prostitutes, admirable little Toulouse-Lautrecs."[76]

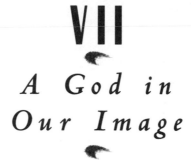

VII

A God in Our Image

If God made us in His image,
We've done as much to him.

IN 1929, unhappy in love, Magdeleine Peyronnec solicited admission to a convent and was accepted as a novice Carmelite. A strong-minded young woman of good family, she would leave the convent the following year when she found that the young man she thought she had lost was there for the taking. In the meantime, she passed ten or eleven months in a secret world that had changed little—and probably for the worse—in several centuries.

On arrival at the convent Magdeleine had to give up her stockings and her "modern combination" in crepe de Chine and lace for a sacklike tunic in heavy brown linen, a rigid whalebone collar, and a stiff coif. There were no underpants, no means of holding up the rough wool stockings that sagged below her knees, no hankie either, unless one had a cold.[1] We may envision her cell from the Customary Rules of the cloistered Dominicans of Lourdes, less stern than those of Magdeleine's Carmelites: no windows, a door—generally closed—as only source of light, whitewashed walls, a crucifix, a plank set on four uprights for a bed, a straw pillow, a palliasse "for those who need it."[2] Sleep fully dressed with collar and with bonnet to discipline quiescent body, though unshod. Beside every cell a smaller cell containing the *tinette*, an uncovered tub for night soil, emptied every three days by a nun in penitence (in 1932, three Trappists at Laval died of emanations whilst emptying the convent cesspits with slop basins).[3] No wash-stand, soap, or toothbrush. Ablutions, carried out with a rag already used by others and dipped in a little water, touched only hands and face. On the first Thursday of each month a special basin was brought round the cells for nuns to wash their feet—no higher than the ankles. All other parts were out of bounds; cleaning or touching them would be a mortal sin.* As for the hair, novices were lent a comb twice a week to disentangle it without any washing. For menstruation, there was shredded linen that could be tied with a piece of string. Washing clothes was not encouraged either. Presumably as a tribute to Saint Benedict Labre, patron of filth and fleas, Magdeleine wore her original tunic, unwashed, unchanged, for the duration of her novitiate.[4]

Dominicans respected silence and, in its honor, recommended the use of fragmentary sentences left unfinished, and of signs. Carmelites made a vow of silence, and furniture was supposed to collaborate. Whenever possible, chairs were manufactured in the convent, their seats and backs in plaited straw, their legs tipped with felt to minimize the sound. The pittance of both orders was meager and vegetarian. Dominicans specified "perpetual abstinence from meat, sauce or gravy made with meat, or dishes cooked with meat." It was bad enough to keep up and care for a miserable body destined to turn to dust. One was not supposed to enjoy the process.[5] It was presumably in this spirit that Carmelites periodically engaged in flagellation and that in the months following her vows, every Carmelite was expected to apply poultices of hot grease or fat to her breasts at bedtime. "Thirty or forty days of this will turn them into flaccid pockets."[6] In the same spirit, though less painfully, the crosses Carmelites wore or gazed at bore no figure of the Christ. No image of nakedness was to meet their eyes.[7] Dominicans appear more sophisticated. Reference to the outside world was discouraged, but they could read *La Croix*. Hence No. 110 of the Dominican Rule: "Given the sovereign respect that we owe to every image of our God, the Sisters will carefully remove it from *La Croix* every time they des-

*Shared by many orders, "the holy and implacable hatred that we all nourish toward our body" carried broad implications. Interviewed in the 1970s, an old nun remembered the popular locution "dirty like a Carmelite" and insisted that it was no slander. "We were afraid to wash simply because we were afraid to touch ourselves. Above all, to look upon ourselves." *Spiritual Instructions for Sisters of Charity* (1884), vii; Catherine Baker, *Les Contemplatives* (1979), 278. In a volume dedicated to religious decorum, *Bienséances religieuses* (1935), 189, Father Jules Blouet, *supérieur du grand séminaire de Coutances*, criticizes those nuns who do not bother to keep clean, urging them to wash hands and face conscientiously, to avoid dirty teeth (unseemly), and to consider sensibilities that strong body odors or the smell of feet might offend.

tine that newspaper to a purpose that is unclean or simply disrespectful. These images of the cross may be burnt."⁹

The rule goes into remarkable detail. It counsels keeping out of drafts (hankies, as we know, are in short supply), it instructs nuns to remove the trace of spiders or other insects they may have had to squash, it allows no more than a spoon of miraculous Lourdes grotto water every day, it requests Sisters to wash their hands sufficiently so as not to soil the rag they use to dry them, and it offers counsel: "[I]t is not absolutely prohibited to pet cats and dogs, but such caresses must always be offered with a religious moderation." When Magdeleine entered her convent, 909 women's religious orders lived in 3,218 establishments scattered throughout France: some 130,000 nuns and novices, three times the number of secular priests, six times that of male regulars. Contemplatives like the Carmelites were in a minority, and so were cloistered nuns in general. Many religious tended the sick, the old, the poor; many trained for missionary work abroad; over 30,000 taught, though legal problems make precise numbers hard to establish. Still harder to encompass are the multiple small companies and communities of dedicated laywomen with no habit or cloister, and often no vows, yet consecrated to a life of prayer, humility, charity, and obedience. Active in Lyons after 1929, the Company of Saint Angela Merici welcomed unmarried women of mostly modest background—accountants, teachers, nurses, shop assistants—eager to combine spiritual commitment and good works. The Pious Union of Lay Sisters of the Sacred Heart of Jesus, which recognized both secular and regular members, some married, some single, tended to recruit among the provincial upper classes. The significance of such societies, slight when taken one by one, is hard to determine. They are mentioned here as a reminder of widespread commitments and activities that were then and are still largely ignored and that yet affected lives and social conditions more profoundly than limited membership and visibility might suggest.¹ˑ

The rules of this swarm of associations varied widely, and so did their willingness to move with the times. Missionary orders, for example, Elisabeth Dufourcq has told us, were pioneers in using typewriters and wireless telegraphy. Such venturesomeness, though, was far from common. By the 1950s, however, twenty years after Magdeleine Peyronnec's adventure, even conventual rules revealed revolutionary changes: Telephones are mentioned; radios are in use; vegetarianism has widely been abandoned. Some orders had started on that road in 1938 or 1939 already. Most, however, at

least ideally, maintained a firm distance from the world, insisted on auster-
ity, abstinence, penitence, mortification of the body, and inculcated a sharp
sense of sin in the young women they sought to teach and guide. There
were still *pensionnats* in the 1930s where washing above the knees was prohibited. And many a convent school between the wars was like the one
where bathing without a shift if one bathed at all was a major transgression.
"Mademoiselle," a young reprobate was told, "you have committed an
abominable sin . . . you have bathed naked. Remember, Mademoiselle: the
Holy Virgin herself never saw herself naked!"[11]

All this would be no more than anecdotal if so many daughters of the
upper classes did not attend schools where persons who professed rejection
of the world sought to prepare them to operate in a world better rejected.
The girls were taught by nuns many of whom had themselves been trained
in stricter times, before the First World War, and who counted their real
successes in the number of religious vocations inspired by their teaching.
The nuns' chief interest was less instruction than education: preparing
Christian wives and mothers, not women who would have to earn a living
and face the everyday realities of life. Meanwhile, in thousands of village
schools they also prepared the daughters of the people for employment appropriate to their station.* Thus the daughter of a small farmer of Vallet
(Loire-Inférieure), born in 1924, entered school at the age of seven and left
when she was ten for domestic service in a "bourgeois" family "like many of
her fellows." That may have been why parents with children who would
have to face material realities squarely gradually abandoned religious institutions, while their social betters continued to favor them.[12] In the thirteen
years from 1925 to 1938 the number of Catholic colleges in the country
doubled, that of their students more than doubled, so that in 1938 more
than one quarter million boys and girls attended secondary Catholic institutions. Outside the secondary, however, Catholic schools had a hard row
to hoe: By the eve of war only about one French child in five enjoyed a
Catholic elementary education. Outside especially Catholic areas, private
schools closed or only soldiered on thanks to subsidies from wealthy families or from the parish priest.[13]

Yet many a parish would have found it hard to come up with a subsidy;

---

*On the other hand, when teaching country girls, nuns, who had themselves escaped their rural condition
and valued their French cultural capital highly, tended to wean their charges from their home languages
and cultures and to inculcate the "refinements" of a national culture far less limiting than the one so many
village girls dreamed of bolting. See Michel Lagrée, *Religion et culture en Bretagne* (1992), 264.

many a parish did not even have a priest. In the Berry in 1930 nearly one third of parishes in the diocese of Bourges had no officiating minister. By 1936, 211 of 500 parishes lacked a pastor. More would come to lack one if things went on as they had been doing: In 1939 seventeen priests had died, six had been ordained; by that year three quarters of the priests were over fifty.[14] At Besançon, in an observant region, the archbishop had to issue advice for parishioners without a parish priest. The fact is that the job grew steadily less attractive. Most village priests were poor—poorer than teachers, whose average nine thousand francs a month looked well beside the priest's two to four thousand francs. In certain mountain communities the priests were poorer still, but they did not do much better in prosperous areas like the Seine-et-Oise. In 1930 nearly a third of rural parishes had no resident minister. By the end of the decade Pierre Hamp sketched a Christmas party near Paris where ladies talked of slimming and of diets, while others commented that country priests lost weight without special effort; soon there would be no more "cassocks" to celebrate village mass.[15]

Personal and social identity included religious provenance, but religious identification kept shrinking. Better than nine in ten French babies were baptized Catholics, but only one third of adults observed their religious duties once a year, at Easter, while civil burials and civil marriages continued to increase. In the department of the Seine in 1937, 23,223 civil marriages far outnumbered 18,124 religious ones. Baptism shrank more slowly: 94 percent in 1930, 80 percent in 1970. Religious burials receded a bit faster: 70 percent in 1930, 64 percent in 1935. On the whole, though, rituals and their performers waned more or less in step.[16]

The long-term trend, however, appeared less obvious in the 1930s than the revival of religious activity that turned the interwar years into the Indian Summer of French Christendom. Around the twenties' ending, the number of annual ordinations rose significantly: 838 a year in 1930, more than 1,200 a year between 1935 and 1939. Men entering the priesthood during that decade did so in greater numbers than any age-group since the 1880s. Overall, the steep decline in vocations and ordinations that followed the prewar separation of Church and State had been stemmed, indeed reversed. There were almost twice as many seminarians on the eve of the Second War as there had been just before the First War (9 percent more than in the halcyon years at the century's beginning) and 31 percent more ordinations in the mid-30s than there had been between 1909 and 1913—more than that when compared with the twenties.[17]

In the diocese of Rouen young priests had never been so many since the Second Empire: nearly half of the clergy under the age of forty in 1938. Relatively fervent regions like Lorraine, Anjou, or Rouergue, where recruitment had fallen less or had stabilized, showed real improvement. Indifferent dioceses like that of Perpignan showed impressive recoveries. In spiritually arid Limousin, where clerical numbers had dwindled for half a century, the proportion of priests per ten thousand population fell by a quarter between the wars, but the number of ordinations went up: Limoges ordained fifty-nine priests in the 1920s, sixty-five in he 1930s; Tulle rose from forty-two to fifty-seven. Women's religious fervor, traditionally superior to that of men, also progressed. In the Hérault, after 1927, the rate of monastic vocations doubled and even tripled all over the department with the exception of Béziers, where, one fin de siècle missionary had predicted, if Christ were to return to earth, the Bittérois would gladly crucify him. In the Beauce, around Chartres, women's church attendance, stagnant or falling, began to rise after 1931, and so, more unexpectedly, did that of the men.[18] Consumption of books showed similar oscillations: During the 1920s books on religious subjects as a percentage of total books published fell from 7.8 in 1923 to 3.1 percent in 1929, then rose to 6.4 percent in 1934. A best seller like François Mauriac's *Life of Jesus* (1936) unloaded 150,000 in a few months.[19]

Few read Mauriac as faithfully as the readers of *Cœurs vaillants* (valiant hearts)—the Catholic children's weekly—read their magazine. Born in 1928, a decade later *Cœurs vaillants* sold two hundred thousand copies, thanks especially to the cartoon series of Tintin and his dog, Milou, creations of Hergé, who had made his start in Belgian boy scout publications. *Cœurs vaillants* offered adventure and travel stories, useful information, the tale of the Lord's passion in cartoon form, edifying stereotypes (stupid and brutish Germans, stupid and brutish Bolshies), and good advice: Stay away from cinemas *(porte de ciné, porte d'enfer)*, from illustrated magazines and dailies with red titles, from bad company that can be recognized by its "modern aspect: short hair, bare arms, ultra-short dresses." It even, after the fashion of the times, launched a sort of uniform for its readers: beige shirt with a scout-type scarf in green and orange.[20]

As important or more so was Catholic Action: the myriad clubs and associations that carried Catholic spirit, charity, and a variety of activities throughout the land. Once restricted to narrow morality, religion now was to affect all life. Œuvres—good works—had always been a part of normal

Christian life and Church activity, but until the turn of the century they had been largely left to individual initiative. Diocesan bulletins since 1900 reveal plenty of *œuvres,* but most of them dedicated to raising money or to advance the spiritual development of the faithful. Groups, societies, of either sex, focused on prayer; sporting or social activities are not in evidence. Then, at the very end of 1905, came the separation of Church and State, and the Church embattled became increasingly activist. The Ligue de Résistance des Catholiques Français was set up in 1906; in 1907 a Catholic Defense Committee called on the faithful in all parishes to organize; a patriotic League of French Womanhood followed the same year. "Moaning is sterile. We must ACT!" the *Semaine religieuse* of Nevers trumpeted on January 5, 1907. Parish priests were encouraged to publish regular bulletins. Catholic militants were urged to organize workers, shop assistants, students, all the young. Priests tucked up their cassocks, encouraged games, started up sporting clubs. By 1939 the Gymnastic and Sporting Federation of French Church Clubs counted thirty-six hundred clubs and half a million members.[21]

This activism grew after the war, when priests and monks, now veterans back from the firing line, set up militant leagues and Edouard de Curières de Castelnau, a Catholic war hero who had lost three sons in the fighting, headed a national Catholic Federation. But grass roots activity was only just beginning, and it would be the thirties that saw an extraordinary effort to mobilize Catholics in a variety of clubs, societies, leagues, fraternities, sororities, study circles, courses, retreats, and prayer circles.

On the sporting front the Church held a strong lead. Introduced by some private schools before the Great War, games were to enter the program of public schools only in the later 1950s. Secular gymnastic societies, reflecting the prejudices of educational authorities, tended to reject ball games and adopted them only in the later twenties in order to compete with parish clubs, which had introduced them to attract the young. Priests had soon discovered the attractive possibilities of sports and games, at least for young males. Female sports, as Pope Pius XI recalled in 1933, led almost inevitably to indecent behavior and display. When decently attired, women could indulge in gymnastic exercises and even play basketball, but shorts were sinful and competition was discouraged as threatening the softer feminine virtues. Males, on the other hand, could engage in competitive games that developed manly virtues, a sense of fair play, and parish solidarity. Parish football was a serious draw, and it also helped emancipate the players. In

1933 the minister of Saint-Priest-sous-Aixe (Haute Vienne) wrote to his bishop to complain that the football club he had founded "claims the right to go play far away without me, even without my permission." There was no knowing where such willfulness might end.[22]

The same emancipating spirit presided over the youth movement that the Church founded in 1928 and 1929, which actually spread and began taking root after 1931. One wonders whether the condemnation of the Action Française in 1926, cutting bright young Catholics off from a movement that drained them for twenty years, did not make them available for alternative activities. This seems to have been the case with Edmond Michelet (born 1899), future Resistance leader and minister of General de Gaulle. A fervent Catholic from Brive, in southern Limousin, Michelet first pursued his ideals as a Camelot du Roi but resigned from the Action Française around 1928 to concentrate henceforth on another kind of militancy in the Catholic Association of French Youth (ACJF), where he would meet like-minded militants like Georges Bidault and René Pleven. But this is speculation. Furthermore, the movements of the 1930s were designed to let peasants and workers run their own show—and even girls were treated on an equal (though chastely separate) footing. They catered to young rurals (Jeunesse Agricole Catholique—JAC), students (Jeunesse Etudiante Chrétienne—JEC), workers (Jeunesse Ouvrière Chrétienne—JOC). A feminine JOCF appeared in 1930; founded in 1936, the JACF soon attracted more members than its male counterpart.

This kind of Catholic action differed from traditional church clubs in that it sought first of all "to reconquer society for the Church." The world was learning to do without God; it had to be taught it couldn't. Pope Pius XI had called for an apostolate not of priests but laymen, "one comrade reconquering another of the same milieu." The first apostles among workers would be workers; the apostles of business and industry would be industrialists and businessmen. In working-class neighborhoods this meant that the accent shifted from guidance by those allegedly wiser and more experienced to group and professional initiative and self-reliance. A new emphasis on the centrality of Christ in clerical training and ecclesiastic language eased the passage from the suffering Christ to the laboring Christ and then to the suffering workman, suggested a *Christ ouvrier*, developed a mystique of labor, pride in its dignity and that of a job well done.

If reality loomed too far from the ideal, it was the job of Christ's disciples to alter and reconquer it for his Church. The late 1920s and the early thirties produced a crop of writings that focused on a working class dechristianized or never exposed to true Christianity and on the need for Catholic action to bridge the chasm that gaped between the workers and the Church. Saving souls involved saving bodies, too, improving the conditions in which the bodies suffered. But to do this, one had to experience these conditions at first hand, share the lives, labor, and adversities of the insulted and the injured, not merely preach to them. In Paris, Lyons, Lille, and elsewhere, priests recognized the need to contact those whom traditional religious institutions barely touched, to pursue them into the working place and share their existence. "Poor priests for poor people, worker-priests for working people."

Father Armand Vallée, "the red priest of Saint-Brieuc" who organized the first Christian unions in the Côtes-du-Nord after having lived awhile with the unemployed, has been mentioned as the first of worker priests. A more likely candidate for the distinction took years to achieve his ambition. Ordained in 1926, Hadrien Bousquet stubbornly struggled for permission to work in industry alongside other workers. In June 1939 his superiors finally allowed him to take a job at the Ivry ironworks, outside Paris, without revealing his true identity. In August of that year he was called up for war service. So, in a country where the image of the Church remained that of the Right at prayer, few priests actually achieved their populist aspirations before the war broke out. But they helped lay the groundwork for the postwar apostolate of worker priests.[23]

New attention paid to working people also refurbished the value of useful tasks performed by like to like. Not charity from one's betters but self-help: jobs for the jobless, aid for the unemployed, practical courses, professional orientation, professional dignity. Human dignity too. One JOC song invited working people to hold their heads high: *"Sois fier ouvrier, et relève les yeux! / Tu n'est pas esclave ou machine!"* (Be proud, workingman, and raise up your head / Neither slave nor machine, you have been misled!). By 1939 the JOC and JOCF in the Nord alone counted twenty thousand members. Nationally the JOC hovered around forty-five thousand, the JOCF boasted more than that, working-class sympathizers were four or five times that many. The JOC periodical *Vie ouvrière* sold 179,000 copies on the eve of war.[24]

The most important gains achieved by their efforts may have been the most modest. The JOC set out to save souls, but it was most effective in turning the workplace into a slightly more civilized, more livable space.

When they stood up against cursing, hazing, bullying, the exploitation of apprentices and of women by workmates and superiors, working Christians notched up small victories as they reshaped heroic aspirations to practical levels.

Meanwhile, Catholic action in the countryside meant that better Christians should become better and more efficient farmers. The JAC was out to rechristianize the countryside by playing on countryfolk's interests and by insisting on what would improve the lives of working peasants: agricultural training, professional and technical progress. And just like sports clubs, young farmers' associations produced a new point of view. Paternalist hierarchies based on social position and on age were going to give way to meritocracy based upon effort and achievement. "The peasant world needs leaders who are peasants," declared *Le Rayon*, the JAC monthly of the Loire Inférieure, in November 1933. The JAC alone "can give the peasantry the leaders that it waits for." That was what it would do, laying down the groundwork for sea changes to come when the young of the 1930s had time to grow to manhood. In Burgundy by the 1970s the mayors and assistant mayors who came from the ranks of young rural Catholic activists were two or three times as numerous in church attendance as other villagers who showed up for Easter observance once a year.[25]

Women and the young were perceived as important, not for pragmatic ends only but for spiritual reasons, too. Social transformation, spiritual progress, religious reconquest, all went hand in hand. And the Church advanced on all fronts. Thus in the Nièvre, studied by Guy Thuillier, the Ligue Patriotique des Femmes Françaises counted 11,500 *ligueuses* in 1932, the Ligue Féminine d'Action Catholique 17,000, who worked in 216 parishes of the department's 300 communes. In Nevers itself in 1930, besides a host of religious orders like the Sisters of the Holy Family, the Sisters of the Assumption, the Little Sisters of the Poor, and the nuns of Saint Gildard, 150 *dames de la charité* aided "the hidden poor," 1,600 patriot ladies functioned as an informal labor exchange, finding jobs for the men and homework for the women, scores of Noëllistes visited sick and old, provided layettes for expectant mothers, helped washerwomen and domestic servants in sickness or in need. In an age when private charity and private patronage continued to play an important role, these beneficent ladies, guided by priests, by nuns, by local activists, constituted a prominent part of the social landscape, yet one that is stubbornly ignored because statistically invisible.[26]

More visible than the charitable, and easier to recognize at a glance, were the boy scouts, another recently founded organization. Inspired by the movement that Robert Baden-Powell had invented in Britain, the Eclaireurs de France and the Eclaireurs Unionistes had been set up in 1911, only a few years after the first Scouts in Britain had appeared. Since the Eclaireurs de France accepted all comers, the Church branded their neutrality as irreligion—hence necessarily close to Freemasonry. The *unionistes* were of Protestant inspiration, thus naturally indigestible for good Catholic families. The Church's first stance on scouting was therefore to dismiss it as Protestant or anticlerical, infantile, and un-French, a passing fad not needed by Catholic youth that sports clubs and gymnastic societies served perfectly well. Then came the war. Catholic lads who had lived and scouted abroad came home and pressed for something that Catholic youths could join. The first scout patrol—the Entraîneurs Catholiques de France—appeared in 1916; the Fédération des Scouts de France followed in 1920.

Fastidious *entraîneurs*, finding British scout uniforms "too untidy" and their scarves vulgar, replaced them with a military-style uniform of reseda green color, a tie, and a hat with brim raised *à la française*, decorated with a tricolor cockade. By 1920 this extraordinary accoutrement had given way to ordinary khaki garb; by 1925 clerical reservations had been replaced by clerical interest. The Soviet Komsomols, remarked Monsignor Landrieux, bishop of Dijon, had shown the power of youth organizations. What pagans did, Christians could do better. Addressing the first congress of Catholic scouts, Monsignor Landrieux exhorted them to become the leaders of the working masses. Leaders or not, by 1929 the federation counted twenty-five thousand active members who enjoyed the sort of camaraderie and informality rarely to be found in bourgeois families of the day: bare legs, bare arms, open shirts, an "American" hat, camping and tramping through forest and fields, exercise taken in the form of games, and a youthful hierarchy of their own.[27]

Girl guides too were cherished for the possibilities of social infiltration that they offered. At Lyons in the 1930s one Jesuit led a troop from the immigrant quarter of Monplaisir that was made up mostly of Armenians, Poles, and other foreigners on whom locals tended to look down. At Nevers, meanwhile, a woman social assistant who launched both scout and guide troops found that the ceremony of raising the flag and saluting it brought charges of fascism. Patriotic display in 1936 aligned one with one political camp against the other. But social and political friction did not intimidate enthusiasts: That year Catholic scouts counted fifty-five thousand members. A hundred thousand Catholics had passed through the Scouts' ranks since 1920, and best of all, scouting had become "a hothouse of priestly and religious vocations."[28]

More broadly, though, Catholic scouts reflected rather faithfully the mentality and aspirations of the Catholic hierarchy and of a significant portion of its flock. Scouting too was a lay apostolate to be pursued in office, workshop, school, street, or countryside. Opposed to the modern world and to its degenerative forces, *les scouts de France* placed themselves under the patronage of Saint Louis and of Charles Péguy, both hopeless anachronists who sought their ideal future in the past. Scout troops adopted the names of knights and heroes: Bayard and du Guesclin; Georges Guynemer, the legendary flier; Hubert Lyautey, the no less legendary colonial pioneer. Older *routiers* (Rover Scouts) ranged across France on foot, praying, singing, camping, rediscovering the "real and profound" nature of their country. On the road and round the campfire, they learned civics and chivalry, elitism and respect for leadership. Led by army officers, polytechnicians, and notables or their offspring, scouts and *routiers* represented a reaction against secularism, democracy, urbanism, machinism, and mass society with its facilities and fads. No wonder that Philippe Laneyrie, who has studied them with patience and sympathy, describes them in the 1930s as "a bourgeois movement of military-feudal aspect."[*29]

No wonder, either, that scouts and ex-scouts should in due course provide many of Vichy's youth leaders. Georges Lamirand, Pétain's durable secretary for youth from 1940 to 1943, came from Social Catholic activism, and his first team drew heavily on Catholic syndicalists, JOCists, and scouts. General de la Porte du Theil, who created the Chantiers de la Jeunesse, had become a scoutmaster in 1928, when he was a lieutenant colonel, and had gone on to head all scouts of the Paris region. When placed in charge of the disoriented draftee class of 1940, he let his scouting experience inspire him. Henri Dhavernas, the engineer who was first to head

---

*Yet curiously, the values of scouts and rovers reflected those that Republican educators steadfastly preached before 1914: cleanliness next to godliness, manliness and manly bearing, simplicity, straightforwardness, moral vigor, naturalness and natural demeanor, friendship, loyalty, independence, respect. Ostentation, affectation, self-indulgence were rejected. Self-discipline and group loyalty replaced authoritarian rule; learning by play and by example of one's fellows replaced uniformities and restraints imposed from above. Democracy was meritocratic elitism in action—*la carrière ouverte aux talents*. It seems that Republican values had been internalized more widely (and more thoroughly) than suspected.

Vichy's other major youth service, the Compagnons de France, was also a scout leader, and it has been remarked that despite, or perhaps because of, German hostility to the scouts, the *style scout* was very much in vogue during those days. Nor should this seem surprising. Religion and patriotism apart (but how can one ignore them?), scouting offered everything to attract the more idealistic Vichy militants: cult of the leader, uniforms, ceremonial, healthy activity in the open air, internalized discipline, manly virtues, team spirit, a sense of service, adventure and community, rejection of rival ideologies—capitalist, Fascist or anti-Semitic—woodcraft, campfires, and singing (several Compagnons de la Chanson graduated from the Compagnons de France!). Chroniclers of Vichy in its first idealistic incarnation have commented on the role played by officers and on the militarization of the youth they led. After a second look, one wonders whether it was not rather a scoutization of the military that occurred. It would not have been a bad kind of training, after all.[30]

Not unconnected with scoutism and with the vogue for open-air activities were youth hostels, where Catholics were among the pioneers. In 1929, twenty-two years after youth hostels had appeared in Germany, Marc Sagnier, veteran left-wing Catholic and pacifist, set up the first French hostel, to be replicated only in 1933 by the Secular Youth Hostel Center supported by teachers and trade unions. In Church as in secular hostels the mixture of sexes, the girls wearing shorts appeared revolutionary and provocative. Traditional Catholics, indeed most of the French, were shocked by the nudity and promiscuity of the hiking young. Some peasants refused to sell milk to girls who displayed their knees. Hikers and cyclists approaching villages would stop so the girls could pull skirts over the shorts they wore. But young people never looked back.[31]

The youth activities that the Church promoted warranted the publication of original guides like the hefty *Nos jeunes* (1930), which outlined the organization of youth clubs, of discussions, of games and theatricals, of film shows (it was vitally important, warned the *Semaine religieuse* of Bourges, not to underrate the importance of movies), holiday camps, study circles, scout troops, parish bulletins. . . . In 1900 the good works that the diocesan bulletin of Nevers had featured ran a narrow gamut between propagation of the faith and support of poorer churches. By 1936, besides expectable prayer groups and spiritual development, it featured the activities of the ACJF, JOC, JAC, JEC, and JIC (Jeunes de l'Industrie et du Commerce—essentially shop assistants), holiday camps, school supporters, young Catholic women, women shop assistants. Equally revealing, the schoolteachers' union and the left-wing monthly *Ecole libératrice* had begun inweighing against what they described as the deadly activities of the lay-teaching *Davidées* in elementary schools,* against JEC propaganda in secondary schools, against JAC and JOC missionary work among peasants and industrial labor, against Social Catholicism—church clubs, sports clubs, popular libraries, the lot.[32]

Denunciations of this "immense conspiracy . . . the political traffic of religious prejudices—unbearable, insolent and violently anti-Marxist and anti-Soviet—"testified that Catholics did not remain inactive. That was just as well from their point of view since the religious wars were flaring up again and would go on flaring. As André Siegfried wrote in 1930, no man of the Left believed that the Church could honestly work with the Republic. Few men of the Church, for that matter, believed that the Republic or republicans would ever honestly work with Romanism. Incidents between ministers and anticlerical local authorities reenacted those of more embattled days a quarter of a century earlier. All over Brittany in the early thirties manifestations and countermanifestations inspired by the performance of anticlerical plays created "a climate of ideological war" from Landerneau and Quimper to Rennes. In 1935 at Keryado (Morbihan) the mayor prohibited the saint's day procession, the age-old *Pardon* that had been authorized by the courts. In Franche-Comté in 1938 the rise of anticlerical vandalism worried the archbishop: calvaries broken, statues mutilated or thrown into the river, holy vessels profaned.[33]

Radicals had reopened hostilities in the mid-twenties, but Catholics were prepared to match them in prejudice and combativity. The men who guided French dioceses and a good many parish priests had started out at the turn of the century, when conflict between Church and State had been most intense. The bishop of Angers, Monsignor Rumeau, ruled his diocese

---

*After reading and rereading René Bazin's novel *Davidée Birot* (1909), the story of a lay schoolteacher whose conscience calls for a faith that fits her personality and needs, Mlle. Marie Silve converted to Catholicism and founded the Association of Christian Laywomen Schoolteachers: les Davidées. In 1916 it began to publish a monthly bulletin. By 1930 Marie Guillot, "Les Davidées," *Révolution prolétarienne*, (December 5, 1930), 327, estimated its numbers at eight thousand.

That year, addressing the congress of the Ligue de l'Enseignement, the militantly anticlerical Marceau-Pivert accused the Davidées of being "innocent dreamers enrolled in an army of murderers and fanatics" and a threat to secular state schools. To defend them, a twenty-five-year-old doctoral student, Emmanuel Mounier, would publish his first polemical article, "Une amitié spirituelle: Les Davidées," *La Vie spirituelle* (April 1931), and begin to plan what, in 1932, became his life's work, the magazine *Esprit*.

from 1898 to 1940. The archbishop of Auch, who resigned in 1934, had been in office since 1907. Stubborn friend of the Action Française, the archbishop of Rouen, Monsignor du Bois de la Villerabel, was seventy-two years old when Rome deposed him in 1936. There were many like them whose words and policies reflected their age, or their mental age. At Nantes, the bishop, Le Fer de la Motte, who also remained a devotee of the Action Française after its condemnation in 1926, protected the parish priests who refused to accept Rome's verdict, kept Nantes between 1925 and 1935 in something like civil war between clericals and secularists: meetings and countermeetings, processions and counterdemonstrations.[34]

For the faithful, indulgence was not unheard of: Chocolate could be eaten in Lent; duck—waterfowl assimilated to fish—could be eaten on Fridays. But tolerance had its limits. The 1920s had resounded with ecclesiastical condemnation of lascivious dances—tango, fox-trot, Charleston—which were not only sinful but likely to keep wanton wenches from marriage and childbearing. By the 1930s bishops had more serious matters on the mind. In 1933 the bishop of Nice grappled with the poisonous scandal of *nudism*—meaning scanty bathing suits whose wearers would soon be deprived of sacraments and religious burial. Equally up-to-date, in 1932, the seventy-five-year-old bishop of Quimper, Monsignor Yves-Marie Duparc, had attacked the "abominable disorder" of public transport where persons of different sex sat far too close. He also, more ominously for the young, censored ballroom dancing, prohibiting the faithful of the Finistère from dancing after dark or in other than open spaces. Parish priests threatened those who owned or managed ballrooms with excommunication.[35]

The unbaptized would never find a husband: "We have enough animals in our stables, we do not need any in our homes." On an everyday level, priests and religious publications reminded the faithful that "purchase is a social act." Catholics should not take their money to those who were foes of the Church, not even, if possible, to individuals and enterprises who stinted their support for the Church. Catholic consciences were committed to patronizing Catholic tradesmen and to employing workers who voted the right way, or whose husbands did.[36]

Lord Acton, a son of the Church himself, once described Catholics as people who believed facts to be matters of opinion and opinions to be facts. One opinion French Catholics always regarded as a fact was the devilishness of Freemasonry and the tight hold on the country that Masons had established. Masonic anticlericalism ran the gamut from civil burials to the tune of songs like "Frou-Frou" and "La Madelon" to Holy Friday banquets that cocked snooks at Lent (at Limoges such annual banquets came to an end only in 1972) to godless educational policies and other similar horrors. Episcopal denunciations of "the Masonic Mafia" attributed the shootings of February 6 to a Masonic plot, the murder of Louis Barthou to godless schools and pagan teachers, and warned that once religion had been stifled by its foes, private enterprise and private property would be next.[37]

Anticlericals gave as good as they got, and the Left's revulsion against "reaction and fascism" after February 6 contributed to reviving anticlericalism, too. As at Miramont (Lot-et-Garonne), where *Le Réveil miramontais* described itself on its masthead as "an anti-Fascist publication of lay defense," many local anticlerical organizations altered their appellation. All over the country *comités de défense laïque* became *comités de défense antifasciste*. Inevitably they brought their militant secularism along; new antifascism was old anticlericalism writ large. Catholics meanwhile, campaigning against pornography, for example, found themselves working hand in hand with leagues like the Jeunesses Patriotes or the Croix de Feu, which were glad to participate in defense of the moral order.[38]

As the elections of 1936 approached, most of the hierarchy tried to keep from overtly taking sides, but its electoral directives placed it where everyone expected. Catholicism *was* the Right at prayer. Consistent in condemnation of Communists, Socialists, and godless Radicals, the Church had to oppose the Popular Front. The future looked menacingly dark, the hours tolled the knell of what little liberty was left, the bishop of Nevers, Monsignor Patrice Flynn (born in 1874), told his flock. Popular Front success would place religious liberties in peril, destroy families and savings, abolish social order. Choosing a good candidate, or one that was least bad, was crucial, warned *L'Union catholique*, monthly bulletin of parish committees. Voting could not be conscientiously avoided; abstention, if not a sin, would count at least as a misdemeanor. Despite such efforts, the results of the first ballot looked bad: "Dark Sunday!" titled *La Croix Angévine*. Just before the second ballot *La Croix* wondered aloud what monster universal suffrage "drunk, doped," would bring forth: "It is all about you . . . your children: your little house: the little garden you dreamed of leaving them: Bolshevism threatens everybody."[39]

When it was clear that the country had "handed itself over to revolutionary parties," the Church circled the wagons. June, fortunately, offered great feasts—Corpus Christi on the fourteenth, the Sacred Heart on the nineteenth—where Catholics could show the flag or, at least, the banner. A common front of prayer faced a common front of Satan—Freemasonry and Communism combined. One faith was mobilized against another, and not for the first time. In isolated communities of the Perche, in Eure-et-Loire, where Saint Marcou, who heals the scrofula, is specially invoked on May 1, some pilgrimages to his shrine seem to have been initiated around that time. At Frazé in 1930, at Soize a few years later.[40] Would priests have sponsored them to counter the Reds' Labor Day?

Now, in beleaguered 1936, at Paray-le-Monial in Saône-et-Loire, "a vast movement of prayer and supplication to the Holy Heart of Jesus" was set afoot that would be taken up as far as Brittany and the north. Waning semireligious practices and local traditions could also be revived to reinforce the faith, like the *Feux de la Saint-Jean,* pagan fires lit on Midsummer Eve that the Church had long discouraged and now encouraged instead. In the dioceses of Quimper and Saint-Brieuc, bishops ordered Breton to be taught in Catholic schools, along with the history and geography of Brittany. And everywhere news of the Spanish Civil War contributed apocalyptic visions: massacres of clergy and of the faithful, "new martyrs." By fall 1936 a pastoral letter signed by five French cardinals made it official: Internal troubles, economic crisis, the specter of war to come, anguish and general disarray—France lived grievous moments.[41]

Fortunately, French battles could still be waged with voting bulletins. In February 1937 the listening public would vote to elect representatives to management councils that controlled the programs of state radio stations. France counted some 4,200,000 radio sets declared and paying state tax, besides a great many others neither declared nor paying. Voting would be by mail ballot restricted to those who had paid their fees and who bothered to register in time for polling. The system was denounced for being based on a monetary franchise and for excluding those many, especially working people, whom it left without a vote. Yet coming nine months after the general elections, the poll was nevertheless recognized as "a third ballot," and the opposing camps took it seriously. Radio Liberté stood for the Popular Front, but especially for the Communist party, some of whose leading figures ran under its label. The radio elections, argued *L'Humanité* (December 28, 1936), should be the occasion for inflicting yet one more defeat on the forces of reaction. In fact, they were about the Left's hope that control of the airwaves might counterbalance the Right's dominance of the printed press. That was not to be. Radio Famille accused Radio Liberté of politicizing radio (as who wouldn't?), and it opposed its own allegedly "national" standards to the Left's allegedly "political" ones.[42]

Radio Famille represented a coalition of the Right that the Socialist *Populaire* denounced as "Fascist and conservative." *Le Populaire* was not far wrong: *Gringoire* and *Je Suis Partout* supported Radio Famille, as did the Action Française and La Rocque's PSF. But the core of the drive was the Catholic Church. *"Organisez! Organisez!"* clamored the diocesan bulletins. And organize they did, successfully.[43] In February 1937 Radio Famille candidates were elected in the majority everywhere except at Toulouse. Half the registered listeners had abstained, and there is reason to believe that even on the Right, voters cared more for quality of entertainment than for morality or political orientation. But all sides had agreed that the voting was for or against the Popular Front. The identification of Catholics and the Right had been reaffirmed, yet there were those who denied it.

My old teacher, the Cambridge historian Denis Brogan, liked to cite the signboard of a small town café as symbolic of the Third Republic: AUX ANCIENS ROMAINS ET AUX JEUNES CYCLISTES. In the 1930s, as in earlier years, the country was split between young wheelmen representing change and ancient Romans who stood for an older order. So was the Church. In winter 1936 the Dominican *Vie intellectuelle* had published a special number entitled "Is God on the Right?," then had gone on to argue that he was not. "Do not believe the deliberate confusion of Catholic principle and right-wing ideology," pleaded the progressive review; "do not enclose the Church within the barbed wire confines of a political party."[44] Elections had furnished the answer to the Dominicans' question and to their pleas: Progressive Catholics had run as Christian Democrats, and they had lost. Spectacularly, Georges Bidault, editorialist of the Christian Democratic *Aube*, had been badly beaten at Domfront (Orne) by a great-grandson of Beaumarchais strongly supported by the local clergy; Francisque Gay, founder and director of *L'Aube*, had suffered an even more humiliating defeat in the Chouan country of Cholet (Maine-et-Loire).

Although Christian Democrats were not on the Right, their position in the spectrum of political opinions was not necessarily on the Left. Most Catholic deputies between the wars divided between Right and center groups of a variety of shadings. Some were for the Action Française, and some against it; some were keen on siding with the workers, some even sympathized with the Socialists. Most of the men loosely described as Christian Democrats joined the Popular Democratic party (PDP), which was hardly democratic, and not popular either, except in a few constituencies. Yet they presented themselves as Social Catholics, and their favorite slogan—"Neither Right nor Left but Forward!"—suggested an alternative to Catholic conservatism. Partisan of organic togetherness, the PDP was anti-individualistic, hierarchic, social, and corporatist.

One of its members once remarked that the only good parts of the program of La Rocque's Parti Social Français were those that had been copied from the PDP—and one can see why. But one can also see why paler copies of more forceful movements would not do too well. The PDP included in its narrow confines men like the deputy mayor of Sarrebourg, Emile Peter, who after 1936 moved to La Rocque's PSF, and the Béarnais Auguste Champetier de Ribes, who voted against Pétain in 1940 and spent his early sixties as a leader of the Resistance in his region. Spread-eagled between conflicting versions of Catholic (or patriotic) politics, the party elected sixteen deputies in 1932, eleven in 1936: hardly an encouraging showing. Most of its representatives were comfortable in the center and did not much like the Popular Front. There was little chance of their rocking the ideological boat of the Right.[45]

The real rocking started in 1931, after the encyclical *Quadragesimo anno.* The Church henceforth tolerated, sometimes even encouraged more militantly democratic activists, and this meant that Catholic progressives were heard from more often. Sympathetic to the Left, to peace, to international understanding, to social reform; opposed to warmongering nationalism, which they denounced as neopagan, opposed to royalists who when they ran down the republic also ran down France, a wing of the Dominican order made clear that wherever God might stand, his children were not all found on the Right.[46] So did secular priests like the abbé Louis Rémilleux in Lyons, who, as early as 1931, organized a parish committee to fight unemployment. Within two years Rémilleux and his friends managed to find stable jobs for 432 men, helped 5,171 others with 36,107 days' employment, served 7,032 free meals. More eminent ecclesiastic figures made the same point. Particularly interested in social questions, the archbishop of Paris, Cardinal Verdier, launched a church-building program to fight joblessness. In 1932 he offered a first loan at 5 percent to build sixty new churches and chapels in the Paris region and quickly raised thirty million francs. In 1935 a further seventy million francs to the same end were covered in half a day. By 1939, 110 churches and chapels had been built in the Paris suburbs, providing work to thousands of unemployed. Achille Liénart, bishop of Lille, cardinal in 1930 when he was forty-six, was another social-minded prince of the Church, sympathetic to labor, famous for helping the families of local strikers when in need and for encouraging Catholic unions. In 1936, after Salengro's suicide, he had not hesitated to condemn the criminally defaming press. Before and after that he defended his JOC against attacks from Castelnau's reactionary Catholic Front. Red for the Right, for the Social Catholics he was the workers' bishop. Neither he nor Verdier was a man of the Left; quite the contrary, but that was not evident at once.[47]

Much more deliberately controversial would be the forerunners of what after the Second War became the Popular Republican Movement (MRP). In 1932 Francisque Gay, who had been a member of Marc Sagnier's Sillon, founded *Aube*, a daily that attracted some twelve thousand subscribers and in which wrote little-known young men like Hubert Beuve-Méry, future editor of *Le Monde*, and Georges Bidault, future prime minister of the Fourth Republic. The spirit of Francisque Gay had a great future, but in the 1930s that was all it had. In spring 1935, when Gay launched an appeal for Christians to come together, he circulated it privately to three hundred persons only, for fear of the reactions that a public airing might set off.[48]

Another periodical born in 1932, the monthly *Esprit*, would leave a strong mark on Catholics and on intellectuals generally. Its founder, Emmanuel Mounier, was only twenty-seven at the time, a member of that self-assertive nonconformist generation that we have met before, reacting against what he and they denounced as the spiritual and political apathy of their time. Aggrieved by "the paganization of the immense Catholic herd," Mounier hoped to show Christians and non-Christians a less caricatural image of what Christianity was about: heroes, sacrifice, honor, comradeship. Not necessarily democracy, though, or people-worship: "[M]asses do not make history, minorities of believers forge values that act on the masses." Mounier stemmed from the antiliberal and anticapitalist tradition of social Catholicism, and he condemned the dissolute individualistic world born of the Renaissance, the Reformation, and the Revolution, seeking a third way between individualism and Marxism. As practiced by Christian Democrats, Christian Democracy was not it. Mounier found the PDP too moderate, lukewarm, flabby, and its trust in a liberal and parliamentary republic that he thought out of date, naive. What he proposed and what *Esprit* expounded was a pre-Existentialist philosophy he called Personalism. Basically, Personalism affirmed a person's sense of responsibility, of being free to choose and act, whatever trammels the universe opposed to his subjective freedom. Personalism was Christian but nondenominational, left-wing but moralistic, antimaterialist but interested in economics: "The Revolution will be economic or it will not be. The Revolution will be moral or it will not be." For the disillusioned Marxist Georges Lefebvre, writing in 1935, *Esprit* was the best of French publications. Yet disillusioned Marxists and illusioned Catholics did not create a tide. Even more than *Aube*, *Esprit* (with fifteen hundred subscribers in 1936) was destined to remain semiconfidential for another decade.[49]

What made Social Catholics important to the Church was that while right-wing Catholics were committed to the Right first, and conservative Catholics were Conservative, Social Catholics were specifically Catholic in inspiration and in references: Youth movements, peasants', workers', and women's movements were Christian initiatives about Christian activities in the world of men. Among the most important of these initiatives was the Federation of Christian Trade Unions (CFTC), founded in 1919 and boasting some 150,000 members by 1936. From 1919 on, in Catholic areas like the black country of the north, Communists and the Communist trade union (CGTU) on one side faced Christian militants and CFTC on the other side. Rival world views were incorporated and mirrored in a network of associations. At Halluin (Nord), the former held the town hall and ran its activities from the Maison du Peuple—mutual assistance societies, *Fraternelle* insurance, symphony orchestra, *Sport ouvrier*—while the House of Free Unions housed the CFTC, Catholic mutual aid and insurance societies, cooperatives, and study groups. Even though Halluin's president of the Enfants de Marie belonged to the Communist party, competition and suspicion were strong, rapprochements rare.[50] In 1935 and 1936, in working-class communities like Clamart, to the west of Paris, the "open hand" that Communists offered to Catholics mobilized a dozen Catholic organizations and the priests of the three local parishes within the Communist Municipal Council's committee to aid the unemployed. That sort of sporadic cooperation did not prevent the large lay unions, CGT and CGTU, from coming together in June 1936 to exclude the Catholic CFTC from the Matignon negotiations, as they would try to exclude it from union shops thereafter. Neither would it prevent the CFTC from soaring from 150,000 to 400,000 members in the year after Matignon, thanks largely to members of the JOC, who joined it in large numbers.[51]

Willy-nilly, Catholics, when not self-propelled toward the Right, were driven there by the entrenched hostility of the Left. Most, though, needed no driving. In May 1935 the reactionary Jean Chiappe ran for election to the Paris Municipal Council from the very Catholic bourgeois neighborhood of Notre-Dame des Champs. The National Front, the Right, the Church supported him; *Aube* and *Esprit* opposed him. A Catholic friend of Mounier and of Gay ran against the ex-prefect. It was no fight at all: Chiappe won by ten votes to one. That prestigious prelate Monsignor Baudrillart, once head of the Catholic Institute and now a cardinal, made clear that any rapprochement with the Left was suspect. "As for me," he told Francisque Gay, "I vote for Fouché"—Napoleon's unprincipled minister of police of whom Chiappe was a reincarnation.[52]

For Baudrillart, as for General de Castelnau, who led the most militant of Catholic organizations, the Popular Front was sheer bolshevism and the progressive Catholics of *Aube, Esprit,* or the Dominican *Sept* were tarred with the Bolshy brush. Pope Pius XI had taken a personal interest in *Sept*'s publication when it first appeared in 1934. François Mauriac, Gabriel Marcel, Jacques Maritain, Paul Claudel wrote for *Sept,* but that was not enough to protect it, or perhaps too much. Castelnau's Catholic National League particularly disliked pink priests who flirted with subversive notions, like the social teachings of the Church, or pacifism. When in March 1935 *Sept* criticized the idea of a two-year term of military service, too long and too aggressive for its taste, Castelnau in *L'Echo de Paris* attacked those pacifists whose naïveté condemned France to "being slaughtered in the name of the Holy Father." Taking up the cudgels in *Esprit,* Emmanuel Mounier had answered the hero who lost his offspring in the war: "General, three sons, isn't that enough?" What *L'Echo* denounced as an "abominable apostrophe" was worse for the high regard in which Castelnau was held, some people even talking of his beatification. Instead of halos, though, the old general was vouchsafed revenge.[53] Quick action in June 1936 saved *Sept* from papal condemnation for trying to be evenhanded between the Left and Right. It would succumb after another year of official hostility, even while its sales had continued to grow.

An honest belief that progressives were Communist moles made traditionalist Catholics attack them whenever the opportunity arose. Thus, when, in spring 1936, shortly before that year's elections, a young professor of letters at the Catholic University of Lille, Pierre-Henri Simon, brought out a book, *Catholics, Politics and Money,* suggesting that Catholics might vote against rabid fellow Catholics, he got into serious trouble. Faced with a choice between a clerical nationalist and a secular personality that was neutral on religion, between Philippe Henriot, for example, and Gaston Bergery, Simon declared that he, as a Catholic, would vote for the latter because he was less destructive. Writing for the Catholic National League, Castelnau swiftly attacked Simon's "divisive activities" and called for his punishment. Villain for some, hero to others, Simon got away with the scare. The hierarchy was more measured than its militant minions; Simon's superior, Cardinal Liénart, protected the professor's right to speak—even write—his mind. But the Catholic Left was clearly marginalized and hardly encouraged to express itself.[54]

Those who were free to express themselves were foes of communism, that "essentially perverse doctrine with which no conciliation was possible," as the *Semaine religieuse* of Besançon pointed out (January 27, 1938). Foes also of other "incarnations of evil": Masons, of course; teachers in godless schools ("poison of the countryside" a priest would call them in 1932); sometimes even Jews, those frequent incarnations of malice. As *La Croix* pointed out in September 1936, Spain's calvary could be attributed to Jews sent from Moscow to teach Reds how to kill priests, monks, and nuns. After the Pope's condemnation of "exaggerated nationalism" and of racism in 1938, the Catholic press began to denounce Nazi persecutions, even to remind its readers that after the Jews it might be the turn of Catholics. But that did not discourage normal activities. On Maundy Thursday and Good Friday, Holy Week offices continued to remind the faithful about the unregenerate nature of the Jews; the grim invocation Pro perfidis Judaeis continued to strike home; fraternities continued to be founded that were designed to pray for the conversion of Jews to the true faith. And there was general relief when the Action Française, condemned by Rome in 1926, was rehabilitated in 1939.[55]

What this comes down to is that whatever the progressivism of some Catholics, the popular mind continued to associate the Church and the Right. That the popular view was roughly correct may be seen in the close relations the Church was to maintain with the Vichy regime. Mainstream Catholicism, of course, was fiercely patriotic. Its attitude to Gemany varied only in the intensity of its suspicions. At Munich time the bishops urged firm hearts and civic duty, then recommended prayer. But the fact that first Daladier, then Paul Reynaud included a leader of the PDP in their cabinets—Champetier de Ribes, senator of the Basses-Pyrénées—illustrated the drift away from religious war and back to national union. As 1938 ended, the archbishop of Besançon thanked God for deliverance from the double peril of foreign war and internal revolution but wisely continued orisons for the maintenance of peace. By then peace could do with any help it could muster. The bishop of Nevers looked ahead: If the French knew what defeat would mean, they would stop devouring each other and try to unite. But "could they unite?" asked the *Semaine religieuse* of Nevers in April 1940, and answered that union was not easy. The war against Germany had not put an end to religious friction any more than it had to political divisions, of which, in any case, they were an integral part. Diocesan bulletins through 1939 and 1940 continued to reflect local griefs and national dissensions.[56]

Then came defeat—not quite, as Maurras put it, a divine surprise, but, as in 1871, explained as providential. "France's calamities," opined the rector of Questembert, "provided a providential occasion to reforge Christendom" where it had gone to pot. Conveniently for the soldiers who now ran the show, priests everywhere clamored that the war had been lost by godless schoolteachers, or else by the stupidity of universal suffrage, or else by failures in Church discipline. A major cause of the country's punishment, Canon Chaplain of Lambézellec informed the diocesan school inspector, was the profanation of Sunday. Chastisement was well deserved. Resanctify the Lord's Day, and all would change for the better. French sins justified divine punishment, wrote Monsignor Saliège, archbishop of Toulouse, who would become a cardinal at the Liberation for his Resistance activities. Given how the victory of 1918 had been wasted, what would the French have done had they been granted victory in 1940? Better penitence. The annual pilgrimage of Rocamadour at the end of June would in 1940 be "penitential": dedicated to accepting the country's harsh ordeal "in a spirit of reparation."[57]

The progressive Cardinal Liénart became an ardent supporter of Philippe Pétain, perhaps because of the subsidies that Vichy now provided to Catholic schools. So did Alfred Cardinal Baudrillart, who shortly before had found in Hitler "our only sheet anchor against Bolsheviks and Communists." Most of the episcopate took similar positions, declaring their "veneration" for Pétain and calling on the faithful to support his endeavors. They were hardly exceptional. Most of the French supported Pétain, at first with hope and then with resignation. Why should their Church be different?[58]

The intra-Catholic war meanwhile continued. *Aube* and *Esprit* were prohibited; Mounier, who wanted to "arm French souls against Nazi contamination," was imprisoned. Traditional Catholics continued to denounce progressive heretics like him, his friends, and those of *Aube*. Christian Democracy, resistant to reaction, bred resistants to the order that reaction introduced: Edmond Michelet in Corrèze, Charles d'Aragon in the Tarn, Maurice Byé and Etienne Borne in the Haute Garonne, and those still better known, like Maurice Schumann and Georges Bidault. Some of the most visible collaborators—Henriot, Brasillach, Darnand—were also visible Catholics. Numerous members of Darnand's militia died crying, "Long Live Christ the King," at their execution. But Catholics who fought Vichy and the Germans were even more visible; 216 priests were killed or executed, 118 members of the Catholic student association, too. The role they and their fellows played in the Resistance defused what hostility to the Church there was. As one Catholic wrote to the bishop of Marseilles, without their courage to disobey their pastors and follow their consciences "neither you nor most of your fellow bishops would sit in your seats today."[59]

"It's a real bother, said God. When the French won't be around any more, there are things that I do, there won't be anyone to understand them." But Charles Péguy, who wrote these words, never thought, though well he might have done, that the French, who understood so well the things God did, fathomed them in a variety of ways. Catholics did not agree among themselves, sometimes within themselves. Would Péguy, the Christian patriot, have been in London with de Gaulle or in Vichy with Pétain? Both claimed him for their own, as they claimed God. And God could have been on the Right with either.

As it was, the Catholic MRP won a quarter of the votes cast in 1945; with 28 percent of the votes cast in the elections of 1946 it became the foremost party of the Fourth Republic. But not for long. What the *Canard enchaîné* called the *Mouvement des Révérends Pères* withered. Young cyclists and ancient Romans frequented the same café but drank at different tables. A Catholic party had no future, Left or Right.

VIII

Cultures

Never, when life itself wastes away, has there
been more talk of culture and civilization.

—*Antonin Artaud*

I*N JUNE* 1932, when Edouard Herriot, a devotee of educational reform, set up the first cabinet of Lebrun's presidency, what had since 1801 been called the Ministry of Public Instruction was given a new name: Ministry of National Education. The politics of education often consist of flogging a dead horse, and so they do in France, except that there dead horses have a way of remaining very much alive. Educational reform had caused much intellectual debate in the 1920s; educational issues—not least the clash of godless and godful schools, though largely unresolved—refused to go away. Public and private, lay and secular institutions had long competed with one another and for the attention of political parties. After the war new questions arose that turned about the further democratization of elementary schooling and the greater accessibility of secondary education. But costly plans for longer compulsory school attendance had been set aside. And socially subversive plans for secondary access based on merit rather than on parents' ability to pay fees had been beaten back. The ministry's new label mirrored the postponed aspirations of reformers but also the national tendency to treat words as acts. The country, Herriot thought, was ready to move past the modest reach of mere *instruction* to the higher aims of *education* that not only forms and trains but brings out and develops latent possibilities. Careers once limited to the talents of a select few would now be opened to the popular many.

Whatever Herriot's hopes and those of his education minister, Anatole de Monzie, little was achieved. Democratizing education was pregnant with implications that raised the hackles of cultural and social elitists, of Catholics, and, if the truth be known, of primary school teachers, who feared their *déclassement*. The pedagogic ideal of one single school—not primary and secondary systems separate in standards and expectations—encouraging talented children to the limit of their abilities had become a political hobbyhorse of the Left. The Right, unimpressed by democratic claims for the *école unique*, denounced the same old eagerness to monopolize education, eliminate not only obstacles to the advancement of the meritorious but rivals for the opportunity to mold their minds. Where the Left clamored for greater freedom, the Right warned against didactic dictatorship. Monzie argued hard that the same educational structure for all did not mean the same education, that monopoly need not rule, or quantity, but quality: selection, orientation, diversification. His proved to be fine plans, condemned to remain just that.

Within months, in any case, Herriot's cabinet went the way of others. And while Monzie retained his office till 1934, his first priority proved to be managing budget cuts. In that context, arguing from economy, he introduced coeducation in primary schools—a move revolting to his Catholic friends—and reaffirmed the abolition of tuition fees in public high schools. His plans for prolonging schooling by a year, from thirteen to fourteen, were to be realized in 1936 by Jean Zay, the Socialist, who took Marcel Abraham, Monzie's *chef de cabinet*, to head his own team.

Prolonging compulsory school attendance was one way of absorbing the potentially unemployed. Abolishing tuition in the secondary was more debatable; a democratic measure, it offered dangerous competition to Catholic colleges by making public high schools more attractive because free. Tuition-free secondary education did not recruit many more offspring of peasants or of workers, but it did facilitate access to scions of modest social groups: employees, artisans, lower civil servants. As opportunities for gainful employment shrank, attendance in public lycées rose impressively: 86,000 boys and 33,000 girls in 1931; 140,000 and 60,000 respectively in 1939. The intake of private schools also rose, but more slowly: from 97,000 in 1931 to 103,000 in 1939. Figures vary, and so do statistics; but the tendency (and the different rates of growth) seem clear. More striking, however, than the growing numbers is the small proportion of young people attending secondary school at all: 5.6 percent of their age-group in 1931, 6.7 percent in 1936—figures to be compared with ten times as many in the 1970s or, as significantly, with the enrollment of preschool *écoles maternelles* that served greater numbers of small children than those of adolescents accommodated by lycées.[1]

Until the reforms of the Popular Front, many lycées of the Third Republic did not differ much from those of the Second Empire: The curriculum and its preponderance of Latin, Greek, and ancient history had changed little; so had the discipline, whose severity accented the war between students and ushers *(pions)* and the "atrocious ragging" of the latter by the former. Like ecclesiastics, lycée professors iterated and inculcated the values of an age gone by—the years when they had made their studies and when their studies made them. That may be why so many of their charges proceeded to revolt when opportunity offered. But just how far did revolt carry, and how deep did it go? After the Great War, the philosophy taught in lycée philosophy classes stressed the stern pessimism of Pascal, but culminated in Bergson. Henri Bergson (1859–1941) was recognized as the great foe of nineteenth-century materialism and determinism, his work the affirmation of indeterminacy and liberty, the freedom to make things new. Emphasizing initiative, energy, élan vital (the vital spirit and the vitality of the spirit), Bergson legitimated creation and innovation, including the possibility of a creative God, and that of a nature less determined, less subject to reasonable reasoning than it had been thought. Didactic philosophy, avant-garde science, school textbooks, and the inchoate yearnings of young and not-so-young people searching for beliefs coincided, and coincided further with the contemporary Catholic quest for up-to-date justifications.

As scientific thought deserted solid entities for energy, radiation, forces, pulsions (what one art critic called the poetics of discontinuity), those who looked on religion as superstition and on science as religion began to be sidelined. Like the cinema, philosophy demonstrated that time and space were separate spheres no longer. Like art, philosophy suggested that experience could plumb intuition, instinct, or the unconscious, in a kind of sensual divination. *"Credo quia absurdum,"* Saint Augustine is alleged to have declared: "I believe because it is absurd." Now, what had been absurd became believable. Matter and spirit no longer contradicted each other; religious speculation could be presented as no more outrageous than philosophical conjectures. Religion, like science, now could respectably lead to relative absolutes: After Einstein, to believe in the absurd lay at the heart of science and religion both, and Bergson had guessed at this before the science and the mood of postwar Europe had imposed it.

In 1926 Pétain's future minister of education, Jacques Chevalier, then teaching philosophy at Grenoble, capped his trilogy of masters of French thought—Descartes, Pascal—with a study of Bergson. Reedited in 1934, the twenty-second edition of Chevalier's *Bergson* appeared in 1941, as if every major national crisis called for the relics of the saint to be trotted out. In 1927 the Nobel Prize for Literature had confirmed the world stature of a figure whose major works lay far back enough to secure admittance to official textbooks. Welcoming or critical, all recognized him as ushering in a new era, one when philosophers could be as interested in religion as in other aspects of reality and experience. In 1942 still, when in a German prisoner of war camp the Catholic Jean Guitton offered a course on recent French thought, Bergson's philosophy would be presented as its culmination. "People were waiting . . . there was a need. . . . Bergson responded to this need: he reemphasized intelligence, he reemphasized spiritual values, he suggested a return to sources and recalled [the crucial role of] energy."[2] Was this Bergson presented *à la mode* of the thirties—and, clearly, of the forties? Or is it evidence that the philosophy of the schools will sooner or later mark even unwilling scholars?

There was one more thing. Passage through a lycée's narrow gates offered a ticket of admission to social and economic promotion. In a mid-thirties novel a spy among the troops would be ferreted out because he quoted Virgil when his false identity gave him a humble origin: Latin was a luxury.[3] So was what society recognized as culture. And culture had little to do with learning. In higher as in secondary education, academic success was based on memory, on learning texts and lectures by heart, on law courses that ignored the realities that laws affected, on lectures in political economy that heeded neither political nor economic life, on histories of thought where German, British, French ideas were approached separately, according to the program that happened to be taught that year, as if ideas or their carriers never talked to each other across national boundaries, as if intellectual activities took place in oases far from the living world.

This is not an abstract issue. We have all heard how badly France's rulers fared on the economic front. If we leave aside the possibility that the problems they failed to solve were insoluble, the weakness of French legislators and officials, many of them highly cultivated men, was less their ignorance of economics than ignorance of how economic problems relate to history, to institutions, to circumstances and personalities. Their ignorance had been taught. Teaching at every level stressed factual data; learning at its supposed best was rather like getting the telephone book by heart. Putting data to use would be the subject of subsequent reflection that, oftentimes, never got its turn. Despite Bergson, students were trained to think in logical sequence, not in context (which might disturb the elegance of the logic). Economists, like philosophers, were strong on principle, ignorant of process, weak on practice. Pure and applied economics did not communicate. Engineering apart, pure and applied science seldom did either. Ingenious inventions, practical innovations withered on the branch or were left to others. Context-hungry economists, historians labored in isolation. They wrote but were little read; they spoke but were little heard; their turn, as with many others, would come after the war. Meanwhile, learning was about passing competitive exams, and culture was about ornament, not practice.

University attendance was a luxury, too, the more so as university tuition doubled, and attendance fell from eighty-one thousand in the early thirties to seventy-six thousand from 1935 to 1939. Few of these undergraduates completed their degrees. In 1938 the total number of diplomas awarded in French universities, from the BA *(licence)* to the doctorate, did not reach sixty-five hundred. Yet even these pitifully small numbers stirred public concern. "We don't just suffer from material overproduction," complained *L'Echo de Clamecy* in 1935, "but from intellectual overproduction too." And it quoted the senator reporting the national education budget, the Protestant Jean Philip, "envisaging the rush to the University with anguish." Nearly seventy-two thousand students, including eleven thousand foreigners and seventeen-thousand women, "hurled themselves into it this year." What would they become? "The intellectual proletariat of today, the rebels of tomorrow."[4] Jean Philip was not so far wrong. Like the marshal's baton that Napoleon's soldiers carried in their knapsacks, rebellion lay coiled in many a schoolboy's satchel and would spring up at the first chance. Witness the youthful self-assertions of the thirties, the refusal of (their parents') bourgeois culture, the critique of (their and their friends') bourgeois families, the anti-intellectual rejection of academic intellectualism and reason that mark the 1930s even more sharply than they had marked earlier decades.

ECONOMIC AND political crisis encouraged intellectual earnestness, even occasional grimness, or else a frivolity almost equally listless, though more nihilistic. Cruel times inspired or justified them. Already before the slump, amateur futurologists had predicted the decline of print before the rising popularity of phonographs and of the cinema. *"Ceci tuera cela."* Depression confirmed these premonitions. When belts have to be tightened, cultural expenses are the first to go. Publishing, which had done well in the 1920s, was hit hard. People read less than they had done in 1930 and 1931, or at least they bought fewer books; they even borrowed fewer books from public libraries. Between 1928 and 1932 unemployment in book industries grew two and a half times; jobless days almost quadrupled. Between 1927 and 1937 production of printed matter fell by one third.[5] In 1927 the industry had suffered 28 bankruptcies; by 1933 these had risen to 146, the following year to 164. Conditions began to improve after 1937, when bankruptcies were down to 86 a year, but by that time the weaker had gone to the wall or fused with others in order to survive.

Just when the worst seemed over, Popular Front reforms hit publication hard. Labor accounts, or it accounted then, for better than two thirds of a printing shop's production costs. In 1933 a printer made 6.50 francs an hour, by 1938 almost double that. Writers were not so lucky. Some—as they had always done, but rather more shabbily—made ends meet by teaching, editing, writing for the periodical press, or selling their manuscripts to collectors in the manner of Benda, Aragon, and Bernanos. Others frequented the cheap restaurants and reading rooms—Cercle Ronsard in Montmartre, Cercle François Villon in Montparnasse—opened for them by charitable souls. If the price of books rose more slowly than wages, more slowly still than other retail prices, it was because the industry picked up the slack, and authors were first in line. Lower royalties were paid when the traffic would bear it, fewer books were published, and more of them were translations. In Germany and Britain translations accounted for about 2 percent of publishers' lists; in France for 11 percent, and the greatest publishing success of the period was a translation: Erich Maria Remarque's *All Quiet on the Western Front.*[6]

Other imports helped publishing limp back to prosperity. It was in 1930 that Paris discovered Disney's *Silly Symphonies,* born in 1929, and in them Mickey Mouse, good-natured incarnation of the American spirit. Colored, ebullient, exciting children's weeklies inspired by American models, featuring American comic strips, appeared first with the *Journal de Mickey* in 1934, then with *Robinson* in 1936. Tarzan, Buck Rogers, Flash Gordon, Dick Tracy, Popeye, and Mickey himself, of course, inhabited fantasy landscapes that were exciting and unfamiliar. They sold well. So did *Marie-Claire*, inspired by American women's magazines, and *Confidences*, inspired by *True Stories*, which would be the most widely read periodical in the bunkers of the Maginot Line. Equally popular, and equally important to the industry, mystery, and detective stories which had been around since Baudelaire translated Edgar Allan Poe, now found a popular market. The detective story came in as an English importation, the first mystery series was launched in 1927, and translations of Agatha Christie evoked the enthusiastic compliments of Jean Cocteau. After 1932 collections and periodicals devoted to detective stories abounded, not least the series in which Fayard was to launch the genre's greatest success: Georges Simenon's Inspector Maigret. Between February 1931 and July 1932 Maigret would feature in one title every month—a tribute to his creator's facility and to the public's favor. There would be 102 Maigrets published between 1930 and 1972, and Simenon became another Jules Verne: the most widely read author of his time.

Although they were turned out by a Belgian writer over twoscore years, the Maigret series provide a treasure trove of commonplace information about conditions and atmosphere of the 1930s in which they are firmly set. Maigret, Jules, son of the bailiff of a noble estate, born in 1887 in the central department of Allier, had hoped to become a doctor and became a policeman instead. In 1913 the young constable was transferred from his humble Paris police station to police headquarters at the quai des Orfèvres, where he would rise to head the Police Judiciaire, equivalent of London's Scotland Yard.

Inscrutable and often brooding, Maigret has married a plump, cheerful Alsatian, Louise, whose cooking goes straight to his heart. Robust and with an appetite to match, the *commissaire* is a glutton and an epicure. Wherever he goes, he samples the fare, savors it, remembers it. His adventures sketch a gastronomic geography of France, and since food and drink clearly outrank sex, his marital relations appear less amorous than dietary. Typical of many Parisians who are also provincial immigrants, the Maigrets live in a small apartment on the boulevard Richard-Lenoir, between the place de la Bastille and place de la République, but respectably closer to the latter. A petty bourgeois address, not far from popular Belleville and from the cemetery of Père Lachaise, yet within walking distance of the inspector's office on the quai. Equally typical, the couple have bought a house in the small town of Meung-sur-Loire, not far from Orléans. There, when Maigret retires, he is left to chafe at enforced leisure and to learn to play nap and other card games within the circle of regulars at the local café. Until that day the savory meals prepared for him are often left uneaten, and Louise Maigret, preoccupied with unspecified household tasks, is left to collect the picture cards that come in coffee packets, hoping to put three complete sets together and thus win a walnut bedroom suite.

However widely read, fictional evidence can never be conclusive. But the basis of the character's success was Maigret's unexceptionality, the closeness between Maigret's experiences and those of readers, who could identify their world with his. As a countryman born, Maigret begins the day with soup before he learns to take coffee for breakfast, and tucks in two more meals a day, not counting numerous snacks. But it is his thirst that is most prodigious. Like pulling on a pipe, a dram helps the creative reverie that is part of his detection method, but it advances sociability as well, offering opportunities for chats, inquiries, the gathering of a sense of place. No wonder that liquor flows through Simenon's pages: not the scotch that accompanied the author's typing, but a long list of normal *consommations,* taken while standing at a zinc-covered counter or sitting unobtrusively near by. Where Maigret passes, Sancerre, Vouvray, every kind of white wine, Calvados, Cognac, pastis, absinthe—where it is still illegally manufactured— and beer, pints and pints of beer, make up astonishing processions. The Brasserie Dauphine, down the street from his office on the quai, will send up beer and sandwiches, though he prefers to do his consuming on the spot. Failing the Brasserie, any bar will do, café, tabac, inn, tavern, nightclub, dining car, or private home where a drink is offered.

Domestic life, especially outside Paris, continues primitive. At Sancerre, in summer 1930, the inspector finds the maid on her knees polishing the floor whilst all the time the household staff runs to draw water from the courtyard well. At Saint Fiacre, north of the capital, the inn that he visits in 1932 is lit by oil lamps. Only the local château has a generator for electric current that provides "weak, hesitant light." Another inn outside Moulins a few years later has neither electricity nor gas; heating and cooking are done with wood, lighting with portable lamps or candles. In the suburbs of Paris, at Bourg-la-Reine, one character lives in a house whose electric light bulbs are set in luminaries that had just recently been used as oil lamps. Nor does he use banks or checks.

Outside the larger centers cinemas are rare. At Meung-sur-Loire in 1938 people talk about how nice it would be to get one. Telephones are seldom found in normal private homes; most cafés boast one, but not all garages. Doctors have telephones and own another rare contraption: an automobile. Local police, still getting around by bike, if not on foot, can boast few cars. Maigret himself does not own a car. He uses public transport, walks, or hails a taxi.

Domestic activities are much in evidence. The rich have personal servants, lots of them; more modest households, like that of the Maigrets, make do with a maid of all work, while the concièrge, ubiquitous in apartment houses and a rich source of information for police, may well double as a household aide. Washing is still done by the river or in the municipal washhouse. When he looks out of his office window at the Seine, Maigret sees a *bateau-lavoir* with public washerwomen hard at work. Bodily hygiene is another matter. At Moulins, on the eve of war, an honorably known lawyer who sports a golden chronometer in his waistcoat pocket "rarely used the bathroom. . . . A basin in a cupboard, a glass for the toothbrush, and a comb suffice."[7] Maigret himself, whose apartment at the beginning of the series boasts no bathroom, uses a tub for major ablutions. One likes to think that as the prospering household acquires the apartment that adjoins their own, broader domestic vistas include better opportunities for ablution.

Washing apart, Maigret leads a clean life and remains true to his equable, long-suffering wife. Surrounded by adulterers, pimps, and prostitutes, the *commissaire* has an unobtrusive, not to say nonexistent, sex life. His social life is almost as light. Politics and current events intrude but rarely, as if Simenon knew that his readers wanted a break from them. A war widow appears who goes to the ministry to collect her pension; there is a butcher who, when he wins at cards, evokes friendly slurs and is called *fachiste*; there are Jews—greasy, sinister, foreign, or all of the above—and there is quietly pervasive prejudice against foreigners: "What the devil are all these foreigners doing here?"[8] as a judge asks his clerk. There are also hints of political scandal, of official interventions in police inquiries, but passion for justice triumphs, or at least, truth will out.

Which reminds us that Maigret is a policeman, the best kind of policeman: gruff but with a heart of gold, taciturn but thoughtful and imaginative. The best of policemen, however, are not above roughing up their charges, beating up a suspect. *Passage à tabac* remains standard procedure, and it sometimes works. But even law-abiding citizens rash enough to argue over a parking ticket may be arrested and beaten up.[9] The police are part of a world where physical violence remains frequent. For politicians, journalists, actors, authors, critics, or simple civilians with some social standing, fencing remains a useful skill, dueling an unexceptional adventure. The diplomacy of seconds settles many a dispute, but the press chronicles the most visible encounters right to the eve of war.[10] Others exchange less formal blows. Men fight, women fight, too many foreigners pull knives, mostly on each other; couples fight too, though never the Maigrets. The cool darkness above the boulevard Richard-Lenoir's broad pavement carries no hint of bourgeois voices raised in anger. Only the detective superintendent's snores and his wife's soft breathing.

In an interview of 1938 Henry Bernstein, the successful playwright, complained that France's crisis was one of stupidity: "[F]ew men of talent today are less than fifty years old."[11] That was unfair, but not ununderstandable. In 1938 Maigret would be fifty-one years old, like Blaise Cendrars, Louis Jouvet, Marcel Duchamp, Le Corbusier, and the permanent secretary of the Quai d'Orsay known in literature as St. John Perse. Paul Morand, Marcel Jouhandeau would be fifty-two, François Mauriac and André Maurois fifty-three, Jean Paulhan fifty-four, Giraudoux fifty-six, Bernstein himself sixty-two. Those whom Bernstein and his kind would read tended to repeat themselves or someone else: Malraux, Drieu La Rochelle echoed the self-centered heroics of Maurice Barrès; François Mauriac ("a sacristy cockchafer," Jean Paulhan had dubbed him[12]) kept on revealing the digestive problems of constipated Catholic families; Jean Giraudoux was producing intellectual embroideries for sensative souls; Paul Morand specialized in gamy exoticism; the pieties of populist writing, from Pierre MacOrlan's *Quai de Brumes* to Eugène Dabit's *Hôtel du Nord*, dragged out the romantic marginalism of nineteenth-century naturalism.

There was Céline, of course, whose *Voyage to the End of Night* had scored a great success in 1932, but whose cumulative sales were only moderate (112,000 by 1938) and whose "rude and obscene" language riled fastidious readers. Céline, unfortunately, went to pot. In 1936, the expurgated version of his *Death on the Instalment Plan* was described as a long, painful voyage to the end of literature; in 1937 the delirious verbal waterfall of his *Bagatelles pour un Massacre* embarrassed critics by its raw prejudice and even more by its unbridled vulgarity. In 1938 *L'Ecole des cadavres* was worse: anti-Semites did not need to plough through thickets of verbiage to know whom they detested. There was, on the other hand, a coming young college teacher called Jean-Paul Sartre, whose *Le Mur* published in the *Nouvelle Revue*

Française of July 1937 had drawn the editor Jean Paulhan's praise: Sartre would be someone, Paulhan wrote to André Suarès. One year later, with *La Nausée*, he was.[13] But the consecrated leaders of literature would not come to grips with the modern world, let alone accept it. Duhamel rued its presence; Valéry sang its demise; Claudel denied its existence. The effort and the triumph of André Citroën's automobile expeditions through the Sahara or Tibet did not seize their attention. Nor did psychoanalysis, which the president of the Psychoanalytical Society, founded in Paris in 1926, declared was not yet adapted to the exploration of the French mind.[14]

We have seen how uneasily Georges Duhamel had gazed upon the United States. Typically for his generation, Duhamel (1884–1966) was a science graduate and medical doctor who had never practiced medicine except in uniform, during the war. He had spent his life as a man of letters; poet, novelist, critic, he would end as a member of the Académie Française, presiding over the great cultural machine of the Alliance Française, recognized as the "ambassador of French spirit and intellect." The spirit did not include the technological aspects of a vulgar industrial civilization that Duhamel, when he could not ignore them, rejected, rejoicing when—as in the United States—he saw them crumble and crack. In 1933 a new Duhamel novel, *Le Notaire du Havre,* opened the multivolume saga of the Pasquier clan: "the accession of a French family to culture. The formation . . . of that French elite, risen from the people, and which remains the elite despite economic and social tragedies."[15]

Its hero is Laurent Pasquier, a biologist by profession but even more a cultivated bourgeois, just like his author and just like the typical (or ideal) members of the reading public. But Laurent's tale, like that of his family, ends in 1931, precisely when Duhamel's (and Laurent's) "chronicle" began to be written. Like Roger Martin du Gard's great chronicle of times past *Les Thibault* (1922–1940), like Jules Romain's *Men of Good Will* (1932–1947), which culminates in the Great War and peters out thereafter, Duhamel's Pasquiers seem to focus on "the first developments of the great crisis of civilization . . . that presently convulses the world"—the crumbling of moral values, the triumph of destructive materialism, the failures of science. When the sixth volume of the series reaches the year 1930, science is not just bankrupt, it's running wild. "What are you tring to do?" asks one character of another. "You're trying to keep people from dying. What a dirty joke! If science prevents people from dying, there won't be anything for them to eat. They will have to make war and kill each other."[16]

What happened to biologists in real life could be seen from the career of

Alexis Carrel (1873–1944), a Lyonnais Catholic fascinated by the cures of Lourdes, who in 1912 was awarded the Nobel Prize for work that he had carried out at the Rockefeller Institute in New York. In 1935 Carrel's *Man the Unknown* was the nonfiction success of the year. There and in other lectures and writings, Carrel argued the profound biological sources of personality and social order, the genetics of class distinctions as of genius or crime, the supremacy of heredity over democracy, the need to develop eugenics (the science of the production of fine offspring) and to replace the anachronistic ideal of popular sovereignty by something more appropriate to the age. The wonders and achievements of science had not improved men or made them happier. Lourdes was as good as or better than a lab. The time had come to assert truly scientific concepts: develop the hereditary potential of individuals, suppress social classes and replace them by biological classes, substitute *Biocracy* for Democracy. Carrel's chance to work in that direction came when he retired from the Rockefeller Institute and returned to France in 1939. Marshal Pétain, helped by Carrel's old employers, set up the modestly titled Foundation for the Study of Human Problems, which was abolished in 1944, the year of Carrel's own death. The heretical scientist lies buried in the Breton isle of Saint-Gildas, where he had spent many happy holidays with Charles and Anne Lindbergh.[17]

POLITICS FARES better when based on repetition of familiar themes. Literature is about originality, and so are the other arts. The most original painter of the decade and the most underrated was Raoul Dufy (1877–1953), whose luminous color and sketchy forms did a great deal to popularize modern art. Like his friend Matisse, Dufy had been a Fauve before the war but then, in the great national decorative tradition, had drifted into printmaking and design. In the 1930s, without giving up painting, he began to design tapestries, especially for the great manufacture of Beauvais. They were not hard machine-made works but handmade weaves, and quite opposed to the spirit of those years: expensive, charming, shallow, and beautifully exuberant.* Woven, painted, or sketched, Dufy's works were, as Coc-

---

*Dufy was helping to revive a dying trade. Of twenty-five hundred tapestry workers working in France in 1925, only a corporal's guard survived ten years later, by which time twenty-three hundred had deserted the sinking craft. The last teaching shop for apprentices closed in 1933. The Popular Front sought to revive the métier, but revival, at Aubusson, Beauvais, and elsewhere, would be slow. See Jean Lurçat, *Tapisserie française* (1947).

teau said of them, offered like a bouquet. Like many contemporary products, they radiate nervous energy; unlike most, they reflect real enjoyment of
the world they sketch. In 1937, for the exposition where Picasso exhibited
Guernica, and the Delaunays great bright machine-age shapes, Dufy painted
a great mural, appropriately for a pavilion called the Palace of Light. *La Fée
électricité* (the electricity fairy) melds power generators and Olympian gods,
wheat fields and winds and windmills with laborsaving or leisure-filling machines: a bright compendium of contemporaneity.

As this suggests, the Depression affected established artists only little.
Their works fell in price, as did all consumer goods, but nowhere as sharply
as stocks or bonds. Indeed, some contemporary canvases began to be valued
as safe investments: *valeurs refuges.* Even so, those in a position to do so
looked abroad, especially to the United States, where private collections
and public institutions like the New York Museum of Modern Art,
founded in 1929, were buying and exhibiting Picassos, Braques, Matisses,
and Légers. Younger painters, meanwhile, like their American counterparts,
could afford neither canvas nor paints. Some kept body and soul together in
dingy lodgings by gathering greens in the fields and lumps of coal from the
railroad track. Others who were better known, like Marie Laurencin,
painted watercolors on order, and even powder compacts, to make ends
meet.[18] In 1935 an exchange salon was set up in Paris where painters unable
to sell their works could exchange them for goods: silk stockings, eau de
cologne, even packaged nails that the artists would then try to sell from
door to door. In 1936 the Association des Dames Françaises lent its facilities to an "Intellectual Social Center" that offered biweekly distributions of
food, clothing, and medicines to needy artists and intellectuals. But none of
these and similar initiatives went very far. Some painters reacted to these
straits by limiting their esthetic explorations to publicly acceptable forms,
others by introducing politics into their art: no more decoration, only socialist realism.

A few among the young, like Edouard Pignon (b. 1905), son of a miner
who himself worked in mines and industry, found Socialist realism horri-
ble: "photographically and stupidly expressed," immediately realist but
avoiding real ideas.[19] Yet choice was limited. Lots of artists (and even more
nonartists) in those days talked about "art for the people," dreamed of
sculpting or painting for a classless society—meaning a society of workers
only. Most of the art inspired by such ideals was abstract; much of it was
banal; little of it spoke to the people whom it claimed to address. "The

people"—workers, peasants, petty bourgeoisie—wanted something they could recognize, whose workmanship they could respect, whose depictions came close to the realities they knew. Pignon, member of a Communist trade union, working in some factory when he was not unemployed, remembers the artistic faith of those days: the link between modern art and revolution, the yearning of young painters to express their social politics on canvas, the way abstractionists "conceived social painting only through the modern liberties of painting. They obstinately wanted to paint for the people. But it's hard to tell how the people welcomed their work." Pignon himself testifies that the people ignored the abstractions committed in its name, while the Communists, Socialists, syndicalists who captained the people cared little for such products. Even Picasso's *Guernica* was greeted with derision ("no technique, won't last, daubed with enamel paint"). "As for the working class, in fact, it never saw it."[20]

Like Picasso, Pignon knew how presumptuous it is to try to paint down to what one calls the people, *or* to want to raise it to one's imagined level. "The artist works first for himself and for his needs. If the drama of a time concerns him, it will pass into his work. There is no painting for the people, there's simply painting, and one day the people will recognize itself in it. . . ."[21]

This would have been the wish of the much older Fernand Léger (born 1881), enchanted by the people, by a poetry of labor that laborers ignored, by the organization of bodies, buildings, leisure, and machines, all part of a fascinating folklore admired from the outside. The decorative gaiety of Léger's paintings pleased, their exaltation of popular scenes suggested respect and self-respect. But the collectors and collections that admired and acquired his works were hardly "popular."

Pignon's words apply more strongly to an artistic nebula recognized as ferrying new departures: the Surrealists. Surrealism is important because its enterprise was about everything new and about making everything new: action and reaction, creation and subversion, aggression—preferably verbal—enthusiasm and excess, alcohol—aperitifs, *digestifs*—and drugs, the extraordinary and vice versa, fantasy, banality, mystery, pranks, transgression and moral rigor, childish diatribes, subtle plays on words, humor and humorlessness, jazz and silent movies, a Catherine wheel art in black and white just like its metaphysics.

The Surrealist movement as such had been founded by a very few young men, quite unknown at the end of the war and little noticed for a long time thereafter: André Breton (born 1896), Philippe Soupault (born 1897), Louis Aragon (born 1897), Paul Eluard (born 1895). Breton, their leader, had studied medicine and psychiatry, read and met Sigmund Freud, and was determined, as his first manifesto declared in 1924, to free thought "from any control by reason or any esthetic or mental preoccupations." Intrigued by mental illness, Breton dismissed distinctions between dream and reality, reason and madness, objectivity and subjectivity. His followers were to board the unconscious like pirates and turn it on all its seams: unfetter instincts, surprise prejudices, short-circuit superficial experience, liberate reflexes. The first step in this direction was to apply the lessons of Freudian psychoanalysis, either by the use of automatic writing or drawing (doodling by a sensitive hand being more authentic than academic representations) or by the jolt that things seen or done in this manner administered to conformist bystanders.

Surrealism was about provocation, but impudence or transgression needs to attract notice, and most Surrealist activities remained confidential. That was no longer so when, with support from the wealthy Vicomte Charles de Noailles and his wife, Marie-Laure, they embarked on filmmaking. In 1929 Luis Buñuel and Salvador Dali's *Un Chien andalou*, a savage attack on society and religion intended as a call to revolution, proved a great hit in art houses and ciné clubs, but stirred little reaction beyond them. So, in 1930, Buñuel repeated the offense and aggravated it in *L'Age d'or*. Charles de Noailles, who subsidized this film, too, as he did Jean Cocteau's *Le Sang d'un poète*,* was drummed out of the Jockey Club. More important, reactionaries reacted as Surrealists had hoped. Staged as a Surrealist demonstration, with paintings, posters, and photographs by Dali, Max Ernst, Yves Tanguy, Joan Miró, Man Ray filling the theater's lobby, *L'Age d'or* loosed savage attacks on society and religion that roused the radical Right to defend public morality. Members of the Ligue des Patriotes, the Ligue Antijuive, and the Action Française attacked the cinema. Artwork was slashed or defaced; seats were broken, shows interrupted by shouts and by smoke bombs; fistfights broke out; spectators were battered. At mid-December 1930, a week after the opening, showings were suspended by order of the authorities, and the film was confiscated.[22]

---

*Cocteau insisted that *Le Sang d'un poète* was not a surrealist film, quite the contrary: deliberately made "in opposition to the surrealists, who were his deadly enemies at the time." Margaret Crosland, *Jean Cocteau* (London, 1955), 89.

Unfortunately such cinematic scandals, with the publicity they brought, were condemned by the modernity they reflected. Cocteau's *Sang d'un poète* had been among the first French sound films, but the technology of sound made costs prohibitive. The eroticism, masturbation, profanation, sadism of Surrealist films would have to wait for the better days when industry recognized them as commercial, and provocation had to direct its energies elsewhere.

The alternative was ready to hand. Esthetic and social rebellion looked much the same. Political revolution had to accompany poetic revolution. Surrealism's call to organized revolt, its penchant for radical invention led a number of its adherents, eager to smash old stifling bourgeois structures and create a new world and a fresh view of things, toward communism. Eluard, Aragon, briefly Breton himself joined the Communist party. There was no evident connection between surrealism and communism beside agreement that the old must be destroyed before a better world could be built. But there was a coincidence. From the first, surrealism had sought to combine artistic creation and revolutionary action. Socially subversive, declared admirers of Sade and of Saint Just, Surrealists admired the real practical revolution going on in Russia, but they found adherence to communism constricting. Few could bear it for long. Asked to address a party cell about the Italian economic situation, Breton had flunked out on statistics. It had been too much. So while Surrealists as individuals might toe the party line, they could and would not do it as a body. As long as they held high the flag of an alternative, less straitlaced revolution, these intellectuals discouraged by Communist confinement to economic and social domains would be reassured that true revolution also covered "love, dreams, madness, religion and art."

In 1930 surrealism was getting its second wind—the first of several. That was when André Breton published his *Second Manifesto*, which speaks of "the soon to come, inevitable world catastrophe" but also makes very clear that you could be a real revolutionary without joining the Communist party. On the other hand, if, as the Surrealists insisted, the revolution was Surrealist, surrealism saw it as its duty to support the revolution. July 1930 would see the appearance of a new review, *Surrealism in the Service of the Revolution*. Printed in the first number was a telegram to Moscow, assuring fellow revolutionaries in Russia of Surrealist help in case of imperialist aggression. It didn't take long, however, before the review soiled its copybook by printing a letter that denounced "the cretinizing wind that [blew] from Soviet

Russia."[23] Breton, enjoined to break with the letter's author, refused and was officially cast into outer darkness. He would not be allowed to address the International Writers' Congress for the Defense of Culture that was held in Paris in 1935, and his fellow Surrealist, René Crével, unable to persuade the Communist organizers to change their minds, committed suicide.* The refusal of authority and constraint that drove Surrealists into communism had forced the Communists to drive them out.

The speech Breton never delivered and Crével never heard protested against Soviet endorsement of nationalism in that year's pact with France: "We Surrealists, we don't love our Fatherland." They certainly did not love bourgeois democracies and their allies, nor did that opinion vary. In the Spanish War, Surrealists opted for the anarchists; in French politics they exalted civil war and condemned international conflict; in the Moscow trials they denounced the abject police enterprises which they found far worse than the Nazis' Reichstag fire. Surrealist politics were puerile, but they were consistent. The marriage of dream and revolution would be more potent and more influential in realms for which their talents fitted them—media more malleable than political society.

The real Surrealist revolution must be sought in the domain of plastic invention. Everything had begun at the turn of the century, when, for a pioneering few, apparent solidity turned to fairy dust: Words, sentences, forms, associations began to be manhandled by cheeky, nonconformist trolls; perception began to turn to insight, visual conventions to plastic virtualities, vision to revision. That was when the likes of Alfred Jarry and Guillaume Apollinaire challenged formal language, cubism challenged perspective, and when Marcel Duchamp presented familiar objects (bicycle wheels, coat hangers, bottle drying stands) as works of art that he called ready-mades. Then came the war, and eccentricity caught fire. Surrealism was to prove one of its brightest embers.

In the 1920s there had been Max Ernst (born 1891), Man Ray (born 1900), Joan Miró (born 1893), Yves Tanguy (born 1900). In the 1930s new converts arrived: Salvador Dali (born 1904), the Catalan who read Jacques Lacan's 1932 dissertation on Paranoia and Personality and turned its intellectual farrago into delirious images, René Magritte (born 1898), the Belgian who painted a pipe with a legend that asserted it was not a pipe

*On a piece of paper found beside the corpse one word was scrawled: *dégoût* (disgust). See Jean Cassou, *Une vie pour la liberté* (1981), 103–05, for the circumstances of Crével's suicide.

(but an image), then contributed a piece of cheese whose title affirmed that it was a piece of cheese; the Swiss Alberto Giacometti (born 1901), who, trying to give sculptural form to emotions and erotic themes, produced objects and mobile objects. The surrealist exhibition of 1936 featured his work, along with Jean Arp's torn papers, Alexander Calder's mobiles, and Meret Oppenheimer's fur-covered spoons, cups, and saucers.*

Use of untraditional substances, and the untraditional treatment of traditional substances, had begun at the very end of the 1920s, when Pablo Picasso learned from Julio González, a fellow Spaniard and a gifted metalworker, how to weld iron to create "drawings in space" out of pieces of scrap metal. Sketches and paintings, the artists' familiar media, could now be re-created in three dimensions, not just two; colanders and other kitchen utensils, iron scraps, wire springs, strands of metal could move beyond the ready-made suggestions carried by Duchamp's "found objects" to improvise richer allusions, forms, motifs. And the lightness of these new arrangements, poised in the air, could transform the sense they gave of movement and of uplift into actual freedom to move, as did the delicate small-scale wood and wire constructions that Alexander Calder built. By 1937 the Spanish pavilion that housed *Guernica* also contained, in the middle of its courtyard, a fountain by Alexander Calder in which the slow, heavy, brilliant movement of mercury replaced the flow of water.

The possibilities of imaginative revolution appeared infinite. Collages, invented by Picasso before the previous war, invaded not only the three-dimensional works of Arp and of Max Ernst but literature: John Dos Passos's *42nd Parallel* of 1930 was to be soon translated and passionately read by the likes of Sartre and Beauvoir. Unbeknownst to the public masses or to the private connoisseurs, the arts were rewriting the chronicle of contemporary consciousness. Surrealism and its cousins offered art's answer to the challenge of technology and rationalization, incorporating their symbols and materials but also appropriating the suggestions of science. Time and space were reordered; chance—its importance confirmed by the improvisations of jazz jam sessions—was recognized as a fundamental element of creation; letters and numbers, divested of their original meaning, were transmuted into visual matter; logic—recognized as restrictive—was

---

*Large sections of the public, indifferent to the experiments of dyed-in-the-wool Surrealists, would be exposed to their humor in the drawings of cartoonist Jean Effel, depicting fairy teachers explaining to fairy students the work of "realist" writers like Andersen and Perrault, or mushroom priests preaching to a mushroom congregation that poisonous fungi go to hell, edible ones to heaven.

replaced by clairvoyance; the noncontradictory coalescence of apparently contradictory elements, forms, values subverted clear distinctions. Surrealism would corrupt the cult of culture, modify the notion of art, introducing what used to be thought shoddy, gimcrack, unclean: soiled materials, crumpled packages and papers, foul matter. While all around politics became increasingly surreal, Surrealist arts imitated contemporary politics by draining words of their original meaning, exploiting signs and symbols for their affective charge, incorporating the most effective clichés of publicity, mobilizing color, shape, motion, action, and their messages in the service of idiosyncrasy.

Is it the fate of successful novelties to triumph as they self-destruct? To most contemporaries Surrealist activities, when noticed, were enigmatic and their ends obscure. Breton and his friends wanted to be subversive; whenever they were noticed, they were misunderstood. Though their explorations lie behind the artistic norms of the twentieth century, their worst punishment must be that their achievements now preside over the interior decoration of bourgeois households or, at least, of their children's rooms.

The politics of plastic artists remain irrelevant unless explicative legends accompany their works. That is not so when the material used is words and when the words are used so that they can be understood. "Whether he wants it or not," as one critic wrote in 1930, "a writer today is forced to take political parties into consideration."[24] However much Julien Benda grumped at their betraying their vocation, intellectuals could not resist good causes: Peace between nations, European union, international understanding, social justice, the welfare of the wretched or of the fatherland, defense of morality or civilization in a myriad versions claimed one writer after another, or the same one at different times. Antoine de Saint-Exupéry, a gentleman, could afford to keep his heart on the left, his acquaintances on the other side. His friend and fellow flier Jean Mermoz, disgusted with political shenanigans, marched with La Rocque's Croix de Feu. Drieu de La Rochelle oscillated between surrealism, communism, and what in a book of 1934 he called *Fascist Socialism*, before joining Jacques Doriot, who was both Socialist and Fascist. In 1939 Drieu described his ideological pilgrim's progress in *Gilles*, which remains the best description of a French Fascist's intello-sentimental ventures. Sartre's friend Paul Nizan traveled a less convoluted road from Fascist league to Communist party, where he argued the case against corrupting workers by instilling them with the culture of their masters. Virgil, Racine, or Picasso were for the effete; let only the bourgeois suffer from them![25] Jacques Prévert, on the other hand, the populist son of a Bonapartist father, remained a lucid rebel all his life. The name of the greatest popular poet the Surrealists produced is associated with scripts like those he wrote for *Le Crime de M. Lange* and *Les Enfants du paradis,* and with the lyrics of "Les Feuilles mortes," but most of his work consists of parodies, poems, plays, and children's stories, for those who had no letters: little people, including working folk, for and about whom he writes.

Then there was a chain-smoking young man whose talk gushed like a millstream, whose writing began to attract attention when *Man's Fate* won the Goncourt Prize in 1933. Born in 1901, André Malraux had flirted—or at least socialized—with Surrealists but could not stomach psychoanalysis or summon much interest in the unconscious. His novels are about things and experience as they become visible to his characters, and about characters taking shape through perceptions, experiences, and actions; but they are about much more than that.

The French title of *Man's Fate*—*La Condition humaine*—was taken from Pascal: "Let us imagine a number of men in chains, and all condemned to death, and some of these men having their throats cut every day in sight of their fellows, and those who remain recognizing their own fate in that of their companions and, as they wait their turn, staring at each other full of anguish and without hope. Such is the picture of man's fate." For Pascal, the plight that he described asserts the vanity of life. For Malraux, it suggests life's challenge but also the vast distance between modern circumstances and those that, not so long before, had defined the novel. Balzac, Flaubert, and their descendants described a fixed physical context and situated in it characters that were themselves defined by understandable moralities, positions, roles. Malraux, however, had read Stendhal, whose characters exist in function of their consciousness and their actions, and whose young heroes do not endure destiny but strive to make it. He had read Dostoevsky, whose characters inhabit an absurd world where every moral precept is open to question. He had read Maurice Barrès, fascinated by the freedom to be asserted when you create a "Me" in opposition to the world.

As a result, the novel *à la Malraux* is not a work of art, or a social comment, or a document about life and mores, just a report about ways we live or are condemned to live, about our appointed lot, our destiny, our doom. *Man's Fate,* which turns around abortive revolutionary activities in Shanghai, is about psychology, conspiracy, loneliness, betrayal, and failure sporadically overcome by fraternity. Men and women live alone but die together is

one mythical message of the book. If that be so, why can't they live together, too, recognizing that they need each other?

The way Malraux writes makes no claim to paint reality or analyze men
and women—not even "man" in given time and place. In Malraux we find
no omniscient narrator, no givens, no stability, no world made ready for
characters to fit in, no world view to offer reassurance or grounds for criticism. The author contributes little imaginative input. Characters see only
what they see, not what the author is in a position to describe. The first
result is that the character becomes a sort of camera, and in the absence of
authorial comment, what the reader learns is narrowly focused, choppy,
limited, subjectively selected. Action alone reveals settings and scenery; the
novel is no longer a tale, but an experience shared. Instead of established
identities, firm values, a structured world, this kind of novel portrays beings
in search of the lucid acceptance of our doom in Pascal's universe.

Here was a style—rapid, nervous, abrupt, reportorial—that seemed to
fit the swift, choppy, unsettled contemporary world whose anguish it assumed. Its politics spoke of contemporaneity. As Napoleon said and Malraux liked to repeat, "Tragedy, nowadays, is Politics." It addressed the tormented young, contemptuous yet desperate for salvation, suggesting that
their exigencies be turned upon themselves, their criticism should become
self-criticism, their aspirations should lead to self-mastery. "Between 18
and 20," Malraux once told a friend, "life is like a market where one buys
values not with cash but with acts. Most men buy nothing."[26] Malraux invited readers to remedy that, suggested it could be remedied, and the message of his highly political books was a moral one, not terribly different
from those of contemporary nonconformity, activism, or *planisme*.

After all, the plans that we saw multiplying in these same years were less
about substance than about doing something: the excitement of replanning
and remaking the world, society, mankind. Malraux's novels are about self-
creating, self-consuming selves in a disquieting, hostile environment, dis-
covering that life can be lived (and gained even while lost) by way of self-
affirmation. The knight seeks not a princess but himself, and the
opportunity to forge himself through his actions. As knights rode out to
seek adventure and identity, Malraux's characters seek to conquer existence,
endow life with meaning, seize control of it and of themselves if only for a
moment. How? In a world that escapes them, they accept responsibility for
their acts, including their inaction. We are not what our parents, society,
school, even our past have made us. We are what our acts make us, and

make ourselves anew with every act. Our acts commit us; action and commitment simplify our situation because they subordinate complexity of detail and experience to the essential: To thine own self be true. Being human
is being responsible, and dignity comes with responsibility accepted.

Four years younger than Malraux, much uglier but just as brilliant, Jean-
Paul Sartre had also been struck by the absurdity of a world whose inhabitants continued to believe was accessible to reason. The world as Sartre saw
it, as Malraux and many Surrealists saw it, was not accessible to reasonable
explanation, not shaped by some intrinsic order, not governed by provi-
dence or progress, but simply by what we call chance, contingency, sheer
casual luck. Objects, individuals, societies, history have no meaning, no significance, no end; they do not "make sense." Or only the sense we give them
and that we give ourselves. Existence precedes essence; being precedes consciousness and the values that consciousness secretes. We are not determined, but condemned to freedom, which is simply awareness of this condition and of the need to keep redefining ourselves and the world around.
In a disorderly, disintegrating world, a few brave souls were drawing the
harsh conclusions of reflection.

Here was a noble and demanding creed appropriate to the difficulty of
the times. It practiced and preached rejection of detail, of compromise, of
evasions. In the midst of wars and revolutions, on the eve of still more terrible crises, the existential novel minimized everyday life, glorified its transcendence, issued an invitation to heroism. That meant that its practitioners
would not be numerous. Malraux went to fly and fight in Spain on the
Republican side and wrote about the Spanish war in *Man's Hope* (1937). But
the public preferred more accessible entertainment, like the great success of
1934, Gabriel Chevalier's *Clochemerle.* That novel turns about the epic struggle between a mayor and a priest over the construction of a public urinal in
the shade of a village church. Old-fashioned comic realism rehashing familiar themes was more attractive than heroic new forms.

When it ventured beyond undemanding levels, the cultural consumption
of the 1930s favored the mannered men of letters over less mannerly men
of action: delicious decorators like Jean Cocteau, sophisticated aphorists
like Giraudoux. Born in 1882, Jean Giraudoux had been publishing since
before the war, but his rather precious writing began to attract attention
only when it coincided with the postwar mood—indolent, indulgent and
self-indulgent, and with political fashion which favored Franco-German
rapprochement. Giraudoux's puns, witticisms, and wordplay, his flippant

refusal of rules and disciplines while carefully remaining within the limits of good taste appealed to the rising acceptance of moderate transgression and to the vogue of the unconscious, folly, and illusion. He offered entertainment enhanced by literary style and wit. All this served him well, but only moderately until he began to write for the stage. Between 1928 and 1944 Giraudoux finished fifteen plays that combined the wit of Noël Coward with the literary culture of the initiated, his public being invited to spot frequent allusions to classic literature and contemporary events and to enjoy the easy persiflage: "In this country that has so many journalists but no press, that has liberty but no free men, where justice each day belongs a bit less to judges and a bit more to lawyers. . . ."[27] They loved it.

Giraudoux is very French: facile but seldom superficial, show-off but discreetly so, prodigal—lavishing culture, talent, jests, and wordplay while inviting admirers to share his enjoyment, and wildly contemporary in his classical, biblical, or fairy-tale references. In 1928 his first success, *Siegfried*, had been about Franco-German understanding, and *Ondine* (1939) managed to return to that theme, at least in part. Written in 1936 and left unfinished, *The Gracchi* was about civil conflict; designed to play during the exposition year, *Electra* would remind spectators of the Spanish Civil War. Both pleaded that life could continue only at the cost of forgetting, compromises, forgiveness. But Giraudoux's most contemporary play, also his most successful, was *La Guerre de Troie n'aura pas lieu.* Opening in 1935, in the wake of the Stresa Conference and in the thick of the Abyssinian War, the play with its Cassandras and Hectors and Ulysses was recognized at once as a metaphor of present tensions and present threats. Hector, who seeks to avoid war for Troy, is identified as a pacifist veteran; his debate with Ulysses evokes that of Briand and Stresemann at Locarno; the pacifist message of the play rejoiced one camp and infuriated the other. Paul Claudel found "this apology of cowardice and peace at any price repugnant."[28] Most of those who applauded in 1935 and subsequent years saw in the play an announcement of their fate: Try as you may, destiny cannot be circumvented; however great a hero's determination, the gates of war cannot be kept shut.

Much of the theater of the 1930s consisted of commentary on very current themes. In 1929 Edouard Bourdet's *The Weaker Sex* had been hard on the rich metics who invaded Paris; by 1934 his *Hard Times* had turned around French characters, their wealth threatened by the seething slump: "a composite mass in process of decomposition," as Colette described the plot. In March 1934, reviewing Georges Berr's *School for Taxpayers*, one of whose characters "has seen his fortune melt in a few months, like everybody else," Colette noted that the Internal Revenue had joined scatology and adultery as one of the favorite subjects of vaudeville. In May that year Alfred Savoir, "a great dramatic author" who had produced a lot of comedies and farces, brought out *Le Joli Monde*, inspired by the Stavisky scandal. The play took fifteen days to write. The years 1936 and 1937 featured ill omens like the "Green Table" of the Ballets Joos, created in 1932, when it seemed less appropriate and dominated by death. A slew of death-related productions endorsed the message of Henri Bernstein's *Voyage*, whose young pessimists announced "wars, economic catastrophes, grief and mourning."[29] No wonder that theater, claiming to be in crisis, fell back on reviving classics from the seventeenth to the nineteenth century (Dumas was a favorite) and on translations from the English—Shakespeare and Noël Coward, J. B. Priestley and Emlyn Williams. Fame and its cash payoff, however, were left to the authors of vaudevilles, such as André Monézy-Eon, creator of classics like *Bibi-la-Purée*, or *Il est cocu, le chef de gare*, and of operettas like *Sidonie Panache* (1931) and *The Black Tulip* (1932), whose royalties outdid Victor Hugo's.

About those years Simone de Beauvoir remembered "the mediocrity of theatre disgusted us, and we did not go there often."[30] Sartre and Beauvoir went to the cinema (which we shall soon encounter) and to music halls. That was where the Paris public had discovered Raimu, the comic from Marseilles destined to become a famous actor, and where they would soon discover another busker from the south, the singer Yves Montand. That was where, also, they first heard the blues, and ragtime, and dixieland, played by black orchestras like Dudley's Famous Charleston Jazzband, listened to the clarinet of Sidney Bechet, applauded and asked for more when a "Charleston Baby" called Josephine Baker hoofed a wild Charleston to the tune of "Yes Sir, That's My Baby!" Blacks were rare in Paris, their dances exotic, their rhythms bewitching—no more, though, than Miss Baker's belly dance (later deleted), her "superb brown thighs," and evidently the rest of her, since Janet Flanner of *The New Yorker* remembered Baker in her final number "naked except for a pink flamingo between her thighs."[31]

The new star thrilled the general public, and ads promoted hair products *pour se bakerfixer les cheveux;* but sensitive ears were pained. Gide asked where music was going, and answered: toward barbarism. Ravel, who loved the new sound, as did Honegger and Darius Milhaud, called his dog Jazz.

Leading the French delegation to the Lausanne Conference of 1932, Edouard Herriot (who had written on Beethoven) was only interested in talking about jazz.[32] The young Sartre dreamed of being a jazz musician. The Hot-Club de France would be set up in 1935, but jazz only passed from the domain of intellectuals and aficionados to that of the mass public when, after the mid-thirties, the big bands of Count Basie, Duke Ellington, Glenn Miller, Benny Goodman moved swing from brothels to ballrooms and made it truly popular, hence commercial.

The sound of American ballroom music and of swing came to France on sound tracks and on records, which had been perfected in the late twenties. The thirties, especially the later thirties, witnessed an extraordinary craze for phonograph music, whose power, sound, and integrity of reproduction had improved and which mass production made generally accessible for private as for broadcast use. American songs were for dancing. For listening, many preferred crooners like the soupy Tino Rossi ("Marinella," 1936), old-fashioned sentiment like that of Edith Piaf ("Mon légionnaire," 1935), escapism ("Have Fun! Don't give a damn! Life is so short!" 1933), wry comments on the present ("Tout va très bien, Madame la Marquise!" 1935) or invitations to youth and fantasy ("Je chante" or "Y'a d'la joie," 1937). These last ditties were the work of a bright young warbler called Charles Trenet (born 1913), lover of jazz and films, especially American films. Al Jolson, the Singing Fool, whom he had admired in *The Jazz Singer*, provided him his nickname: *Le Fou chantant.* Trenet's most famous admirer, Yves Montand, would take over the moniker as he took over Trenet's latest success: "Boom! Oh when my heart goes Boom . . ." for his debut in 1938. But Trenet's songs recall less American ditties than Marc Chagall and, more especially, Dufy: flying lovers, levitating postmen, curés on bicycles, sunlit pastures, playful nudes, enchanted settings. The youth, fancy, whimsy, gaiety, humor, and hope so signally lacking during those dreary years were available on the boards.

And on the screen.

Cinema had been born in France, and it had prospered greatly. Before 1914 French producers had pioneered western films with the help of at least one French cowboy star, and their products were sold worldwide—not least in the United States, where domestic producers sought to loosen the French grip on the American market with "buy American" campaigns. The war speeded the rise of the American movie industry, but silent films could be enjoyed—hence sold—under any clime. Then, in 1927, the first sound film, *The Jazz Singer*, had been released in the United States, and its effects on the French industry proved catastrophic. In 1929, when Jolson first sang his "Mammy" on a French screen, the country had only two theaters equipped to show sound films. Worse, it had no sound stages, and most early French talkies were going to be produced abroad. But in 1930 real French sound films appeared, including Abel Gance's *The End of the World* and René Clair's *Under the Roofs of Paris*. The Duhamels, viewing their first talkie that year, found it frightful, ridiculous, ugly: "We leave halfway through."[33]

Whatever the merits of Dr. Duhamel's opinion and that of his spouse, what had until 1930 been an entertainment for intellectuals and for the lower classes soon turned into mass entertainment. Movie theaters outdistanced the attraction of music halls, in which they had been born. No less that of theaters, where seats cost about ten times the price. In 1930 the French turned out ninety-four feature films; in 1931 half as many again.[34] Yet, though sound attracted ever-growing audiences, it hurt French producers. The national market was too small, the industry too fragmented. German studios were less artisanal and better organized; the Americans and the British enjoyed far vaster markets, where films could be amortized before they were sold abroad. The introduction of dubbing dismayed the cognoscenti, pleased the general public, but aided only those films that benefited from a good distribution machinery. France did not excel in that field.

It is little wonder that from 1930 on, anxious voices were raised about the danger to French artistic production, incidents occurred in theaters that showed English-language films, "glories of the French university" expressed dismay about "naïve, artless American scripts" which were about to crush French enterprise and intellect, the press called for protection. The *Revue des Deux Mondes* denounced American colonization of French cinema, *L'Illustration* warned of the American hold—"invasion," "hegemony."[35] After 1933 the trickle, then the flood of Central European refugees aggravated the situation. In Paul Morand's *"France la doulce, (sweet France),"* first published that very year in Emmanuel Berl's leftish *Marianne*, all film producers are Jewish, Greek, Romanian, Armenian . . . "In defending the French," declares the author in an introductory note, "I simply claim for them the rights of minorities." Morand was poisonous, but he was not mendacious. In 1934, of 430 films opening that year, 327 were foreign, less than a quarter French. And about 30 of these last had been made by foreign technicians and by refugee directors like Max Ophuls, Fritz Lang, Robert Siodmark, G. W. Pabst.*[36]

Financing was a jungle or, better still, a bog. The French, at least until recently, have been bad at developing credit institutions or credit instruments that would be reasonably accessible. This may be why, whilst a majority of personnel in French film unions went on relief, coproductions, especially with Germany and Italy, flourished. Until 1938 French stars and French directors worked in Berlin, where the UFA studios sometimes produced films solely in French versions.† On the eve of war Abel Gance worked in Rome. At home things were too difficult. By the mid-thirties Pathé, Gaumont were in receivership, and most films were produced by one-shot corporations, their financing provided at high interest rates by British banks and insurance companies. Despite exports hampered by the high cost of French-made film stock, and with their preferred recipe of protectionism and import quotas limited by fear of foreign reprisal, producers went on struggling against the competition. But financing at reasonable cost only became available by state intervention under the Popular Front and after it.[37] It was Jean Zay who commissioned a report on the industry that would recommend state financing, eventually implemented first under Paul Reynaud, then under the Vichy regime. It was Jean Zay too who founded the first *cinémathèque*, who initiated special credits financed by a tax on admissions, who abolished double features to make more room for French shorts, who funded five *national* prizes to supplement the *Grand Prix du Cinéma français*, instituted a few years before, and who, to compete with Mussolini's film festival in Venice, prepared a national festival, at Cannes, that was supposed to see its first opening in September 1939.[38] This was the background against which French films were made, and it added to the darkness of a mood reflecting not just contemporary events but also the doldrums of the industry.

Of two thousand French films shot between 1930 and 1950 only a

---

*To cite only the better-known German émigré directors working in France in the thirties, William Wilder made one film, Fritz Lang and Ernst Lubitsch two each, Ophuls seven, Pabst eight, Siodmark eleven or twelve. Ginette Vincendeau, "French Cinema in the Thirties" (University of East Anglia thesis, 1985), 103–04. Ibid., 55, Vincendeau notes that in 1934 twenty-six foreign cameramen were at work, while forty-seven French ones were jobless.

†Edwige Feuillère's recollections, *Les Feux de la mémoire* (1977), devote Chapter 6 to the crucial role that UFA and Tobis Klangfilm played in the making of French versions and the mutually profitable employment of French actors, writers, and directors, whom she describes as "immigrant labor" in Germany.

quarter survive, and most of those that we still view are more or less glum. Although one can't be sure, René Clair (born 1898) might be the one exception. Most of Clair's films oscillate between populist sentimentality (*Under the Roofs*, 1930; *The Million*, 1931; *Bastille Day*, 1932) and anticapitalism (*The Last Billionaire*, 1934). Clair's gags and fantasy had dipped in Surrealist waters, but his anti-Fascist satire produced financial difficulties. He went to England to make *The Ghost Goes West*, then to Hollywood, and returned to filmmaking in France only after the Second War. Jean Renoir (born 1894), whom we regard so highly, was seldom successful commercially. His *Crime of Mr. Lange* (1936) reflects the resentments and hopes of 1936, when it was shown. The script by Jacques Prévert turns around the sins of wicked capitalists and the enterprise of likable and determined working folk aided by younger, more forthcoming capitalists. It is about a printing shop left in the lurch by the defection of its crooked manager, saved by a young man's comic strip that chronicles the adventures of a cowboy, Lucky Luke, and catches the public's fancy. And it is about the young man's public-spirited murder of the villain. Slow, though pleasing, the film would be eminently forgettable (as audiences found it) but for its simple and straightforward view that evil is best dealt with by elimination, after which good copes with the rest, a stance that history has not so far endorsed.

La Vie est à nous, which Renoir made on the heels of *Mr. Lange* and which did not benefit from a Prévert script, is simply arty Communist propaganda. The social criticism of *La Régle du Jeu* (1939) fell worse than flat among whistles and catcalls, closed after three weeks, and was then banned as demoralizing. *La Grande Illusion* (1937) was to be the exception that proved the rule. No French producer had agreed to finance it, yet it turned out the year's artistic and financial success. The great illusion of the title is war, or national dissensions, but the film is really about all divisions that set men apart—class, race, nation, social category (being an aristocrat, a banker, a mechanic or a Jew)—and their transcendence in comradeship, friendship, love. And it is about war or, rather, against it. Renoir, a veteran who had been wounded twice, set out to make a film that was pacifist, and this the French censorship recognized when in 1939 it prohibited its showing. Yet paradoxically the success of *The Great Illusion* was partly *tricolore*, as the public rose to sing the "Marseillaise" along with the prisoners who sang it on the screen—and sang it sometimes with arms outstretched, giving the Fascist salute.[39]

The Great Illusion was the culmination of a long line of pacifist films, beginning with Abel Gance's *J'Accuse* of 1919 and including a slew of imports like Lewis Milestone's *All Quiet on the Western Front* (1930). But the most discreet, hence effective, pacifist propaganda came from newsreels, in which fashion parades and bathing beauties increasingly intersected with views of current wars announcing the war to come, or films like Jacques Feyder's *La Kermesse héroïque* (1935). Behind its visual references to Dutch seventeenth-century paintings, the film that English speakers know as *Carnival in Flanders* pointed up the virtues of cowardice which preserves life and property: Timorous burghers, resourceful women folk, Spanish soldiers more interested in making love than war, collaborate to save a town from pillage and slaughter. Coolly received in Paris, attacked in Belgium, whose honor it besmirched, the film was a smash hit in Germany and Britain before winning an Oscar in Hollywood.

Carnival was humorous and lively. It would be hard to say the same of other notable products of those years. Alan Williams's history of French filmmaking speaks of "the brooding, angry pessimism" that informed the "poetic realism" of Julien Duvivier, Marcel Carné, and their like and of the appeal that their bleak-minded films held for French audiences in the 1930s. The terms *populism* and *populist* seem to have been coined in 1929, and their practitioners were as busy on the screen as they were in print, presenting miserable life among the more or less miserable: prostitutes, pimps, dolorous lovers, and a variety of felons who testified to social mismanagement, scuttled aspirations, sentiments melting into sentimentality. Carné's *Hôtel du Nord* and *Quai des Brumes* in 1938, his *Jour se lève* in 1939 were naturalistic denunciations of a life where happiness was more unattainable than coconuts at a fair. Looking back at those days, Carné described *Le Jour se lève* as his blackest film, and no wonder: *"tout le monde vivait dans la désespérance*—everyone lived in despair."[40]

Yet, as *Paris-Soir* pointed out, "the cinema public wants to laugh."[41] To laugh or to relax, and there American products led the pack—absurd with the Marx Brothers, enchanting with Rogers and Astaire, intoxicating with musical comedies, charming with Disney's *Silly Symphonies,* spellbinding with his first feature, *Snow White,* which Paris was to discover in 1938. *The Great Illusion* headed the hit parade of 1937 with Duvivier's *Pépé le Moko* in seventh place, but the eight other films on the list were comedies or features about sport, love, or mystery. The following year *Quai des Brumes* came second, after *Snow White.* Other films on the hit parade provide less searing entertainment or else patriotic inspiration. To make *Pépé le Moko*, Julien Duvivier, refused assistance by the French Foreign Legion in North Africa, had obtained the help of a Spanish colonel named Francisco Franco. The military authorities proved more cooperative with makers of upbeat, martial-minded films that enlisted the resources of the navy (*Alert in the Mediterranean*), the army (*Legions of Honor*), or the military academy (*Three from Saint-Cyr*), all about the honor and efficacy of the French forces. Of the fifteen most popular films in 1936 and 1937 almost half featured military or naval heroes. Portrayals of dedicated officers leading brave, reliable men found an enthusiastic public. *Alert in the Mediterranean* made the hit parade of 1938, *Legions of Honor* received the grand prize of French cinema, and one reviewer suggested that *Three from Saint-Cyr* should be shown to the Germans: It would give them second thoughts about taking on the French.[42]

The French themselves appeared more eager to take on enemies at home. Ambient prejudice soon seeped into their films, which, like other media, reflected the rising tide of xenophobia and anti-Semitism. One schoolteacher in Christian-Jaque's charming schoolboy mystery story of 1938, *Les Disparus de Saint-Agil*, repeats, "I don't like foreigners! Foreigners mean war!" The following year Sacha Guitry's entertaining *They Were Nine Bachelors* would sketch a France "literally invaded by metics." "They had better get out!" Another—mild—success of the same year made the same point. In *Derrière la façade*, a policeman faces Erich von Stroheim, a nasty, dishonest foreigner who has just been naturalized: "If you don't like the way you're treated, get yourself naturalized in your own country!"[43]

As a historical document the arts, like the life going on around them, reflect confusion and offer a mixed testimony. On one hand, nagging adversity suggests superficial solutions: xenophobia, social protest, patriotic revival. On the other, it incites helpless participants to escapism. Neither will solve irresoluble problems. Collective action, political, military, social, was destined for failure in the end. Collective quandries, it would seem, could only be faced on the individual plane. Personal commitment, responsibility, creativity, honor alone offered a little hope amidst growing despair. Not placing blame on foreigners, politicians, capitalists, or collectivists. But that only became clearer after 1940, and even then to far from all.

IX

The Nightmare of Fear

For the last four years we have lived in this
nightmare of fear.

—*Julien Green*

IN 1931 an American chemical warfare specialist reported back to Washington on his tour of Europe. During the past year, he noted, there had been considerable talk of war, apparently unrelated to specific motives. "The war talk in Europe is or has been altogether a matter of fear," and fear seemed to focus on the belief that "the next war [generally expected for 1932] will see the widest possible use of chemical agents as well as all other available scientific means of destruction." The report forwarded a special number of the French magazine *Vu* for February 1931, entirely devoted to chemical or "scientific" warfare, and a similar issue of the German *Die Woche* for April. "It is likely that the German issue was copied after the French."[1]

Why in the midst of peace, in the absence of major crises, in the wake of the Kellogg-Briand Peace Pact should this be going on? Could it be ascribed to the economic depression, as one quotation in the report suggests: "A chance to make some money," when everything else is bankrupt? Or to gas mask manufacturers making "use of this chemical warfare agitation to boost their sales"? The writer preferred a third explanation. There is, he explained, "a powerful agency in Europe now actually promoting publicity of this kind. This is the International Red Cross, which to aid its campaigns of education of the populace in chemical warfare protection, has set up a special information bureau at Geneva. The International Red Cross Program is of course for orderly and systematic instruction of the people in all that protection against chemical warfare means. . . . It is not unnatural, however, that journalistic enterprise here and there will make capital of this for sensationalism."

Beginning in the 1920s and rising to a crescendo in the thirties, books, articles, posters, brochures, and every kind of propaganda made people aware of the danger of air attack, bombs, chemical and bacterial warfare, the need for and the possibilities of "passive" and active defense against air attack. And as our American intimated, in 1929 the International Committee of the Red Cross had created an International Documentation Center on Airborne Chemical Warfare, whose educational campaigns lent authority to the general jitters.*[2] But if one were to pinpoint a start for so diffuse and multiple a phenomenon, it would have to be the publication in 1921 of Giulio Douhet's *Il Dominio dell'aria (The Command of the Air)*. Brilliant and opinionated, Douhet championed the strategic use of air power and tirelessly asserted the role bombing could play in disorganizing and annihilating an enemy, ravaging his towns, terrorizing the population, destroying military and industrial installations. A French translation of Douhet's book only appeared in 1932—ten years before the English version. By then, however, his theories and other similar ones had made their way in military literature and in the popular press.

---

*Once a diplomatic protocol solemnly condemning chemical warfare and bacteriological warfare had been signed at Geneva in 1925, the International Red Cross declared the fight against them a high priority, and the *Revue internationale de la Croix-Rouge* introduced a regular feature on chemical warfare, air-raid precautions, and the protection of civil populations. International meetings and a host of exhibitions, publications, demonstrations, processions, courses, exercises that enlisted local authorities, churches, scouts, and sporting clubs kept the menace in the public eye. So did the Germans, whom the Treaty of Versailles deprived of a military air force and who found it politic to emphasize the dangers of air and chemical warfare. At the World Disarmament Conference of 1932 the French delegation proposed League of Nations control of military and civil aviations, the banning of incendiary bombs, of gas and germ warfare, and the prohibition of all shelling or bombing beyond certain frontline areas. Widely acclaimed, this admirable initiative sank without trace, as did the dream of disarmament when Germany walked out of the Disarmament Conference (September 1932), then out of the League of Nations (October 1933). The terror of unrestricted warfare seemed confirmed. Thereafter simulated raids and battles in the air designed to test defenses in Britain, France, Italy, and Germany received wide press coverage. So did the conclusion that France's inspector general of territorial defense, General Duchêne, drew from their experience: "We shall never manage to protect urban populations adequately." *Revue internationale de la Croix-Rouge* (July 1934), 673, for Duchêne; (October 1934), 801, for "the general assumption" that the protocol of 1925 would be ignored; *"Quel serait le caractère d'une nouvelle guerre?"* Enquête organisée par l'union interparlementaire (1932) for the views of influential experts.

In late 1929 several Chamber of Deputies debates turned around the organization and safety of the nation's borders, sharpening fears of aerial warfare and persuading a wide public that "the next war . . . will be in the air." After 1930 especially, prophets of air warfare outbid each other in describing the horrors of coming conflicts in which armies in their fortified shelters suffered little, whilst in their rear towns and countryside lay in ruins; bombed, burned, gassed, littered with the corpses of civilians: "ten million, fifteen million, twenty million corpses," as Socialists were told in their National Congress of 1931. The more enthusiastic the advocates of air power, the more frightful their predictions. For René Chambre, author of *A History of Aviation* (1933), bombers were properly unstoppable. "We shall never prevent the enemy from bombing our towns, flooding them with incendiary bombs, toxic gases of every sort, microbes. A hundred planes each carrying a ton of asphyxiating shells would cover Paris with a gas sheet twenty meters high, all in an hour."[3]

As our American expert pointed out, civil defense itself causes civil disquiet. Exercises simulating gas attacks on cities, air-ground maneuvers simulating air raids on Lyons, Toulon, Dunkirk, Nancy spurred features in the press that magnified the sense of danger. The possibilities of surprise attacks were dire; the only parry against them would be preventive attacks impossible to envisage in a peaceful democracy or else the threat of massive reprisals. The defense debate was slipping into nightmare. Air war, wrote Paul Pascal, professor of chemistry at the Sorbonne, was a return to barbarism. It was certainly an encouragement for defeatism.[4]

The growing agitation over bombers and destructive bombing may also have been a pacifist ploy. Didactic enterprises sponsored by the Red Cross or the Ligue de Protection Aérienne set themselves limited ends. The terror tactics of pacifism deliberately set out to scare. In 1930 the Frankfurt Conference of the Women's League of Peace and Freedom stressed the relation between war and gas attacks. In 1930–1931 appeals of the Ligue Internationale des Combattants de la Paix (International League of Fighters for Peace, LICP) described in apocalyptic terms the "cities destined to incendiary bombs, deadly gases and annihilation" and the populations succumbing to "mortal panic, terror and misery." Norman Ingram, historian of French pacifism during these years, believes that it was the LICP which "brought home to hundreds of French towns and villages the pacifist message that the next war would be the last." An apocalypse, as Louis Gillet predicted in 1934.[5]

Last war or not, many thought of it as proximate. The *Journal* of Julien Green, the delicate Franco-American writer, is full of rumors of war for the end of the month, panics, images of catastrophe. "The people I see have fallen prey to panic," he notes in 1932. "This happens three or four times a year." And in 1934: "Life is impregnated with this general fear." Did militant pacifism bring the provinces in line with Paris on this score, as Ingram seems to suggest? In 1932 Emile Servan-Schreiber, a well-connected journalist, contrasted the calm provinces with Paris, where somber people talked only of catastrophes. But a reading of provincial newspapers in 1933 and 1934 reveals regular lecture series concerned with civil defense and well-attended meetings on the effects of air attacks and poison gas.[6]

Just how effective such activities proved can be seen from the efforts of business, industry, and private families to secure safe haven outside imaginary killing grounds. "For Sale. Far from invasion routes, house in the West, between Laval and Angers . . ." In October 1932 *L'Œuvre* denounced this ad published in *L'Est Republicain;* but in 1933 the family seat of the ducs de Brissac, near Limours in the far southwest, would be sold to a power company, Sud-Lumière, "which sought a refuge for its archives in case of war," and by 1934 the administrative authorities of the University of Strasbourg were making plans for evacuation to Clermont-Ferrand should war break out.[7]

In his splendid *Autopsy of a Defeat* Ladislas Mysyrowicz has lined up an impressive (and depressing) tally of quotations that etch the pervasive fear of war, of sudden war, of air attacks, bombing, and gassing. The press bears him out: In spring 1933 alone, cartoons show men discussing airborne perils, incendiary bombs, gas masks. Through 1934 and 1935 the Paris and provincial press publishes advertisements for protective products, photos of policemen carrying or wearing gas masks, indications on where these can be bought. In 1935 police and civil authorities distribute posters and brochures: "Precautions to be taken against bombs from planes" and "Instructions for protection against air attack." Julien Green's diary records the passage of policemen and their explanations: "(masks, shelters, don't panic, stay calm, everything). I wonder when and how we shall escape from this hideous age."[8] In 1936 air-raid shelters are in the planning stage, the sheltering possibilities of the metro actively discussed. Thereafter the subject never drops out of sight. Accounts of fighting, first in Abyssinia, then in Spain, confirmed the fearmongers' worst fears. That was what made the destruction wreaked on Guernica by German bombers especially impressive, and pacifists did not fail to point out how far more dreadful the effect would be of a full-scale raid, not by fifteen or twenty planes "but hundreds and thousands."[9]

A few months after Guernica, François Nourissier walked around the Pavilion de la Défense Passive with his mother while visiting the exposition and still remembers how its sirens and other ominous exhibits seemed to announce the imminent coming of a war.

The relentless bombardment with frightening news and rumors, more damaging than most surprise attacks, makes one wonder why civil defense turned out so ill prepared. In March 1939, in the wake of Prague's fall, "passive defense" was still "being organized," and although the comte and comtesse de Pange were able to collect their gas masks in the hall of the Gare des Invalides, respirator supplies fell far short of the levels required for general public distribution. Moreover, a portion of the gas mask stock came from Czechoslovakia, so the shortage was likely to get worse unless, as the *Canard enchaîné* suggested, civilians could be persuaded to make their own gas masks.[10]

The essence of tragedy, Alain once said, is the expectation of catastrophe. After 1930 the expectation of catastrophe was in the air. For Marshal Foch, the Treaty of Versailles was no more than a twenty-year truce. Officially since 1935, unofficially well before, the Germans, whom the treaty restricted to an army of one hundred thousand and no heavy armament at all, were rearming. Britain and France knew about it but officially ignored the treaty breaches. It was difficult to argue against German claims to equal treatment with other powers, awkward to match a secret rearmament that remained no secret. Deliberate leaks and alarmist articles stirred fears of Franco-German conflict. The *Journal* of Green, again, swarms with grim notes. Everywhere he goes, he notes in October 1930, the talk is all about the next war. "In salons, in cafés, that is all one hears with the same tone of horror. Some expect it in two months, others less pessimistic grant us another year of peace. . . ."[11] The wails of pacifists who had been crying "Wolf!" since the Great War's ending became increasingly anguished. In September 1930 the *NRF* dismissed present peace as "a latent war smouldering beneath the treaties." Two years later, in July 1932, Romain Rolland himself announced that war was coming.[12]

Uncontrollable war on the other side of the world confirmed both fear and impotence. In September 1931, defying the concert of nations, Japan had begun its bloody progress across Manchuria and North China; in October its planes had bombed Chinchow, leaving it in flames; in February 1932 its troops had taken Shanghai. Asian war might have encouraged talk of disarmament. At any rate, in February 1932, just as the League of Nations crumbled before the determination of the Japanese, an international Disarmament Conference opened at Geneva. The French delegation offered a comprehensive plan for the reduction and limitation of armaments—especially air forces, and the sorts of commercial planes that could be converted into bombers. Pierre Cot, France's minister for air, proposed abolishing national air forces altogether and internationalizing civil aviation. Naturally, plans of this sort got nowhere. Nor did the Disarmament Conference itself, fated to fizzle in a flood of hypocrisy and hot air. But the conjunction of German rearmament, mayhem in Asia, economic dislocation, the rise of Nazism in the German elections of 1932, and the attention focused on all these issues by the Disarmament Conference helps explain the catastrophism of the early thirties.

The impact of events was bolstered by a rash of pacifist war films and alarmist publications. *Nothing New on the Western Front* in 1930, Abel Gance's *End of the World* in 1931, were but the best known.* Once again, war seemed just over the horizon. Crises in Europe, clashes in China brought the threat home. "War is possible," affirmed a special number of *Plans* in July 1931, and the *Nouvelles littéraires*, discussing *La Fin de l'après-guerre?*, doubted that much was left to end. More likely, as a translation of Ludwig Bauer's title suggested, *War Is for Tomorrow.*[13] In January 1932 Eugène Dabit recorded his feeling that the anguish of it all was stifling him: "Monstruosity . . . crime . . . failure . . . It is with this perpetual anguish of a stupid death that we have to act, love, create." He could not. In November: "I write badly: I don't feel like writing. The war may break out at any time." In counterpoint

---

*In 1933 H. G. Wells's novel *The Shape of Things to Come* traced the fate that lurked in the near future: air war, pestilence, and a return to barbarism amid the ruins. The impact of Alexander Korda's 1936 film of the same name was vastly greater. It began with the devastation wrought by worldwide war, graphically described the plague and armed anarchy that followed, and ended on a dubious note of utopian salvation as a rocket carried human colonists to more peaceful conditions in outer space. The Canadian actor Raymond Massey, who starred in the film, remembered that the model spaceship to salvation had been designed by the same German rocketry experts who designed the V-1 and V-2 weapons that bombed Britain in 1944 and who were brought to work in NASA's jet propulsion laboratory. More immediately the English poet David Gascoyne's *Journal* testified to the persuasiveness of Korda's images: "Are the scenes of H. G. Well's [sic] prophetic film going to materialize . . . ?" he asked himself in 1938. "Dense ranks of bombers zooming across the sky, famous buildings tottering in flame and smoke, . . . stampeding crowds." See Raymond Massey, *A Hundred Different Lives* (Toronto, 1979), 192; David Gascoyne, *Paris Journal 1937–1939* (London, 1978), September 27, 1938.

Green noted "the madness that consists of expecting the war for the end of the week. For the last four years we have lived in this nightmare of fear."[14] Many seem to have talked about it, thought about it, been haunted by it: Elie Halévy, Jean de Pange, André Chamson . . . "It was in 1932," notes Henri de Montherlant, returning from a long stay in Algeria. "I felt at once that war was imminent." His notebooks of that year are full of the obsession. It keeps him awake at night. The *Canard* harps on what it likes to call "the next last war." Dabit too: "How happy I could be without this thought of war." Everyday life, Green notes, "is as it were impregnated by this general fear."[15]

In 1932 Montherlant admits to himself that most of those around him still "do not give a damn . . . they know there is a menace . . . but bury their heads in sand." Pange and his friends recognize the threat but judge it to be less than in 1914. By 1935 (Hitler announced German rearmament in March) Pange sees "all France obsessed by the thought of German aggression." Montherlant too hears men in the street speak of the particular day of the mobilization when they would have to join their units. Dabit, reminded by a gendarme's visit that in case of mobilization he leaves "immediately and with no delay," explodes in despair against "this odious menace that weighs upon our lives." Servan-Schreiber, back from his summer holidays, hears a young woman declare that she's holding off ordering her fall wardrobe: "You can imagine, with this talk of war." What with the radio and with other media, news came too thick and fast. The world, thinks Servan-Schreiber, lives on its nerves and nerves are getting frazzled.[16]

This was the mood when Giraudoux's *La Guerre de Troie n'aura pas lieu* was first performed in 1935. Jacques Body tells us that its author meant to call it "Prelude," and we know that the prophecies of Cassandra, the ill-fated negotiations of Hector and Ulysses were indeed a prelude to far worse events. In 1936 the Germans reoccupied the Rhineland as the French stood by. Henri de Kerillis, the nationalist journalist and foe of pacifist pygmies, published *Français! voici la guerre.* War was no longer for the morrow: "War comes. War is here." And the French were fated to face it from a position of weakness: "In March 1936 France began to lose the next war."[17]

The thirties are littered with lost opportunities, and it would seem that each persuaded someone that war after it could no longer be avoided. The year 1932 was early in the process, 1935 more convincing, 1936 a bumper year. That was when the prudent discovered the value of even quite modest maladies and began to collect the medical certificates with which to avoid service. For individual Frenchmen, Montherlant noted with much disgust and some injustice, war meant "They're not going to get me." Nor were "they" Germans, but the military: "War for [the Frenchman] consists in getting away from them by all possible means. *There* is the great struggle beginning." Others were less readily impassioned. Françoise Giroud remembers Louis Jouvet in 1937: "War is absolutely crazy. But there will be no war." Many agreed. Then came the Anschluss, the ides of March again: "March 13, 1938 . . . the end of the peace." That summer Montherlant, half-jokingly, told a young friend: "[D]on't worry about your future—in a year you'll be killed in the war." The lad replied: "That's what my mother tells me." A reminder, if one were needed, that there were mothers too, daughters, wives. In her large house full of children and servants Edmée Renaudin found herself always tired, anxious, oppressed, afraid of death, given to sudden wakings and to long insomnias.[18] It was the fear of war.

SOLDIERS SHARED the sense that France was vulnerable, and this made France more vulnerable still. Through most of the 1920s the French talked softly and carried a small stick. Their army was understaffed, undermanned, underpaid, and overrated. Their foreign policy pretended first that Germans could be forced to execute the provisions of Versailles, then that it didn't matter if they didn't. One thing no one bothered to pretend was that force existed to be used. As a Communist deputy eager to cut military expenditure asserted, "You don't want any more victories. It follows that you're building an army to prevent defeat." Renaud Jean was right: The conquering, offensive doctrines that caused so many deaths between 1914 and 1918 had been discarded. Soldiers had learned that enemy fire kills. They distrusted the offensive doctrines of the prewar Staff College, the emphasis on vitalism and will, the predilection for charges with the bayonet. The dominant doctrine now was that "the power of the defensive constitutes the most important and least questionable lesson of the war."[19] Prudence, protection, avoidance of risk: The army would be ready, but to do nothing much. Was that why, in February 1932, the former Ministry of War became the Ministry of Defense?

Their major task henceforth to avoid invasion, soldiers forgot that attack at times could be the best defense. As the American military attaché advised his superiors, "fear of another invasion . . . dominates all France's military

Holidays with pay were both a novelty and a
great success, even if comfort was moderate
at best. Even when stony and muddy, cheap
beaches were better than none—

Roger Viollet

so was a chance to camp and fish on the
banks of the Marne, the Loire, the Seine,
or even by a roadside. Young families
with a tandem were on top of the world.
It's a safe bet that the scarves worn by the
trio in the photo were red. No wonder
that critics were wrinkling their noses.

Henri Cartier-Bresson/Magnum Photos

Henri Cartier-Bresson/Magnum Photos

Crimes of Holidays with Pay

1. "Third-class carriages are chock-full!"
   "It's intolerable! All these people on paid holidays are dangerously weighing down the train!"

2. "What a past, these popular holidays! Can you smell that one, how she poisons the roadway with her cheap perfume?"

3. "Horrors! We can't stay here. They swim in our ocean; they breathe our air; they're using our sun to get brown!"

4. "Kiki, don't go near those persons; you'll catch fleas!"

5. "I don't understand! The rooster is crowing well before dawn."
   "Naturally! You can't imagine that these bastards crisscross the country without propagating their ideas of disorder!"

6. "You see! I told you that if you take your holidays among these Reds, you risk becoming the target of painful misunderstandings."

...d'autant plus que les travailleurs ayant obtenu le congé payé se répandent à travers le pays.

MEFAITS DES VACANCES PAYEES

— Les wagons de troisième classe sont bondés!

— C'est intolérable! Tous ces gens en congé payé surchargent dangereusement les trains!

— Quelle peste, ces vacances populaires! Tu sens celle-là comme elle empoisonne la route avec son parfum bon marché?

— Oh! Horreur! Impossible de rester ici! Ils se baignent dans notre océan, ils respirent notre air et se font brunir par notre soleil!

— Kiki, n'approche pas ces individus, tu vas attraper des puces!

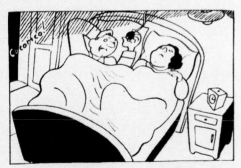

— Je n'y comprends rien! Le coq chante bien avant le lever du jour.

— Parbleu! Tu penses bien que ces salopards ne vont pas à travers le pays sans propager leurs idées de désordre!

— Tu vois! Je te le disais: à vouloir prendre des vacances parmi ces gens aux idées rouges, on risque d'être l'objet d'une pénible confusion!

R. Dubosc

Unions gave the Exhibition
of 1937 a rough time.
Above, a strike by building
workers on the Expo site,
trying to reedit the spirit of
1936.

Below, the delayed but nevertheless completed product, with the Soviet pavilion in the left foreground facing the German pavilion on the right. Both are *virile*, monumental, massive, and redolent of memories of imperial Rome.

Roger Viollet

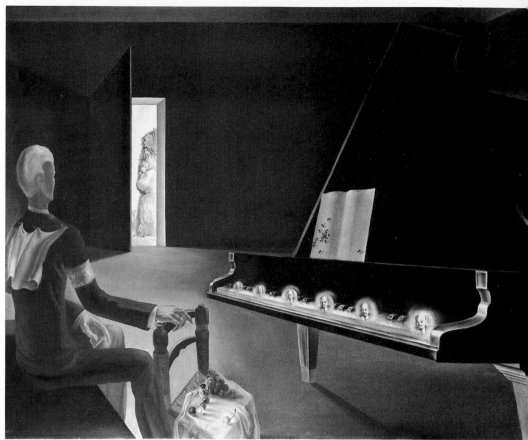

Thanks to government patronage, they and
many others rediscovered murals (and in the
process teamwork, for the walls they had to
cover were huge), experimented with poly-
chromatic colors, declared (as Picasso did)
their horror of a world "sinking in an ocean
of pain and death."

For artists, the Exhibition was a sort of Popular Front WPA. Robert Delaunay helped design the Palace of Air and Railroads, Sonia Delaunay helped decorate it. Léger painted the Palace of Discoveries, Dufy the Palace of Electricity. Friend of the poet Federico García Lorca, Salvador Dalí (1904–1989) had worked with Buñuel on *Un Chien Andalou* in 1928 and brought his "paranoic-critical" paintings to Paris in 1929. In *Six Apparitions of Lenin on a Piano*, painted in 1931, he managed to connect his revolution paranoia with Lenin, whom he found as surrealistically fascinating as he soon would find Fascist dictators.

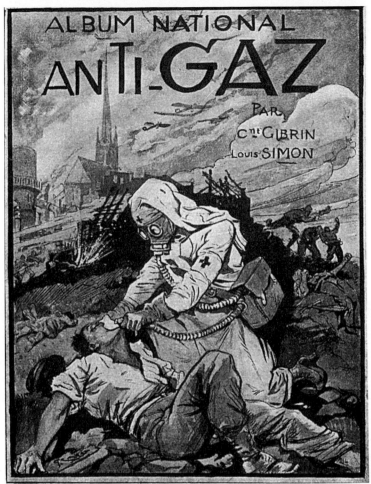

Charles Lavauzelle & Cie.

Picasso's vision of Guernica had less impact than
newsreels of the real-life nightmare that terrorized
and intimidated millions. But, all through the thirties,
pamphlets and exercises designed to anticipate air
attacks and gas warfare by building up civil defense
spread fear throughout the land. The more one prepared for war, the more one dreaded it.

As the Popular Front ran down, and peace with it, pacifism became more frenzied, anxiety more searing, pacifist meetings more passionate. But the disarmament they called for would leave the country morally and physically unprepared.

David Seymour/Magnum Photos

Within a few short years, a sort of peace was to return to France in the wake of German tanks, driving floods of refugees before them. *Left,* in May 1940, we see a mother and daughter fleeing their small town. Givet—in the Ardennes, and a few weeks later, in mid-June, poor Parisians, their belongings piled in hand carts, crossing a deserted Place de la Concorde on their way to the South and safety.

policy." Colonel Jean Fabry, an authentic hero, crippled, decorated, bore the American out. Speaking in the Chamber of Deputies in 1930, he described the imprint that the war had left: "Twelve years after the war we are still unable to throw off this fear [of invasion]. . . . It is in our blood: time will not alter it."[20]

What military planners feared most was a surprise attack. Against sudden offensives that would catch the military machine off its guard, only fortifications could preserve the country. That was a formula which appealed to pacifists suspicious of warmongering soldiers, to soldiers whom politicians kept on a short leash, to banking and business interests looking forward to profitable orders. In December 1929 a law—subsequently amplified—authorized a first four-billion-franc credit for the fortifications that became known as the Maginot Line after the then war minister, André Maginot. When Maginot died in 1932—of a typhoid fever caught eating oysters—the line was well on its way. It had been envisaged as extending from the Swiss border to the North Sea. Strategic and budgetary considerations pared it down, so that it petered out where the Luxemburg border did, at Longuyon, some thirty miles east of Sedan. The "natural barrier" of the Ardennes hills and forests was supposed to deflect attack thereafter toward the Belgian plain, where the expected clash between French and Germans would take place.[21]

Not everyone found such calculations convincing. Critics who accepted a defensive stance (not all did so) expressed concern at a fortified line that lacked permanent works along the Belgian border. Senate committees regularly called for fortification of the northern border. They were answered that constructing them would suggest a French stand on their own frontier, with Belgium left in the lurch if and when attacked. They were told that the Belgian plain was the best place to meet and defeat the aggressor. They were also told that fortifications past Sedan and on to the North Sea would cut a destructive swath through heavily built and populated areas difficult to evacuate in case of war. Some thought these were just excuses: "The present financial difficulties of the French government would appear to be the principal reason why the extension . . . cannot be seriously considered at present."[22] Articles in the press and government discussions continued to the next war, but the General Staff dragged its feet. Though in 1931 the Belgians made clear their lack of enthusiasm for military collaboration, and though in October 1936 they repudiated a French military alliance that looked more like a risk than a guarantee, military planners continued to dream of the kingdom as a foreordained battleground on which the French armies, their flanks protected by the Maginot Line at one end and the North Sea at the other, would face and defeat the enemy in their own good time.

It was true that after 1932 or 1933 costs of rearmament limited their choices. Short of men, they had invested in fortifications. When they needed men, they lacked the funds they had invested in cement *and* the military doctrine that would permit defense to become effective. But if the preparedness proved imperfect, propaganda made up for much of it. The mass of the French public was readily persuaded that it could sleep safe behind its cement walls. As Philippe Nord, the mystery writer, made an officer on the Maginot Line insist, "Really, isn't that so . . . it's totally impregnable?" One doubts if it ever was, but we shall never know. What seems less doubtful is that faith is blind. When, in 1936, the minister of war inaugurated the fort that guarded the Rhine bridge of Kehl, leading to Strasbourg, he found that its heavy gun, too large for its turret, could not be installed. In spring 1938, when Jules Moch briefly held the portfolio of Public Works, he discovered that Maginot power lines could function only at the sufferance of the Germans. The Ministry of War and that of Public Works had not talked to each other about power supplies for the fortifications on which so much depended. The oversight was remedied in the nick of time.[23]

Of course, the fortified lines were never meant to be purely defensive. But that is how they worked, in military doctrine and on civilian minds.[24] Lack of confidence in French forces and in their will to fight had built the fortifications in the first place. Once built, they became a factor in the weakening of those they had been meant to reinforce. Too many political decision makers were veterans respectful of military hierarchy, unwilling or unable to question it too long. We shall soon see that soldiers were ultimately responsible for their failures. But political decadence—failure of thought and of policy—must also bear some responsibility for military defeat.

In March 1933 Winston Churchill outraged friend and foe in Britain's Parliament when he exclaimed, "Thank God for the French Army!" It is not clear that by 1933 the French Army was much to thank God for. The American military attaché seems to have been convinced that the French kept it up "as the outgrowth of [their] fear of Germany" and for no other reason. Its defensive strategy made it incapable of aiding the country's allies in Eastern Europe, hence of functioning as an extension or support of foreign policy. After Locarno, when France and Germany mutually guaranteed their common border but no others, after the Maginot Line and its statement of a timorous attitude, few could doubt that France lacked the means and will to carry out the principles its foreign policy asserted. "Would we be so crazy," the war minister, General Louis Maurin, asked the Chamber of Deputies in March 1935, "as to advance beyond our fortified barrier to I know not what adventure?"[25]

Had they been bent on military adventure, what would they use for it? All serious observers since the 1920s argued that the army ill compared with its predecessor of 1914, that Germans were superior in training and morale, the British ahead of it in modernization. Military service, reduced to eighteen months in 1923, had been cut to twelve months in 1928. It would be upped to two years in 1936, to compensate for the hollow classes born between 1915 and 1920—a quantitative improvement that would have been more effective had quality been maintained. But when depression struck, the defense budget was first in line for cuts. Half the economies of 1933 came from defense—among them five thousand regular officers and a quarter of the regular troops, backbone of every army. The years 1934 and 1935 would see further cuts, until morale, not brilliant in the twenties, plunged still lower. Once so high, the image of the military in the public eye darkened and shrank. Pacifism and antimilitarism went hand in hand. Senior officers were depressed; other ranks depressing. In 1932 Marshal Lyautey told Suzanne Borel, the future Mme. Georges Bidault, how the soldiers lining the route of President Doumer's funeral looked to him: "Lopsided, ill built, unable to stand up straight, they were a wretched lot!" Shortly before that, Doumer—while still alive—had heard of the two strapping sons of a prominent politician held up by a man with a toy gun while cycling through Brittany. They had handed over all he asked, including a bicycle. Doumer was shocked: "To put their hands up, what a humiliation! Young lads! Frenchmen! . . . *there* are fine recruits for you!"[26]

Testimony varies, of course. Some returned from their military service remembering apathy in the ranks and inefficiency among commanding officers. Others retained the image of a powerful, admirable body. Young Frenchmen admired their army, remembers Michel Debré. Pierre de Calan agrees, as does another future *inspecteur des finances*, Christian de Lavarenne. Four fifths of the French must have lived in the belief that their army was the strongest in the world. Was it the units they served in or their social class? Lavarenne recalls Gamelin asserting, *"On rentrera dans l'Allemagne comme dans du beurre.*" Did Maurice Gamelin really believe or say that Germany presented no greater obstacle than a hunk of butter? It does not sound like the chief of the General Staff as we know him.[27]

Son and grandson of generals, bright, erudite, courteous, diplomatic, great amateur of good food, Gamelin (1872–1958) was a prudent military bureaucrat and a pessimist, not a leader. Léon Blum, who admired him, found him "intelligent and limited."[28] But behind Gamelin stood Pétain, hero of Verdun, protector of poilus, another master of indecisiveness except in defense of his personal interests. Both men—Pétain relayed by Maxime Weygand in 1931, then by Gamelin in 1935, at the head of the military establishment—preached the defensive dogma, opposed overemphasis on newfangled tanks and planes, dismissed intelligence that did not fit their preconceptions. Born in 1867, Weygand, who had been Foch's chief of staff, had known men who had served on the staffs of generals who served the Revolution and Napoleon. Older still, Pétain, born in 1856, had grown up under the Second Empire of Napoleon's nephew, his mind forged in another age. The earliest photos in the family album showed the marshal's sisters wearing crinolines. Childhood experience should never be discounted, but personality predicted worse. Timid, suspicious (rather like Daladier, but shrewder), Pétain, declared an aide who knew him well, was a bull without horns.[29]

Then it had been Pétain who refused to fortify the northwestern border, who declared the Ardennes—Shakespeare's Forest of Arden—impenetrable, who stood by whilst armament credits were reduced. It would be Pétain who nurtured that brash young apostle of mechanized warfare Charles de Gaulle, then shunted him aside when he pressed too hard for his views. It would be Pétain who, in 1939, contributed to Louis Chauvineau's *Is an Invasion Still Possible?* a preface arguing that cement could withstand motorization, that defense could maneuver more rapidly than attack, that France could build a second Maginot Line and a third to back up the first, though evidently not a continuation where it was not wanted. Professor of fortification and director of the School of Military Engineers, General Chauvineau was, if not the father, at least the uncle of the Maginot Line. The spirit of his argument and of Pétain's preface was wholly defensive: Attack may bring a win, but for how long? Attack could bring defeat; what do you do then? Better play it safe.

Clemenceau had evaluated such types: "[W]hen heels click, minds close." Bertrand de Jouvenel, who knew whereof he wrote, felt that it would be hard to imagine the intellectual isolation of the officer corps between 1930 and 1940. Here, too, the evidence varies. Reading Simone de Lattre's account of her husband's life, the officers we encounter seem neither idle nor mediocre.[30] But regulars like Jean de Lattre de Tassigny and Alphonse Juin were few, their numbers further diminished by attrition and budget cuts. Although the cuts of the early thirties were going to be restored by Popular Front governments after 1936, the shortage of officers of all ranks, and of specialist officers especially, continued to draw comments in 1938.[31] With armaments being modernized, at least in theory, with supplies and communications growing more complicated, with theories of combined operations beginning to be aired, the role of regular officers and of non-coms grew, while their preparation to train reservists and recruits or deal with masses recalled in the event of mobilization lagged.

Even those leaders like Jean de Lattre, eager to improve morale, seem to have concentrated on creature comforts: refurbishing barracks, installing showers, replacing mess tins with crockery, setting up reading rooms and canteens.[32] Initiatives of this sort were highly overdue, but where they came they only addressed part of the problem. An army's morale is one third creature comforts, two thirds self-confidence born of hard training and obstacles overcome. The former were in short supply; the latter was seldom in evidence. French and foreign observers were struck by the caution of the fighting troops. In 1934 a confidential report on army morale referred to the debility (atonie) that deprived it of vitality, found weariness among officers, unenthusiastic docility among other ranks. Others concurred. "Reconnaissance units show excessive timidity," noted Americans, "while infantry advances at a dangerously slow pace." The German attaché was more cruel: "Has the French infantry forgotten how to attack?" American officers attached to elite tank units in the mid-thirties found the food excellent, differed about the training (some speaking highly of it, others judging it neglected), were surprised at the paucity of office equipment (few or no typewriters, all paper work done by hand) and even more by the absence of sports and games. One captain, after three months with a tank regiment at Angoulême, reported that though horses were available, no officers rode and "most of the captains are much overweight."[33]

An army is as good as its officers. Sartre may not be the most reliable witness on this score, but he was not alone to find his leaders "incompetent . . . conceited ninnies." What was worse, they were stuck in the mud. Postulant for an army commission, Guy de Carmoy was faced with an examination question: "To what extent should a soldier take initiatives?" After reflection, and against his better judgment, Carmoy answered: "Within the limits of army regulations and of orders received." He got the highest grade. Taken as a whole, the officer corps left something to be desired. And no wonder: Pay was poor, promotion slow, prestige dim. Senior officers who may have performed heroically on the Marne or Somme had aged since then. Duroselle, depressed by their poor quality, points out that in 1940 French colonels nearing their sixties faced German colonels of forty.[34]* A law of 1920 had set retirement for senior officers at sixty-two but kept those who commanded armies until seventy. A lot of their underlings had been the bright middle-aged men of a conflict whose lessons they applied when they themselves were old and tired. Too many were worn out because they stayed on as long as possible in order to avoid the ridiculously low retirement pay. Whatever the reasons, the effect was dim, and dimmer still because of latent hostility between general and subordinate officers, between staff officers and those who had come up in the trenches, between different—sometimes very different—generations. Longtime Socialist Minister of Education Jean Zay, mobilized between September 1939 and June 1940, noted disastrous impressions: an immense administrative machine, its cogs solely preoccupied with promotion, evincing no interest in modern strategy or tactics. Debré confirms. The army of the later thirties remained what it had been: "the respected bastion of a blind conformism."[35]

Conformism need not be blind to stifle. Dominant doctrine was just as reasonable as the theories challenging it; moreover, it was founded on experience. In 1934 Lieutenant Colonel de Gaulle's *Towards a Professional Army* had taken issue with ruling dogmas but also implicitly challenged the great democratic tradition of the nation in arms. A citizen army had once been an irresistible force. It was less so now that its ranks held a horde of pacifists, ill trained in routine-bound barracks. France, pleaded de Gaulle, could never match German numbers. It could hope to outmatch them qualita-

*In a recent study a high-ranking army officer and professor at the Ecole de Guerre judges the officer corps as being of high quality but notes the advanced age of too many reserve officers and concludes that with many junior officers over forty, numerous units went into fire led by men whose physical resistance was necessarily diminished. Other ranks, too, were overage and, sometimes, overweight at the war's beginning, the Wehrmacht's average age stood below thirty, that of French troops over forty. Nor was this any wonder since woefully short of men, the French called up reserves back to the class of 1909. Pierre Rocolle, *La Guerre de 1940* (1990), I, 192, 202, 205.

tively, however, in the training and equipment of a mechanized, motorized, armored force of one hundred thousand volunteers. Such notions fluttered too many dovecotes. De Gaulle's elite force could become a praetorian guard; it was certainly undemocratic and antiequalitarian. Worse still, its aggressive implications went against the strongly held beliefs of the hierarchy. When a new *Infantry Combat Handbook* was published in 1938, the strongest argument in its favor would be that it did not *innovate* but "preserved from oblivion" the lessons of World War I. Those lessons had been defensive. As General Maurin reassured the Chamber, offensive doctrine "cost us quite dear enough, for us to avoid it henceforth. (Loud applause) How can one believe that we still think of offensives, when we have spent billions to set up a fortified barrier?"[36]

The year 1935, when these words were spoken, opened the dangerous period of the "hollow years," when army recruits were about halved in number. Also a depressing demographic interlude, when the number of deaths in France actually outnumbered births. No wonder that faced with German aggression, military doctrine insisted on reassuring images and a defensive stance. It would be this mentality that limited the possibilities of armor and hemmed it within the limits of timidity. Emile Servan-Schreiber had been struck by a newsreel where images of a military review at Nürnberg suggesting "the incredible military renaissance of a Germany going full steam ahead" contrasted with shots of a Montmartre race in which the prize went to the *slowest*, and with coverage of French maneuvers. "Soldiers drinking plonk, cavalry charging as it had done 100 years before, not one tank, not one motorized unit. If the Germans paid to choose our films, they couldn't have done better!" The Germans did not need to pay; their rivals manufactured enough demobilizing doctrines and images for two. As late as July 1939 the authoritative *Infantry Review* published an article rejoicing that French doctrine on motorized warfare had withstood all temptation to depart from the hard-learned lessons of 1917–1918, which prohibited the use of armor without close infantry support. "During this time all other armies were falling for the seductions of speed, for the promising charms of brilliant cavalcades [of armor]. . . . It took a lot of courage to resist the contagion. . . ."[37]

Resist it they did. In 1922 one deputy, an ex-artillery captain, had declared that "you can recognize a modern army by its smell: it smells of petrol, not of horse manure." But horses and their partisans knew how to hold their own. When, in the middle thirties, Roger Goetze, born in 1912, did his military service at the Artillery School in Poitiers, his class still wore spurs. "Not very convenient for driving a truck, but what do you expect . . . ?" The general officers of the cavalry, in whose hands motorization lay, were "usually" members or officials of horse-breeding associations. By 1932 a cavalry division consisted of two horse brigades and one motorized brigade. Many of their officers, Americans reported, believed that "perhaps they have already gone too far on the lines of motorization."[38] Timidity and thrift shaped that attitude. All that the French could think of was to replace open trenches, muddy and dangerous, by more comfortable, less fragile installations. From 1930 to 1939 they labored to carry out this ideal but could not pay both for concrete and for mechanized arms. Yet when this has been said, strategy and tactics go beyond mere means. The quarrel was about what was best to do, not how to pay for it. The horse, argued an article of 1935 in a military review, is the only true cross-country conveyance that obstacles fatal to vehicles will not stop. Besides, France had plenty of fodder but little oil. Too dependent on imported oil already, complete mechanization would place it at the mercy of forces it could not control. It would also ruin the farmers, who were hard hit already, and the garrison towns whose economy turned around horse manure. When in July 1936 the War Ministry replaced horses with motorized vehicles in tactical units, Lunéville lost its three cavalry regiments. For the city of twenty-four thousand and for the countryside around, "it was catastrophic." In the *Action française*, which many officers read, General Lavigne-Delville warned against substituting engines alimented by foreign fuel for the national horse fed by national oats. There was little fear that this would happen soon. In 1937 budget allocations for military transport fuel stood at 30 million francs, those for fodder over 128 million.[39]

In November 1939 the American ambassador, William Bullitt, thought that the General Staff believed the only way to win the war was by a combination of air attack supplemented by tanks. He must have been talking to the Germans. For those who made military policy in France, tanks remained mobile gunships to be used in support of infantry. This moderately antediluvian position had been reinforced a couple of years earlier when armor had failed to open Franco's way into Madrid. German tactics might offer "catastrophic" successes; the French-style combination of armor and infantry promised "limited but certain gains." In the *Revue de France* a military commentator rejoiced to see that aviation, tanks, and motorized units used by themselves could not bring victory. "So much the better!" The famous *Panzerdivisionen* were nothing but scrap iron. Reassured, one could turn back to serious things like horses.[40]

Which was just as well, since mechanized transport limped. Mobilized in September 1939, Raymond Abellio would find the matériel of his infantry division what it had been twenty years before, its transport all horse-drawn. Civilian vehicles—cars, trucks, vans—requisitioned at mobilization broke down one after the other, and there were no spare parts or tools to get them going again. Armor too, after Spain, was treated as a moderate priority only. *Le Temps* burbled about the failure of German armor in the Polish campaign. Intelligence, having studied the Germans' massive use of armor and dive bombers against infantry, drew the right conclusions, but these did not fit the views of the High Command. Speaking to an American officer, a major of the General Staff insisted several times that "the tank is finished as an offensive weapon."[41] Bernard de Margerie, in the Third Hussars, rode off to war quite literally. When the hussars were motorized, he was transferred to one of the few horse regiments left, the First Light Cavalry (*Chasseurs à cheval*), who rode into Belgium on May 10 only to be cut to pieces by German tanks. About the same time as the light cavalry, the Thirty-seventh Tank Battalion of the First Armored Division engaged the Germans near Philippeville. Of thirty-three tanks going into action, seven came out. Personnel losses had been light. The battalion commander, Major de Cissey, was wounded when his tank was hit by the shell of a French 75. De Cissey's son, a young aviator, believed most of the losses should be attributed to breakdowns.[42] They may have been due also to running out of gas, just as delays in going into action were sometimes due to long refueling stops.

The practical effects of military doctrine came out in other ways. Combined operations, however talked about, remained an alien idea. As late as 1938 "no specific measures in this direction have been reported." Air strategy and tactics were planned with no reference to ground or naval forces. These in their turn maneuvered as if there were no danger from the air. Foreign observers admiring the evolutions of army units were nevertheless surprised by their indifference to cover: "[T]hey would have made a wonderful target for attack aviation." But attack aviation also was a foreign concept. Americans, Germans, later the British too, had attack machines: fighter planes. The French, who believed in bombers, had few. By 1938 the Americans noted efforts to produce more pursuit planes because "bombers must be intercepted and destroyed."[43]

This reminds us that French air power influenced policies largely by its absence. In January 1938 the respected commander of the First Air Corps, General Joseph Vuillemin, reported to his minister that in case of conflict "French aviation would be crushed in a few days." He was equally categorical two months later, when addressing the Permanent Committee of National Defense: The air force would be annihilated in fifteen days.[44] The catastrophic situation reflected serious disparities of intellect and nerve between French generals and their German counterparts but also, and above all, the prejudices of stubborn military mandarins. Dominant figures like Pétain and Weygand looked on the air arm as an auxiliary of land armies, useful for reconnaissance and tactical support, useless when it came to strategic operations. In paradoxical alliance with fiscal conservatives appalled by the cost of building an effective fighting force and with pacifists revolted by visions of aerochemical devastation, the Ministry of Defense and the General Staff dismissed Douhet's lurid fantasies of strategic bombing and throttled all attempts to build a large modern air force.*

Though military expenses began to rise after 1934 and rose steeply after 1936, keeping steadily ahead of the British,[45] what Herrick Chapman calls the holy alliance of military conservatism and financial orthodoxy made sure the air force got no more than a trickle of the new credits. By 1937, when one third of the British defense budget went to the Royal Air Force, its cross-Channel counterparts received only one sixth of the French. Committed to a tactical air force, not a strategic one, the soldiers saw to it that in combat the army would control the greatest part of air force strength and use that in unimaginative ways.[46]

The air force's troubles, however, went beyond military doctrine and military rivalries. Full of brilliant designers and skilled craftsmen, the aeronautical industry was a shambles, a congerie of small firms incapable of facing the world of modern productivity and unwilling to test its waters. An autonomous Air Ministry had been set up by Poincaré in 1928, within days of the minister of commerce responsible for aeronautical affairs losing

---

*In March 1930, a few months after the general's death, the *Rivista aeronautica* published Douhet's "The War of 19–," in which a sudden German attack on France and Belgium by armored divisions supported by overwhelming air power destroys the allied air forces in the first hours of fighting, breaks up road and rail traffic, and leaves more than a hundred important centers "in flame and smothered in clouds of poison gas which in some cases were carried by the wind, spreading death and terror all around the countryside." See Giulio Douhet, *The Command of the Air* (Washington, 1983), 295–394, and, for the quotation, 391. Douhet acknowledged these were barbarous methods but made clear that they brought victory. For skeptical readers, his predictions fell in the category of science fiction.

his life in a plane crash. It was steadily headed by committed and enthusiastic men. From 1928 to 1940 five of the eight ministers who led it had been aviators during the war, and Pierre Cot, the longest-lasting (1933–1934, 1936–1938), who had been a combat artilleryman, learned to fly when he took over his department. All air ministers tried to stimulate research, innovation, reequipment, productivity; all but the last seem to have failed. Good intentions could not triumph over ingrained conservatism, Malthusianism, and financial caution.

Things began to change for the better when Pierre Cot, the nonconformist firebrand, took over for the second time in a Popular Front cabinet dedicated to rearmament. During his first tenure he had forced the country's five airlines to merge into one—Air France—if they wanted indispensable state subsidies to continue. Now he set to replacing superannuated generals with younger men and, most pressing, to modernizing the industry that represented "the outstanding weakness in French aviation."[47] But Cot was tarred with the brush of his leftish sympathies, which complicated personal relations both with his air staff and with management, while his reforms made things worse before they could get better.

Nationalization with a view to rationalization of aircraft production replaced the morass of small producers with a welter of larger ones hobbled by conflicts with both state and labor. Through 1937 production instead of rising fell. So did morale, while confusion and labor troubles increased. A Curtiss-Wright engineer inspecting French factories that turned out aircraft engines found laggard workmen and a lot of work done by hand that machines could have done faster. After 1938 the efforts of Cot's successor, Guy La Chambre, obtained funding of accelerated production schedules, but these remained most impressive on paper. In the shadow of German aggression and primed by generous government subsidies, industry was not unwilling to follow La Chambre's new plan but still found it hard to change its ways. Into May 1940 report after report strikes the same note: In aircraft factories equipment is poor; machines are too few; parts are hammered, filed, drilled, fitted by hand; resources are wasted; workmanship is unimpressive. Nine months into the war gigantic efforts had just succeeded in raising output from about five hundred planes a year to as many a month. But by then it was too late.[48]

The problem list goes on. Communications presented another serious drawback to battle-worthiness. General, later Marshal, Joffre had refused to use a telephone. Pétain would attribute France's unprecedented defeat in

1940 to the substitution of electronic communications for carrier pigeons. He would have done better to blame the failure to substitute electronics. In 1935 American observers of mechanized maneuvers in Champagne drew attention to what they considered their "outstanding lesson: the extreme difficulty of maintaining control over a mechanical force due to inadequate means of communication."[49] For Crémieux-Brilhac, "the army seems to ignore radio." Its transmissions relied on field telephones and on liaison by officers, runners, motorcyclists. Radio equipment was nonexistent or else awkward. In September 1939 the gendarmerie of Alsace and Lorraine misunderstood its orders and prematurely massacred all the carrier pigeons of three departments. The General Staff got its news of the Polish disasters from German broadcasts caught on a hotel radio set. The duc de Brissac describes the generalissimo Gamelin "isolated without radio in a bunker of the fort at Vincennes." When General Weygand took over command from Gamelin late in May, "[h]e discover[ed] with amazement that the transmission center of the General Staff has no radio sender or receiver." A French liaison officer entering Belgium on May 10, 1940, was covered with flowers by the Belgians but could not get his superiors on the telephone. His first report, as Claude Paillat recorded, would be carried by a motorcyclist. The following day, May 11, General Prioux's message to the High Command would be sent by carrier pigeon: "a colombogram."[50] Pétain's blame had been premature.

In 1891, jotting down notes for *La Débâcle*, Emile Zola insisted that the crushing defeat of 1870 had been fatal: a historical necessity. "On one side Germany with its discipline, its science, its new organization . . . on the other France, weakened, no longer keeping up with change, bound to make every mistake and making them in effect." The book, which appeared in 1892, contains passages that made painful reading half a century later. The infantryman Maurice Levasseur, a patriot scarcely doubting eventual victory, can't help feeling uneasy at what he sees about him: inaction, lack of foresight, an inextricable mess, but, above all, a slow paralysis that, starting from the top, "would invade the whole army, disorganize it, annihilate it, casting it into the worst disasters without its being able to defend itself." France, Zola concluded, died of routine and folly; it did not keep up with the modern world. *La Débâcle*—downfall, collapse, disaster—was the inevitable title for an account of what ensued. "It was so because it could not be otherwise."[51]

X

The War Nobody Wanted

It is bad manners to expect victory when
you don't feel like fighting.
—*CHARLES PÉGUY*

You have never considered what manner of men are these with whom
you will have to fight, and how utterly unlike yourselves. They are revolutionary, equally quick in the conception and in the execution of every
new plan; while you are conservative—careful only to keep what you
have, originating nothing, and not acting even when action is most urgent. They are bold beyond their strength; they run risks which prudence
would condemn. . . . Whereas it is your nature, though strong, to act
feebly; when your plans are most prudent to distrust them; and when
calamities come upon you to think that you will never be delivered from
them. They are impetuous, and you are dilatory; they are always abroad,
and you are always at home. For they hope to gain something by leaving their homes; but you are afraid that any new enterprise may imperil
what you have already.

THIS IS NOT Henri de Kerillis speaking but Thucydides' version of the
Corinthian ambassadors' talking the Spartans into going to war against an
aggressive Athens. It is also a good description of the mood in which the
French faced a formidable enemy.

France's fortunes in war and its approach to war are indissoluble from the run-up to it. But the run-up itself was part of the experience. Before catastrophe came, a phony peace preceded phony war. "We live in a strange intermediate state between peace and war," Henri Lefebvre wrote a fellow leftist in April 1939.[1] One of the strangest aspects of this uncertain time are the contradictory signals sent by the powers that be: Daladier and Reynaud wanted rearmament to move full speed ahead; the Foreign Ministry under Georges Bonnet insisted that all go easy on Hitler and Mussolini.[2] Fashion greeted "the conjunction of Venus and Mars" by designing *tailleur* costumes "clean cut and with a military air," but also flouncy petticoats and corsets with whalebone stays. With summer, *Femina* recommended *"Défense passive"* sunglasses against too strong a glare. The cinema was even less equivocal. Films dark with foreboding were increasingly spelled by inspiriting features—*Trois de St Cyr, Gunga Din*—and by newsreels that bulged with armaments.[3]

Counterpart of uneasy times, "the greatest criminal of our days since Landru" was being tried at Versailles. Convicted of murdering ten women and one boy, Henri Désiré Landru had been executed in 1922. Arrested in December 1937 for crimes committed between July and November of that year, a German interloper, Eugen Weidmann, had confessed at once but waited fifteen months to be brought to trial, then three more before his execution. The tale of Weidmann's sins was simple. With three accomplices, he had preyed on tourists brought to Paris by the exposition: They robbed and killed an American dancer, Jean de Koven, an Alsatian girl, a visiting German, a taxi driver, and several others. Their spoils, as so often happens, had been relatively modest, but the manner of operation and the murderer's cool detachment impressed a public less habituated to criminal violence than half a century before, or since.[4]

Weidmann's trial, otherwise unexceptional, had been marked by orders to curtain off the lower part of the public gallery so as to preserve the sobriety of a court that would otherwise be faced by the distracting revelations of "very short skirts." On March 3 the monster—more frightening for being recognized as intelligent and sensitive—had been condemned to death. The sentence of an accomplice similarly condemned having been commuted, the German was left to face his doom alone, in the small hours of Saturday, June 17, under the guillotine in front of the Versailles prison. Two hundred visitors' permits had been given out, but the "repugnant crowd" described with lip-smacking disapproval by a prurient press made a night of it. Clustered on roofs, at windows, on trees, and on the ground, thousands joined in the long, frantic wait that turned into a "filthy spree": smell of frying chips, clamors, jostles, whistles, catcalls, clucks, filling the soft springtime night.[5]

A few months later at a summer spa Hervé Alphand met one who had been there: Louis Louis-Dreyfus, whom he describes with some hyperbole as the richest man in Europe. Everyone needs a relaxation now and then, Louis-Dreyfus confided. It had been hard to get up so early, but it was worth it. "Weidmann's execution was edifying, purifying. I did not regret it." However edifying the saturnalia might have been, a decree of June 26 abolished public executions. In July the next murderer to be guillotined, a thirty-four-year-old mechanic who merely knifed his mother-in-law and wife to death, would have his head cut off in a prison courtyard. Pending "scandalous manifestations" on a more grandiose scale, the French would be denied the acrid zest of one another's deaths.[6]

Meanwhile, the weeks between Weidmann's trial and his execution had proved eventful. The horoscope of March 16 announced an uncertain day "when we risk lapses of judgment and even of good sense . . . many small vexations." Confirming the predictions, on that day Hitler occupied the rump of Czechoslovakia, which had been sacrificed six months before. Smaller vexations came while the government dithered over letting the Germans take over the Czech Paris Embassy. Only British ire appears to have prevented their finally doing so.[7] Having accepted humiliation in September 1938, it seems that there was no end to the humble pie the democracies, would ingurgitate. On March 22 Lithuania was forced to cede Memel to Germany; on April 7 Mussolini, not to be outdone by his ally, invaded Albania. The weekly illustrated *Match*, featuring the Italian occupation of the little kingdom, carried an article on German industry by Bertrand de Jouvenel in which the reporter asked a German officer what raw material the Germans found most tempting: "Steel is master of the world. Most tempting for us is the iron ore of Polish Silesia and that of French Lorraine. But everything in due course!"[8]

The Spanish war, begun in 1936, was petering out. Barcelona fell in January; in February Franco had been recognized; Spanish refugees were streaming across the Pyrenees, creating serious practical problems and concerns even more acute than the material difficulties they raised. The president of the Chamber's Foreign Affairs Committee complained that five hundred thousand had arrived in France, only a small proportion of these had returned, hundreds of thousands remained to be dealt with. "The presence on our territory of numerous foreign elements is not only a financial burden, but a serious impediment to public order and national security." Those who could not be persuaded to go back would be parked like cattle in camps not far from the border that became a byword for odious discomfort. Over the gate of one, framed between French flags, could be read the inscription: CAMP DE CONCENTRATION DE ST.-CYPRIEN. Below that: VIVE LA FRANCE.[9]

Previous crises had courteously allowed the general public to draw breath from one to the next. Now they tumbled furiously in each other's wake. On March 31, piqued by Bohemia's demise, Britain guaranteed the territorial integrity of Poland; on April 13, after Albania's fall, Britain and France extended the same guarantee to Romania and Greece. On April 28, Hitler, in a torrential speech over three hours long, broke with Poland while threatening it with the worst. On April 30 Russia proposed a military alliance against Germany (allied negotiators traveling by sea were to reach Leningrad on August 10). Then, on the fourth of May, the leftist daily *L'Œuvre* published an explosive article by the Neo-Socialist pacifist Marcel Déat, "Do We Have to Die for Danzig?" To his own question Déat returned a loud No! French folk had not the slightest wish to die for "Poldavians" or for anybody else. The convoluted conflicts of people far away were not their affair. Why should they lay their lives down for them? Nor were the facts at issue simply black or white: Munich had been, in principle at least, about the self-determination of Czechoslovakia's Germans, the Sudeten. Danzig was German, too; the Polish Corridor, which cut through German territory to link Danzig with Poland, was a geographical and political aberration. Why should the French be dragged into a war they didn't want, for a cause that on the face of it ought to be peacefully settled?[10]

The desperate urge for peace brought other uncertainties to the fore. The British alliance could prove a broken reed. It had done so before, when the British repeatedly failed to support French resistance to German breaches of the Versailles peace. In any case, French and British did not get on that well. Plenty of French found little to choose between British and Germans. "The English get on my nerves," one of Edmée Renaudin's neighbors told her in May.[11] As for a Russian alliance, there were certainly those who believed that a pact between France, Britain, and Russia would intimidate Hitler and discourage further aggressions on his part. But the guarantees handed to Russia's neighbors on a platter gave Poland and Romania support without requiring them to provide facilities for Russian intervention against Germany. Above everything else, most of the French except the Communists considered Bolsheviks as bad as Nazis, indeed worse. Respectable rightists would not sit at the same table as Communists, let alone stand shoulder to shoulder with them.[12] The idea of a war against the Germans about some other country's interests and on the same side as Muscovite predators seemed revolting. Better think again?

In April a Gallup poll had found 51 percent of the American public expecting war that year; by May the proportion had fallen to 32 percent. *Paris-Soir* explained American reasons for relaxing: No one on either side had enough money for war. The money would be forthcoming. At mid-May Paul Reynaud's new national defense loan brought in six billion francs in six hours.[13] Even without the Russians, a firm attitude, refusal to make more concessions would prevent further land grabs. The Germans, in any case, "were tired of their regime, it wouldn't survive the war." The French meanwhile had other fish to fry. The 150th anniversary of the Great Revolution evoked appeals—from Herriot among others—to avoid civil war. Otherwise it attracted no more attention than the decree-law postponing by two years the general elections due to be held in 1940 and thus prolonging the tenure of the present Chamber by two years. The thirty-second cycling Tour de France took off without German or Italian riders, to be won by a Belgian. The military parade of July 14, in which French and British units marched past in unison, was drenched by showers, and yet the crowd was large and enthusiastic.[14] That same month a national survey revealed that only one in six refused to fight for Danzig, while 76 percent were ready to use force in its defense. The silent majority seems to have been less passive and less defeatist than the noisy minority.[15]

July turned out a month of arrests and rumors of arrests designed to scotch German propaganda. But holidays were coming. Nobody was sure if they would be interrupted, if passive defense sunglasses would have to be exchanged for more active garb, but the August sun saw three million French make for mountains, beaches, or the countryside. Those who could afford it trundled with them the newly published translation of *Gone with the Wind* or else the latest number of *Femina*, more portable than *Autant en emporte le vent* but just as decorative with its predictions of bustles and bows, *drapés, poufs*, facings—more complicated fashions for complicated times.[16]

The Nazi-Soviet Pact of August 22 drove ritual August features off uninspired front pages: "All Paris on holiday." "At Divonne, the capital of repose, happiness is untroubled." French Communist leaders too were on holiday—Maurice Thorez on the Mediterranean coast, Jacques Duclos in his native Pyrenees—and *L'Humanité* still called for a Franco-Russo-British pact. It ignored that Moscow had changed course in the spring, even while luring on the Westerners it distrusted.[17] The Nazi-Soviet Pact sealed the prospect of war. On August 25 reservists only recently released from the Munich mobilization were being recalled again. The dollar, gaining 10 percent, reached forty francs. The Communist *L'Humanité* and *Ce Soir*, which had just glorified Russia's pacific gesture ("Silence to the anti-Soviet pack!"), were suspended. Censorship came into force, and newspapers began to appear peppered with blank spaces.[18] Holidaymakers were making tracks for home. On September 1, while *Je Suis Partout* headlined A BAS LA GUERRE, VIVE LA FRANCE, German troops invaded Poland; on September 2 general mobilization was announced; on September 3 Britain and France declared war on Germany—the French six hours later than their allies. That day Hervé Alphand marked the first Sunday of the war by lunching at Larue's splendiferous restaurant. The following day Anatole de Monzie noted in his diary: "This Sept 4, France at war does not believe in the war."[19]

That was one way of putting it, and it cut close to the bone. Many of those who thought that a firm attitude would discourage German aggressiveness were surprised to find that firmness had not worked. Many felt that if a war was to be fought, the Germans were the wrong enemy altogether. Some simply panicked, fighting to get home from Brittany or Savoy, "the expectation of catastrophe reflected in their faces," or to get out of cities slated for destruction: "If you are a mother, your *duty* is to leave Paris." Most simply did their duty, whatever that duty was.[20]

There are as many versions of the mobilization of 1939 as there are of patriotism in the 1930s or of the Battle of France in 1940. We have accounts of a mobilization that worked like clockwork, others that stress the Communists in railway stations yelling, "Don't go!" and, "Peace! Peace!" My own impression is close to that of the prefect of the Rhône in Lyons who, in September 1939, reported "something between resolution and resignation." Much of the evidence bears him out, although it leans rather toward the latter term. "Resignation," remembers Pierre de Calan, "Resignation," echoes Bernard Cazeaux. "Most men are as indifferent to the fate of Poland as they had been to that of Czechoslovakia. All obeyed but did no more than obey. Besides, no one could see the sense of the venture. . . ."[21] Another recurring term is *pagaille*—a shambles. Calan remembers a prodigious shambles. So does Léonce Chaleil, a truck driver in an Alpine unit. So does the duc de Brissac.[22] But large movements of troops and matériel are bound to be chaotic, and evidence suggests that they settled down into the institutionalized "shambolism" of military life.

Dispatched to cover the first day of mobilization at the Gare de l'Est, one journalist returned to his editor reporting no enthusiasm but a resolute mood. The editor sighed: "One can see that they have nothing to lose. . . ." That gives a class-cultural sense of the gap between chatterers and the steady, stoic mass. But of course, it's more complicated. Coming on the heels of mobilization and demobilization in September–October 1938, the call-up of 1939 was taken as a replay that would also end in a settlement. Reservists, often drunk, lived in the expectation of another Munich. Believing that he would be back home in a few days, François Bizard, called back from army leave, did not even bother to say good-bye to his parents. The anticipated air bombardments never materialized. "Thus far," William Bullitt noted on September 8, "a curious unreality about the war."[23] Perhaps the war itself was a false alarm?

Many hoped that it might so prove. Daladier, who had no sympathy for Poland ("a vulture") and no confidence in it ("stupid"), expected German bombardments so terrible that the public would drive him from political life and probably kill him. But, then, few in government doubted that things would go badly for Germany's foes, and events proved them right. On September 18 Russian troops entered Poland. On September 19, *Paris-Soir*, which had been publishing installments of Agatha Christie's *Ten Little Niggers*, printed the last: "And then there were none." By the end of the month Poland had been devoured. The French were unworried. Reynaud had assured them that victory would be theirs because their side was strongest—*Nous vaincrons parce que nous sommes les plus forts*—and the Stock Exchange held fast. So did the army, ready and formidable, but not to be risked in mere fighting, as Giraudoux explained to the American Club in a lecture entitled "Why We Make a War, and Why We Do Not Make It."[24]

The second alternative was more evident than the first. If the songs that people sing or listen to with pleasure are anything to go by, resignation reigned. The song heard everywhere was a mopey romance, "J'attendrai . . . ," while attempts to strike up "Marseillaise" or "Madelon" evoked derisive hoots, at least in soldiers' cafés. One of the winter's great successes was a ditty that Maurice Chevalier sang at the Casino de Paris, depicting the French Army as a mirror image of French society:

Le colonel était d'Action Française,	The colonel an Action Française royalist,
Le commandant était un modéré,	The major just a middling moderate,
Le capitaine était pour le diocèse,	The captain sided with the diocese,
Et le lieutenant boulottait du curé.	The lieutenant loathed clergy and *noblesse.*
Le juteux était un fervent socialiste,	The sergeant major wildly socialist,
Le sergeant un extrémiste convaincu,	The sergeant was a rabid radical,
Le caporal s'inscrit sur toutes les listes	The corporal voted for all comers
Et le deuxième class' au PMU.	The private was for football pools an' all.
Le colonel avait de l'albumine,	The colonel had an albuminoid surfeit,
Le commandant souffrait du gros colon,	The major's colon was a filthy mess,
Le capitaine avait bien mauvaise mine	The captain looked like hell had frozen over
Et le lieut'nant avait des ganglions.	The lieutenant's ganglions needed redress.
Le juteux avait des coliques nephrétiques,	The sergeant major ailed with renal colic
Le sergeant avait le pylore atrophié,	The sergeant from a strangled hernia,
Le caporal un coryza chronique,	The corporal's eczema was chronic
Et le deuxième class' des cors aux pieds.	The private's bunions were anathema.
Et tout ça fait d'excellents Français,	And all this makes excellent Frenchmen
D'excellents soldats	Excellent soldiers
Qui marchent au pas;	Who march in step.
Ils n'en avaient plus l'habitude. . . .[25]	They hadn't been used to it. . . .

There wasn't really that much marching to get used to. Mobilization soon turned into general immobilization. Five million men had been called up, a quarter of the male population, most of whom had nothing to do after four or five in the afternoon, little enough during the rest of the day. Their main concern became how to get out of uniform or, at least, out of the lines. "The war," noted a staff lieutenant on November 7, "we don't think of it." The bombing, the gassing, the microbes, all the nightmares of previous years seemed to have been set aside along with peace. The press talked about a war of nerves, but nerves had been more on edge before September than they were during the following months.[26]

The archbishop of Besançon denounced a disquieting situation: No great battles, few dead or wounded; "many seem to forget that we are at war." Many, of course, would rather that they weren't. Joseph Peschadour, Socialist deputy of Corrèze, asked his neighbor Monzie, in the government, to do something about it: "Is there a war? Are we at war?" Wasn't the state of war a formality to be brought to an end? Failing a declaration of peace, politicians acted as if business were normal; parliamentary commissions discussed the possible abolition of first-class compartments in passenger trains, worried about the winter sports industry and the winter season on the Côte d'Azur, proposed replacing puttees with leather leggings. In October 1939 the General Staff, dissatisfied with the fare it was getting, posted all available chefs in uniform to its quarters at Meaux. *"Enfin, nous allions avoir des chefs."* If people knew how their war was run, Daladier confided to his friends at dinner, they would have thrown us into the Seine long ago.[27]

How should they know? Why should they care? The press was reassuring or else silent. Censorship prevented untoward hostility to the Germans, prohibited articles arguing for the Reich's dismemberment or suggesting that Hitler was a bloody fool, excluded references to an anti-Fascist war in case Mussolini's feelings should be hurt.* Paris was much more pleasant; the traffic was light; a lot of shops had closed as during the holidays, then opened again with little sense of a change. Confectioners sold boxes shaped like gas masks but containing sweets. Stationers stocked packets of small flags of all nations, including that of the enemy with its black swastika on a white ground. Horse races suspended at the start of hostilities started again. Wages and prices had been frozen as of September 1, 1939, but prices were creeping up while the minister of agriculture refused to restrict consumption. Wartime rationing would only be introduced two months before the Germans attacked. Edgar Ansel Mowrer, the war correspondent, returning to Paris at the end of winter, described a restaurant meal on a day of food restrictions when he did not expect to find much to eat: "a choice between seven kinds of oysters, six or seven kinds of fish including bouillabaisse, no butcher's meat (veal, mutton, beef) and no sausages, 'only' rabbit, chicken and curry; vegetable hors d'oeuvres, caviar, anchovies, sardines; no pastries, cakes or candy, but choice between fruit salad, pineapple with kirsch and *soufflé à la liqueur.* Thanks to a couple of fairly decent wines, we managed to get this sort of thing down."[28] No wonder Mowrer wondered whether the country was at war.

---

*Yet in November 1938 the censor had permitted the sale of toys ridiculing Hitler as Don Quixote charging a windmill, with fat Göring as Sancho in attendance. B.D.I.C. Phototèque, Paris.

"Sheltered behind the Maginot Line," explained *Paris-Soir* on January I, 1940, "the nation is safe and working much as usual."[29] Cinemas, bars, and *dancings* did a brisk trade. The Dutch were debating whether their national painters should paint flowers on their fortifications. The French football team defeated Portugal 3–2. Opinion settled into the belief that there would be no war or that the war would be won without any fighting.* For months the most visible signs of war had appeared in fashion: sober costumes, shorter skirts, epaulets, pajamas and overalls designed for shelter wear, the slate blue of the RAF as a favorite color. Models bore martial names: Spahi for a Lanvin suit, Camouflage for a Schiaparelli coat. Schiaparelli excelled herself, turning out "air raid suits, lastex elastic waists for 'fat and lean years,' *culottes* for cycling, skirts with enormous pockets, dresses with built-in muffs for queuing in the cold, prints representing ration cards, coupons, schedules: Monday—no meat, Tuesday—no alcohol, Wednesday—no butter, Thursday—no fish, Friday—no meat, Saturday—no alcohol, but Sunday—*toujours l'amour.*"[30]

Not everyone who read *Gone with the Wind* was troubled by its tale of victory of a more populous, industrial North over the less developed South which suggested that Germany might be expected to triumph over France for similar reasons. They might have been more troubled by the pacifist epilogue to Roger Martin du Gard's *Les Thibault*, published in January 1940 and by the dying hero's last jottings: "Not acceptance. Indifference. Exhaustion that cancels revolt. Reconciliation with the inevitable. . . . Peace. Let it end. . . . It's simpler than one thinks." It was.[31]

The Germans worked hard to destabilize the country and weaken what will for war there was. From July 1939 France had been peppered with brochures and tracts arguing Germany's case, calling for peace, reminding those who needed a reminder that Britain, once again, was ready to fight to the last Frenchman. "The French risk their lives, the British their machines," went the German jingle. It worked quite well. An army of wine bibbers meshed badly with one that guzzled tea. The British were too well off: Their higher pay, their enviable Players cigarettes, their whiskey irritated. "Anglophobia appears practically general in the French Army," noted Claude Jamet without much regret. All the songs about entente cor-

*In November 1939 Simone de Beauvoir, visiting Sartre at Brumath, not far from Strasbourg, notes: "Sartre is persuaded that there will be no fighting, that it will be a modern war without massacres as modern painting is without subject, music without melody, physics without matter." *Journal de guerre*, 122.

diale to the contrary, "we cannot find much sympathy for each other. These people are more foreign, they seem more far away than the Chinese." German radio broadcasts beamed to France from Stuttgart were more effective still. French radio programs never were much good; news bulletins were soon dismissed as vapid and unreliable. Listeners got into the habit of tuning in to the BBC or else to Radio Stuttgart.[32] That was the fault of the Information Service, created in July 1939 and headed by Jean Giraudoux.

Delay in setting up a Department of Information bears witness to laudable reluctance to manage news and broadcast propaganda. It also inevitably resulted in the sort of disorder that newly set-up enterprises always face before they find their feet, and the disorder affected a crucial aspect of the war effort—or, rather, the nonwar effort. The Nazi propaganda machine had been perfected since the early thirties; the French never got a start. Giraudoux hated Nazis far less than he disliked the ruthless materialism of industrial Germany, far from the old-world charm of the small-scale France he cherished. He had no talent for vulgar propaganda, no mind for administration. His new department became a can of worms full of export rejects: retired officers and diplomats, professors, unemployed journalists, opportunists of limited talent who did not know how to catch—and hold—the general public's ear. Their leader—that delicate spirit, Georges Bernanos had called him—was no better. As a country postman wrote back from the front lines, "It's unendurable. Risk, cold, boredom, but for goodness' sake no more phrases like those of Giraudoux." Personnel was defeatist. Morale was bad. The *commissaire général à l'information* himself was hardly optimistic: "One prepares for war as one prepares for an exam. We shall not pass this one."[33]

One of Giraudoux's broadcasts had to be devoted to praising the Alsatian dialect "that one could hear at this moment [November 10, 1939] in the schools and markets of the Périgord or the Saintonge."[34] Large numbers of Alsatians and some Lorrainers had been evacuated from the combat zone to safer venues inland—safer, but not more comforting. Alsatians and some Lorrainers traditionally spoke their own Germanic dialects, which stirred the inland French antipathy for boches since long before the war. Translated to Franche-Comté and to Dauphiné, to center and southwest, Alsatian and Lorrainer evacuees were regarded as intruders at best, *schleuhs* and boches at worst, and "treated like dirt." Despite official reminders that they were really French, the womenfolk of local servicemen made sure they did not think that they were as good as they. Reports from Vienne, from

Besançon, from Périgueux describe their shoddy treatment of the evacuees. Some blamed them for the war: "If Hitler declared [*sic*] war, it is because he wants to get back Alsace-Lorraine."³⁵

If anything, the menfolk serving in the evacuated zones behaved still worse. In Lorraine Claude Jamet noted "the systematic pillage of all evacuated villages occupied by troops." Keeping his *War Diary* in the autumnal Alsatian countryside, Jean-Paul Sartre noted what he was told: "In the evacuated districts over towards Sarreguemines [Moselle], the soldiers billeted there have smashed everything, crapped in their beds, broken into the cupboards with axes: There's a real obsession with evacuation and looting at Brumath . . . evacuation to them means looting." And here's the colonel's driver describing what he has seen: "Mirrors smashed on the wardrobes; pieces of furniture split by bayonet-strokes; bed-linen looted—what couldn't be carried away is torn. The tiles on the roof are smashed, the silverware has disappeared. In the cellars the lads drank what they could and then, when they could drink no more, went off leaving the spigots of the barrels open; the cellar is flooded with wine. A sewing-machine is split in two. By axe-blows? And yet it was cast iron, says Klein (the driver) sadly."³⁶

Irresponsible soldiers, nomadic military units tend to act destructively. But mayhem on this scale testifies to lack of discipline magnified by prejudice and by prejudicial tales whose truth is less relevant than the frame of mind that generated them. In the evacuated Lorraine village near the German border that Pierre de Calan's infantry unit occupied they found swastikas and portraits of Hitler.³⁷ Passing through Burgundy in September 1939, a train of Alsatian evacuees halted at Paray-le-Monial was observed to have blankets with swastikas hanging to dry at the windows. Fights between servicemen attempting to drag off the Nazi blankets and Alsatians determined to recover their property only broke up when the troop trains made a precipitate departure. How much of this was true, how much was rumor inspired by prejudice or meant to justify it?³⁸ Enough that the tales were there. On both sides. It is small consolation after this to read *The New Yorker*'s A. J. Liebling after a visit to evacuated Strasbourg, eerily empty of people: "[M]ilitary police put up a Christmas tree for the abandoned pigeons of the cathedral: a tiny balsam surrounded by bread crumbs."³⁹

Here was an opportunity for popular education, missed or addressed only with half a heart. Other activities of the Information Office seem to have been to scale, limited to what had been long denounced as brainwashing—*bourrage de crâne*. But war propaganda does not consist of treating adults like children, feeding them slogans and patriotic pap. There was nothing wrong with collecting scrap iron and chronicling sporting events, even when the British beat the French 36–3 at rugby.[40] But a people at war must be prepared for danger, for effort, for exertions of will. Giraudoux and his kind were not made for taking serious things seriously or talking about them in simple, accessible terms. The nonevents of the eight months after September did not help. It was hard to keep minds fixed on a war that did not happen, and the first to find more pressing matters engaging their attention were the leaders of the war that was so hard to find.

A NATION is often more at peace when it's at war. But the phony war was accompanied by an internal peace that was just as phony. Business as usual, or almost as usual, in the country at large reflected politics as usual: intraparty and intracabinet squabbles. Daladier's government of national unity was badly disunited, and the worst friction within it took place between its leading personalities, Reynaud and Daladier.[41] Outside the cabinet also there was less fighting between French and Germans than between French and French, prewar disputes continuing unappeased between Left and Right, but also within each side, each with its bellicists, its pacifists, its defeatists.

Most of the destructive activity, however, seems to have been focused on the Communists. The German-Soviet Pact justified the worst fears of those who always questioned the national loyalty of Communist party members, and Communists did their best to confirm this, conducting a counterwar of stickers, flyers, tracts, underground publications, oral propaganda, all of which called for peace at once and denounced the imperialist war. For the patriots of *Gringoire* who called for death to the Communist traitors, communism was the number one enemy, the Communists were a foreign army camping on French soil. A more attractive crusade was partly displacing a war respectable folks doubted.[42]

Already busy with Spanish republican refugees, police and gendarmerie were set to hunting Communist subversives and then left-wingers identified with the Communists. Given priorities that they could understand, spurred by ministerial circulars, aided by volunteer informers, the forces of order bent their energy to the chase. Their quarries often turned out to be like the alleged Communist of Saint-Céré, accused of hanging a red flag from his window, which turned out to be a rag that signaled for the baker to deliver bread. Then—divine confirmation—came the Soviet attack on Finland on November 30, 1939. This enabled, as the combative Kerillis put it in the Chamber, former apologists for the Nazis to try to turn the war into an anti-Stalinist crusade. The government, hesitant about making war on the Germans, was being pressed to make war on the Russians first. There was talk of an attack on the Caucasus and of bombing Russian oilfields at Baku that supplied Hitler's war. When on March 1, 1940, the Finns asked for a hundred bombers and fifty thousand men, Daladier agreed. A British diplomat in Paris noted that the French contingent was ready to start off. If Swedes and Norwegians refused passage, the Allies should "make a forcible entry."[43]

The Finns preferred to sign an armistice with their aggressors, and Daladier, who had failed to outface either of France's foes, was driven to resignation. As in March 1936 and March 1938, in March 1940 the country faced a foreign crisis whilst in a cabinet crisis. Reynaud was confirmed by 268 votes against 267 opposed or abstaining. Daladier continued in the cabinet as minister of war. Within two weeks the German invasion of Denmark and Norway started. On May 9, in the wake of the Norwegian fiasco, Daladier announced he would give up the War portfolio. The following day war was to begin at last. Bertrand de Jouvenel would find it stupefying that "a great power, at a decisive moment of its destiny, should be as if struck by immobility." It isn't, said Jouvenel, that no one noticed what was going on. It is that all were busy watching each other, "their vigilance absorbed by internal strife."[44]

ON SEPTEMBER 3, 1939, Second Lieutenant Jacques Delmas, twenty-four years old and straight out of officer school at Saint-Cyr, was issued a staff map that showed the north and northeast border and Germany all the way to Berlin. He found the troops idle and dreary, the officers so little in command that they would cross the street to avoid groups of enlisted men they knew would not salute them. Pierre Andreu, a quartermaster sergeant in a Senlis barracks, describes a formless mass obsessively in quest of a soft job or hurrying to get their wives pregnant if they could, to gain brownie points toward demobilization: two years' seniority for every child. Second Lieutenant Hubert Beuve-Méry, commanding a company at the north end of the Maginot Line, considered the war lost: *La guerre est foutue.* American visitors to the Second Army in the same area (Meuse, Ardennes) were struck by their interlocutors' insistence on the troops' high morale. "It occurred to Col. Budd and me that since it was the occasion for so much comment it might not be as good as it's alleged to be. The men at the front presented a rather sorry spectacle of discomfort and dejection."[45]

Sartre was more discriminating. Up in Alsace, he found the war "elusive," life full of rumors, comrades deadly bored. He himself escaped boredom by reading and especially writing: notebooks, letters, about a million words in a few months. The infantrymen he talked to had been determined in the fall, but resolution seeped away through the long months of inaction.[46] We hear of equipment lacking through the long, hard winter, but most seem to have been comfortable enough. The meat consumption of the 3,300,000 men of the military zone was seven times that of German soldiers, four times that of Britain. Bullitt, returning from a visit to the Maginot Line, found Daladier harassed and enervated and advised him that he should go to the front to rest. He would find calm, order, cleanliness, plump soldiers, well kempt, keeping their weapons and their uniforms neat.[47] And bored. No sports, no games, no physical education, as far as one can tell from the newspapers, but a lot of drinking. The wine ration—half a liter (about one pint) a day—had been raised by a quarter liter on January I. Every day, 2,500,000 liters of wine for the services were shipped and distributed: alcohol for an alcoholic nation under arms. Further lickerish floods flowed from a patriotic enterprise dear to the hearts of vintners and of their parliamentary representatives: supplies of free hot wine to warm the troops in winter, le vin chaud du soldat.[48] But spirits did not improve the spirit.

By February 1940 the tone of Sartre's notes has changed. Men who once complained about their comrades' inclination to heroics now say that their mates' morale is low. "It's what I've had occasion to observe everywhere lately." The men are fed up with doing nothing. They predict collapse. "If things go on this way," one declared, "without any fighting, we'll be having a revolution and it'll start with the Army." This change in attitude is echoed by other evidence. In September 1939 Roger Goetze, commanding an artillery unit in the mountains above Briançon, quoted his sergeant major: "We didn't want this war . . . it's not our business but we are at war, you are our leader, you order and we'll follow." A few months later, when there is talk of moving the position: "Don't do it, you can't do it, we've had enough, we want to go home, and we wouldn't follow if you try to do it."[49]

Testimony about the spring of 1940 paints a somber picture of depres-

sion and defeatism among commissioned and noncommissioned officers, as
in the other ranks. The men, Sartre recorded, had no patriotic ideal to sus-
tain them; none had been inculcated in the past score years. They knew they
did not like Hitler or his ideas; but Poland meant nothing to them, and
fighting for democracy meant little more. They carried out their duty and
hoped they could get home soon, but the one became increasingly meaning-
less and the other increasingly distant. One way their disaffection expressed
itself was against officers. French soldiers interned in Switzerland after the
fighting expressed bitterness against officers and noncoms. So did the light
infantry types whom Sartre quotes: restrained but profound hatred, talk of
bumping them off, anger, contempt. It is possible that elite units maintained better morale; it is probable that most men were never asked for the
efforts that would have raised their morale; it is likely that distance in conditions and relations between ranks aggravated class frictions. The conclusion is hard to avoid that the long months of inaction during which a great
war machine was left to run in neutral sapped what resolution there had
been and prepared the rout to come.[50]

Marie-Claire's horoscope for May 10, 1940, was hardly encouraging:
"We shall be subject to austere, indeed grim astral influences. Hostile to
tender hearts, they will be propitious to the cold and calculating. . . ." Just
before dawn that forbidding Friday the cold and calculating Germans attacked Luxembourg, Holland, and Belgium. The real war had begun. It
would not last long. Within three days German armor had crossed the
Meuse River. The Dutch capitulated on May 15, the Belgians on the
twenty-seventh. That night the Paris Opéra offered the first performance of
Darius Milhaud's *Medea*. "The music," Simone de Beauvoir noted, "seemed
very beautiful."[51] A week later Dunkirk, from which over 330,000 troops
had been evacuated by the Royal Navy, also fell, and on June 6 scratch
defensive lines on the Somme were broken through. The Comédie Française put on a play, *On ne saurait penser à tout* (You can't think of everything).
The Germans entered Paris on June 14.

All this time rumors were rife: toxic balloons, poisonous bonbons, fifth
columnists disguised as nuns or postmen, parachutists dropping from the
skies. War correspondents, British airmen escaped lynching by the skin of
their teeth. The censorship cut the running head of *Je Suis Partout*, which
proclaimed LA PATRIE EN DANGER, but Gamelin's order of the day ordered
the troops to win or die.[52] Most of them found both alternatives too dire.

Going into combat near Stenay, a few miles from Sedan, Pierre de Calan recalls seeing with his own eyes the spot where the Maginot Line and its antitank defenses stopped, respectful of the Belgian border: *"Je reste halluciné."* His division, Calan concludes, fought well but proved frighteningly power- less. Like everybody else. The generals blamed the men. French troops, Gamelin's number two man told a British air marshal, "were not fighting as they should. Seven months of inactivity had weakened their fighting spirit." Whose fault was that? But the sixty-eight-year-old Gamelin, though badly shaken and increasingly depressed, could not be sacked in the midst of bat- tle, or so it was alleged. By May 20 the generalissimo, known to his troops as Gagamelin, was out, replaced by the seventy-three-year-old Maxime Weygand.[53]

Foreign embassies were sending their womenfolk off to safe billets. Am- bassador Bullitt proclaimed the morale of French Army and civilians "a vast credit to the human race."* But refugees flooding southward and wounded soldiers returning from the front spread tales of muddle and defeat. A week after German tanks rolled through the impassable Ardennes, Reynaud had called on the country to forge itself a new heart, now, at once. Easier said than done when he and his fellow leaders expected only the worst. Both Paul Reynaud and Georges Mandel, newly appointed minister of the inte- rior, reported Bullitt, "expect a Communist uprising and butcheries in the city of Paris and other industrial centers as the German Army draws near." Could the Americans send tommy guns to fight the Communists off? Two days after this, the same dispatch that deemed morale a credit to the human race spoiled its effect by repeating: "Everyone here believes (from Mandel to Herriot) that the moment the French Government leaves Paris the Com- munists of the industrial suburbs will seize the city, and will be permitted to murder, loot and burn for several days before the Germans come in." Shades of Bazaine![54]

Happily, predictions of this sort were not publicized. Whilst evacuation proceeded at Dunkirk, Parisians took life calmly. The outdoor stamp mar- ket functioned as usual on the Champs-Elysées; children watched Punch and Judy shows or rode old donkeys through the sunny alleys. British ob- servers were exasperated: "They should be digging trenches or doing some-

---

*An American war correspondent expressed a different view. Returning to England from France in June, Robert Nixon of the International News Service described British morale as very high (they stood and fought against any odds and counterattacked at any opportunity) and that of the French as low (they would not stand up to tank and mortar fire and would not counterattack). NA, 2015-1271/15, June 24, 1940. Diversity is the gist of war.

thing . . . we'll end by having to fight Germany alone."[55] The French, at least, were not alone. The saints were on their side. On May 19 Reynaud, who publicly declared his faith in miracles, attended public prayers held at Notre Dame; on the twenty-sixth the relics of Saint Géneviève, who had saved Paris before, were solemnly carried in procession; on the thirty-first, at the Basilica of the Sacré Cœur, France was reconsecrated to the Sacred Heart of Jesus. Old canticles abandoned by a disenchanted age were being dusted off for the emergency:

Dieu de clémence	God of clemency
O Dieu vainqueur,	God of victory,
Sauvez, sauvez la France	Save, save your France
Au nom du Sacré-Cœur.	In the name of the Sacred Heart.

On June 2 a party of General Motors executives visiting the headquarters of the general commanding the Paris air defense found morale to be of the best. Before a delicious lunch with the general and his staff, who were housed in a large château, they heard that the Germans could be stopped with five hundred more fighter planes and six hundred more tanks. On June 7 the last number of *Je Suis Partout* to appear before the Occupation featured an article by Thierry Maulnier, "The Miracle of Flanders," that prophesied forthcoming victory. On June 6 the French front had been broken on the Somme, but the French believed themselves entitled to miracles.[56]

Miracles, unfortunately, favored the Germans, not the French. The battle in the air was lost in the first forty-eight hours, expectably when we remember with what determination the air arm had been kept at heel. Less than 80,000 airmen in all, counting hardly 4,000 flying personnel in France and about one third the aircraft that the Luftwaffe disposed of, hamstrung by battle principles that played down attack in favor of ground support, the air force was a Cinderella. Airmen fought like lions, but they were outmatched despite the equally heroic efforts of their British allies. Figures differ, but it seems that in the end the Allies downed two German planes for every three they lost. Henri Amouroux shows RAF losses in the Battle of France as 1,526 men killed and wounded, 959 planes lost; French ones as 1,493 killed and wounded, and 1,200 or 1,300 planes lost. Extraordinary sacrifices, but to no avail. When, a few months later, American observers tried to explain the collapse in the air, they rejected the excuse of numerical inferiority—itself attributable to faulty planning—and blamed the generals: "[The] head men were too politically-minded; they shared the selfishness and jealousy of the Army and Navy commanders; they found it too easy to procrastinate and, above all, they never really believed that the war would come in their time."[57] Harsh words and in part unjust, but defeat is a ruthless judge.

The air force at least put up a good fight. The record on the ground was less honorable, but here, again, it hinged on minds that lagged behind the times.

Numerically, French armor matched and overmatched the enemy.* But in the High Command no one understood the new mechanized warfare; no one could cope with its speed or adjust the lessons learned in the First World War to the Napoleonic tactics of the Germans. Army engineers seemed to have never heard of road mines, land mines, field mines, mine barriers against tanks. Artillerymen, handicapped by horse traction, had argued long and hard that antitank weapons would prove more powerful than tanks, then neglected to acquire enough of them. Infantry, short of trucks, had to march to battle and engage the enemy when weary and on the wrong foot. Summing up the situation in his brilliant *Les Français de l'an 40* (The French of 1940), Jean-Louis Crémieux-Brilhac rehearses the army's shortcomings: aviation inferior in number and quality; armor adequate in quality and quantity but handicapped by limited range, poor armament, and radio equipment, above all by the way it was used; inferior and insufficient antitank and antiaircraft weapons; inferior or nonexistent means of communication. "Collapse of doctrine, impotence of leadership, crisis of equipment."[58]

Writing two months after these doings, an American captain compared the German army with a great football team: "a powerful line (heavy tanks), a lightning backfield (mechanized units), and splendid interference (bombing planes)." The metaphor must have come easily to Americans, for A. J. Liebling also called on it:

> It must have been a little like one of those football games in which one team seems certain in advance to beat the other by two or three touchdowns, but in which the inferior team plays far below its form. The

---

*James M. Laux observes that in May 1940 the French Army had more than double the number of wheeled vehicles than the Germans. Also more tanks (4,638 against the enemy's 4,060) with thicker armor and heavier guns, hence almost double the armor tonnage of the Germans. *The European Automobile Industry* (New York, 1992), 146–47.

worse the poor devils muck things up, the more confidently the destined victors play, and the result is an unwarranted score. . . . After such a game, the spectators always think the winning team much stronger than it really is and the losers weaker than they possibly could have been.

Edmée Renaudin's uncle Jean could not be as detached: "The bastards, he said, the bastards, the idiots! To have brought us to this!"[59]

The French, it seems, had never heard of getting there firstest with the mostest. And there again Zola's words ring true: "Why this almost general ignorance, this inferiority of our leaders, so perfectly brave, who had to retreat the ones after the others, without even seeming to understand? They found themselves disarmed, and one must add that all went to pieces in their hands, the matériel insufficient and inferior, the troops . . . poisoned by a ferment of indiscipline, unsettled, incapable of victory." If that happened, it was because they prepared it. But if the war was lost, the defeat was still theirs to win.

Soon all agreed that if France lost, it was that it had been betrayed. The Russians had betrayed it by signing with the Germans; the Germans treacherously had signed their pact with Russia; the Communist party betrayed when it chose loyalty to Moscow over the fatherland; the Belgians betrayed when they capitulated; the British had let it down by going home rather than stay to fight and lose in France; metics and Jews had sapped the country's strength. The army had been treacherously entoiled: "never beaten or discouraged," simply let down. When, as the *Times* of London had asked on November 9, 1870, "when will French soldiers learn to say: we are beaten, and not we are betrayed?"[60]

People had begun to trickle out of Paris at the end of May. After the Germans crossed the Somme, they really began to pack. The army was pulling out of the capital, leaving behind hundreds of cars, trucks, guns, new and unused, that Germans would find handy in later campaigns elsewhere. Uniformed stragglers passed through the streets, ragged, dispirited, some of them drunk. By June 10 evacuation had turned into a general *sauve qui peut*. Six or seven million men, women, children were taking to the roads throughout the country, three quarters of the population of Paris among them. Cities like Troyes and Chartres were left practically empty in the mindless flight; tens of thousands of children were lost on the roads. Virginia Cowles, the reporter, described the gigantic civilian exodus in which she joined on June 11, "the first *mechanized* evacuation in history," crawling southward at about three miles an hour. An Englishman who had been unable to secure a car bought one of the last bikes still for sale and got out of Paris on June 14. He noted drinking and drunk poilus and soldiers looting empty villages along the road. Marie-Madeleine Fourcade, part of the same crowd, observed that in the midst of chaos one ritual continued to be observed: When it was time for meals, everyone stopped.[61]

The military meanwhile were dissolving. Units wandered aimlessly, sent from pillar to post or facing the wrong way. Some welcomed leadership; others shunned it. Some looked for action, others fled. *Quand ils reculeront,* Cocteau had observed, *ils ne reculeront devant rien* (When they start to retreat, they'll retreat before nothing).* Defeat justified defeatism. At Guéret in the Creuse, far from the line of fire, Désiré Arnaud, who was trying to administer the department, was astonished by the number of senior officers heading south without their troops. When the Italians bombed the undefended country town, killing 106 and leaving more than 300 wounded, he was glad that the mayor of Fontainebleau had thought to bring along the little town's fire company in his retreat, but found that all the medical officers of a military hospital also passing through had fled. Members of a profession that fought so brilliantly against competing metics did not show as much energy or dedication when it came to minding wounded. They ran.[62]

Facing the enemy involved unexpected risks when the enemy was not always where one expected it. More than one officer trying to put up a fight was shot by his own men. Others were overborne or murdered by civilians eager to avoid trouble. At Montargis the mayor, backed by his fellow citizens, routed a captain trying to defend the town. At Châteauroux the mayor tried to disarm passing troops that belied the white flags with which he bedecked his city. At Vierzon an officer who insisted on defending the outskirts "was killed by the populace which wished to prevent the destruction of the town."[63] Meanwhile, at Saumur, fifty-one cadets of the cavalry school and of Saint-Maixent nearby died trying to defend the passage of the Loire. Ernst Jünger found the French officers unimpressive; but twice as many officers died in these weeks as men, and twelve general officers laid down their lives.[64] Even so, the bravery, initiative, or foolhardiness of some

---

*In a note dated June 1, 1940, Georges Sadoul described the pillage and chaos that accompanied the retreat from the Somme: "an army of drunks commanded by sots" (*armée d'ivrognes conduite par des saoulards*) in which more casualties came from drink than from Germans and more armament was abandoned to carry demijohns than was lost in action. *Journal de guerre* (1977), 258–59. Sadoul's division appears to have borne itself well; hence, probably, his indignation.

could not make up for years of indecisiveness and intellectual idleness, let alone for anachronism among the leadership.

On Sunday, June 16, near Falaise in Normandy, Jacques Le Roy Ladurie ran into the villagers of Damblainville, the priest reading his breviary, the sexton carrying the cross before them. "I had never seen such a procession, mixing handcarts and bicycles, young and old, faithful and miscreants, men and women, cats and dogs . . . on the way to I know not what pilgrimage." The abbé Valdour explained that they were just *going*—"we don't want to be boches"—and refused to listen to Le Roy Ladurie's pleas to turn back home. "They go on their way singing canticles."[65]

That day, at Bordeaux, Reynaud resigned to be replaced by Philippe Pétain. On the seventeenth Pétain sued for an armistice. The British ambassador, Sir Ronald Campbell, had gone to see the marshal earlier in the day and found him completely gaga—an exaggeration, clearly, since Henri Dumoulin, head of the old gentleman's cabinet, remembered that "he had good moments in the mornings." But, gaga or not, Pétain's decision came as a great relief.[66]

Pierre Andreu's cavalry regiment was in the Vendée by then. "My pain was not shared by my comrades, my squadron felt no humiliation. The men jumped with joy. . . . 'So, it's over!' " In the villages the end of fighting came as a deliverance: "[O]ne felt such a shambles, such a rout, it was clear that everything was lost; so just as well capitulate rather than get oneself killed for nothing, like pigeons."[67] Bourgeoisie, upper classes felt very much the same with but few exceptions. At Brive the Social Christian Edmond Michelet produced the first tracts calling for resistance on the seventeenth, the day before Brigadier General Charles de Gaulle's radio appeal from London. At Chartres that same day Jean Moulin, prefect of Eure-et-Loir, attempted suicide. In Paris Thierry de Martel, a distinguished physician, carried it off. But gestures of this sort were few and far between. As a friend of the duc de Brissac remarked, "the French have understood: in 1914–1918, 100,000 prisoners, one and a half million dead, in 1940 the opposite: 100,000 dead, one and a half million prisoners."[68] It wasn't quite like that: Nearly a hundred thousand dead in six weeks is comparable to the death rate suffered at Verdun, and five Frenchmen fell for every two Germans. So people fought, or at least they died. But that was the lesson, the explanation, the common understanding of those six deadly weeks. That, and a short-lived legend of German invincibility.

Only the British refused to understand. "*Everyone* at Vichy, whatever their political views, was convinced that they would fold." There were few in France who, if and when they thought, did not think like Vichy. The Germans behaved correctly, harmed no one, paid for their purchases in cash. The three cannon shots of June 26 announcing the official end of hostilities were welcome, but the country had laid down its arms at least a week before. *Paris-Soir* (a German-controlled edition) suggested what the summer should be about: couture, aperitifs, and shopping. On July 6 the Casino de Paris reopened its portals to the public. On the stage door a new notice hung: ENTRANCE PROHIBITED TO DOGS AND JEWS.[69]

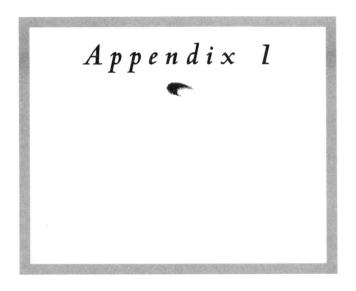

Appendix 1

MILITARY INTELLIGENCE DIVISION
WAR DEPARTMENT GENERAL STAFF
MILITARY ATTACHE REPORT: FRANCE

Subject: French Leadership I.G. No 6210

Source and Degree of Reliability: Direct observation and conversations.

From M.A. Berlin, Germany. Report No. 17,468. August 15, 1940.

In being with and talking to the French officers in German prison camps, one is immediately impressed by their age and physical condition. A large percentage of them are old, broken men, thoroughly dejected and demoralized in spirit. The observation applies to all ranks except that of 2nd lieutenant. Many French officers have had to be hospitalized after reaching German prison camps. German doctors say there was no common illness, just a general condition.

One major general in a hospital was visited. He was an old man suffering from stomach ulcers and had been retired several years before the war. He was recalled to active duty on mobilization and assigned to command a division. This doddering old man held the fate of 15,000 Frenchmen in his hands in the face of one of the best organized and equipped armies in modern history.

After numerous conversations with French enlisted men, there were many charges that their officers shamelessly deserted their units and left them to shift for themselves. The men complain bitterly of the conduct of their officers.

A German officer stated that he actually saw a detachment of several hundred French officers who had marched 35 kilometers without any guard from a prisoner of war dispatch point to a prisoner of war transit station without any guard of any kind (sic) and with apparently none having made their escape. This occurred before the Armistice was announced.

Another German officer stated that he was in a tank unit of about 75 tanks advancing south in the Champagne when they came in the field of fire of a battalion of artillery (French 75's). The terrain here was quite open and gently rolling, ideal tank terrain, but also excellent field of fire for all weapons. The German officer stated that he thought his unit would be wiped out. The tank unit immediately advanced on the artillery battalion at full speed and at a range of 800 meters the artillerymen turned and fled.

Numerous reports from good sources in Switzerland stated that the French Army did very little training during the past winter and that the discipline, clothing, and equipment was [sic] poor.

The change in the high command in the French Army while the British Expeditionary Force, the Belgian Army, and the mobile elements of the French Army were being destroyed near Dunkirchen is well known. German officers have stated the so-called Weygand Line existed only in the newspapers.

A German general related how a French division was retreating toward the south in a long column. The German Air Force blew out the bridges along the routes of withdrawal. The entire division with all of its officers and equipment halted along the road and waited until it was captured.

All of these incidents cannot be charged to poor leadership entirely, but it is believed a spirited, inspired command element would have made a great change in the character of French resistance.

The purpose of this report is to point out the advanced age in all echelons of command, particularly in the higher brackets, and the low physical standards of the commissioned personnel in the French Army.

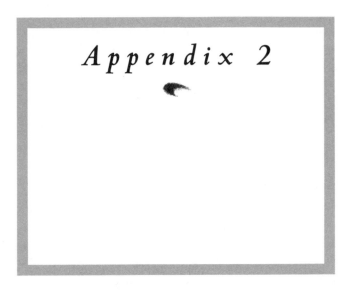

Appendix 2

MILITARY INTELLIGENCE DIVISION

WAR DEPARTMENT GENERAL STAFF

MILITARY ATTACHE REPORT: FRANCE (Aviation)

Subject: General Disposition of French Air Army in May 1940; Summary of Activity Prior to Armistice; Conclusions.

I.G. No. 9920

Source and Degree of Reliability: The following summary is derived principally from Air Ministry information recently received and from conversations held with French aviators since the fall of France; also from office records and observation.

From M.A. France. October 31, 1940.

Information received prior to May 10, 1940, from French official sources was largely exaggerated and overoptimistic. This was official policy. Since the collapse, however, the tendency has been to elicit sympathy by emphasizing the numerical inferiority of French air force personnel and materiel. In other words, information is often colored to suit the French desire of the moment, and actual figures cannot be taken too literally. . . .

Air Defense Command. An additional command, also under Air G.H.Q. but which included certain ground units, was the Air Defense command under

General Aubert. The primary mission of this force was the defense of Paris. . . . This organization was still in the training stage in May, and still acquiring new and badly needed searchlight and sound locating equipment. Reports were received of some successful night pursuit attacks northeast of Paris, but due to shortage of equipment and small-scale operations, the technique employed cannot be said to have advanced beyond the experimental stage. Great difficulty was experienced in coordinating command between ground and air units.

Pursuit units just outside of Paris made frequent training flights at night, but as far as is known, never took part in an actual night engagement.

Army Cooperation Units. Each ground army had assigned to it one group of fighters, one or several groups of observation and reconnaissance, and theoretically one bombardment group. (Verbatim statement of a French staff officer.) These units, due to lack of training and cooperation, as well as to their comparative weakness in the face of hostile aviation, functioned poorly or not at all during the real battle, with the exception of army reconnaissance.

As an indication of the efficiency of observation aviation, a French artillery colonel stated that during the "dull" period of the war, it required 15 days' negotiations to obtain one plane to observe fire for a G.P.F. battery, and that the value of the observation was less than in 1917.

Scattered Combat Units. In addition to the commands mentioned, small pursuit units were scattered throughout France, supposedly for the defense of sensitive points. These were alerted by telephone from Air G.H.Q. when necessary. They came into action with the daily bombardments of airdromes and communication in May, but they were too few and too scattered for any effective concentration. The use only of telephones for this service to the exclusion of radio was an error. With the partial breakdown of the alert system the action of these units became practically independent.

Naval Aviation. The naval air arm operated independently of the Air Army. With equipment almost entirely obsolete its work could consist primarily only of coastal patrols. It participated, however, in one heavy combat, when two dive-bombing squadrons attempted to stop the advance of German tanks toward the Channel. These squadrons, one of which was equipped with the Vought V-156, an aircraft-carrier type, were cited for their bravery, but their losses in two days' operations were over 80%. Obviously these planes were not satisfactory for such a mission.

Modern Bombardment Planes. Most of the modern bombardment planes were in the south of France where new defensive armament installations were being experimented with and installed, and where transition training was being conducted. Many Douglas and Martin bombers were in Bordeaux and North Africa, still unassembled.

Liaison between Air, Land and Sea Forces. Although the activities of the three separate forces, Army, Navy, and Air, were supposedly coordinated and directed by the Minister of National Defense, there was no one who would take command and insist on the necessary cooperation and training which would have made the use of these forces effective in conjunction with each other. This failure to enforce satisfactory liaison was evident also in the lower echelons; artillery and air officers engaged together in the Air Defense Command often issued conflicting orders simply because the mechanics of efficient liaison had not been properly studied. . . .

The pursuit units stationed in the 1st Army Sector bore the brunt of the interception effort. Their well-trained, enthusiastic pilots did a good job, flying many missions daily until they were exhausted. The lack of fresh replacements at this time became evident. (The number of military pilots had been a well-guarded secret.) . . .

Too much reliance had been placed on wire communications between air command posts.

Bombardment aviation had participated in no combat operations prior to May 10. After that date, night bombardment operated over and behind the German lines continuously, using old bombers. Their modern bombers were, they said, too difficult to operate at night from existing airdromes, most of which were too small or rough for safe operations. Day missions were attempted with little success; dive bombing by Breguet 691's and ground strafing by Martin 167's met with heavy losses. German anti-tank guns were used effectively against low-flying aircraft, causing many air casualties. Pursuit units assigned to the support of day bombardment missions complained that they were rarely able to discover the bombardment at the designated rendezvous, indicating the confusion attending the transmittal of orders. . . .

With the advance of the Germans, German aviation appeared in such force that it had mastery of the air in any locality at will. The French lack of modern materiel, trained crews, and efficient control, made successful operations impossible from then on, despite the courage of individual pilots. It would seem reasonable to be cautious in concluding that all the German air methods employed were efficient; with so little air opposition any air operation had a good chance of some measure of success.

Beginning about June 16, with the first rumors of armistice, the air force became politically divided. Most of the combat units were directed to the south of France and later to North Africa, while an undetermined number of bombardment planes, including some entire units, proceeded against orders to England. The British Air Attache in Bordeaux at that time could not advise the many French pilots who came to him to disobey the instructions of the French air command; he did however suggest that there was an excellent airdrome at Amherst.

A night bombardment of Bordeaux took place June 19–20, during which about 50 light explosive bombs were dropped. No military objective was hit. At this time, when Bordeaux was choked with refugees and there was terrific tension, the bombardment was obviously psychological, as the important airdrome at Merignac and the bridges across the Garonne were scrupulously avoided. Well after the departure of the enemy bombers, French pursuit could be heard cruising over the city.

The morale of the French air force then dwindled rapidly to nothing. Air Ministry officials at Bordeaux and at the Merignac airdrome were reluctant to receive foreign air attaches; offices and personnel were in utter confusion.

Each day from June 20 until the Armistice, French planes demonstrated over the city, diving below the level of buildings along the wide boulevards and causing panic among the refugees, few of whom knew whether they were French or hostile. . . .

The underlying reasons for the obvious deficiencies of the Air Army are chiefly political. Numerous changes in Air Ministers, each with his own satellites, encouraged the lack of coordination between the three major forces, and between the aircraft industry and the Air Army. There was no definite broad plan, no basis from which each of the many departments concerned in the building of an Air Army could work with coordination toward a common goal. There were hundreds of individuals with good ideas, but there was no guiding hand to coordinate them.

A doctrine for the employment of the Air Army existed on paper but not in fact. Official propaganda and ministerial complacency had a soporific effect on the public and this extended into the air force personnel itself. Officers in one unit knew little about other units, nor where their own mission fitted into the general picture. It seems clear now that the attitude of mystery exuded by so many officers was a mask for their ignorance.

The Air Army shares in the responsibility for defeat mainly because *it was unable to maintain local air superiority* during any of the crucial stages when its assistance to ground units might have changed the situation. Thus the major default of the Air Army was *a shortage of materiel in the combat area.* Just how effective a greater force of combat airplanes would have been will always be a matter of conjecture. From observation, it can be assumed that there was *a criminal lack of liaison between* the three major forces, but particularly between *the Army and the Air Army.* This resulted primarily in insufficient study of the problem of air-ground cooperation.

Gamelin's defensive policy prohibited bombardment from exhibiting its state of training until after the May offensive. Therefore as an independent striking force the Air Army really never functioned. Defense against the enemy's striking force was deficient in that an adequate warning system coupled with an efficient pursuit-antiaircraft defense set-up was never realized.

Local airdrome defense was inadequate due to a shortage of equipment, and was nonexistent on many airdromes in the center and south of France. The number of combat planes destroyed on the ground was ⅔ that of those shot down in combat.

Organization was topheavy; in the Air Army after the declaration of war, the generals (regulars and those called from retirement) totalled over 100. Places had to be found for all of these; as a result the number and size of staffs increased beyond all proportion to the fighting strength of commands.

Recruiting of pilots and crews failed to keep pace with combat airplane procurement. When the latter began to show some results, even the most inviting propaganda failed to fill the new schools organized after the declaration of war. Physical standards were lowered and laws passed enabling easy transfer from other branches, but the effort had begun too late.

In conclusion, the Air Army fell down because it talked too much and acted too little. Its head men were too politically-minded; they shared the selfishness and jealousy of the Army and Navy commanders; they found it too easy to procrastinate, and above all, they never really believed that the war would come in their time.

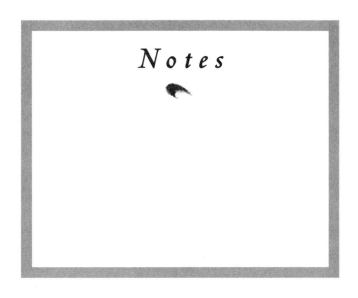

Notes

Interesting Times

1. All quotations are from Thucydides, *The Peloponnesian War*, Book I.
2. L.-A. Prévost-Paradol, *La France nouvelle* (1867).
3. Paul Valéry, *Cahiers*, II (1974), 1503, 1504.
4. Paul Valéry, "Discours de l'histoire . . . lycée Janson-de-Sailly, 13 Juillet, 1932," in *Variété* (1938), IV, 140.

I: A Wilderness Called Peace

1. Alphonse Haensler, *Curé de campagne* (Paris, 1980), 160 (hereafter, when not indicated, the place of publication is Paris); *Paris-Soir-Dimanche*, Jan. 19, 1936; Jean Giono, "Refus d'obéissance," in *Récits et essais* (1989); Claudine Chouez, *Giono par lui-même* (1956), 23; Jacques Body, *Giraudoux et l'Allemagne* (1975), 181–84.
2. Pierre-Edmond Robert, *D'un Hôtel du Nord l'autre* (1986), 29, 31, and Eugène Dabit, *Journal intime (1928–1936)* (1939), 22, 88, 141, 173, 220, 256, 273–74, 286, 300–01, 349–50.
3. Roger Vercel, *Capitaine Conan* (1934), 254; *Gazette des Tribunaux*, Jan. 7, 8, 1937.
4. Antoine Prost, *L'Enseignement et l'éducation en France.* (1981), IV, 137; Ralph Schor, *L'Opinion française et les étrangers, 1919–1939* (1985), 28.
5. Jacques Dupâquier et al., *Histoire de la population française.* (1988), IV, 85, 97; Jean-Jacques Becker and Serge Berstein, *Victoire et frustrations 1914–1929* (1990), 160.
6. Michel Huber, *La Population de la France pendant la guerre* (1931), 422.
7. Yves Simon, *La Grande Crise de la République française* (Montreal, 1941), 17–18.

8. Becker and Berstein, *Victoire.* 156; Dupâquier, *Population.* IV, 97, 98.

9. Jacques Ozouf and Mona Ozouf, *La République des instituteurs* (1992), 129, 104.

10. Antoine Prost, *Les Anciens Combattants/Archives* (1977), 73; Sully Ledermann, "La Mortalité des adultes en France," *Population* (Oct. 4 1946), 675; National Archives [hereafter NA], 2015-1221/2, Nov. 20, 1936; Julie Sabiani, ed., *Le Pacifisme dans les lettres françaises* (Orléans, 1985), 50. The national debt, whose costs represented 37.5 percent of the 1930 budget, also reflected the economic consequences of the war.

11. Janine Bourdin reminds us that in 1938 most Frenchmen in any position of authority were veterans and that 1,500,000 of the 5,250,000 surviving servicemen of 1914–1918 were still in the reserves, liable for eventual call-up. Janine Bourdin and René Rémond, *La France et les Français en 1938 et 1939* (1978), 96–97.

12. Jean Appert, interview, Archives Orales du Comité pour l'histoire Economique et Financière (hereafter AO), I, 1; Prost, *Archives,* 86; Michel Missoffe, *André Tardieu* (1957), 36. Janine Bourdin, *La France et les Français,* 102, quotes the *Journal des mutilés et combattants* (Oct. 9, 1938), admitting that veterans had "doubtlessly emphasized too much their horror of war. . . ."

13. Edmée Renaudin, *Sans fleur au fusil* (1979), 15. Eric Mension-Rigau, *L'Enfance au château* (1990), 39, remarks how the bloodletting of the war unhinged and unsettled the upper classes. One man born in 1915 lost two of three uncles on one side of the family, three out of four on the other side, the fourth being a *grand mutilé.*

14. Simone de Lattre, *Jean de Lattre, mon mari* (1971), 75; NA, 851 1442–2, 1933; Renaudin, *Sans fleur.* 29; *Gazette des Tribunaux.* March 24, 1939. In November 1991 the mass grave in which Lieutenant Henri Alban Fournier—better known as the writer Alain-Fournier—and twenty of his comrades of the 288th Infantry Regiment lay buried was identified and dug up at Saint-Rémy-la-Calonne, in the Meuse forest where they had fallen seventy-seven years before, on September 22, 1914.

15. Pierre Laborie, *Résistants, Vichyssois et autres* (1980), 47.

16. Jules Romains, *Les Hommes de Bonne Volonté, Verge contre Quinette* (1939), 243: "The celebration of Victory was going to be, in the first place, a celebration of the Dead." Philippe Ariès, *L'Homme devant la mort* (1977), 543, echoed the feeling.

17. NA, 2015-1039, Jan. 6, 1930.

18. Annie Kriegel, *Ce que j'ai cru comprendre* (1991), 111–12; Prost, *Archives.* 39; AO, Gaston Cusin, I, 1; Edouard Herriot, *Journal Officiel.* Chambre (Débats) (hereafter JOC), Aug. 23, 1924, p. 3084; *Paris-Soir.* March 26, 1930; Daniel Halévy, *Décadence de la liberté* (1931), 138.

19. Roger Chickering, *Imperial Germany and a World without War* (Princeton, 1975), 14.

20. Raymond Abellio, *Ma dernière mémoire.* II, *Les Militants. 1927–1939* (1975), 14.

21. Students of the Ecole Normale Supérieure were known as *normaliens.* René Belin in Bourdin and Rémond, *La France et les Français.* 217–18.

22. André Levinson, *Nouvelles littéraires,* June 8, 1929; Jean-Baptiste Duroselle, *La Décadence 1932–1939* (1979), 179.

23. Quoted in David Schalk, *Roger Martin du Gard* (Ithaca, 1967), 139, 198–99. See also *Discours à l'Académie Suèdoise* (Stockholm, 1938), 69.

24. Jean Vial, *L'Instituteur* (1980), 215; Léon Emery, *Correspondances.* (Carpentras, 1982), I,

89; Judith Wishnia, *The Proletarianizing of the Fonctionnaires* (Baton Rouge, 1990), 288; André Delmas in Bourdin and Rémond, *La France.* 214.

25. Simon, *Grande Crise,* 28–30; Jean-François Sirinelli, *Intellectuels et passions françaises* (1990), 77; Janet Teissier du Cros, *Divided Loyalties* (London, 1962), 77. On the other hand, some pacifists changed their minds in extremis. Pierre Brossolette and Jean Prévost, militantly antimilitarist at the Ecole Normale, died in the Resistance. Raymond Aron, who had been "passionately pacifist," ended up in London with General de Gaulle. Others, like Félicien Challaye, Georges Demartial, René Gerin, continued to blame France for the sins of the Germans even under the German Occupation.

26. *Marie-Claire.* Supplement *Nos Enfants* (July 1937).

27. AO, Christian de Lavarenne, I, I; Vibraye in Norman Ingram, *The Politics of Dissent. Pacifism in France 1919–1939* (Oxford, 1991), 95–96.

28. Ingram, 98, 181, 185, quotes a number of pacifist militants denouncing the Jewish press, "the bluff of anti-Semitism," the "occult links between Blum, the Socialists, Jewish finance and arms manufacturers." There are many ways to skin a cat.

29. Raymond Aron, quoted in Sirinelli, *Intellectuels.* 484, 486; see also *Le Spectateur engagé* (1981), 26.

30. See note 28, and Guy Thuillier, "Le Pacifisme avant 1939: René Gerin," *Revue administrative.* Albert Thibaudet, *Les Idées politiques de la France* (1927), 203, presented socialism as almost identical with pacifism: "One is a Socialist by virtue of the priority [the party gives] to this problem above all others." Pacifism also drove enthusiasts to join Franco-German clubs, even ones like the Comité France-Allemagne, founded in 1935 to counter anti-Nazi propaganda. As late as 1938 a lawyer like André Weil-Curiel, Jewish, Socialist, and a Mason, remained a member of that association, while Prime Minister Léon Blum maintained the government subsidy that covered the cost of entertaining German visitors vetted by the Nazi regime. Laurence Berteaud Dorléac, *L'Art de la défaite* (1993), 90.

31. See *Libres Propos, Paris-Soir, Canard enchaîné.* Feb. 1933, Sirinelli, *Intellectuels.* 81.

32. Duroselle, *Décadence.* 169; Pivert in *Le Populaire.* May 27, 1936.

33. Giono, *Récits.* 1159, 1160; Jeanson, "A bas l'union sacrée," *Le Barrage.* March 17, 1938, quoted Ingram, *Politics of Dissent.* 225; Alain, ibid., 232; *Canard enchaîné.* Sept. 7 and Oct. 5, 1938.

34. Sirinelli, *Intellectuels.* 119; *L'Œuvre.* Sept. 26 and 27, 1938; *Echo de la Nièvre.* Oct. I, 1938. While many pacifist personalities were veterans who showed bravery in battle, others like Paul Faure, born in 1878, who had avoided service though not too old to fight (Péguy was five years older), may simply have been physically and psychically intimidated by armed conflict. Whilst only Pierre-Bloch, *Jusqu'au dernier jour* (1983), 52, has denounced him as a coward, others who knew him well speak of him as "not very brave." Michel Bilis, *Socialistes et pacifistes* (1979), 89.

35. Proust, *A la recherche du temps perdu.* IV, 194; Giono, *Précisions* (1939), 46, 16, 18.

36. Delmas (future deputy of Montauban), quoted in J. P. Cuvillier, *Vincent Auriol et les finances publiques du Front Populaire* (Toulouse, 1978), 3; René Modiano in Abellio, *Les Militants.* 312.

37. *Journal de l'abbé Mugnier. 1879–1939* (1985), 575.

II: Economy, Economies, Economists

1. Martin Wolfe, *The French Franc between the Wars, 1919–1939* (New York, 1951), 181, 27, and passim.

2. Wolfe, 51; *Semaine religieuse de Saint-Brieuc.* July 15, 1921. Jean Patat and Michel Lutfalla, *Histoire monétaire de la France au XXe siècle* (1986), 28.

3. See Jacques Ozouf and Mona Ozouf, *La République des instituteurs* (1992), 49; *Confidences.* July 8, 1938. In 1932 André Bouton, a Sarthe neighbor of Joseph Caillaux's, would publish a comfortless review: *La Fin des rentiers.*

4. A passionate Wagnerian, the surgeon named his son Wilfrid Siegfried, and Wilfrid Baumgartner, brilliant son of a brilliant father, went on, as one of the country's senior financial officials, to defend the franc which had let the family down.

5. See *L'Ami du Peuple.* April 18, 1932; André Delmas, *Mémoires d'un instituteur syndicaliste* (1979), 173; Edouard Herriot, *Contre l'absurde déflation* (1933); AO, Jean Filippi, I, 2; *Figaro.* April 25, 1933. See also *Le Matin.* April 19, 1935: "The religion of the franc is nothing but the religion of France."

6. *L'Ami du Péuple.* Oct. 27, 1929; *Réveil du Nord.* Nov. 26, 1929; *Le Temps.* Nov. 7 and 8, 1929; *Paris-Soir.* Feb. 16, 1930; *Le Temps.* Aug. 18, 1930; Reynaud quoted in E. Beau de Loménie, *Les Responsabilités des dynasties bourgeoises* (1963), IV, 455.

7. NA, 2657-C-262/2, Jan. 4, 1932; Commercial Attaché #229, Dec. 16, 1932.

8. *Le Temps.* Sept. 22, 1931; NA, 2657-C-262/2, Jan. 4, 1932.

9. *Berliner Tageblatt.* Sept. 21, 1928; Beau de Loménie, *Responsabilités.* IV, 303.

10. NA, 2081-1492/6, Jan. 16, 1939.

11. Wolfe, *French Franc.* 85, 120; Julian Jackson, *The Politics of Depression in France, 1932–1936* (Cambridge, 1985), I; Robert J. Young, *In Command of France* (Cambridge, Mass., 1978), 23.

12. *Paris-Soir.* Jan. 3, 13, 1930: Bus fares have tripled, aperitifs and gas have doubled, eggs too . . .; NA, 2655-C-225/2, Nov. 21, 1930; NA, Commercial Attaché, #228, Oct. 13, 1930. Bernard Cazeaux, *Le Goût des vacances perdues* (1975), 23, notes the steady rise of the chocolate pastries that he used to buy as a child: from ten cents to twenty and up, until they reached one franc.

13. *Je Suis Partout.* Jan. 3, 1931: "Et maintenant voici la crise . . ." *Ami du Peuple.* Feb. 9, 1932: "Mardi Gras de crise"; Feb. 10, 1932: "Défunt Carnaval."

14. *La Production française* quoted in *Ami du Peuple.* Jan. 23, 1932; *Femina* (Feb. 1932), 34; Michel Margairaz, *L'Etat, les finances et l'économie. 1932–1952* (1991), I, 30; Marcel Marion, *Petite Histoire du second cartel* (1935), 15; NA, Commercial Attaché, #228, March 25, July 9, 1932; #232, Jan. 3, 1934.

15. Hubert Bouin, *Histoire économique de la France depuis 1880* (1988), 89; Jackson, *Politics of Depression.* 29, 30; Ralph Schor, *L'Opinion française et les étrangers* (1985), 555; NA, Commercial Attaché, #228, Oct. 13, 1930, 2736-C-12/2, Dec. 16, 1931 and 2655-C-225/8, Dec. 18, 1932; *Paris-Soir.* Jan. 3, 1930, *L'Œuvre.* Jan. 18, 1933; Dr. Destouches, "Pour tuer le chômage tueront'ils les chômeurs?," *La République.* March 19, 1933.

16. *Petit Troyen.* Jan. 21, 1933; Dr. G. Ichok, *La Mortalité à Paris et dans le département de la Seine*

(1937), 175. Conditions varied widely. At Toulouse, for example, joblessness was dire between 1932 and 1935, whilst in smaller towns not far away, like Revel and Saint-Gaudens, there was little of it. See Pierre Gérard, "La Montée des droites," in *Les Droites et février 1934* (Toulouse, 1992), 67.

17. Jackson, *Politics of Depression.* 30; Alfred Sauvy, *Histoire économique de la France entre les deux guerres,* (1967), II, 121–25; *Nouvelles littéraires.* Sept. 26, 1936.

18. Albert Buisson, president of the Tribunal de Commerce de la Seine, in *Gazette des Tribunaux.* Jan. 28, 1934.

19. Jacques Duboin, *La Grande Relève des hommes par la machine* (1932), 17; Paul Reboux in *Paris-Soir.* Jan. 15, 1931; Charles Spinasse, *La Crise économique. Discours du 27 février 1931* (1931); Paul Faure, *Populaire.* Feb. 9, 1935; Emile Servan-Schreiber, *Regards sur un demi-siècle* (1964), 142; Boutin, *Histoire économique.* ch. 5 passim.

20. Gamelin quoted in *Journal de Saint-Gaudens.* Jan. 23, 1937; AO, Christian de Lavarenne, I, 2.

21. Paul Léautaud, *Journal littéraire.* (1962), X, 21. Also Edmond Jaloux in *Nouvelles littéraires.* Aug. 26, 1933.

22. Edouard Bourdet, *Les Temps difficiles* (1934), 3, 5; *Femina* (Jan. 1934), p. 8.

23. For one example among many see NA, #233, Monthly Economic Review, Nov. 1934.

24. *La Sécurité sociale. son histoire,* IV, *La Mutualité sociale agricole.* 1919–1981 (1991), 91; AO, René Frédet, II, 2; for village autarchy, see Henri Mendras, *La Seconde Révolution française* (1988), 31; for Norman details, J. Le Roy Ladurie's ms. reminiscences, chs. 4, 6, and 7.

25. Sauvy, *Histoire économique.* II, 66; Jean de Pange, *Journal* (1970), II, 126, Aug. 24, 1934.

26. Ozouf, *La République.* 365. It might be worth to remember that 19 percent of all officers had been killed in the war, compared with 16 percent of other ranks. This puts peasant ire in a different perspective. See Colin Dyer, *Population and Society in Twentieth Century France* (New York, 1978), 40.

27. *Skol Vreizh.* no. 7 (April 1987), p. 22.

28. Quoted in Geneviève Gavignaud, *Les Campagnes en France au XXe siècle* (1990), 51.

29. Bouin, *Histoire économique.* 89; *Skol-Vreizh.* 22; Denis de Rougemont, *Journal d'une époque. 1926–1946* (1968), 203.

30. Le Roy Ladurie ms. ch. VII and ch. VIII, 26.

31. Gérard Cholvy and Yves-Marie Hilaire, *Histoire religieuse de la France contemporaine* (Toulouse, 1986), II, 396; Le Roy Ladurie ms., ch. VII, 2, and his pamphlet *Vers une politique paysanne* (1937).

32. Le Roy Ladurie ms, ch. VII and ch. VIII, 9.

33. Ibid., ch. VI, 25.

34. Duroselle, *Décadence.* 80; Christian Baudelot and Roger Establet, *La Petite Bourgeoisie en France* (1974), 47, 56.

35. Bouin, *Histoire économique.* 97; Claude Jamet, *Carnets de déroute* (1942), 77.

36. Wolfe, *French Franc.* 17; Auguste Detoeuf, *Propos de O.-L. Barenton, Confiseur* (1965), 42 (original ed. 1938); Dominique Aron-Schnapper et al., *Histoire orale ou archive orales* (1980), 35–36.

37. Marion, *Petite Histoire.* 15–16; AO, Jean Appert (general director of the Contributions Indirectes. 1937–1939), I, 1; Charles A. Dupuis, *Souvenirs, 1902–1938* (1989), 43; *Œuvre.* Jan. 21, 1933. Charles-Albert Michalet, *Les Placements des épargnants français de 1815 à nos jours* (1989), 233ff; Wolfe, *French Franc.* 102. See also Charles Pomaret, *L'Amérique à la conquête de l'Europe* (1931), 218 (largely ghosted by Pierre Brossolette). Ibid., 209: "In the tariff war, . . . Europe will always face America at a disadvantage."

38. Georges Blondeau, *L'Octroi: Pratique actuelle* (1937), 4, 13, 29, 78–86; Gaston Blancher, *Du remplacement des droits d'octroi et des difficultés d'application particulière à la ville d'Alès* (Montpellier, 1937), 39, 37, 133; *Paris-Soir.* Jan. 18, 1930.

39. NA, Commercial Attaché #230, March 1, 1933; Léautaud, *Journal.* 204–05, May 26, 1936.

40. Michel Bruguière, *Pour une renaissance de l'histoire financière* (1991), 249, 250.

41. Yves-Gabriel Antiphon, *La Loterie, ressource budgetaire* (Alger, 1929); Pierre Coste, *Les Loteries d'état en Europe et la Loterie nationale* (1933), 7–8 and passim.

42. See *Le Réveil du contribuable.* 1929 ff; Auguste Cavalier, *La Révolte des contribuables* (1932); J. A. Coulanges, *Les Mille et Quelques Manières d'égorger le contribuable* (Marseilles, 1935); Fred Kupferman in Olivier Barrot and Pascal Ory, *Entre deux guerres* (1990), 84, 91.

43. For *thésaurisation.* see Duc de Brissac, *En d'autres temps* (1972), 322; Pange, *Journal,* II, 37, June 1, 1931; NA, Commercial Attaché #232, Annual Economic Report for 1933, Jan. 30, 1934, and #237, July 13, 1936; *Semaine religieuse de Saint-Brieuc.* Jan. 1, 1937, "Thésauriser: une mauvaise affaire," *Journal de la Nièvre.* Jan. 1, 1935; *Echo de Clamecy.* Jan. 12, 1935.

44. AO, Gaston Cusin, II, 2; Pierre de Calan, II, 1; Claude-Joseph Gignoux, prefacing a posthumous collection of Jacques Bainville's economic writings, *La Fortune de la France* (1937), and in *Je Suis Partout.* Aug. 5, 1933. Gignoux was undersecretary for the economy under Laval in 1931, edited the *Journée industrielle.* presided over the Confédération Générale du Patronat Français, and wrote regularly for *Je Suis Partout.* Antoine Pinay, *Un Français comme les autres* (1984), 23; Gilbert Floutard, "La Crise à Toulouse," in *Les Droites et février 1934* (Toulouse, 1992), 77; NA 2736-C-13/1, July 16, 1936.

45. Margairaz, *L'Etat.* 67; NA, 2015-901/60, March 27, 1934 and 2015-901/67, July 31, 1934. Marshal Pétain, minister of war, facilitated short-term reenlistments for soldiers about to be discharged who feared unemployment in civilian life. To what extent was the increase of military service from twelve to eighteen and then to twenty-four months justified by fear of unemployment?

46. Bouin, *Histoire économique.* 96 and passim; Bernard Hazo, *Le Mouvement ouvrier à Trignac* (Nantes, 1976), 48–59; *Petit Troyen.* Jan. 2, 1933.

47. Bouton, *Fin des rentiers.* 304; Lucien Romier, *Promotion de la femme* (1930), 117. *Paris-Soir.* Feb. 28, 1932; *Gazette des Tribunaux.* June 10, 1936; NA, Commercial Attaché #249, March 7, 1939.

48. Wolfe, *French Franc.* 77; Judith Wishnia, *The Proletarianizing of the Fonctionnaires* (Baton Rouge, 1990), ch. 10; Rougemont, *Journal.* 229; Margairaz, *L'Etat.* 45; Julian Jackson, *The Politics of Depression in France 1932–1936* (Cambridge, 1985), 110.

49. See *Le Democrate du Gers.* May 15 and June 15, 1934; *Echo de la Nièvre.* July 27, 1935; *Echo*

de Clamecy. Aug. 17, 1935; AO, Cusin, I, 2: "Les manifestations contre les décrets de Laval étaient suivies en province par des gens très bien. . . ."

50. AO, Guy de Carmoy, I, I and II, 2; Jean Filippi, I, 2: "connerie majeure, c'est ça qui a fait le Front Populaire." Filippi had helped to prepare the decrees of 1935.

51. Georges Politzer, *Cahiers du Bolchevisme.* Feb. 15, 1936.

52. Wolfe, *French Franc.* 213, 218; Ralph Schor, *Nice et les Alpes Maritimes de 1914 à 1945* (Nice, 1980), 126, 128.

53. Emile Moreau, *Souvenirs d'un gouverneur de la Banque de France* (1954), viiff; Pange, *Journal.* 291–92, Margairaz, *L'Etat.* 224; *Le Populaire.* June 13, 1936; NA, 2610-66-127, Dec. 12, 1931, and 2610-66-180, Sept. 8, 1934.

54. *Vu,* Oct. 5, 1934, "Tout va bien en Angleterre." See also *Paris-Soir.* Feb. 22, 1934: "La Cherté des prix français." According to F. A. Haight, *French Import Quotas* (London, 1935), 69–70, wholesale prices of wheat, butter, eggs, and coal were double and sometimes triple in France.

55. Margairaz, *L'Etat.* 53; Jean Chiappe, *Discours à MM les Commerçants de Chaillot-Dauphine* (*Salle d'Iéna.* Aug. 28, 1936), 14–17; Duroselle, *Décadence.* 218.

56. AO, Filippi, II, 2; *Canard enchaîné.* May 11, 1938: *"Enfin la baisse des prix! On trouve du franc à moins de deux sous."* The franc's weight in gold grams, 0.3 in 1914, had fallen to 0.065 after the devaluation of 1928. By 1939 it stood at 0.027.

57. *Paris-Soir.* Feb. 6 and 19, 1930: "Lutte contre la vie chère"; Odette Louis, *Les Magasins à prix uniques* (1935), 18.

58. *Paris-Soir.* Jan. 25, 1931, for Galeries Lafayette's full page ad: "BAISSE GENE-RALE"; *Œuvre.* Jan. I, 1933; *Semaine religieuse de Saint-Brieuc.* March 1936.

59. Bouin, *Histoire économique.* 92; *Ami du Peuple.* Jan, 3, 1932; NA, Commercial Attaché #230, Jan. 8 and Jan. 31, 1933. That same year *Œuvre.* April 15, 1933, deplored the clouds of salesmen, representatives, and canvassers trying to sell appliances or insurance.

60. AO, Calan, I, I; Pierre Hamp, *Et avec ça, Madame?* (postwar ed., 1946), 50, 54, 122–23; Pierre Yung, *La Vente à tempérament en France* (1933), 39, 147.

61. Louis, *Les Magasins.* 92.

62. Richard Mutz, *La Vente* (1934), 211; Louis, *Les Magasins.* 97, 70; Alain Leenhardt, *Les Magasins à prix uniques* (1935), 1–2, 9, 78, 143. For a description of the "Prix-Fix" of Roubaix as a center of working-class sociability, see Maxence Van der Meersch, *Pêcheurs d'hommes* (1939), 12–16.

63. Evariste Curtil, *Des Maisons françaises d'alimentation à succursales multiples* (1933), 9, 352, and passim: Gabriel Chevalier, *Les Héritiers Euffe* (1947), 19 and passim.

64. Hamp, *Et avec ça.* 131–34; Fernand Jouas, *Les Ventes au Rabais dans le Commerce de Détail* (1934), 42, 43, 50; Curtil, *Des Maisons.* 99; *Petit Troyen.* Feb. I, 1933, and March 16, 1934; *Echo de la Nièvre.* June 19, 1937.

65. Hamp, *Et avec ça,* 81, 83; Catherine Rein, "Structures d'emploi et marchés du travail dans l'agglomération parisienne," in Susanna Magri and Christian Topalov, *Villes ouvrières 1900–1950* (1989), 204.

66. Jouas, *Les Ventes.* 121.

67. Jamet, *Carnets.* 24, 25.

68. *Paris-Soir.* March 7, 1934.

69. Bouin, *Histoire économique,* 94; A. Desqueyrat, *Classes moyennes françaises* (1939), 90; Philippe Laneyrie, *Le Taxi dans la ville* (1979), 20–30.

III: Plus Ça Change

1. NA, 2610-66-127, Dec. 1931, 261066-180, Sept. 1934, Sept. 1936.

2. *Paris-Soir.* Jan. 1, 1930; also Jan. 5, 1933.

3. Not for all, when rag dolls dressed by Patou or Poiret and costing two hundred to eight hundred francs (several months' wages for a maid) were the height of fashionable interior display. The doll's trousseau "must be constantly renewed, since she and her mistress follow fashion together." Mona Clarke, *Regarding the French* (New York, 1925), 56. For servants, see Geneviève Fraisse, *Femmes toutes mains* (1979), esp. 15, 17; Pierre Guiral and Guy Thuillier, *La Vie Quotidienne des domestiques en France au XIXe siècle* (1978), esp. 245.

4. Eric Mension-Rigau, *L'Enfance au château* (1990), 101.

5. NA, 2610-66 Jan. 4, 1927; Edmée Renaudin, *Sans fleur au fusil* (1979), 18; Fraisse, *Femmes.* 28.

6. Pierrette Sartin, *Souvenirs d'une jeune fille rangée* (1982), 29, 81; Pierre Hamp, *Une nouvelle fortune* (1926), 87; Paul Gerbod, "Les Coiffeurs en France," *Mouvement social* (Jan. 1981), 72. *Echo de Clamecy.* Jan. 26, 1935, carried a hairdresser's advertisement: "*Lavatory Moderne. Maison Pot, près de l'Hôtel de Ville, Corbigny. Salon pour dames et messieurs. Ondulations.*"

7. Hamp, *Nouvelle fortune.* 80.

8. Claude Arnauld in O. Barrot, P. Ory, *Entre deux guerres* (1990), 312–13. For a sample Depression party, see Elsa Maxwell's account of the *fête champêtre* she put on in Baron Nicky de Gunzberg's mansion in the Bois de Boulogne: *RSVP* (1954), 155.

9. *Illustration.* Aug. 22, 1931, Sept. 15, 1934; *Femina* (Feb. 1930), 8, and (April 1930), 43; *Paris-Soir.* Feb. 17, 1931.

10. *Femina* (Dec. 1932), 33, (May 1936), 29 ff, (Aug. 1936), (Feb. 1938); *Nouvelles littéraires.* April 11, 1936.

11. Henriette Nizan, *Libres mémoires* (1989), 41, 123; Jean de Pange, *Journal.* II, 183, Nov. 19, 1932; Louis Merlin, *J'en ai vu des choses* (1962), 145; Pierre Nord, *Double Crime sur la ligne Maginot* (1951), 86. For Pange, things went from bad to worse. On Feb. 13, 1939, going to hear *The Magic Flute* at the Opéra, he was dismayed "to see that all elegance had disappeared." No more evening dresses, not even dark outfits, and many men in colored suits. *Journal* (1975), IV, 323.

12. *Marie-Claire* (March 26, 1937).

13. Colette, *La Jumelle noire* (1991), 219.

14. *Marie-Claire* (April 30, 1937); *Match* (1939); Colette, op cit., 313; Leon Paul Fargue, *Piéton de Paris* (1939), 36.

15. *Paris-Soir.* March 18, 1930; Hamp, *Nouvelle Fortune.* 41; P.-W. Fouassier, *Pour le boulanger, 9, Nos jeunes* (1930), 184: "When electrical energy is available, one shouldn't

hesitate to use it." Some people simply did not choose to use it. Thus Mme. P. L. who died in 1945 at the age of sixty-five, the wife, then widow of a teacher in the Normal School of Commerce, owned a house in that Lorraine town. In her own apartment until her death she used only oil lamps because she disliked the glare of electric light.

16. Michel Bruguière, *Pour une renaissance de l'histoire financière* (1991), 219, 222, 224–25; Raymond Abellio, *Ma dernière mémoire* (1975), II, 196; Henri Noguères, *La Vie quotidienne en France au temps du Front Populaire* (1977), 112. One apostle of electrification, Lucien Babonneau, *Energie électrique en France* (1948), 254, concluded that if current development plans were successfully carried out, France would "thus attain the living standards of those happy peoples where man eats his fill . . . and defies heat and cold in a conditioned atmosphere." Such desirable times were still far off in 1948.

17. *La Nation*. Nov. 25, 1925, quoting Pierre Monicault, deputy of the Ain; *Paris-Soir* May 22, 1939: "Enemy of progress, a farmer near Flers shoots dead a worker repairing a power line and expresses no regrets."

18. *Petit Troyen*. Jan. 7, 1933.

19. André Burguière, *Bretons de Plozévet* (1977), 157; Pierre Jakez Hélias, *Le Cheval d'Orgueil* (1975), 480.

20. Guy Thuillier, *Pour une histoire du quotidien au XIXe siècle en Nivernais* (1977), 128, 129; Jean-Pierre Goubert, *La Conquête de l'eau* (1986), 95.

21. *Productivité française* (March 1952), 7, 9, 22.

22. *Marie-Claire* (July 23, 1937); *Femina* (1939), begins to feature monthly Kelvinator ads: "cold in the service of comfort"; *Match* (June 1, 1939). In Simenon's *Le Cheval Blanc* (1938), 37, the Arbelet family of Nevers had no refrigerator but talked of buying one.

23. *Marie-Claire* (Sept. 2, 1938).

24. Catherine Bertho, *Télégraphes et téléphones* (1981), 303–10 and passim.

25. AO, Pierre de Calan, III, 1; Claude Lévi-Strauss and Didier Eribon, *De près et de loin* (1990), 251; Emile Servan-Schreiber, *Regards sur un demi-siècle* (1964), 63; *Gazette des Tribunaux*. April 19, 1931.

26. Suzy Borel, *Par une porte entrebaillée* (1972), 192; AO, Christian de Lavarenne, I, 1; Calan, III, 1; Pierre-Joseph Richard, *Histoire des institutions d'assurance en France* (1956), 214; Raymond Millet, *L'Ange de la révolte* (1938), 30; Paul Léautaud, *Journal littéraire* (1962), X, 191, May 19, 1933: "saloperie de TSF . . . goujaterie du téléphone . . ."; *Journal de l'abbé Mugnier* (1985), 495.

27. Philippe Lamour, *Cadran solaire* (1980), 87; *Gazette des Tribunaux*. Feb. 12, 1932; *Nouvelles littéraires*. March 25, 1933; *Journal de la Nièvre*. Oct. 1, 1934.

28. Cécile Meadel in Régine Robin, ed., *Masses et cultures de masse dans les années trente* (1991), 55; Maurice Barthelemy, Introduction to Jean Giraudoux, *Messages du Continental* (1987), 23–24.

29. *Paris-Soir*. Jan. 21, 1930; Hubert Lafont and Philippe Meyer, *Le Nouvel ordre gendarmique* (1980), 48; Hamp, *Nouvelle Fortune*. 46; *L'Illustration*. Nov. 16, 1929; *Paris-Soir*. Jan. 16, 30, 1930 and Jan. 3, 1931. Noguères, *Vie quotidienne*. 275, tells us that in January 1938, 960 parking tickets were written in Paris, compared with 400,000 in every month of 1976.

30. *Le Matin*. May 1, 1928; Duc de Brissac, *En d'autres temps* (1972), 271.

31. Simone de Lattre, *Jean de Lattre, mon mari* (1971), 49–50; *Gazette des Tribunaux*. March 30, 1932, and March 1, 1937; *Petit Troyen*. Jan. 2, 1933; Jean-Claude Chesnais, *Histoire de la violence* (1981), 319; *Echo de Clamecy*. Aug. 17, 1935; *Petit Sarthois*. March 17, 1934; Le Roy Ladurie, ms., II, 15; Lucien Dubech in *Candide*. Aug. 20, 1931.

32. Simenon, *Maigret chez le Ministre* (1954), 158; "Il ne conduisait jamais. Il avait essayé . . ."; AO, Eugène Demont, II, 2; *Nouvelles littéraires*, Oct. 3, 1936.

33. Denis de Rougemont, *Journal d'une époque* (1968), 167–69.

34. Léonce Chaleil, *La Mémoire du village* (1989), 293; Jean Lhôte, *La Communale.* (1957), 21; Patrick Fridenson in Barrot and Ory, *Entre deux guerres.* 510, 504–05; Bertho, *Télégraphes.* 310.

35. NA, Commercial Attaché #228, July 1, 1930, #230, Jan. 6, 1933, #235, Nov. 19, 1935; *Excelsior.* Jan. 1, 1932.

36. Paul Leglise, *Histoire politique du cinéma français: Le cinéma et la IIIe République* (1970), 174; Janine Bourdin and René Remond, *La France et les Français en 1938 et 1939* (1978), 28; *Le Film.* May 24, 1941; *Bulletin de statistique de l'industrie cinématographique.* Jan. 1, 1941.

37. Jacques Copeau in *Nouvelles littéraires.* Aug. 20, 1932; Marcel Pagnol in *Paris-Soir.* Jan. 6, 1934; *Illustration.* April 18, 1931; *Canard enchaîné.* May 4, 1938.

38. Julien Gracq, *La Forme d'une ville* (1985), 157 and passim.

39. See *Paris-Soir.* Jan. 5, 1930, and again on Jan. 16, 1933, on the massive numbers of horses imported to be slaughtered for meat: nearly thirty-two thousand in 1931. The slaughterhouse in the rue Brancion had to be extended to cope with growing numbers of horses.

40. Hamp, *Nouvelle Fortune.* 207; AO, Louis Franck, I, 2. Between 1929 and 1934, Franck was associate director of the State Tobacco Manufacture in Lille. The fourteen hundred employees he directed were relatively well paid but "lived in terrible conditions." Franck observes that they did not think about their living conditions or complain about them. "Physical conditions did not concern them." Habit is a wonderful thing.

41. See *Henri Sellier 1919–1969* (1970), 7, 12, and P. Grunebaum-Ballin, ms. speech delivered Dec. 1, 1962, p. 3.

42. Suzanne Cribier, "Le Logement d'une génération de jeunes parisiens à l'époque du Front Populaire," in Susanna Magri and Christian Topalov, *Villes Ouvrières* (1989), 114, 115, 119; Jean Vial, *Journal de Classe, 1927–1977* (1978), 21. Cribier, 123, adds that in 1983 Mme S would be awarded a lodging in an *habitation à loyer modéré* (moderately priced lodgings), where she experienced her first bathroom and elevator.

43. Goubert, *La Conquête*, 161, 20, 207.

44. AO, Hervé Alphand, I, 1: "hotel infect"; Lavarenne, I, 1, "inconfort stupéfiant." Could it be that the inspectors' country tours taking place between May and October were limited by unheated hotels becoming unlivable in bad-weather months?

45. *Petit Sarthois.* April 20, 1935; Henry Bordeaux in *Paris-Soir.* July 1, 1937. But even Bordeaux testifies to dubious manners and repugnant toilets in the hostelries he exhorts.

46. Goubert, *La Conquête.* 253; Marie Rouanet, *Nous les filles* (1990), ch. 1.

47. Dr. G. Ichok, *La Mortalité à Paris et dans le département de la Seine* (1937), 5, 15, 36; *L'Inceste en milieu rural* (1977), 15–16; Catherine Rollet-Echalier, *La Politique à l'égard de la petite*

enfance sous la IIIe République (1990), 555; Chesnais, *Violence.* 111–12, 120, 185–86, 163–64, 79–80, 56.

48. Françoise Thébaud, *Quand nos grandes-mères donnaient la vie* (Lyons, 1986), 39; Sully Ledermann, "La Mortalité des adultes en France," *Population* (Oct. 1946), 664; B. R. Mitchell, *International Historical Statistics, Europe 1750–1988* (New York, 1992); Jean-Louis Gay-Lescot in *Cahiers de l'I.H.T.P.,* No. 8 (June 1988), 55.

49. François Lebrun, ed., *Peurs et terreurs face à la Contagion* (1988), 426; Dr. Arthur Vernes, *S.O.S. Pour la défense de la race* (1936), 14, 15; Ichok, *Mortalité,* 178. Dr. Marcel Léger, *Une Calamité publique qui devrait disparaître!* (1932), 4, 11; A. Touraine et Fouassier, "Dix ans d'abolitionnisme à Strasbourg," *Bulletin de la société française de dermatologie* (Nov. 1937), 1–15; Drs. Cavaillon et Destandau-Barral, "Le Service social à l'hôpital dans la lutte contre le péril vénérien," *Revue française de puériculture,* (1936), 1, 36–37.

50. Lebrun, *Peurs.* 213; Sully Ledermann, *Alcool, Alcoolisme, Alcoolisation* (1956), 34, 78, 117; André Mignot, *L'Alcoolisme* (1955?), 68.

51. Jean Yole (Dr. Robert), *Maintien de la jeunesse rurale à la terre* (Niort, 1933), quoted in Jean Peneff, *Ecoles publiques, écoles privées dans l'Ouest* (1987), 149.

52. Mignot, *Alcoolisme,* 9, 61, 65, 84–85; Ledermann, *Alcool.* 130–31, 220; Chesnais, *Violence.* 159.

53. Ichok, *Mortalité.* 59; Ledermann, *Alcool.* 117.

54. *Comité d'histoire de la Sécurité Sociale, Colloque sur l'histoire de la Sécurité Sociale 1980* (1981), 98 and passim: Gilles Henré, *Histoire de la Mutuelle générale des PTT* (1991), 176, 180; Lebrun, *Peurs,* 215. To hear Louise Weiss tell it, the declared foes of alcohol may have been more concerned with their turf than with their propaganda. When the successful journalist showed the director of the Antialcoholic League her articles attacking harmful beverages, her interlocutor was alarmed: "Ah! where would we be if everybody chose to meddle with antialcoholism?" *Mémoires d'une européenne* (1970), III, 21.

55. See Patricia E. Prestwich, *Drink and the Politics of Social Reform: Antialcoholism in France Since 1870* (Palo Alto, 1988), ch. 7, esp. 202–27.

56. *Journal de la Nièvre.* April 1, 1934; *La Mutualité sociale agricole, 1919–1981* (1991), 261; Guy Thuillier, "Les Institutions médico-sociales en Nivernais en 1930," *Colloque sur l'histoire de la Sécurité Sociale 1982* (1983), 199–203.

57. Goubert, *Conquête.* 156, 163, 141–42; also Stephen Hecquet, *Les Collégiens* (1960), 23.

58. *Œuvre.* Jan. 19, 1933, Feb. 1, 1939; *Canard enchaîné.* Feb. 1, 1939; Marcelle Auclair, *Mémoires à deux voix* (1978), 303 ff. A letter in *Confidences.* Aug. 4, 1939, confides: "My daughter only washes herself on Sundays. Monday she cleans her face and, beginning Tuesday, she only takes time to get her makeup off and replace it copiously. . . ."

59. Nizan, *Libres mémoires.* 160, 176; *Confidences.* Oct. 28, 1938; Pierre Citron, *Giono: 1875–1970* (1990), 150; Goubert, *Conquête.* 82.

60. Yves Lambert, *Dieu change en Bretagne* (1985), 118, 434.

61. Hélias, *Cheval d'orgueil.* 160, 162, 483–84; Burguière, *Bretons.* 163–64.

62. Jacques Kergoat, *La France du Front populaire* (1986), 12. Data about conditions of labor are drawn from Daniel Bertaux and Isabelle Bertaux-Wiame, *Enquête sur la boulangerie artisanale* (1980), I, 76.

63. Bertaux, *op. cit.,* I, 63, 65 and II, 30.

64. Ibid., II, 82, 92, 94; P.-W. Fouassier, *Pour le boulanger* (1939), 7.

65. Bertaux, op. cit., II, 99, 108.

66. Pierre Hamp, *Et avec ça, Madame?* (1946), 9–11.

67. Fouassier, 27; Bertaux, *Enquête, pour le boulanger* I, 23, 34, 58.

68. Yvonne Verdier, *Façons de dire, façons de faire* (1979), 20; Yvonne Charrier, *L'Evolution intellectuelle feminine* (1931), 242; M.-M. Davy, *Les Dominicaines* (1934), 227–28; *Marie-Claire* (March 12, 1937).

69. Roger-Henri Guerrand, *La Libre maternité* (1971), 101; Jean Rabaut, *Histoire des féminismes français* (1978), 278 and passim: Bertie Albrecht, *Le Problème sexuel.* (six numbers, 1933–1935); Madeleine Pelletier, *Le Droit à l'avortement* (1931), *La Femme vierge* (1933).

70. Nizan, *Libres mémoires.* 164. Legal access to birth control came only in 1972.

71. *Semaine religieuse de Besançon.* April 14, 1938, and esp. Dec. 29, 1938; Marcelle Auclair, *A la grâce de dieu* (1973), 76–77.

72. Pierre Andreu, *Le Rouge et le blanc* (1977), 33; Fargue, *Piéton.* 36 (young men of 1938 prefer quarts Vittel to women); *Paris-Soir.* May 5, 1937, "L'Affaiblissement viril."

73. *Mutualité sociale agricole.* 127; Bertaux, *Enquête.* II, 76.

74. Pierre Bassac, *La Fécondation volontaire: Une révolution dans la vie sexuelle* (1935), 155–57, 163.

75. R. P. Mayrand, O.P., *Un problème moral: La Continence périodique dans le mariage suivant la méthode Ogino* (Voyron, 1934). See also Dr. J. N. J. Smulders, *Méthode Ogino-Smulders: De la continence périodique dans le mariage* (1933).

76. Prost in Antoine Prost and Gérard Vincent, eds., *A History of Private Life* (Cambridge, Mass., 1992), V, 80; *Marie-Claire* (March 19, 1937).

77. *Marie-Claire* (March 5 and 26, May 28, 1937); *Paris-Soir.* Feb. 6, 1936.

78. Guy Thuillier, *Les Femmes dans l'administration depuis 1900* (1988), 41 ff, 61. As *Marie-Claire* (June 25, 1937), declared, with money so unstable, today "the moral dowry is far more important than the dowry in bank notes." Lucien Romier's *Promotion de la femme* (1930), 141, had made the point that "materially, at any rate, marriage was no longer the only normal means of existence to which a woman could aspire."

79. Duroselle, *Décadence.* 19–20; Suzanne Cordelier, *Femmes au travail* (1935), 156; *Humanité.* Feb. 23, 1920; *Œuvre.* July 1, 1939.

80. *Colloque sur l'histoire de la Sécurité Sociale 1989* (1990), 69; Pauline Bernège, *Le Ménage simplifié ou la vie en rose* (1935), 14. Bernège also advised her readers that they could halve the labor of washing up by using a plate rack, and recommended folding ironing boards and electric or gas irons that did not have to be heated on a burner. Ibid., 42, 268. Which suggests the obvious: a middle-class readership with the means to follow her suggestions.

81. Clarke, *Regarding the French.* 94; AO, René Frédet, II, 1; Yvonne Kniebiehler, *Nous les assistantes sociales* (1980) ch. I; Mension-Rigau, *L'Enfance.* 41; *Femina* (Feb. 1936): "Paris travaille"; Cordelier, *Femmes.* 5.

82. Kniebiehler, *Nous les assistantes.* 30, 151–53.

83. Thuillier, *Pour une histoire.* 159; Sylvie Zerner, "De la couture aux presses," *Mouvement social* (July 1987), 3, 6.

84. See Dominique Aron-Schnapper et al., *Histoire orale ou archives orales?* (1980), 39; Guy Thuillier, "Le Musée de Nevers," *107e Congrès National des Sociétés Savantes.* Brest 1982, (1983), II, 167–69.

85. Suzanne Cantineau, *Les Carrières féminines* (1933); Cordelier, *Femmes.* ix.

86. Cordelier, *Femmes.* v, vi, xiii.

87. Ibid., 108, 156–57; *Nouvelles littéraires.* April 10, 1937; *Gazette des Tribunaux.* March 7, 1934; Thuillier, *Les Femmes.* 69. See also Dominique Terrail, *Mon métier d'homme* (1953), ch. iv, for doctors resenting feminine competition.

88. Henré, *Histoire de la Mutuelle.* 140–41.

89. Henri de Montherlant, *Carnets 1930–1944* (1957), 282–83.

90. Chevalier, *Héritiers Euffe.* 393; *Paris-Soir.* July 4, 1937.

91. *Ami du Peuple.* Feb. 12, 1932; *Echo de Clamecy.* March 9, 1935; *Paris-Soir.* April 25, 1936. See also Louise Weiss's articles in *Petit Journal.* May 26, 1937 ff.

92. Louise Weiss, *Mémoires d'une européenne.* (1970), III, 116, 122, 129–30, 132–33, 204; Steven Hause and Anne Kenney, *Women's Suffrage and Social Politics in the Third French Republic* (Princeton, 1984), 250, 268.

93. Clemenceau, quoted in Weiss, *Mémoires*, 54. Meanwhile, old partisans of women's liberation developed doubts about its effects. Women were affirming their personality all right, grumbled Victor Margueritte in *Nos égales* (1933), vi, but "the new equality consists largely of a leveling downward: females begin to resemble males in their least noble aspects."

94. *Marie-Claire* (June 25, May 14, 1937). But Thuillier, *Femmes*, 76–77, reminds us that while the law of 1938 modified some of the spouses' rights and duties, it reaffirmed the husband's right to oppose his wife's working "in the interest of marriage and the family"—a right that civil law continued to recognize at least into the 1940s.

95. Jean Stoetzel, "Une étude du budget-temps de la femme," *Population* (Jan. 1948), quoted in *Productivité française* (March 1952), 4.

IV: Foreigners

1. Arthur de Gobineau, *Les Pléiades* (1874), I, 7.

2. Ralph Schor, *L'Opinion française et les étrangers, 1919–1935* (1985), 34–35; André Kaspi and Antoine Marès, *Le Paris des étrangers* (1989), 14–15, 30.

3. See Jean-José Frappa, *A Paris sous l'oeil des métèques* (1926), 206 and passim; *Le Matin.* Jan. 1926, for series on "Paris, l'hospice du monde"; *Paris-Soir,* Jan. 9, 10, 1930.

4. See Urbain Gohier, *Paroles d'un Français* (1930), 279–87: "La France aux barbares." Schor, *L'Opinion*, 179, calls *L'Ami du Peuple*'s contents an anthology of xenophobia.

5. Camille Mauclair, *L'Ami du Peuple*, Aug. 15, 1929; Mauclair, *Les Métèques*, 10, 111, 141, 146; also his *Crise de l'art modern* (1944). Novelist, poet, journalist, and critic, Mauclair (1872–1945), who had been a friend of Mallarmé's and one of the first supporters of Dreyfus, turned racist and anti-Semitic in the late 1920s and collaborated under the Occupation.

6. Schor, *L'Opinion.* 34–35, 641; Pierre Milza, ed., *Les Italiens en France de 1914 à 1940* (Rome, 1986), 17, 323; Janine Ponty, *Polonais méconnus* (1988).

7. Schor, *L'Opinion*, 556–57. For less hostile reactions see *Echo de Clamecy*, July 6, 1935, and Pierre Dominique in *Nouvelles littéraires*, Feb. 25, 1939.

8. *Progrès de Lyon*. Feb. 28, 1926, and June 6, 1927; Milza, *Les Italiens*. 32, 323, 326–27, 442–43.

9. Milza, *Les Italiens*. 29, 31, 102, 332, and Caroline Wiegandt-Sakonn, ibid., 439. See also *Figaro*, Jan. 3, 1930, *Humanité*. Jan. 9, 1930, and *Le Matin*. Jan. 10, 1930, about Italian anti-Fascist terrorists arrested by French police and their cache of explosives.

10. Ponty, *Polonais*. 297.

11. Ibid., 290; J.-C. Bonnet, *Les Pouvoirs publics français et l'immigration dans l'entre-deux-guerres* (Lyons, 1976), 264. Marcel Gillet and Yves-Marie Hilaire, *De Blum à Daladier. Le Nord/Pas-de-Calais 1936–1939* (Lille, 1979), 185, show that between 1931 and 1936 the number of Poles in that region had fallen from 200,000 to 150,000.

12. Jean Chiappe, *Discours* (1936), 22 and passim; Raymond Millet, *Trois millions d'étrangers en France* (1938), 9, 30–31, 73, 76 and passim; René Gontier, *Vers un racisme français* (1939), 227. Foreigners were in fact responsible for a far higher proportion of crimes, and not least crimes of violence, than their share of the population. See Bruno Aubusson de Cavarlay, "La Justice pénale en France (1934–1954)," *Cahiers de l'IHTP* (April 1993), 91.

13. *Action française*. Dec. 13, 1932; *Le Couvre-chef* (Sept. 1933); Ralph Schor, *Nice et les Alpes-Maritimes de 1914 à 1945*. (Nice, 1980), 151–52.

14. Marcel Livian, *Le Régime juridique des étrangers en France* (1936), 15; *Humanité*. Dec. 24, 1933.

15. Schor, *L'Opinion*. 561, 564; *Humanité*. Dec. 24, 1933, Sept. 29, 1937; David Weinberg, *Les Juifs à Paris de 1933 à 1939* (1974), 175.

16. Schor, *L'Opinion*. 562, 584.

17. Ponty, *Polonais*. 317; *Etudes démographiques: Les Naturalisations en France* (1942), 45; *Echo de Clamecy*. June 1, 1935.

18. Georges Mauco, *Les Etrangers en France* (1932), 543; Kaspi, Marès, *Paris*. 18; Schor, *L'Opinion*. 366, 603; Henri Noguères, *La Vie quotidienne au temps du Front populaire* (1977), 78. Pierre Hamp, *Braves Gens de France* (1939), 189, 192, comments harshly on foreigners (like Dr. Roubinoff, an exploitative crook) who come to practice in France with insufficient training. More convincingly, Erich Maria Remarque's *Arch of Triumph* (New York, 1945) turns about the Paris life of a highly qualified German surgeon exploited by his French colleagues. Ravic, Remarque's hero, has no papers and no license to practice in France, but Paris doctors are only too glad to have him do their work for a pittance and leave to them the credit and the gain.

19. Schor, *L'Opinion*. 611, 724.

20. Ibid., 358; *L'Illustration*. Nov. 11, 1933, Feb. 3 and Dec. 14, 1935; *Canard enchaîné*. Feb. 10, 1932; *Echo de Clamecy* April 11, 1936.

21. Marcel L'Herbier quoted in *Canard enchaîné*. April 21, 1937; Jacques Feyder by Henri Jeanson in *La Flèche*. April 22, 1938; Fernandel in *Petit Journal*. Nov. 5, 1937.

22. *Ami du Peuple*. May 31, 1930; *Paris-Soir*. Feb. 2, 1931; *Holmes-Laski Letters* (Cambridge, Mass., 1953), II, 139. One might add that Charles Baudelaire, the translator of Edgar Allan Poe, had grumbled against Americanization, too.

23. *Paris-Soir.* Jan. 5, 1936; Georges Duhamel, *Scènes de la vie future* (1930–35), 84–90; Pierre Hamp, *Une nouvelle fortune* (1926), 88; Schor, *L'Opinion.* 162 and passim.

24. André Siegfried, *Les Etats Unis d'aujourd'hui* (1927); Duhamel, *Scènes.* 19, 25.

25. Duhamel, *Scènes de la vie future,* 11, 25, 29, 33. See also Kadmi-Cohen, *L'Abomination américaine* (1930).

26. Georges Duhamel, *Le Livre de l'amertume: Journal 1925–1956* (1983), 163, Nov. 19, 1930.

27. Dominique, *Nouvelles littéraires.* July 12, 1930. Paul Morand, *Champions du monde* (1930), 177. See also 239: "The more we lend money that's not paid back, says one American, the less we are loved. The French detest us." Ther is no evidence that the author disagrees with this view.

28. Paul Achard, *A New Slant on America* (Chicago, 1931), 12, 103, 203.

29. *Nouvelles littéraires.* Jan. 10, 1931, May 16, 1931. Fernand Léger, the painter, no longer young but young at heart, bore witness to the attraction. New Yorkers were "magnificent barbarians capable of digesting reinforced concrete and nails," he reported in 1931, praising "this new world that suits me so well." *Lettre à Simone* (1987), 29, 36.

30. Arnaud and Dandieu, *Le Cancer.* 11, 15–17, 19–20, 49, 53, 57, 65, 68, 93, 94, 152, 213, 215–24, 232–33.

31. J. B. Duroselle, *La Décadence* 1979), ch. 7: "L'Amérique et la France," and especially 181, 206, 216, 227.

32. *La Révolution nécessaire* (1933), iii.

33. Octave Noël, *Le Péril américain* (1899), I, 48; Charles Pomaret, *L'Amérique à la conquête de l'Europe* (1931), 3, 223–25; Gilberte Brossolette, *Il s'appelait Pierre Brossolette* (1976), 48. For more on postwar attempts to modernize French industry and society and how these foundered in the thirties, see Richard Kuisel, *Ernest Mercier: French Technocrat* (Berkeley, 1967).

34. Hergé, *In America* (1932); Arnaud and Dandieu, *Le Cancer.* 232, quoting *Bulletin de la Compagnie Cottonière.* Aug. 11, 1931; Tardieu speaking at the Bal Bullier, April 7, 1932. In 1936, still, one store in Le Mans (Sarthe) was called Les Stocks Américains. On June 26, 1937, the *Journal de Saint-Gaudens* reported that a Russian plane trying to fly from Moscow to Paris had been forced to land in Vancouver in the state of Washington.

35. Hamp, *Nouvelle Fortune.* 104.

36. Robert Lacour-Gayet, "Souvenirs d'un jeune inspecteur des Finances," *Études et documents.* 1991, III, 441.

37. NA, 2437-C-128/I, Nov. 29, 1932.

38. Emmanuel Berl, *Frères Bourgeois mourez-vous? Ding! Ding! Dong!* (1938), 59; Duroselle, *La Décadence,* 52.

39. See the comments of Jean Zay in *Souvenirs et solitude* (1987), 162–63.

40. Lacour-Gayet, "Souvenirs," 428–29, 434, 440, 443–44. See also AO, Jean Appert, IV, 2, I, 2.

41. Duhamel, *Le Livre.* 331.

42. *Ami du Peuple.* Jan. 21 and 23, Feb. 6, 1932; *Figaro.* Jan. 20, 1932; Céline, *L'Ecole des*

cadavres (1938), 66, 74. The old nationalist André Chéradame, *Sam, à votre tour, payez!* (Mayenne, 1931), 23 ff, argues that American press and opinion are dominated by German Jews and by Jews sympathetic to Germany. For more details, see David Strauss, *Menace in the West: The Rise of French Anti-Americanism in Modern Times* (Westport, Conn., 1978).

43. Schor, *L'Opinion.* 613.

44. Quoted ibid., 182. Late-nineteenth-century anti-Semitism had capitalized on dormant prejudice; the Dreyfus Affair had publicized and spread it; the comradeship of the war had stilled it; economic crisis brought all the old stereotypes out again.

45. Berl, *Interrogatoire par Patrick Modiano* (1976), 17.

46. Paul Morand, *Bucarest* (1935), 160–61; Paul Léautaud, *Journal littéraire* (1962), XII, 50, 57, 116, 213; Marcel Jouhandeau, *Comment je suis devenu antisémite* (1936–39); Pierre Assouline, *Simenon* (1992), 277, 285; Simenon, *Les Caves du Majestic* (1939); for Brasillach, Dominique Arban, *Je me retournerai souvent* (1990), 68–69, and Geraldi Leroy, in *Intellectuels des années 30* (1989), 256; for Arland, see Louis-Albert Revah, *Julien Benda* (1991), 234, and *Nouvelle Revue française.* Feb. 1, 1938, 303–10; for Jaloux, *Journal de l'abbé Mugnier* (1985), 573.

47. Jacques Body, *Giraudoux et l'Allemagne* (1975), 329–30; AO, Jean Filippi, I, 1.

48. Schor, *L'Opinion.* 79.

49. Emile Delavenay, *Témoignage* (Aix-en-Provence, 1992), 73; Jean-Marie Cardinal Lustiger, *Dare to Believe* (New York, 1986), 39; Susan Zuccotti, *The Holocaust, the French and the Jews* (New York, 1993), 23.

50. *Semaine de Suzette.* Dec. 20, 1934; Paul Morand, *France la Doulce* (1934), 51; *Petit Bleu.* May 9, 1932.

51. Michael Marrus and Robert Paxton, *Vichy France and the Jews* (New York, 1981), 36; Albrecht Betz, *Exil et engagement* (1991), 89–92.

52. Betz, op. cit., 109; *Emigrés français en Allemagne: Emigrés allemands en France 1685–1945* (1983), 129. Reading Arthur Koestler's memoirs of those years, one realizes how many of the more visible and audible exiles were Communists or Communist sympathizers and how many anti-Fascist associations functioned as Communist fronts. *The Invisible Writing* (London, 1954), 198, 231, and passim.

53. Morand, *France.* 48, 129; *Candide.* Jan. 25, 1934; *Je Suis Partout.* April 22 and 29, 1933, Oct. 13, 1934, Feb. 9, 1935.

54. Buré in *L'Ordre.* March 8, 1933; Coty in *Figaro.* April 2, 1933; Thälmann in *La France et l'Allemagne 1932–1936* (1980), 169.

55. Harry Paul, ms., "Science on the Right," 16; *Figaro.* May 18, 1933, "Le Communisme au Collège de France"; and press comment in *Œuvre.* April 10 and 13, 1933; *Echo de Paris.* April 19, 1933; *Echo de la Nièvre.* April 22, 1933. As Thomas Glick and his contributors have shown in *The Comparative Reception of Relativity* (Boston, 1987), 113, 137, and passim, Einstein's theories did not receive a warm welcome among the French scientific community.

56. Jean de Pange, *Journal* (1965), II, 261, April 1, 1933, and 268, April 15, 1933: "Hitler? Lui faire crédit."

57. Stephen Schuker, *Jews in Modern France* (Hanover, N.H., 1985), 145, 170; Weinberg,

Les Juifs. 52, 157; *Croix Angévine.* Feb. 11 and 18, 1934. Himself a Jew, Henri Bergson watched the rise of "a formidable wave of anti-Semitism that would break upon the world" and attributed it "in great part, alas!" to "a certain number of Jews entirely deprived of moral sense." terms that could apply to the likes of Stavisky but more likely to the role of Jews in Bolshevik Russia. See Philippe Soulez, *La Gauche et les philosophes* (1992), 101.

58. *Candide.* Oct. 10, 1935; *Action française.* Aug. 22, 1936; *Je Suis Partout.* July 17, 1939.

59. Raymond Abellio, *Ma dernière mémoire* (1980), III, 48–49; *Je Suis Partout.* aug. 7, 1938. Not just the Left either. In *François de Wendel en République* (1976), 549, Jean-Noël Jeanneney shows the great industrialist inclined to discount warnings of Nazi menace and rising German power when these came from Jews. If his friend and political ally Georges Mandel supports the British alliance, Wendel asks himself in the mid-1930s, is he not being carried away "by his Jewish hatred against Germany"?

60. Alain, *Correspondance avec Élie et Florence Halévy* (1958), 311, Aug. 6, 1936; *Echo de la Nièvre.* Sept. 24, 1937; *Correspondance Jean Paulhan et André Suarès, 1925–1940* (1987), 208–09, Nov. 19, 1938. Uncompromising humanist and rationalist, Julien Benda (1867–1956) was a prominent and prolific figure perhaps best known for his *Trahison des clercs* (1927), which denounces the mobilization of passions as political forces and the descent of intellectuals into the political arena, where they abandon higher principles that it is their mission to defend for short-term intoxications.

61. Marrus and Paxton, *Vichy France.* 40; Weinberg, *Les Juifs.* 212–223. Hostility to Jews also grew because Jewish entries from Poland and other nearby countries where anti-Semitism grew steadily worse were becoming more numerous, and illegal entries may have outnumbered legal ones. Ponti, *Polonais.* 319, estimates eighty to ninety thousand by 1939. Poles in general did not have a good press in the fall of 1938, when Polish miners in the Nord were credibly reported to have paraded with shouts of "Heil Hitler!" Gillet and Hilaire, *De Blum.* 202. Ponty, 346, refers to similar reports and rumors in many parts of France.

62. Berl and Modiano, *Interrogatoire.* 126; Céline, *Bagatelles.* 86; *L'Ecole.* 25.

63. Arland, *Nouvelles Rome française.* Feb. 1, 1938, 303–10; Jacqueline Morand, *Les Idées politiques de Louis-Ferdinand Céline* (1972), 47, plausibly links Céline's paranoiac pacifism and his equally paranoiac anti-Semitism.

64. Maurice Pujo, *Comment La Rocque a trahi* (1938) and the anonymous, undated *La Rocque et les juifs;* Pierre Pierrard, *Juifs et Catholiques Français* (1970), 273, for the Pope's explicit words, which probably explained Céline's dubbing Achille Ratti "Isaac Ratisch."

65. It was under the provisions of this so-called Marchandeau decree, named after the minister of justice who signed it, that some of the more anti-Semitic portions of Drieu La Rochelle's *Gilles* were censored in October 1939 and only restored under Vichy. The integral edition of the work would be published in 1942.

66. Arban, *Je me retournerai.* 83–84; Le Roy Ladurie, ms., CVII, 6; Claude Lévi-Strauss and Didier Eribon, *De près et de loin* (1990), 41–42; AO, Louis Franck, III, 2.

67. Pierre Laborie, *Résistants, Vichyssois et autres* (1980), 16.

V: The Decadence

1. J.-B. Duroselle, *La Décadence* (1979), 15.

2. NA, file 851, #1442-1, Feb. 20, 1930.

3. *Holmes-Laski Letters* (Cambridge, Mass., 1953), II, 932, April 2, 1927.

4. Daniel Halévy, *Décadence de la liberté* (1931), 89; Eric Mension-Rigau, *L'Enfance au château* (1990), 84; for Caen, J. Le Roy Ladurie, ms., I, 15.

5. Peter J. Larmour, *The French Radical Party in the 1930s* (Stanford, 1964), 63, 66.

6. In fact, as Larmour stresses, ibid., 60, the Radicals whom he met did not read Alain or reflect his mistrust of the state. Jacques Kayser, active in party affairs through the twenties and the thirties, never heard references to him. Kayser in *Tendances politiques dans la vie française* (1960), 70. Larmour's dominant impression of Radical thinking was of "a rather sentimental and unsystematic eighteenth-century belief in progress." One should add Larmour's general assessment of the party and the men whom he studied: "As a group they were curiously admirable. Most were honest; many very earnest . . ." and some highly cultivated; "and that makes the tragedy of their failure more profound." Op. cit., 55.

7. Déat, *Perspectives Socialistes* (1930).

8. Alain, *Correspondance avec Elie et Florence Halévy* (1958), Aug. 29, 1934.

9. Letter of May 28, 1925, quoted in *André Tardieu* (1957), xvi.

10. Yves Simon, *La Grande Crise de la République française* (Montreal, 1941), 47.

11. *Le Nationalisme français* (1966), 17: *"une méditation sur une décadence."*

12. The man in the street remained steadfastly irreverent. To cries of *"La France aux Français,"* wags replied: *"Le homard à l'Américaine."* Henri Noguères, *La Vie quotidienne en France au temps du Front Populaire* (1977), 119.

13. Raymond Aron, *Mémoires* (1983), 103.

14. *Les Derniers Jours* (Feb. 1927).

15. Jean Chiappe, *Paroles d'ordre* (1930), 21; Julien Benda in *Nouvelles Littéraires*. Oct. 17, 1931; Henry de Jouvenel, *La Paix française* (1934, but printed in 1932), 352; Raymond Abellio, *Ma dernière mémoire* (1975), II, 109.

16. *Décadence de la nation française* (1931), 10–12, 18–20, 27, 40, 46, and passim.

17. Simone de Beauvoir, *La Force de l'age* (1960), 139; Barthélémy Montagnon, *Grandeurs et servitudes socialistes* (1929), 57; NA, Commercial Attaché, Paris #232, Annual Economic Report for 1933, Jan. 30, 1934, refers to "the American model of managed economy appealing only to marginal groups like the Neo Socialists."

18. Gérard Brun, *Techniciens et téchnocrates en France* (1985), 36.

19. Pierre Andreu, *Le Rouge et le blanc* (1977), 89; Dorsay (Pierre Villette) in *Je Suis Partout*. Jan. 9 and March 26, 1932.

20. *Je Suis Partout*. Oct. 14, 1933.

21. See *Nouvelles littéraires*. May 11, 1935, and Oct. 24, 1936 for articles glorifying Henri de Man; Richard Kuisel, *Capitalism and the State in Modern France* (Cambridge, 1981), 119.

22. AO, Gaston Cusin, II, 1. That may explain the flow of works devoted to the New Deal: Bertrand de Jouvenel, *La Crise du capitalisme américain* (1933), Hyacinthe Dubreuil,

Les Codes de Roosevelt (1934), Robert Marjolin, *Les Expériences Roosevelt* (1934), Georges Boris, *La Révolution Roosevelt* (1934), André Philip, *La Crise et l'économie dirigée* (1935), and many more.

23. Bloch-Lainé, *La France restaurée* (1986), 50. The major actors in the postwar plan testify against this view. Jean Monnet, *Mémoires* (1976), 278, writes, *"Nous nous mîmes au travail sur une table rase,"* but that does not mean there were no memories of prewar debates. Philippe Mioche, *Modernisation ou décadence?* (Aix, 1990), 17, believes Monnet had no time to pay attention to *planisme.* More specifically, Robert Marjolin, *Le Travail d'une vie* (1986), 61, finds the product of prewar *planistes* pitiful: a tissue of generalizations accompanied by invocations of virtue and civic spirit—"A sort of pre-Pétainism." In effect, the term *National Revolution* appeared in *L'Homme nouveau* (Sept. 1935), a journal close to Romain's *Groupe du 9 juillet.*

24. *Le Rajeunissement de la politique* (1932), 182–83.

25. *Holmes-Laski Letters.* 1222, 1300; Duroselle, *Décadence.* 483.

26. *Ami du Peuple,* quoted in NA, 2657-C-222/2, Aug. 30, 1928. See also 2657-C-222/3, Aug. 31, 1928.

27. Bainville, *Doit'on le dire?* (1939), 279–81; also *Les Conséquences politiques de la paix* (1920).

28. *Nouvelles littéraires.* Oct. 11, 1930: "Le Silence de l'Allemagne."

29. Jules Sauerwein, *Trente ans à la une* (1962); NA, 2172-1238/1, Jan. 12, 1931. When in 1928 Georges Loustanau-Lacau wrote a book that warned against reviving German military power, the General Staff had forced him to cut out offending passages. *Mémoires d'une français rebelle* (1948), 69.

30. *Revue hebdomadaire.* July 1931, 97–98: "La Fin de l'après-guerre"; NA, 2657-C-259/3, Dec. 8, 1931.

31. Louis Loucheur, *Carnets secrets 1908–1932* (1964), 171.

32. AO, Louis Franck, III, 2, remembers how widely Hindenburg's election against Hitler was regarded as a French success by the general public, by diners at the Cercle Militaire of Lille, and by Léon Blum.

33. Lacretelle in *Nouvelles littéraires.* May 20, 1933; Duc de Brissac, *La Suite des temps* (9174), 23; Duroselle, *Décadence.* 21.

34. Louis Artus, *Paix sur la terre.* mentioned in *Nouvelles littéraires.* Jan. 9, 1932; Buisson in Daniel Guérin, *Quand le fascisme nous devançait* (1955), 6.

35. *Gazette des Tribunaux.* June 20, 1934; Paul Léautaud, *Journal littéraire* (1962), X, 287. On the other hand, Konrad Heiden's *History of National Socialism* was translated and published in 1934, with a preface by Julien Benda. Georges Bataille (who had begun to study fascism and write about it as early as 1933) borrowed Heiden's book from the Bibliothèque Nationale, where he worked, in August 1935 and returned it in January 1936. *Lettres à Roger Caillois* (1987), 53. Some things never change!

36. Horace de Carbuccia, *Le Massacre de la victoire* (1973), I, 172–73; Denis de Rougemont, *Journal d'une époque* (1968), 159–60.

37. For the Papins, see *Paris-Soir.* Feb. 4, 1933 ff (and Feb 14, "Un beau crime, svp!"); for Nozière, *Gazette de Tribunaux.* Oct. 14, 1934, and *Humanité.* Oct. 12, 1934.

38. Dell, *My Second Country, France* (London, 1920), ix.

39. NA, 2657-C-209, Dec. 18, 1936, "Venality of the Press."

40. Pierre Cot in *Le Rajeunissement.* 160; Dell, *My Second Country.* 24; NA, 2657-C-209, Dec. 18, 1936, "Venality of the Press." Duroselle, *Décadence,* 203, 205, quotes a *Time* magazine estimate of 1938 that the French press was the most venal in the world and Daladier's estimate that four fifths of it lived on subsidies.

41. Laurent Greilshamer, *Hubert Beuve-Méry* (1990), 59 ff; Jean Galtier-Boissière, *Mémoires d'un parisien* (1961), II, 295.

42. Larmour, *Radical Party.* 58, makes the point that a free press service distributed articles to provincial publications, giving them about twenty times the readership of the newspaper where they had originally been published.

43. See *Petit Parisien,* July 28, 1926: *"L'Escroc Stavisky arrêté à Marly. . . ."*

44. Larmour, *Radical Party.* 48. Stavisky himself had contributed to a Radical finance organization, the Comité du Commerce et de l'Industrie, also known as the Comité Mascuraud, after Alfred Mascuraud, senator of the Seine from 1905 to his death in 1926, who had founded it in 1898 to help fight the Nationalists. The committee's president, Louis Proust, was expelled from the party for his role in the Stavisky Affair.

45. *Figaro.* Jan. 21, 1934; NA, #851 reel 1442-2, Jan. 29, 1934.

46. D. W. Brogan, *The Development of Modern France* (London, 1940), 660.

47. NA, #851, reel 1442-2, Special report of Jan. 9, 1934; *Paris-Soir.* Jan. 1, 4, 20, 1934; *Nouvelles littéraires.* Feb. 17, 1934.

48. Dell, *My Second Country.* 89–90; *Le Peuple.* Jan. 10, 1934; *Canard enchaîné.* Jan. 10, 1934; AN #851, reel 1442-2, Jan. 11, 1934.

49. *Nouvelles littéraires.* Jan. 13, Feb. 3, 1934; *Paris-Soir.* Jan. 12, 13, 17, 1934; *Vu.* Jan. 31, 1934.

50. NA, Commercial Attaché, #232, Economic reviews of Jan. and Feb. 1934; file 851, #1442-2, Jan. 13, 1934; 2857-C-286/1, Jan. 16, 1934.

51. Suarès in *Nouvelles littéraires.* Feb. 17, 1934. See Alain Laubreaux in *Vu.* Feb. 14, 1934: At the Comédie-Française some cry against Coriolanus; others against Chiappe. One account has the public in better seats applauding the tribunes, one man in the second balcony trying to whistle them down. A voice from the orchestra seats: "Perhaps the gentleman is a deputy?" The curtain had to be brought down.

52. *Détective.* Jan. 4, 1934; on Daladier, A.O., Cusin, II, 2.

53. Henry Charbonneau, *Mémoires de Porthos* (1967), 97.

54. Serge Berstein, *Le 6 Fevrier 1934* (1975), 157. For July 21, 1926, see NA, 2657-C-206, July 27, 1926: "[F]or the first time in many years the breath of revolution animated a Paris crowd. . . ."

55. *Action française.* Feb. 3; *Echo de Paris.* Feb. 6; *Le Jour.* Feb. 5, 1934; Berstein, *Le 6 fevrier.* 140–41.

56. *Humanité.* Feb. 6, 7, 8, 1934; *Illustration.* Feb. 17, 1934; André Thirion, *Révolutionnaires sans révolution* (1972), 388–89; Léautaud, *Journal.* X, 276, Feb. 7, 1934. In December 1898 the twenty-six-year-old Léautaud had sent a contribution to the fund that Drumont's *Libre Parole* opened to commemorate Major Henry, with the comment: *"Pour l'ordre, contre la justice et la vérité."* Pierre Quillard, *Le Monument Henry* (1899), 172. The man of letters who loved dogs and cats more than his ilk found little reason to change his mind in years to come.

57. Lilian Mowrer, *Journalist's Wife* (New York, 1937), 318–19; AO, Pierre de Calan, II, I and Jean Filippi, II, I; Jean de Pange, *Journal* (1970), III, 27.

58. *Ouest-Eclair*. Feb. 8, 1934; NA, file 851, #1442-2, Feb. 7, 1934; *Journal de Montélimar*. Feb. 10, 1934.

59. *Croix Angévine*. Feb. 11, 1934; AO, Désiré Arnaud, I, 2; *Vu*. Feb. 21, 1934. Provincial reactions after echoes of the sixth had reached them were more lively (see the March police reports quoted in Ralph Schor, *L'Opinion française et les étrangers*. 1985, 637), but occasionally exasperated: *Journal de Montélimar*. March 24, 1934. Even so, the strikes and marches of Feb. 12 appear to have been good-natured. "We had a lot of fun," noted one militant schoolteacher in Bourges, where three thousand marched. *"On s'est payé la tête de Bourges et des bourgeois."* Claude Jamet, *Notre Front Populaire* (1977), 22.

60. For Barthou's last hours, see Robert J. Young, *Power and Pleasure: Louis Barthou and the Third French Republic* (Montreal, 1991), 224–25; also Suzy Borel, *Par une porte entrebaillée* (1972), 113, 179.

61. Léautaud, *Journal*. X, 320, Oct. 10, 1934. But Colette, *La Jumelle noire* (1991), reviewing a revue on Oct. 21, speaks of a black week: *"stupeur . . . tristesse."*

62. A *Figaro* editorial on March 8, 1934, called the Radical party "a syndicate for the exploitation of France by all means including crime." For the continuingly "highly dangerous situation" and the boos, see NA, 1442/3, Nov. 5, 1934.

63. NA, 851, reel 1442/2, Feb. 8, 1934. Also *Paris-Soir*. Feb. 9 and 10, 1934.

64. Bertrand de Jouvenel, *Après la défaite* (1941), 121. André Delmas, *A Gauche de la barricade* (1950), 9, and Jean-François Sirinelli, *Intellectuels et passions françaises* (1990), 91, both use the same parallel. A then young magistrate of the Conseil d'Etat, serving in the cabinet of the minister of commerce, remembers Jean Mistler, collapsed behind his desk, repeating: *"La république est foutue."* Pierre Laroque, *Au service de l'homme et du droit* (1993), 103.

65. AO, Cusin, II, 2; André Delmas, *Mémoires d'un instituteur syndicaliste* (1979), 235–41; Andreu, *Rouge et blanc*. 84; *Gazette des Tribunaux*. Feb. 13, 1935; *Petit Troyen*. Feb. 11, 1935: *"Après l'insurrection fasciste."*

66. *Paris-Soir*. Feb. 22, March 20 and 30, 1934; *Croix Angévine*. June 3, 1934; Copeau in *Nouvelles littéraires*. March 24, 1934; Léautaud, *Journal*. X, 290, March 14, 1934.

67. *Paris-Soir* and *L'Intransigeant*. March 21, 1934; *Femina*. (Feb., March 1934); *Paris-Soir*. Feb. 9, March 6, 1934.

68. Dominique Borne and Henri Dubief, *La Crise des années 30* (1989), 125; Danielle Tartakovski, "Stratégies de la rue, 1934–1936," in *Mouvement social* (April 1986), 32.

69. NA, 1442/3, June 18, 1935: "Extraparliamentary Ligues have so far proved thoroughly ineffective and their prestige has been weakened."

70. See Jacques Bardoux, *Le Drame français: Refaire l'etat ou subir la force* (1934), 20. Appropriately, on Feb. 6, 1958, to commemorate the events of twenty-four years before, a commando of the neo-Fascist Jeune Nation was to place a bomb in the lavatories of the National Assembly.

71. For the verdict, see *Paris-Soir*. Jan. 18, 1936.

72. William Bullitt, *For the President. Personal and Secret* (New York, 1972), 104, April 7, 1935. On Nov. 24, 1936, p. 184, Bullitt writes again to report that Blum, Herriot,

Claudel, "everyone" are "convinced that war is about to arrive" either in 1937 or, certainly, in 1938.

73. Stalin may have been willing to go farther. In 1943, at Vichy, Laval told Raymond Abellio how Stalin had very seriously suggested that he, Laval, should lead the future Popular Front. *Ma dernière mémoire.* II, 150.

74. Just how traumatic Stalin's turnaround proved can be seen in Léon Emery, *Correspondance* (Carpentras, 1982), I, 114–21. For the Right, see *Je Suis Partout.* May 4, 1935.

75. See *Echo de Clamecy.* Sept. 21, 1935, reporting the suicide of a twenty-seven-year-old man in Sheffield, in fear of what might derive from sanctions.

76. Yves Simon, *La Campagne d'Ethiopie et la pensée politique française* (1936), 25; *Croix-Angévine.* Nov. 17, 1935: *"Les Abyssins sont-ils chrétiens?"*

77. Cot in *Démocratie savoyarde.* March 21, 1936; *Correspondance Jean-Paulhan et André Suarès* (1987), 194.

78. Jean Zay, *Souvenirs et solitude* (1987), 71–73; Paul Stehlin, *Témoignage pour l'histoire* (1964), 39, 85–86; Judith Hughes, *To the Maginot Line* (Cambridge, Mass., 1971), 248 ff.

79. Stehlin, op. cit., ch. IV,; Emmanuel Monick, *Pour mémoire* (1970), 80–81; Jacques Chastenet, *Quatre Fois vingts ans* (1974), 230. When a French friend assured the Mowrers, "Next time we mobilize," Edgar inquired, "Why not now?" "Mon cher . . . a mobilization costs a lot of money . . . are we ready for that just now?" Lilian Mowrer, *Journalist's Wife.* 348. On the other hand, at the Jockey Club, the general opinion on March 7 seems to have been: *"Ils sont chez eux."* The Germans were free to do what they liked in their own country. Pange, *Journal* (1975), IV, 226.

80. See Alfred Fabre-Luce, *Le Grand Jeu. 1936–1939* (1962), 61.

81. For Pius XI, Duroselle, *Décadence.* 179; for French reactions, AO, Hervé Alphand, I, 2, and Guy de Carmoy, III, I; for Americans, NA, 1442/3, April 15, 1936. Janine Ponty, *Polonais méconnus* (1988), 348, cites a Polish memorandum of May 7, 1936: "France holds an ever-diminishing place in Europe. . . . The nation grows old . . . The lack of patriotism and the bad will typical of the rentier spirit permit no reaction. . . ."

VI: A Famous Victory

1. *Mein Kampf* (Boston, 1943), 107.

2. Alexander Werth, *France in Ferment* (London, n.d.), 263.

3. Ibid., 279.

4. Peter Larmour, *The French Radical Party* (1964), 187; Marcel Gillet and Y.-M. Hilaire, eds., *De Blum à Daladier. Le Nord/Pas-de-Calais* (Lille, 1979), 35; Werth, *France in Ferment.* 289.

5. Herriot in *l'Œuvre.* Oct. 6, 1934; Larmour, *Radical Party.* 174.

6. *Paris-Soir.* April 2 and 3, 1936; Chautemps in *Le Temps.* Oct. 19, 1935; Aubaud in Serge Berstein, *Histoire du parti radical* (1982), II, 355.

7. Danielle Tartakowski, "Stratégies de la rue," in *Mouvement social* (April 1986), 57; Gillet and Hilaire, *De Blum.* 30; *Paris-Soir.* April 23 and 30, 1936.

8. NA, # 1442/3, May 11 and 14, 1936.

9. Jacques Kergoat, *La France du Front populaire* (1986), 357. For an account of the strikes at Roubaix, see Maxence van der Meersch, *Pêcheurs d'hommes* (1940), 162–251, where the musical background is largely provided by Ray Ventura's 1935 success "Tout va très bien, Madame la Marquise. . . ."

10. Henri Noguères, *Vie quotidienne en France* (1977), 125; *Paris-Soir.* June 22, 1936; *Skol Vreizh. Images du Front populaire* (April 1987), 49, 51; Alain Laubréaux, *La Terreur rose* (1939), 27; Lilian Mowrer, *Journalist's Wife* (New York, 1937), 175; Paul Léautaud, *Journal littéraire* (1962), XI, 209–13.

11. *Dossiers de l'Action populaire.* June 1936; *L'Aube.* July 1, 1936; *Etudes.* July 5, 1936; *Echo de Paris.* June 3, 1936. See also Paul Christophe, *1936. Les Catholiques et le Front populaire* (1986), 89, and Jean-Noël Marchandiau, *L'Illustration 1843/1944* (1987), 257.

12. Annie Kriegel, *Ce que j'ai cru comprendre* (1991), 98.

13. Jean Galtier-Boissière, *Mémoires d'un parisien* (1961), II, 310; Jean de Pange, *Journal* (1970), III, 428; Bullitt, *For the President.* 197; Léautaud, *Journal.* XII, 70; *L'Œuvre.* May 4, 1936, and AO, Pierre de Calan, II, 1.

14. *Nouvelles littéraires.* Sept. 26, 1936. A relentless campaign in the conservative and reactionary press had accused Salengro of deserting to the enemy during the First World War. But the slander had been launched by the Communists: See *L'Enchaîné.* Feb. 6, 1931 and *Le Prolétaire* of 1920.

15. NA, #1442/3, April 15 and May 14, 1936.

16. *Nouvelles littéraires.* Aug. 8, 1936; Commercial Attaché, 38 #244, Economic conditions in France, 1937, 69; #2736-C-16/1, Jan. 26, 1937.

17. NA, Commercial Attaché, 38 #244, 90 and #238; Halévy, *1938* (1938), 13.

18. For the establishment of a Comité National de Surveillance des Prix, see Louis Franck, "Quand le contrôle des prix était une politique artiste," *Annales des mines* (June 1987), 34–44. But farmers continued to look askance at the advantages workers gained, while they worked more for less, feared rises in equipment and fertilizer prices, and resented the rural projects of the Popular Front (Wheat Board, social insurance) as representing state intervention. At Limerzel (Morbihan), the locals slashed the bicycle tires of visiting holidaymakers. Yves Lambert, *Dieu change en Bretagne* (1985), 186.

19. J.-C. Asselain in Jean Bouvier, ed., *La France en mouvement, 1934–1938* (1986), 177; Noguères, *Vie quotidienne.* 97–98; Mowrer, *Journalist's Wife.* 369–70.

20. *Nouvelles littéraires.* April 10, 1937; Asselain, *op. cit.,* 181 and passim.

21. NA, Commercial Attaché, 38 #244, Economic conditions in France 1937, 32; Michel Margairaz, *L'Etat, les finances et l'économie* (1991), I, 456.

22. Margairaz, *op. cit.,* 408 ff, 421; Bertrand de Jouvenel, *Après la défaite* (1941), 87, 89–91.

23. Margairaz, *L'Etat, les finances,* 232; *Paris-Soir.* Jan. 12, 1937; Gilbert Hatry, *Louis Renault, patron absolu* (1982), 266; Michel Chabot, *L'Escarbille* (1978), 218.

24. *Femina* (1930), xxiii; Jean-Pierre Goubert, *La Conquête de l'eau* (1986), 116.

25. René Lacoste, *Plaisir du tennis* (1981), 16, 22.

26. Pierre Hamp, *Une nouvelle fortune* (1926), 203, 205.

27. On the Tour, see Pierre Chany, *La Fabuleuse Histoire du Tour de France* (1983), 245 and passim. Among the songs it launched one may cite "Le Tour de France" (1930), "La

Môme biclo," and "Les Champions de la route" (1931), "P'tit gars du Tour" (1932) and "Le Tour qui passe" (1933): *"Voilà le Tour qui passe/Saluons ces champions/C'est l'av'nir de la race/de cinq grandes nations: faut qu'on les applaudisse/mais dans l'fond de not'cœur/nous souhaitons que le vainqueur/soit desormais un p'tit Français."*

28. P. Arnaud and J. Camy, *Naissance du mouvement sportif associatif en France* (Lyons, 1986), 267. This is not to underrate the attractions of rugby, whose devotees were most numerous in the southwest. In 1934 Marcel Aymé published "Sporting," the story of the rivalry between the gymnastic society L'Espérance of Castalin, patronized by the Radical-Socialist deputy of the little town, and the rugby club Le Sporting, founded and subsidized by the candidate of the Right, Dr. Dulâtre. When, against all expectations, the Sporting wins a match against a visiting Paris team, Castalin shifts its loyalties from gymnastics to rugby, and "the election of the good doctor was assured." Reprinted in *Commentaire* (Autumn 1993), 451–58.

29. Barthélémy in *Journal Officiel.* Chambre, Débats, Dec. 15, 1938, 1825.

30. Mowrer, *Journalist's Wife.* 324.

31. Jean-Louis Chappat, *Chemins de l'espoir* (1983), 182; Jean Zay, *Souvenirs et solitude* (1987), 61.

32. Chappat, *op. cit.,* 164–65, 167. For his cultural initiatives, see *1936. Léo Lagrange* (1980), 22, 23; Mowrer, *Journalist's Wife.* 401. It was under Lagrange's aegis that a traveling library, the Bibliobus, was launched in the Marne in 1937. Kergoat, *La France.* 366–67, says that within two years it touched more local readers than all of the department's school libraries. One of Zay's initiatives was to celebrate the traditional old maids' feast of Saint Catherine as a *fête nationale des midinettes* by reserving for young dressmakers and milliners all official boxes in state theaters and operas. Zay, *op. cit.,* 114.

33. Noguères, *Vie quotidienne.* 158, 168–69; *Confidences.* Nov. 25, 1938; *Semaine religieuse de Besançon.* Feb. 2, 1939. Some of Lagrange's initiatives found the ground prepared for them. Hairdressers, always keen on sports, had developed their own flying clubs since 1930 and started to hold annual air shows in 1932. Paul Gerbod, "Les Coiffeurs en France," *Mouvement social* (Jan. 1981), 81.

34. Christophe, *1936.* 115; Chappat, *Chemins.* 175.

35. Ralph Schor, *Nice et les Alpes Maritimes* (1980), 138; *Le Petit Niçois.* Sept. 25, 1935; *Le Peuple.* June 27, 1939.

36. *Le Populaire.* Sept. 8, 1937; *Confidences.* Aug. 19, 1938.

37. But Zay combined all the characteristics hated by the Right: A Jew on his father's side, a Protestant on his mother's side, he was a Mason and a dedicated man of the moderate Left.

38. Bullitt, *For the President.* 174.

39. André Delmas, *Mémoires d'un instituteur syndicaliste* (1979), 335–36; Emmanuel Berl, *Interrogatoire* (1976), 61; Bullitt, *op. cit.,* 173; Raymond Abellio, *Ma dernière mémoire* (1975), II, 110.

40. Martin Wolfe, *The French Franc between the Wars* (New York, 1951), 213.

41. See Margairaz in *Etudes et documents.* (1991), III, 583–98; J.-B. Duroselle, *La Décadence* (1979), 444.

42. A. J. P. Taylor, *English History 1914–1945* (Oxford, 1965), 351.

43. *Echo de Clamecy.* Aug. 22, 1936.

44. See Jacques Bardoux, *J'Accuse Moscou* (Nov. 1936) and Wladimir d' Ormesson, *L'Europe en Danger: Le Communisme c'est la guerre* (1936). Christophe, *1936.* 141.

45. *Canard enchaîné.* May 12, 1937.

46. Claude Farrère, *Visite aux Espagnols* (1937), 11, 14–15; also his *Souvenirs* (1953), which reflects strong anti-Masonic and anti-Communist sentiments.

47. For this and below, see AO, Gaston Cusin, III, I, III, 2, IV, I.

48. See NA, 2724-S-16/6, April 2, 1937, quoting *Action française.* April I, 1937.

49. *Echo de Clamecy.* March 16, 1935; *Humanité.* Feb. 12 and 19, 1937; NA, Commercial Attaché, 38 #244, Economic conditions in France 1937, 36.

50. See press of March 17, 1937, ff and NA, 1442/4, March 17, 1937, 2736-C-18/1, March 25, 1937.

51. *Gazette des Tribunaux.* July 29, 1938; Pierre Lucius, *Les Chantiers de l'Exposition ou le laboratoire de la révolution* (Laval, 1937), 3, 5, and passim; J. Verger, *L'Exposition a-t-elle été Sabotée* (1937). Michael Seidman, "The Birth of the Weekend," *French Historical Studies* (Fall 1981), 266–69, paints an equally depressing picture of low productivity, cost over-runs, sabotage, and utter indifference to the entreaties of the government, the Socialist party, or even the Confederation of Labor. Workers overall, writes Seidman, took twice as long to complete a job in 1937 as they had done in 1936: One job that could be finished in 78,710 hours took 264,700 hours; another took 256 hours instead of 123.

52. For samples see *Echo de Clamecy.* July 25, 1937; *Echo de la Nièvre.* July 24 and 31; *Paris-Soir.* July I and II, Aug. 12, 1937. Edmond Labbé, *Exposition internationale des arts et techniques dans la vie moderne: Rapport général* (1940), II, 111–12, 496–99, 506–07.

53. *Gazette des Tribunaux.* March 10, May 7, 1937.

54. See François Broche, *L'Assassinat de Lemaigre-Dubreuil* (1977), 11–21; Pierre Péan, *Le Mystérieux Docteur Martin 1895–1969* (1993), 91–115 and passim; NA, 1442/5, Nov. 20, 1937, and Jan. 11, 1938; Bullitt, *For the President.* 241; Brasillach, *Œuvres complètes.* X, 542.

55. Larmour, *The Radical Party.* 165.

56. Duroselle, *Décadence.* 445. Robert Frankenstein, *Le Prix du réarmament français* (1982), 96, argues convincingly that the effort to improve national defense made the bad financial situation worse. Without rearmament, the budget deficit would have begun to shrink early in 1937 and weighed less heavily on national revenue. Once again, Blum had no luck: He did the right thing and reaped only failure.

57. Duroselle, op. cit., 447, 457; Emmanuel Chadeau, *L'Industrie aéronautique en France* (1987), 161–62; Antoine de Saint-Exupéry, *Pilote de Guerre* (1942), 92.

58. Larmour, *The Radical Party.* 221 ff; Jean-Thomas Nordmann, *Histoire des radicaux* (1974), 124; Albert Bayet, *L'Œuvre.* Jan. 5, 1940.

59. *Paris-Soir.* July I, 1937; NA, 1442/5, Jan. 12 and 27, 1938; Bullitt, *For the President.* 250.

60. Larmour, *The Radical Party.* 227.

61. NA, 1442/5, March 13, 22, 1938; 2657-C-260, March 28, 1938; Bullitt, *For the*

President. 268; *Je Suis Partout.* April 1, 1938. Eduard Beneš (1884–1948), Czech states-man and longtime foreign minister, had become president of Czechoslovakia in 1935, after Thomas Masaryk left that office at the age of eighty-five.

62. NA, 1442/5, Sept. 8, 1938; 2657-11-90/87, Sept. 19, 1938, quoting Lindbergh letter dated Sept. 13, 1938.

63. Jean Calvet, *Mémoires* (Lyon, 1967), 125; Delmas, *Mémoires.* 350; Galtier-Boissinère, *Mémoires.* passim.

64. Henry Miller, *Letters to Anaïs Nin* (New York, 1965), 149–52.

65. Michel Debré, *Trois républiques pour une France: Mémoires* (1984), I, 98–9; Henri Boegner, *Oui patron* (1976), 53; Yves Simon, *La Grande Crise de la République* (Montreal, 1941), 40; *Echo de Clamecy.* Oct. 15, 1938.

66. Duroselle, *Décadence,* 355; Joseph-Vincent Ducatillon, *Une renaissance française* (1939), 28; *La Frontière.* Dec. 12, 1938; Edgar Ansel Mowrer, *Triumph and Turmoil* (New York, 1968), 290.

67. Duroselle, *Décadence.* 386, inists that Jewish ministers were invited to the German Em-bassy reception; Zay, *Souvenirs.* 170–71, that they were not invited to an unspecified reception, which I take to be that of the Quai d'Orsay. No wonder that Lindbergh described the French as "a corrupt and demoralized nation." *Wartime Journals of Charles E. Lindbergh* (New York, 1970), 81.

68. Jacques Laurent, *Histoire égoiste* (1976), 152; AO, Jean Filippi, III, I; Simone de Lattre, *Jean de Lattre, mon mari* (1971), 129.

69. AO, Guy de Carmoy, III, I, quoting General Pennès, assistant to the chief of Air Force General Staff (see also Georges Bonnet, quoted in Duroselle, *Décadence.* 354); Bullitt, *For the President.* 297–300.

70. NA, 1442/5, Oct. 4, 1938; 2657-11-90/97, Oct. 4 and 90/98, Oct. 6, 1938. An-other highly relevant remark came from Jean-Paul Sartre, who, after noting that every-body had collapsed like hot-air balloons, pointed to the consequence: "[M]any say that the Russians will turn toward the Germans, and it's not impossible." *Lettres au Castor, 1926–1939* (1983), 215.

71. Debré, *Trois républiques.* I, 141, 145 (Debré was a member of Reynaud's cabinet): Mar-gairaz, *L'Etat.* 477, 485; Alfred Sauvy in René Rémond and Janine Bourdin, *Edouard Daladier chef de gouvernement* (1977), 95.

72. *Ere nouvelle.* Dec. 1, 1938; NA, 2657-C-260, March 28, 1938; Berstein, *Parti radical.* II, 564.

73. Students reacted to Fascist claims and demonstrations with their own: *"Venise aux Français, la Sardaigne aux Français, le Vésuve à la France, l'Italie à la Corse, le Négus au pouvoir . . ."* Ralph Schor in Pierre Milza, ed., *Les Italiens en France* (Rome, 1986), 103.

74. See Patrick Marnham, *The Man Who Wasn't Maigret: A Portrait of Georges Simenon* (New York, 1993), 152.

75. Larmour, *Radical Party.* 245 ff; Gillet and Hilaire, *De Blum.* 215–16; *Le Grand Echo.* Jan. 20, 1939. See Emile Roche in *La République.* March 23, 1939: "Threats . . . have done more to wake love of our colonies than ten years of propaganda."

76. Sauvy in Rémond and Bourdin, *Edouard Daladier.* 94; Debré, *Trois républiques.* I, 161–62.

VII: A God in Our Image

1. Magdeleine Peyronnec and Jean-Benoît Marcy, *J'ai été Carmélite* (1935), 36 ff.

2. *Coûtumier du Monastère des Moniales dominicaines de Lourdes* (Toulouse, 1938), 229.

3. Peyronnec, *J'ai été Carmélite.* 76–78, and press, July 12, 1932.

4. Ibid., 130–32, 161. Holy poverty reinforced rejection of the body. Catherine Baker, *Les Contemplatives* (1979), 36, cites a sixty-nine-year-old Carmelite who confirms that she and her fellows did not wash their teeth and that she wore only two robes throughout her conventual life. *"Mais chez les pauvres c'était pareil";* The poor had it no better.

5. *Coûtumier.* 190–91, 198, 222, 206, 209, 212.

6. Peyronnec, *J'ai été Carmélite,* 270. For Carmelite "penitence and mortification" see Baker, *Contemplatives,* 200–03, concerning flagellation instruments ("disciplines"), and ch. 9 passim.

7. Ibid., 64.

8. *Coûtumier.* 399.

9. Ibid., 397, 401–02.

10. NA, 2657-C-231/2, Oct. 11, 1928; Claude Langlois, *Le Catholicisme au féminin* (1984). 309–10. I am indebted to Mme. Elisabeth Dufourcq for some of the figures or their confirmation. For Saint Angela Merici, see Geneviève Fourquet, *Une aventure de fidélité* (1990); for the Pious Union, *Constitutions des oblates du coeur de Jésus* (Moulins, 1982). But these are only two among a host of others, most of them unsung and unrecorded.

11. Elisabeth Dufourcq, *Les Aventurières de Dieu* (1993), 382; *Constitution des Dominicaines enseignantes de Toulouse* (approved in 1953, printed in 1954); Odile Arnold, *Le Corps et l'âme* (1984), 81, and for the quotation, Jean-Pierre Goubert, *La Conquête de l'eau* (1986), 221. One must not generalize, however, or overrate the modern spirit; discussing the newly founded Dominicaines de Saint Jacques, who divided their time between contemplation and study, M.-M. Davy, *Les Dominicaines* (1934), 227–28, commented: *"Il faut le reconnaître, peu de femmes sont capables de travailler intellectuellement."* Thirty years after Davy, Marlène Tuininga talked to a cloistered nun in a rural abbey of the 1960s who rose at four, went to bed at eight winter and summer, slept on a palliasse and ate no meat. *Les Religieuses* (1969), 14.

12. Paul Guiral and Guy Thuillier, *La Vie quotidienne des professeurs en France* (1982), ch. VIII; Jean Peneff, *Ecoles publiques, écoles privées dans l'Ouest* (1987), 66, 212.

13. Peneff, op. cit., 15; Gerard Cholvy and Yves-Marie Hilaire, *Histoire religieuses de la France contemporarine* (Toulouse, 1988), III, 354; Louis Pérouas, *Refus d'une religion, religion d'un refus en Limousin rural* (1985), 149–50.

14. *Semaine religieuse de Bourges.* 1930, 2; Guy Devailly ed., *Le Diocèse de Bourges* (1973), 226–27.

15. *Semaine religieuse de Besançon.* June 13, 1940; Alphonse Haensler, *Curé de campagne* (1980), 234, also 151; Adrien Dansette, *Histoire religieuse de la France contemporaine.* (1951), II, 632; Pierre Hamp, *Braves gens de France* (1939), 150.

16. Dansette, op. cit., 624; François-Isambert, *Archives de sociologie des religions.* no. 9 (1960), quoted in *Histoire de l'édition française* (1986), IV, 271.

17. Cholvy and Hilaire, *Histoire religieuse.* III, 20; Fernand Boulard, *Essor ou déclin du clergé français* (1950), 31, 41, 232; Julien Potel, *Les Prêtres séculiers en France* (1977), 36.

18. Nadine-Josette Chaline, *Des Catholiques Normands* (Roanne, 1985), 215; F. Boulard, *Matériaux pour l'histoire religieuse du peuple français.* I (1982), I, 118, and III (ed., Gérard Cholvy, 1992), 13, 29, 53; Louis Pérouas, *Les Limousins, leurs saints, leurs prêtres* (1988), 179–80; Bernard Gouley, *Les Catholiques Français aujourd'hui* (1977), 15; Serge Bonnet, *Sociologie politique et religieuse de la Lorraine* (1972), 148.

19. *Histoire de l'édition.* 84, 272; *Croix Angévine.* Aug. 29, 1937.

20. *Cœurs vaillants.* Oct. 20, 1928, July 26, 1931, and *passim.*

21. Cholvy and Hilaire, *Histoire religieuses.* III, 35.

22. Michel Lagrée, *Religion et cultures en Bretagne* (1992), 428; Pérouas, *Les Limousins.* 188–89.

23. Pierre Pierrard, *L'Eglise et les ouvriers en France* (1984), 519–20; Emile Poulat, *Naissance des prêtres ouvriers* (1965), 188–208; Michel Launay, *La J.O.C.* (1984), 76; *L'Abbé Armand Vallée, prêtre social* (1950).

24. Van Der Meersch, *Pêcheurs.* 143; Yves-Marie Hilaire, ed., *Histoire du Nord/Pas-de-Calais de 1900 à nos jours* (1982); Cholvy and Hilaire, *Histoire religieuses.* III, 31–32. Dufourcq, *Aventurières,* 457, quotes Louis Canet, charged with religious affairs at the Quai d'Orsay, who regarded Catholic Action as a new "pontifical fascism." For a less nervous view of its spirit and activities, see Abbé Félix Klein, *Nouvelles Croisades de jeunes travailleurs* (1934).

25. Boulard, *Matériaux,* I, 91.

26. Guy Thuillier, "Les Institutions médico-sociales en Nivernais en 1930," *Actes du 107e Congrès des Sociétés Savantes* (1983), 217–18, and *L'Imaginaire quotidien au XIXe siècle* (1985), 54–55. Ill visible also are the doings of Social Catholic activists like Andrée Butillard, whose Women's Civic and Social Union, founded in 1926, battled attempts to force women out of the job market and fought hard for subsidies paid directly to women who stayed home and raised children. See Butillard, *Le Travail de la mère hors de son foyer* (1933), Henry Rollet, *Andrée Butillard et le féminisme chrétien* (1960), and Karen Offen, *Women and the Politics of Motherhood in France* (Badia Fiesolana, 1987), 8, 13, which drew my attention to this appealing figure.

27. Joseph Despont, *Pionniers du scoutisme* (1964), 15–18, 43–44, 72; *Nos jeunes* (1930), 593; Philippe Laneyrie, *Les Scouts de France* (1985), 87. No wonder that in straitlaced Chambéry the father of Paul Touvier, the future *milicien,* forbade his children to join the Catholic scouts, tainted by Protestantism. René Rémond et al., *Paul Touvier et l'Eglise* (1992), 40.

28. Yvonne Kniebiehler, *Nous les assistantes sociales* (1980), 189; Jacqueline Roubert, "Recherches sur les activités socio-éducatives," *Colloque sur l'histoire de la Sécurité Sociale* (1992), 228–29; Paul Vigneron, *Histoire des crises du clergé français contemporain* (1976), 153, 155; André Latreille and René Remond, *Histoire du catholicisme en France.* (1962), III, 605; Laneyrie, *Les Scouts.* 131, tells us that on the outbreak of war there were seventy-two thousand Catholic scouts, including sixty-five hundred scoutmasters and

eight thousand Rover Scouts. Anxious about these successes, the Socialists launched the Red Falcons and the Communists the Red Pioneers (followed in 1937 by Communist scouts). None of these formations reached the thousand-member mark.

29. Laneyrie, op. cit., 94; Pierre Schaeffer, *Les Enfants de Cœur* (1949), 145 and passim. There were also scout-like initiatives that competed with the scouts, like the Companions of St. Francis, pilgrim hikers founded in 1927 by a Lyonnais priest, Joseph Folliet, to combine spirituality, good humor, comradeship, and fresh-air adventure that would spur enterprise and energy. See Jean Barbier, *Joseph Folliet, 1903–1972* (1982). Folliet did not like scouts, and his Companions stressed poverty, democracy, and spiritual development. They had no uniforms, no ritual, but their general activities are very reminiscent of those of other youth organizations.

30. Robert Hervet, *Les Chantiers de la jeunesse* (1962), 20–21; Cholvy and Hilaire, *Histoire religieuse*, III, 86; Laneyrie, *Les Scouts.* 140 and passim.

31. Henri Noguères, *La Vie quotidienne en France au temps du Front populaire* (1977), 176; Etienne Bécart, *Pourquoi.* Feb. 1976, 14.

32. *Semaine religieuse de Bourges.* 1930, 43; *Semaine religieuse d'Auch.* Jan. 6, 1934, 10; Paul Gerbod, *Les Enseignants et la politique* (1976), 68–69; Jean Guitton, *Les Davidées* (1967); Gérard Lurol, *Mounier I* (1990), 45–51.

33. Lagree, *Religion.* 150–51; *Semaine religieuse de Saint-Brieuc*, March 19, 1937; *Semaine religieuse de Besançon*, Feb. 24, 1938.

34. Peneff, *Ecoles publiques.* 199 ff.

35. *Semaine religieuse de Bourges*, March 1930; Pierre-Marie Dioudonnat, *Les Ivresses de l'Eglise de France* (1976), 141–42, 179–80; *Canard enchaîné.* March 30, 1932; *Skol Vreizh* (April 1987), 25. In 1937 Paul Touvier's father, a strict Catholic, refused to believe that his son could possibly have seen, as Paul affirmed, a priest in a swimming suit. Rémond, *Touvier*, 38.

36. Pérouas, *Refus d'une religion.* 128; *Annuaire catholique de la région brestoise* (Brest, 1938), 1–2.

37. Pérouas, *Les Limousins.* 207; *Semaine religieuse de Auch*, Jan. 27, April 14, Sept. 1, Oct. 27, 1934. That Masons occupied positions of influence and power in the land is not in doubt. See Pierre Chevallier, *Histoire de la Franc-Maçonnerie française.* (1975), III, 159–63, for their domination and colonization of the Social Insurance administration.

38. Yvon Tranvouez, *Un curé d'avant-hier* (1989), 126–27; Jacques Kergoat, *La France du Front populaire* (1986), 45; "Lettre d'Annecy," *Revue des lectures* (Sept. 1935).

39. Paul Christophe, *1936: Les Catholiques et le Front populaire* (1986), 45 and passim; *Semaine religieuse de Nevers*, Jan. 4, 1936, May 2 and 9, 1936; *Semaine religieuse de Saint-Brieuc*, April 24, May 22, 1936; *L'Union catholique.* April 1936; *La France catholique.* May 16, 1936; *Croix Angévine.* May 3, 1936; *La Croix.* May 2, 1936.

40. *Semaine religieuse de Nevers*, May 9, 1936; Alban Bensa, *Les Saints guérisseurs du Perche-Gouët* (1978), 209.

41. *Semaine religieuse de Saint-Brieuc*, June 6, June 26, July 31, 1936; *L'Union catholique* (Oct. 1936); *Semaine religieuse de Nevers*, summer/autumn 1936; *Semaine religieuse de Nantes*, Nov. 7, 1936.

42. The fullest accounts of the radio elections are to be found in André Tudesq and Elie Cazenave, "Radiodiffusion et politique: Les Élections radiophoniques de 1937 en

France," *Revue d'histoire moderne et contemporaine* (Oct. 1976), 529–55, and in Christophe, *1936*, 181–87. The issue had first been raised in 1934, over the government's decision to oust Sunday services from the broadcasts of Radio-Paris, nationalized that year; see *La Croix* and its provincial editions, e.g., *Croix Angévine*. Jan. 21, 1934.

43. See *Semaine religieuse de Besançon*, Feb. 4 and 13–20, 1937; *Semaine religieuse de Nantes*, Feb. 15 and May 30, 1937.

44. *Vie intellectuelle*. Feb. 25, March 10, 1936. Private experience sometimes proved the Dominicans right. In 1936 the twenty-year-old Françoise Vandermeersch joined a religious order in order to share the poverty and privatious of workers striking against her factory owner father. Her father and mother, meanwhile, though badly hurt by the nine-month strike, continued to contribute to the strikers' support at weekly collections, as Cardinal Suhard demanded, and to help their own striking workers whose womenfolk came asking for alms. *La Vie en face* (1976), 69 ff.

45. Chaline, *Des catholiques*. 194.

46. AO, testimony of Christian de Lavarenne, I, 1; Maxence Faivre d'Arcier, I, 2, Roland de Margerie, I, 2; Joseph-Vincent Ducatillon, O.P., *Le Vrai et le faux patriotisme* (1933), 18, 80, 86, also his *Une renaissance française* (1939). A patriotic Frenchman, Ducatillon, who in due course became Dominican provincial of France, was violently attacked by the Action Française.

47. Vigneron, *Histoire des crises*. 177; Paul Lesourd and Claude Paillat, *Dossier secret: L'Eglise de France* (1968), II, 463.

48. Francisque Gay, *Pour un regroupement des forces d'inspiration Chrétienne* (1935); Christophe, *1936*, 27; Georges Rougeron, *Les Familles politiques au conseil général de l'Allier* (1977), 11.

49. *Mounier et sa génération* (1956), 150, 152; M. Trebitsch, "Correspondance d'intellectuels," *Cahiers de l'IHTP*. no. 20 (March 1992), 79.

50. Pierre Letamendia, *La Démocratie chrétienne* (1977), 21; Louise Weiss, *Mémoires d'une européenne*. III (1970), 196.

51. Noguères, *Vie quotidienne*. 38; Cholvy and Hilaire, *Histoire religieuse*. III, 41; *Syndicalisme*. July 1, 1937.

52. *Esprit* (April 1935); Christophe, *1936*, 33–34.

53. René Rémond, *Les Catholiques, le communisme et les crises* (1960), 246; Sept, March 1, 1935; *Echo de Paris*. March 9, 1935; *Esprit*. April 1, 1935; Mounier, 161; *Echo de Paris*. April 27, 1935.

54. *Echo de Paris*. May 8, 1936; Christophe, *1936*. 48–61, 71–72. Contemporary of Sartre, Nizan, and Raymond Aron at the Ecole Normale Supérieure, Simon (1903–72) was a militant of the student radical Right and a leader of the Jeunesses Patriotes before shifting toward *Esprit* and the Catholic Left.

55. *Semaine religieuse de Besançon*, Jan. 27, 1938; *La Croix*. Sept. 20, 1936; *La Croix*. May 25, Aug. 17, Sept. 17, 1938; *Semaine religieuse de Besançon*, Jan. 5, 1939; *Semaine religieuse de Nevers*, July 22, 1939; Pérouas, *Refus*. 134–35.

56. *Semaine religieuse de Nevers*, Jan. 14, May 20, 1939; *Semaine religieuse de Besançon*, Jan. 4, June 6, 1940; for Munich Sept. 29, Oct. 6, 1938; *Croix Angévine*. Sept. 3, 1937, June 11, 1939; *Semaine religieuse de Nevers*, April 13, 1940; *Semaine religieuse de Besançon*, Sept. 7, 1939; *France catholique*. Oct. 27, 1939.

57. Yves Lambert, *Dieu change en Bretagne* (1985), 187; Tranvouez, *Un curé*, 77–78; Mounier, 278; Pierre Laborie, *Résistants, Vichyssois et autres* (1980), 153; *La Croix.* June 28, 1940.

58. Christophe, *1936*, 50; Jean-François Sirinelli, ed., *Histoire des droites en France* (1992), III, 221.

59. Paul Christophe, *1939–1940: Les Catholiques devant la guerre* (1989), 27; Claude Miche-let, *Mon père Edmond Michelet* (1971); Cholvy and Hilaire, *Histoire religieuse.* III, 112–13, 115.

VIII: Cultures

1. Alain Norvez, *Le Corps enseignant et l'évolution démographique* (1977), 34–36; Antoine Prost, *Histoire générale de l'enseignement et de l'éducation en France* (1981), IV, 23, 220; Claude Goyard, *Histoire de l'administration de l'enseignement (n.d.)*, 53.

2. James Smith Allen, *In the Public Eye: A History of Reading in Modern France, 1800–1940* (Princeton, 1991), 63; Pierre Andreu, *Le Rouge et le blanc* (1977), 27; Jean Guitton, *Regards sur la pensée française 1870–1940: Leçons de captivité* (1968), 16.

3. Pierre Nord, *Double crime sur la ligne Maginot* (1951), 221.

4. Prost, *Histoire générale*, 243. *Echo de Clamecy.* Jan. 12, 1935.

5. Victor Perot in *Crapouillot.* May 1, 1920; Raoul Toscan, "Nevers en l'an 2000," *Paris-Centre.* May 5, 1930; Guy Thuillier, *La Bibliothèque municipale de Nevers* (1983), 156; Allen, *Public Eye.* Tables A4, A7; *Histoire de l'édition française* (1986), IV, 80–82.

6. *Histoire de l'édition française*, IV, 78, 216; *Œuvre.* May 9, 1933; Jean-Baptiste Duroselle, *La Décadence* (1979), 196–97.

7. Simenon, *Les Inconnus dans la maison* (1940), 194.

8. "Ceux du Grand Café" in *Œuvres complètes.* IX, 530; *Pietr le Letton* (1931), 150.

9. See Maurice Martin du Gard, *Nouvelles littéraires.* March 8, 1930, about the arrest and beating of Marcel Achard.

10. The subject deserves more attention than it has received so far. See, among others, *Echo de la Nièvre.* March 4, 1933; *Petit Troyen.* Jan. 26, 1934; *Journal de la Nièvre.* April 1, 1934; Paul de Cassagnac, *Allez, Messieurs!* (1937), 14, 22, 236, and passim; Alfred Fabre-Luce, *Le Grand Jeu* (1962), 196.

11. *Nouvelles littéraires.* Feb. 12, 1938.

12. *Correspondance Jean Paulhan et André Suarès* (1987), 165, Feb. 22, 1937.

13. Robert de Traz, *Nouvelles littéraires.* Dec. 30, 1933; René Lalou, *ibid.*, May 23, 1936; Francis de Miomandre, ibid., Feb. 19, 1938; Paulhan to Suarès, op. cit., 174, Aug. 8, 1937; Edmond Jaloux, *Nouvelles littéraires.* June 18, 1938.

14. Marcelin Pleynet, in Olivier Barrot and Pascal Ory, *Entre deux guerres* (1990), 50.

15. Duhamel's ms. note in Paul Maunory, *Catalogue de l'exposition Georges Duhamel* (1984), 21.

16. Georges Duhamel, *Vues sur la chronique des Pasquier* (1951), 53; *Les Maîtres* (1937), 33.

17. Alexis Carrel, *L'Homme cet inconnu* (1935) and *Jour après jour, 1893–1944* (1956), esp. 140–142, 235–36.

18. Raymonde Moulin, *Le Marché de la peinture en France* (1967), 39–40; *La Querelle du réalisme*

(1936), 168, 188. Yet Flora Groult, *Marie Laurencin* (1987) makes the painter appear rather prosperous at that time.

19. Edouard Pignon, *La Quête de la réalité* (1966), 46.

20. Ibid., 30–31, 38–39, 46.

21. Ibid., 48 and ch. II passim.

22. André Thirion, *Révolutionnaires sans révolution* (1972), 283–84. It was also Charles de Noailles who, in 1929, had acquired from Berlin the original manuscript of the Marquis de Sade's *120 Days of Sodom*. A true subversive and a fake revolutionary, Sade was one of the Surrealists' great heroes.

23. René Crével, *Les Pieds dans le plat* (1934/1974), 294. Also André Masson, "Le Surréalisme quand même," *Nouvelle Revue française* (1967), quoted in Francis Marmande, *George Bataille politique* (Lyons, 1985).

24. Marcel Arland, *Nouvelle Revue française* (July 1930), 106.

25. *"Faire lire Racine aux ouvriers? ou Virgile? Quand un ouvrier aimera Picasso, il sera plus efficacement corrompu que s'il aimait Gozzoli."* Quoted in Jacques Kergoat, *La France du Front populaire* (1986), 356.

26. Quoted in Gaêtan Picon, *Malraux par lui-même* (1965), 11.

27. *L'Impromptu de Versailles*, scene 4.

28. *Europe nouvelle*. Dec. 7, 1935; *Politique* (1936), I, 86; *Nouvelle Revue française* (Jan. 1936), 132; Claudel, Nov. 26, 1934, quoted in Giraudoux, *Théatre* (1982), 1493.

29. Colette, *La Jumelle noire* (1991), 57, 69–70, 93, 298.

30. *La Force de l'age* (1960), 64.

31. Janet Flanner, *Paris Was Yesterday* (1972), 133, 132; Jean-Claude Klein in Barrot and Ory, *Entre deux guerres*, 369.

32. Valerie Steele, *Paris Fashion* (New York, 1988), 264; André Gide, *Journal 1889–1939* (1948), 874; André Maurois, *Mémoires* (1970), 224.

33. Georges Duhamel, *Le Livre de l'amertume* (1983), 139. Marcel L'Herbier, *La Tête qui tourne* (1979), 169 ff, dedicates his second chapter to the eruption of talkies, which he and the likes of René Clair rejected as a simple gold rush in which the best images were spoiled by mediocre dialogue, and speech turned out "the blemish of talkies." For much more information see Alan Williams, *Republic of Images: A History of French Filmmaking* (Cambridge, Mass., 1992).

34. Ginette Vincendeau, "French Cinema in the Thirties," thesis, University of East Anglia, 1985, 33.

35. *Paris-Soir*. Jan. 21, 1930; *Revue des Deux Mondes* (Feb. 15, 1930); *Illustration*. June 27, 1931. Paul Leglise, *Histoire politique du cinéma français: Le Cinéma et la IIIe République* (1970), 75, recalls that after the showing of *Broadway Melody*, Gaston Gérard, deputy mayor of Dijon and himself an amateur actor, raised questions in the Chamber of Deputies about measures to deal with "the rapid progress of sound films and the intention of American managers to impose the English language on the French public."

36. *France la doulce* (1934), 9–11; Vincendeau, "French Cinema." 18; Francis Courtade, *Les Malédictions du cinéma français* (1978), 106.

37. Williams, *Republic of Images*. 249; Vincendeau, op. cit., 50–53 and passim. Vincendeau, 34–35, also tells us how many important French films of the thirties were produced in

the Tobis Klangfilm studios, which opened at Epinay in 1929: all of René Clair's films of the early thirties like *Sous les toits de Paris, Le Million, A nous la liberté;* Feyder's *Pension Mimosas* and *La Kermesse héroique.* Julien Duvivier's *Allo Berlin, Ici Paris*. . . . Meanwhile, between 1931 and 1939 the UFA studios in Berlin turned out forty-one French films. As *L'Illustration.* Oct. 3, 1941, commented in a review of Lilian Harvey's *Calais-Douvres, "Louée soit la Ufa!"* (Praised be the UFA!) See also Denis Rolland, "Les Années noires d'Abel Gance," *Guerres mondiales et conflits contemporains* (Jan. 1992), 95 ff.

38. Jean Zay, *Souvenirs et solitude* (1987), 181; Leglise, *Histoire politique.* 167–68, 195–98; AO, Guy de Carmoy, II, I.

39. Joseph Daniel, *Guerre et cinema* (1972), 144; *Canard enchaîné.* Sept. 7, 1938.

40. Williams, *Republic of Images*, 242; Carné quoted in Janine Bourdin and René Rémond, eds., *La France et les français en 1938 et 1939* (1978), 30.

41. *Paris-Soir.* Jan. 3, 1933.

42. John W. Martin, *The Golden Age of French Cinema* (Boston, 1983), 56, 63; Vincendeau, "French Cinema," 189.

43. François Garçon, *De Blum à Pétain* (1984), 184 ff.

IX: The Nightmare of Fear

1. Quotations in this and following paragraph are from G-2 Report No. 30831, July 3, 1931, NA 4-I 2314-93.

2. Louise Weiss, *Mémoires d'une européenne* (1970), III, 206. Lecture demonstrations designed to assuage panic only succeeded in instilling panic. For passive defense more generally, see ibid., 205–29.

3. *Journal Officiel, Chambre, Débats.* Dec. 29, 1929; NA, 2314-85/2, Jan. 8, 1930; Ladislas Mysyrowicz, *Autopsie d'une défaite* (1973), 175; Chambre, quoted by Jean-Marie d'Hoop, *La France et l'Allemagne 1932–1936* (1980), 77.

4. NA, 2081-1179/1–5, Aug. 1930 and Dec. 29, 1930; 2172-1241/1, Feb. 16, 1931; Colonel Vauthier, "Le Danger aérien," *Revue de Paris* (May I and 15, 1930); Pascal in *Nouvelles littéraires.* Nov. 29, 1930. Author of *Explosifs, poudres, gaz de combat* (2d ed., 1930), Pascal believed there were few defenses against air attack, except the serious threat of ferocious reprisals.

5. Norman Ingram, *The Politics of Dissent: Pacifism in France, 1919–1939* (Oxford, 1991), 128, 136, 138, 140.

6. Julien Green, *Journal 1926–1934*, in *Œuvres complètes* (1975), IV, 135, 199, 201, 337–38, 348; Servan-Schreiber, *Regards sur un demi-siècle* (1964), 108–10; *Petit Troyen.* March 24, 1933, and Jan. 19, 1934.

7. *Œuvre.* Oct. 4, 1932; Duc de Brissac, *En d'autres temps* (1972), 18; Carole Fink, *Marc Bloch* (New York, 1989), 168.

8. Mysyrowicz, *Autopsie.* 318–23; *Œuvre.* March 31 and April 11, 1933; *Vu.* July 4, 1934; *Echo de la Nièvre.* April 13 and 20, May 18, 1935; Servan-Schreiber, *Regards.* 165; NA, 2706-C-54/20, Dec. 31, 1935, and 2706-C-54/25, Nov. 9, 1936; Green, *Journal,* 388.

9. René Gérin, "Guernica," *Le Barrage.* May 13, 1937, quoted in Ingram, *Politics,* 221.

10. *Paris-Soir.* March 9, 1939; Jean de Pange, *Journal* (1975), IV, March 21, 1939; *Canard enchaîné.* Feb. 11, 1938, March 29, 1939.

11. Green, *Journal,* 76–77.

12. Julien Benda, *Nouvelle Revue française* (November 1927), 605; Ramon Fernandez, *Nouvelle Revue française* (Sept. 1930), 328; Romain Rolland, *Europe* (July 1932).

13. *Gringoire.* July 25, 1930; *Nouvelles littéraires.* Feb. 7 and March 21, 1931; *Plans.* July 1931; *Nouvelles littéraires.* Sept. 12, 1931, Jan. 16, 1932.

14. Eugène Dabit, *Journal Intime* (1939), 22, 88, 220; Green, *Journal.* 199, 338.

15. Alain, *Correspondance Elie et Florence Halévy* (1958), 370–71; Pange, *Journal.* 371, 396; *Jean-José Marchand interroge Montherlant* (1980), 36; Henri de Montherlant, *Carnets 1930–1944* (1957), 115; Dabit, *Journal.* 220; Green, *Journal.* 338.

16. Montherlant, *Carnets.* 95–96, 219; Pange, *Journal* (1970), II, 178; III, 235; Dabit, *Journal.* 273; Servan-Schreiber, *Regards.* 148–49.

17. Jacques Body, *Giraudoux et l'Allemagne* (1975), 363; Henri de Kerillis, *Français! voici la guerre* (1936), 127; Philippe Lamour and André Cayatte, *Sauvons la France en Espagne* (1937), 20. See also Hervé Alphand, *L'Etonnement d'etre* (1977), 10.

18. Montherlant, *Carnets.* 231, 233, 296; Françoise Giroud, *Leçons particulières* (1990), 47; Pierre Andreu, *Le Rouge et le blanc* (1977), 135; Edmée Renaudin, *Sans fleur au fusil* (1979), 18. On March 14, a few days after the Anschluss, the pacifist and leftist schoolteacher Claude Jamet, a disciple of Alain's, notes: "Deep within all of us, something secretly awaits, I was going to write: hopes for the war." *Notre Front populaire* (1977), 241.

19. *Journal Officiel, Chambre, Débats.* March 15, 1922, quoted by Judith M. Hughes, *To the Maginot Line* (Cambridge, Mass., 1971), 141; *Le Temps,* quoted as "a clear exposition of army doctrine" by the U.S. military attaché, NA, 20151049, May 8, 1933.

20. NA, Military Attaché, 2015-801/28, Jan. 18, 1929; Fabry quoted in G-2 report, 2667-C-20-24, Jan. 3, 1930.

21. NA, G-2 Report, 2667-C-20/34, June 13, 1931; Jean-Richard Bloch, *Destin du siècle* (1931), 179, 180, 188; Robert J. Young, *In Command of France* (Cambridge, Mass., 1978), 31, 153.

22. François-André Paoli, *L'Armée française de 1919 à 1939.* IV (nd), 125, 175; Alphand, *L'Etonnement.* 33; NA, 2667-Y-7/34, Oct. 16, 1933 and 2667-C-20/44, Oct. 28, 1933. See also 2657-194/34, Oct. 31, 1936, suggesting that the French might begin to extend the Maginot Line northwestward to protect Turcoing, Lille, and the northern industrial area. Such guesses led to nothing but reflected widespread wishful thinking.

23. Pierre Nord, *Double crime sur la ligne Maginot* (1951), 50; Henri Amouroux, *La Grande Histoire des français sous l'occupation.* I, *Le Peuple du désastre* (1976), 116; Jules Moch, *Une si longue vie* (1976), 145–46.

24. See Hughes, *Maginot Line.* ch. V.

25. NA, 2657-C-225/4, Aug. 4, 1928; Maurin, *Journal Officiel, Chambre, Débats.* March 15, 1935, quoted by R. Michalon and J. Vernet in *La France et l'Allemagne,* 294.

26. Suzy Borel, *Par une porte entrebaillé* (1972), 81; General Jean Rupied, *Elysée 1928–1934* (1952), 100–102, 182–83. See also NA, 2015-I032/I, Oct. I, 1929, where the

U.S. military attaché unfavorably compares the French Army with its predecessor of 1914, with the Germans (superior in training and spirit), and with the British (more modern). "The martial prewar spirit no longer exists. . . . Fundamentally . . . the Frenchman is not the ardent warrior he was before the war." And 2015-1032/2, Oct. 22, 1929: "[T]he great task is to reestablish the morale of the army. . . ."

27. Nord, *Double crime.* 52; AO, Eugène Demont, II, 1; Michel Debré, *Trois Républiques pour une France.* I (1984), 82; AO, Pierre de Calan, V, 1; Christian de Lavarenne, I, 2.

28. Jean-Louis Crémieux-Brilhac, *Les Français de l'an 40* (1990), II, 375.

29. For Weygand, see NA, 2051-1120/1, June 13, 1932. For Pétain, Georges Loustanau-Lacau, *Mémoires d'un Français rebelle* (1938), 94, 83.

30. Bertrand de Jouvenel, *Après la défaite* (1941), 101; Simone de Lattre, *Jean de Lattre, mon mari* (1971), 81 and passim.

31. NA, 2015-1266, and 1266/1, Dec. 13, 1938, quoting article of General de Cugnac in *Choc,* complaining of officer shortage, and confirming his views.

32. Simone de Lattre, *Jean de Lattre,* 85–86.

33. Report in Paoli, *L'Armée.* 73, 74, 76; Lieutenant Colonel Hurst in *Revue de l'infanterie* (May 1935); Germans quoted in Crémieux-Brissac, *Les Français.* II, 398; Americans in NA, 2015-1204, June 28, 1935, 2015-1197/1, Feb. 25, 1935, 2015-1213/1, Jan. 10, 1936. Pierre Rocolle, *La Guerre de 1940* (1990), I, 215, also found generals in poor physical condition, heavy from lack of exercise, slow in mental as in physical reactions. For dislike of telephones, typewriters, and motorized transport see Lucien Souchon, *Feue l'armée française* (1929), 46–50.

34. J.-P. Sartre, "Merleau-Ponty vivant," *Temps modernes* (Oct. 1961), 304; AO, Guy de Carmoy, IV, 1; J.-B. Duroselle, *La Décadence* (1979), 260.

35. Mysyrowicz, *Autopsie.* 1939; Souchon, *L'Armée.* 52–53; Jean Zay, *Souvenirs et solitude* (1987), 44–45; Debré, *Trois républiques.* I, 142. Add to this, of course, the searing heart searching of Marc Bloch's *L'Etrange défaite,* written in 1940.

36. Charles de Gaulle, *Vers l'armée de métier* (1934); Capitaine Vernier, *Le Nouveau Règlement d'infanterie* (1939), 7–8; Mysyrowicz, *Autopsie.* 21; General Maurin in *Journal Officiel, Chambre, Débats.* March 15, 1935, 1045.

37. Servan-Schreiber, *Regards.* 147–48; "Les Chars français," *Revue d'infanterie* (July 1939), 9–10; Mysyrowicz, *Autopsie.* 27.

38. Jacques Duboin in *Journal Officiel, Chambre, Débats.* March 14, 1922; AO, Roger Goetze, I, 31; NA, 2881-C-101/22, March 23, 1931; 2015-1128/4, Nov. 23, 1932.

39. NA, 2281-C-1/24, March 4, 1935; 2015-1210, Feb. 3, 1936; Jean Lhôte, *La Communale* (1957), 7; *Action française.* Nov. 10, 1931; Mysyrowicz, *Autopsie.* 156.

40. William C. Bullitt, *For the President: Personal and Secret* (Boston, 1972), 383; Robert Nayberg, "Les Conséquences de la bataille de Guadalajara," *Guerres mondiales* (Jan. 1992), 32; Louis Garros in *Revue de France,* (July and Sept. 1937), quoted in Mysyrowicz, *Autopsie.* 142; *Le Temps.* Oct. 21, 1938; General Daubert, "Chars et antichars," *Mercure de France* (Oct. 1937), 297. A sadly symbolic photograph of July 1939 shows the graduation of that year's class of the officers' school, Saint-Cyr Coëtquidan—*promotion "La Plus Grande France":* a group of bare-chested youths on a lawn, brandishing Gaulish swords, carrying Gaulish shields, accoutered in their ancestors' winged helms.

41. Raymond Abellio, *Ma dernière mémoire* (1975), II, 314, and (1980), III, 44–45; *Le Temps.* Nov. 22, 1939; Brissac, *En d'autres temps.* II, 19–20; NA, 2015-1223/13, Nov. 22, 1939; 2015-1271/11, Jan. 12, 1940.

42. AO, Margerie, I, 1; NA, 2015-1223/21, May 25, 1940.

43. NA, G2/183-279, June 16, 1938; 2015-1060, Sept. 13, 1930; 2081-1207/1, Dec. 30, 1930.

44. General Jean Delmas in René Girault and Robert Frank, *La Puissance en Europe* (1984), 129. NA, 2657-11-90/91, Sept. 6, 1938 and 2657-11-90/87a, Sept. 22, 1938, quotes Lindbergh at Munich time who finds the French "pathetic" and France "in a pitiful condition in the air."

45. Robert Frankenstein, *Le Prix du réarmament français* (1982), 20–21. Ibid., 35. In 1934 it accounted for 4.9 percent of national revenue, compared to 3 percent in Britain; in 1938 for 8.6 percent, compared to 8 percent in Britain; in 1939 to 23 percent, compared to 22 percent in Britain.

46. Herrick Chapman, *State Capitalism and Working-Class Radicalism in the French Aircraft Industry* (Berkeley, 1991), 143.

47. NA, 2081-1492/1, May 6, 1938.

48. NA, 2081-1482, April 2, 1937; 2081-1487/2, Jan. 4, 1938; 2081-1487, March 20, 1940; 2081-348/20, April 27, 1940; 2081-348/21, May 2, 1940; 2081-1359, Oct. 7, 1940, for J. Carlton Ward, president of the Fairchild Corporation, visiting France beginning May 29, 1940; 183-314 22, Air Bulletin 13, Aug. 2, 1940.

49. André Laffargue, *Fantassin de Gascogne* (1962), 139–40; Edgar Ansel Mowrer, *Triumph and Turmoil* (Boston, 1968), 309; NA, 2015-1195/5, Nov. 5, 1935.

50. Crémieux-Brilhac, *Les Français.* II, 616–17, 253, 381; Georges Friedmann, *Journal de Guerre* (1987), 45; Brissac, *En d'autres temps.* II, 23; Marc Bloch, *L'Etrange défaite* (1957), 91–92; Claude Paillat, *Le Désastre de 1940,* IV, *La Guerre éclair* (1985), 6, 7.

51. Emile Zola, *Les Rougon-Macquart* (1967), V, 410, 1377, 1411, 1415, 1417.

X: The War Nobody Wanted

1. M. Trebitsch, "Correspondence d'intellectuels," *Cahiers de l'IHTP* (March 1992), 76.

2. Jean-Louis Crémieux-Brilhac, *Les Français de l'an 40* (1990), I, 319. In February 1939 Jean Paulhan wrote to André Suarès that the Foreign Office had warned the *Nouvelle Revue française* it would be taken to court at the first article attacking Hitler or Mussolini, but that had been before the war. *Correspondance Jean Paulhan et André Suarès* (1987), 223.

3. *Femina* (Feb. and March 1939); Alexandre Arnoux in *Nouvelles littéraires.* March 11, 1939.

4. *Paris-Soir,* March 11, 1939; *Gazette des Tribunaux,* March 12, 13, 14, 1939.

5. *Paris-Soir.* March 10 and June 18, 1939; *Match* (June 22, 1939); *Petit Journal.* June 17 and 18, 1939.

6. Hervé Alphand, *L'Etonnnement d'être* (1977), 17; *Gazette des Tribunaux.* July 21, 1939.

7. *Paris-Soir.* March 16, 1939; Georges Duhamel, *Le Livre de l'amertume* (1983), 284–85.

8. *Match* (April 13, 1939). Two days before Italy gobbled up Albania, Albert Lebrun had

been reelected president by 506 votes out of 910, while the Right howled, "A Moscou!" as their opponents retorted, "A Berlin!" It seemed that all parties were committed to the welfare of some country other than their own. Looking back from prison, Jean Zay added his melancholy comment: "What was missing was a man, and there again appeared France's eternal drama." *Souvenirs et solitude* (1987), 320.

9. Jean Mistler, quoted in *Paris-Soir*. March 12, 1939; Jean Sagnes and Sylvie Caucanas, eds., *Les Français et la guerre d'Espagne* (Perpignan, 1990), 399. Mistler could have added that, however horrid their conditions, the 200,000 or 250,000 men, women, and children in internment camps cost the insolvent country some seven million francs a day.

10. Interestingly, *Je Suis Partout*. May 12, 1939, attacked Déat. The issue was not Danzig, but Poland, a real nation, unlike "burlesque Czechoslovakia."

11. Edmée Renaudin, *Sans fleur au fusil* (1979), 19. One year earlier the Vicomte de Pange at the theater had been shocked to hear the public growl disapproval when one character on the stage spoke of the French and the British supporting each other. "Is anglophobia so inveterate?" Jean de Pange, *Journal* (1975), IV, 161.

12. *Paris-Soir*. May 26, 1939. NA, 1442/5, March 9, 1939, reports how the previous day a dozen deputies of the Right invited to lunch with the president of the Chamber, Edouard Herriot, refused to sit at table with their Communist colleagues and left Herriot's residence without lunching.

13. *Paris-Soir*. May 16 and 20, 1939.

14. Pange, *Journal*. IV, 385; Janine Bourdin and René Rémond, eds., *La France et les Français en 1938 et 1939* (1978), 120; *Paris-Soir*. July 11, 15, 30, 1939; Zay, *Souvenirs*. 325.

15. Pierre Laborie, *Résistants, Vichyssois et autres* (1980), 160–61.

16. *Paris-Soir*. August 15 and 20, 1939; *Nouvelles littéraires*. Sept. 2, 1939; *Femina* (May, July, Aug. 1939).

17. *Paris-Soir* Aug. 23, 1939. The Geneva-oriented commissar for foreign Affairs, M. Litvinov, had been dismissed on May 4 and replaced by V. Molotov, who, on May 20, had approached the German ambassador in Moscow suggesting negotiations. To give credit where credit is due, on May 5, 1939, *Je Suis Partout* had predicted a German-Soviet pact.

18. *Paris-Soir*. Aug. 22 and 25 1939; *Canard enchaîné*. Aug. 30, 1939. In *Ce Soir*. Aug. 23, 1939, Aragon glorified the Nazi-Soviet Pact: *"La guerre a reculé hier. . . . Silence à la meute antisoviétique! . . . parce qu'il y a l'URSS on ne fait pas la guerre comme on veut"* (Yesterday war retreated. . . . Silence to the anti-Soviet pack! Thanks to the USSR, one can't just make war as one pleases). *Esprit* called him a buffoon. Jacques Laurent, *Histoire égoïste* (1976), 168.

19. *Je Suis Partout*. Sept. 1, 1939; Alphand, *L'Etonnement*. 21; Monzie, quoted in Laborie, *Résistants*, 59. See also Paul Valéry, *Cahiers*, (1974), II, 1,498: "This Monday—September 3 [sic!], we wake up at war. . . . At the sound, it will be exactly . . . *the end of a World*." Alexis Carrel's diary for Sept. 3: "Second day of mobilization. Biological laws are unforgiving. It is too late. We shall die as a great nation. We shall be beaten as France has never been beaten. . . . We have to act without hope to save what still can be saved." *Jour après jour* (1956), 203–04. Less ominously, Sartre opens a letter to his mistress, dated Sept. 2: *"C'est donc la connerie qui a triomphé"* (So idiocy has triumphed). As

for Uniprix stores, noted Beauvoir, three days later, they advertised: *Maison française—Capitaux français.* Simone de Beauvoir, *Journal de guerre* (1990), 27.

20. *Paris-Soir.* Sept. 1 and 3, 1939; Alexandre Arnoux, *Contacts allemands* (1950), 146.

21. Bernard Cazeaux, *Le Goût des vacances perdues* (1975), 52; AO, Pierre de Calan, V, 1. See also Fernand Léger (the painter, who had fought in the last war), *Lettres à Simone* (1987), 240, on Sept. 2: *"Mobilisation Générale—Ça nous rajeunit."*

22. Jean-François Sirinelli, *Intellectuels et passions françaises* (1990), 130.

23. Zay, *Souvenirs.* 107; *Le Rouge et le blanc* (1977), 143; AO, François Bizard, III, 3; William C. Bullitt, *For the President: Personal and Secret* (Boston, 1972), 368.

24. Bullitt, op. cit., 79, 291, 369, 372–73; J.-B. Duroselle, *La Décadence* (1979), 473; *Paris-Soir.* Sept. 12, 1939; Jean Giraudoux, *Messages du Continental* (1987), 107–08.

25. Georges Sadoul, *Journal de guerre* (1977), 56, 123; R. Cardinne-Petit, *Les Soirées du Continental: Ce que j'ai vu à la Censure 1939–1940* (1942), 52–54.

26. Claude Jamet, *Carnets de déroute* (1942), 28, 36, 52.

27. *Semaine religieuse, Besançon,* Oct. 26, 1939; Laborie, *Résistants.* 73, 85; Jacques Isorni, *Quand j'avais l'âge de raison* (1966), 245–46; Emmanuel Mönick, *Pour Mémoire* (1970), 19.

28. *Correspondance Paulhan-Suarès* (1987), 301; Paul Léautaud, *Journal littéraire* (1962), XII, 313; Henriette Nizan, *Libres Mémoires* (1989), 259; Laborie, *Résistants.* 84–85; Michel Margairaz, *L'Etat, les finances et l'économie.* I (1991), 486; Edgar Ansel Mowrer, *Triumph and Tragedy* (New York, 1968), 302.

29. Georges Loustanau-Lacau, *Mémoires d'un Français rebelle* (1948), 166 and passim, bitterly criticizes the failure to *use* the Maginot Line, around which half a million troops were concentrated, when a tenth of that number would have been sufficient and allowed the rest to be employed on active operations.

30. *Paris-Soir.* Jan. 1, 29 and May 1, 1940; *Hommage à Elsa Schiaparelli* (1984), 49–50.

31. Jacques de Fouchier, *Goût de l'improbable* (1984), 82. Roger Martin du Gard, *Œuvres complètes,* (1955), II, 1,011. More must have read the sixteenth volume of Jules Romains's *Hommes de bonne volonté: Verdun,* published in 1938, with its equally depressing message.

32. Jamet, *Carnets.* 43–44; Laborie, *Résistants.* 61, 81. Sadoul, *Journal,* 53–54, Oct. 9, 1939, notes a cartoon he has seen in *Gringoire:* Old man and old woman debate whether to go to the cinema or listen to Radio Stuttgart *(Alors, qu'est-ce qu'on fait, on va au ciné ou on écoute Radio Stuttgart?).* In Sadoul's view, cartoons published by *Candide, Oeuvre,* and their like about the German broadcasts were an underhanded form of publicity for them.

33. AO, Guy de Carmoy, IV, 1; Laborie, *Résistants,* 82; André Beugler, *Les Instants de Giraudoux* (1948), 141. According to Jacques Body, *Jean Giraudoux et l'Allemagne* (1975), 415, Giraudoux wanted to place a sign in his department's offices: EN RAISON DES CIRCONSTANCES, LE MOT IMPOSSIBLE EST REDEVENU FRANÇAIS (Given the circumstances, the word *impossible* has become French once more). Fernand Léger, *Lettres,* 242, also testifies that ordinary folk showed no interest in "the fine words of Monsieur Giraudoux. It's our kind [artists? intellectuals?] who lean toward the radio set."

34. Giraudoux, *Messages,* 81–84.

35. Jeanne Ancelot-Hustache, *Les Sœurs des prisons* (1933), 182; Pange, *Journal.* III, 267 and

passim; *Confidences.* Jan. 20, 1939; *Les Passagers du solstice* (Thionville, 1990), 27; *Semaine religieuse de Besançon,* Sept. 21, 1939; Dominique Aron-Schnapper, *Histoire orale ou archives orales?* (1980), 40; Jean-Paul Sartre, *War Diaries* (London, 1984), 33, 50.

36. Jamet, *Carnets,* 26; Sartre, op. cit., 32, 49, 153. Corroboration, if needed, may be found in Loustanau-Lacau, *Mémoires.* 168–71, Léautaud, *Journal,* 315, and Sadoul, *Journal,* 92, 93, 164–65.

37. AO, Pierre de Calan, V, 1; *Les Carnets de guerre de Gustave Folcher, paysan languedocien* (1981), 24–25.

38. Henri Amouroux, *La Grande Histoire des Français sous l'occupation* (1976), I, 163, mentions an anonymous letter from Montpon (Dordogne) denouncing "certain evacuees from Strasbourg" for celebrating Hitler's birthday. Inquiries revealed nothing. Alsatian evacuees were obviously unhappy in the Périgord and may have reacted with minor provocations; on the other hand, Jacques Godechot, teaching in Strasbourg in 1933, remembered the penetration of Nazism in the Alsace of those days, and the notice on the door of a famous Strasbourg restaurant: *"Interdit aux chiens et aux juifs."* In *Jules Isaac* (1979), 81.

39. A. J. Liebling, *The Road back to Paris* (Garden City, 1944), 56. Léautaud, *Journal.* XII, 316, mentions that dogs left behind in Strasbourg had been killed by *gardes mobiles.*

40. *L'Auto.* Feb. 26, 1940. For sports fans, April 1940 was full of ups and downs: *L'Auto.* April 9: "the great question of the moment: will the [Olympic] Games of 1940 take place?" *L'Auto.* April 25: "The Helsinki Games will not take place." *L'Auto.* April 13: "So there will be a cycling Tour de France in 1940. We can relax." *L'Auto.* April 19: "No Tour de France this year."

41. *The Diplomatic Diaries of Oliver Harvey, 1937–1940* (London, 1970), 341, 349.

42. See Amouroux, *La Grande Histoire,* I, 129 ff. Crémieux-Brilhac, *Les Français.* I, 185; *Petit Parisien.* Jan. 17, 1940. As George Orwell said somewhere, the quickest way to end a war is to lose it.

43. Laborie, *Résistants.* 91, 94, and passim; Harvey, *Diplomatic Diaries.* 338.

44. Bertrand de Jouvenel, *Après la défaite* (1941), 125. Writing at the same time, Yves Simon, *La Grande Crise de la République française* (Montreal, 1941), 157, insisted that one would never understand the events of the last few years, and those of 1940 too, unless one realized the growth of "a whole class of persons for whom what mattered above all was neither money, nor honors, nor pleasure, nor God, but hatred."

45. Gaston Marchou, *Chaban Delmas* (1969), 27; Andreu, *Le Rouge.* 144–45; Laurent Greilshamer, *Hubert Beuve-Méry* (1990), 139; NA, 2015-1271/8, Nov. 10, 1939. For the men's eagerness to benefit from parenthood, see *Petit Parisien.* Feb. 7, 1940. Amouroux, *La Grande Histoire.* I, 122, reports a soldier marrying the mother of his five children. Making the common-law relationship legal and recognizing his offspring, gave the groom ten years credit toward release from the army.

46. Sartre, *War Diaries.* 47, 204.

47. Crémieux-Brilhac, *Les Français.* I, 432 ff; Jean Chauvel, *Commentaire* (1971), I, 69.

48. For sports and games, see *L'Intransigeant.* March 6, 1940, and *L'Auto.* March 8, 1940. For wine, Crémieux-Brilhac, *Les Français.* II, 432, 463, 468. Louise Weiss's lover, an officer recalled to service in 1939, sighs: *"Toute la troupe est dans les vignes. Elle boit, elle boit,*

elle boit" (All the troops are in their cups. They drink, they drink, they drink). *Mémoires.* IV, *Le Sacrifice du chevalier* (1971), 86.

49. Sartre, *War Diaries.* 208; AO, Roger Goetze, I, 35.

50. Sartre, op. cit., 203, 206; NA, 2015-1271/30, March 19, 1941; confirmed in Sadoul, *Journal,* 90, 131. Also AO, Guy de Carmoy, IV, I; Pierre Naville, *Mémoires imparfaites* (1987), 25, 33–34; Andreu, *Le Rouge.* 146–49. Liebling, *The Road Back.* 31, finds only one man in Paris who predicts disaster, an American who had served in the Foreign Legion and who said that the army was rotten "because the officers were afraid to work the men too hard . . . it would collapse at the first push." As Colonel Larpent, the *Action française's* military columnist, grumbled, "The absinthe army was a good deal better." Pierre Gaxotte, *Les Autres et moi* (1975), 176. Absinthe had been banned during the First World War.

51. Simone de Beauvoir, *La Force de l'age* (1960), 450. On May 1 Paul Reynaud had proclaimed that the French nation was on its way to victory: *"La nation française marche vers la victoire." L'Auto.* May 2, 1940.

52. *Je Suis Partout.* May 24, 1940; Alain Laubréaux, *Ecrit pendant la guerre* (1944), 180; *Petit Parisien.* May 18, 1940.

53. AO, Pierre de Calan, V, I; Harvey, *Diplomatic Diaries.* 358, 360, 369; Jamet, *Carnets.* 95.

54. Bullitt, *For the President.* 440–41, 434; *Petit Parisien.* May 17, 1940.

55. Bullitt, op. cit., 444; Harvey, *Diplomatic Diaries.* 375.

56. NA, 2081-1509/4, June 6, 1940. Pierre de Calan, who lived through those days, refers to the power of the memory of the Battle of the Marne, which stopped the Germans in 1914, and "to the French installed in the idea thay they had the right to a miracle." AO, IV, I.

57. Crémieux-Brilhac, *Les Français.* II, 649–69, esp. 669; Henri Amouroux, *La Grande Histoire.* I, 91, 95; NA, 2081-1509/7, Oct. 31, 1940.

58. Crémieux-Brilhac, *Les Français.* II, 54, 167–68, 654. Like Crémieux-Brilhac, who refers to "an almost total absence of mines" (54), American officers recapitulating the causes of French defeat blame French engineers: "none of them had ever heard of the use of road mines, of mines laid in fields, or of mine-barriers [against tanks]. (NA, 2015-1271/30, March 19, 1941). But Ernst Jünger, *Gärten und Strassen* (Berlin, 1942), 166, speaks of French *Tretminen* stacked at Laon, and more mines protecting the banks of the Meuse (which the Germans were to assault, bridge, and cross) had just been withdrawn beginning May 1, for stocking and verification.

59. NA, 2015-1271/35, Sept. 1, 1940; Liebling, *The Road Back.* 102; Renaudin, *Sans fleur.* 91.

60. Emile Zola, "Sedan," *Le Figaro.* Sept. 1, 1891, in *Les Rougon-Macquart* (1967), V, 1411–12; *Paris-Soir.* May 31, 1940; *Times.* Nov. 9, 1870.

61. Peter Fontaine, *Last to Leave Paris* (London, 1944), 16, 48, 50; Virginia Cowles, *Looking for Trouble* (New York, 1941), 375; AO, Guy de Carmoy, IV, I and Pierre de Calan, V, 2; Suzanne Bidault, *Souvenirs* (1987), 14; Marie-Madeleine Fourcade, *L'Arche de Noë* (1989), 22. For more on looting, see Amouroux, *La Grande Histoire.* I, 334, and Simone de Beauvoir, *Journal de Guerre* (1990), 321.

62. AO, Désiré Arnaud, II, 2. Georges Friedmann, serving in a field hospital, noted how anti-Semitic attitudes persisted among doctors in military hospitals: prejudice, discrimination, isolation of the outsider. "It's practically the only place where you can find [anti-Semitism] among the troops." *Journal de guerre* (1987), 207–08.

63. Crémieux-Brilhac, *Les Français.* II, 687–90, 704; André Beaufre, *Le Drame de 1940* (1965), 265; William L. Shirer, *The Collapse of the Third Republic* (1969), 875; Saul Padover, "France in Defeat," *World Politics.* April 1950, 324–26.

64. Junger, *Gärten.* 169–70 ff; Crémieux-Brilhac, *Les Français.* II, 676. Pierre Rocolle, *La Guerre de 1940* (1990), II, 345: By the end of hostilities, the official figures showed 92,000 French dead and 200,000 wounded; about 45,000 German dead and 111,-000 wounded.

65. Jacques Le Roy Ladurie, ms., V, 28.

66. Harvey, *Diplomatic Diaries,* 392; Dumoulin, quoted AO, Guy de Carmoy, IV, 2; Le Roy Ladurie, VI, I.

67. Andreu, *Le Rouge.* 155; Chaleil, *La Mémoire.* 306; also Fourcade, *L'Arche.* 24: "At last! All that is finished," declares an exquisite old gentleman, the great goldsmith Puyforcat.

68. Duc de Brissac, *La Suite des temps* (1974), 74. See also, AO, François Bizard, I, 2.

69. AO, Maxence Faivre d'Arcier, II, 2; *Paris-Soir.* June 26, 1940; Gilles Ragache, *La Vie quotidienne des écrivains et artistes sous l'occupation* (1988), 142. Sadoul, *Journal,* 395, notes on July 9: "This morning, the French radio: "We have victoriously thrown back the attacks of the enemy, two of whose planes have been shot down." The bulletin refers to the English, and it is really the French radio speaking."

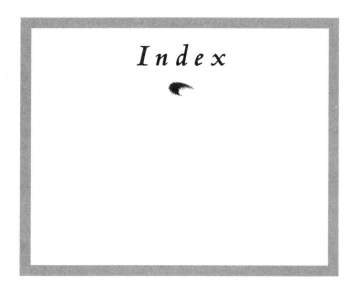

Index

Brasillach, Robert, 102–3, 122*n*, 172
Brecht, Bertolt, 104
Breton, André, 221, 222–23, 225
Breton, Jules-Louis, 51
Briand, Aristide, 8, 125–26, 127, 142, 157, 229
Brissac, duc de, 256, 263, 278
British Expeditionary Force, 282
British Intelligence Service, 139
Broadway Melody (film), 320*n*
Brogan, Denis, 199
Broglie, Amédée de, 58–59
Brooke, Rupert, 23
Brossolette, Pierre, 98, 291*n*
Brother Bourgeois, Are You Dying? (Berl), 121
Brzezinski, Zbigniew, 164
Bucard, Marcel, 119*n*
building industry, 47–48
Buisson, Suzanne, 127–28
Bullitt, William, 142, 151, 153, 163, 164, 174, 178, 252, 263, 271, 273, 309*n*–10*n*
Buñuel, Luis, 221
Buré, Emile, 105
Butillard, Andrée, 85*n*, 316*n*
Byé, Maurice, 206

Cachin, Marcel, 175
Caillaux, Joseph, 108*n*
Calais-Douvres (film), 321*n*
Calan, Pierre de, 51, 247, 261–63, 268, 271–73
Calder, Alexander, 224
Camelots du Roi, 118, 133, 189
Campbell, Ronald, 278
Canard enchaîné, 23, 24, 73, 93, 152, 167, 206, 241, 243
Cancer américain, Le (Aron and Dandieu), 96–97
Candide, 105, 107–8, 128, 326*n*
Canet, Louis, 316*n*
Capitaine Conan, Le (Vercel), 12

capitalism, 19, 35
Carmoy, Guy de, 249–50
Carné, Marcel, 12, 235
Carnival in Flanders (film), 235
Carrel, Alexis, 218, 325*n*
Castelnau, Edouard de Curières de, 188, 201, 203–4
Catelain, Jacques, 93*n*
Catholic Action, 187, 316*n*
Catholic Association of French Youth (ACJF), 189, 194
Catholic Church, 182–206
  Abyssinian War and, 144
  activism and, 188–91
  Acton's description of, 196
  anticlericism and, 197–98
  birth control and, 79
  clergy and, 186–87
  Communists and, 198, 202
  education and, 185–86
  Freemasonry and, 196–97, 317*n*
  Jews and, 109, 194
  Left and, 195, 198–99, 200, 202, 203
  1937 election and, 198–99
  Personalism and, 201–2
  Popular Front and, 197, 199, 200, 203
  Radicals and, 115
  religious orders and, 182–85
  Right and, 199, 202–3, 204
  scouting movement and, 192–94, 316*n*–17*n*
  Spanish Civil War and, 198
  sports and, 188–89
  unemployment and, 200–201, 202
  Vichy regime and, 193–95, 196
  women and, 85, 185, 187–88, 191
  youth movement and, 189–90, 192, 194–95
Catholics, Politics and Money (Simon), 203
Cazeaux, Bernard, 262
Céline, Louis-Ferdinand, 19, 23, 66, 102, 109, 216, 305*n*